A225 The British Isles and the modern world, 1789–1914

The Open University

D1387110

Block 2
Confidence and crisis, 1840–1880

Edited by Donna Loftus

This publication forms part of the Open University module A225 *The British Isles and the modern world, 1789–1914*. Details of this and other Open University modules can be obtained from Student Recruitment, The Open University, PO Box 197, Milton Keynes MK7 6BJ, United Kingdom (tel. +44 (0)300 303 5303; email general-enquiries@open.ac.uk).

Alternatively, you may visit the Open University website at www.open.ac.uk where you can learn more about the wide range of modules and packs offered at all levels by The Open University.

To purchase a selection of Open University materials visit www.ouw.co.uk, or contact Open University Worldwide, Walton Hall, Milton Keynes MK7 6AA, United Kingdom for a catalogue (tel. +44 (0) 1908 274066; fax +44 (0)1908 858787; email ouw-customer-services@open.ac.uk).

The Open University, Walton Hall, Milton Keynes MK7 6AA

First published 2017

Edited and designed by The Open University.

Typeset by The Open University.

Printed and bound in the United Kingdom by Hobbs the Printers Ltd, Brunel Road, Totton, Hampshire SO40 3WX.

ISBN 978 1 4730 0390 3

1.1

Contents

Unit 8 The 'age of equipoise' and the Great Exhibition of 1851

Donna Loftus

Contents

Aims

This unit will:

- explain how and why the mid-nineteenth century is associated with equipoise and optimism
- consider historical debates about progress
- introduce the topics of Block 2.

Introduction

Welcome to Block 2 – 'Confidence and crisis, 1840–1880'. Block 2 covers the mid-nineteenth century, a period still associated with the sort of anxieties you studied in Block 1 but also with increasing confidence that industrialisation would help make the everyday lives of working people better. By way of introduction to Block 2, this unit will demonstrate how confidence and crisis coexisted in the mid-nineteenth century.

The unit begins in the 1840s, one of the most turbulent decades in the history of the British Isles and one that has since become known as the 'hungry forties'. The decade witnessed the Irish Famine (explored in detail in the unit 'Ireland and the Famine': Unit 9) and one of the deepest economic depressions of the nineteenth century, which caused mass starvation, unemployment and unrest across the United Kingdom. There were widespread fears that industrialisation had come to an end and great anxiety about future progress. In the middle of such uncertainty there was considerable controversy about how to deal with the present crisis. Thinkers and politicians, writers and artists debated who was responsible for alleviating distress – some argued that the state should do more, others that **laissez-faire** political economy (ruling out government interference) should be allowed to run its course.

In this context, radicalism flourished; the Chartist movement that you encountered in the unit 'The rise of the working class?' (Unit 3 in Block 1) reached its peak in the 1840s. As revolutions broke out across Europe in 1848, the stability of the nation appeared to be under threat. In Sections 8.1 and 8.2, you will, respectively, consider the rise of radicalism through the Chartist movement and the Anti-Corn Law League, and question how Britain managed to avoid revolution in 1848 when so many other countries did not.

Just three years after the 'year of revolutions', the Great Exhibition of the Works of Industries of All Nations was held in the Crystal Palace in Hyde Park, London. This was a major international event showcasing manufactured items from the United Kingdom and the rest of the world. Historians have interpreted the event as evidence of renewed confidence in industrialisation and its ability to deliver progress and prosperity to the people of the United Kingdom (Purbrick, 2001). Such confidence was, it would seem, demonstrated in the support for the Great Exhibition among a large proportion of the population. Over 6 million visits were made to the exhibition and it was considered a great success at the time and subsequently. In a case study of the Great Exhibition in Section 8.3, you will look at how such confidence in progress was fostered and how consensus between different social and political groups was cultivated. You will also examine how deep this confidence was – were the anxieties and uncertainties of the early nineteenth century still apparent under the pomp and ceremony of the Great Exhibition?

Section 8.4 will go on to explore the social and political reforms of the mid-century and whether other material factors, such as improvements in the standard of living, shaped a new confidence in the future. Then, in preparation for the rest of Block 2, you will briefly consider the tensions that lay behind any social and political consensus and how these re-emerged in the 1860s and 1870s.

As you work through this unit, you'll be asked to think about how the turbulence of the 1840s gave way to increasing confidence in a modern industrial society and whether there is anything in the claim that the mid-century was an 'age of equipoise'. This term was first used by the historian William Burn in 1967 to describe the period between 1852 and 1867 as one of stability, calm and optimism in contrast to the unrest and anxiety of the years before and after. Burn did not claim that there were no disputes in this period; in fact he noted that there were many. However, the mid-Victorian generation was confident that such disputes could be resolved through compromise and that competing interests in politics, economy and society could be held in balance. As Burn said, what he found in studying the mid-century was 'a generation in which the old and the new, the elements of growth, survival and decay, achieved a balance which most contemporaries regarded as satisfactory' (Burn, 1964, p. 17).

The phrase 'the age of equipoise' caught the imagination of subsequent historians because it appeared to explain why there was greater optimism about progress in the mid-century. As you will see throughout Block 2, many of the fears of early nineteenth-century society were not realised: after 1848, working-class radicalism dissipated and Chartism declined. The middle class was on the rise, growing in political influence after the Reform Act of 1832 and the Municipal Corporations Act of 1835, but the landed aristocracy had not been overthrown and peaceful class coexistence looked possible. There were real improvements in everyday life for a number of people as the social reforms of the early period began to have an impact. As the units 'The making of the British middle class' and 'Cities, disease and health' (Units 12 and 13) explain, the new middle class established a power base in industrial towns and cities through civic councils and voluntary associations, and helped to build roads and sewers as well as churches, town halls, libraries and schools. The Factory Acts had been passed to limit the working hours of women and children employed in factories and slavery had been abolished, but global trade was flourishing. As a result, there was increasing faith in the beneficial influence of free trade, greater confidence that a minimal state would represent the interests of all the people and confidence that political economy could be humanised. It became possible, as the Great Exhibition demonstrates, to think of the United Kingdom as a progressive, **liberal** society made up of different people, groups and forces, each playing a role in contributing to the well-being of the whole.

But such a vision was fragile and was, by the 1860s, coming under strain. Depressions in trades reoccurred throughout the mid-century, puncturing prosperity and eroding confidence in a lasting stability. As you will see in Unit 9, the Irish Famine was over by the 1850s but its effects lingered in debates over Home Rule and Irish independence. The unit 'Work, poverty and the new Poor Law' (Unit 10) will show how continued crises over the Poor Law raised questions about inequalities in wealth and whether more needed to be done to keep working people out of poverty. The unit 'Religion, revival and reform' (Unit 11) will look at how the idea of the United Kingdom as peaceable and tolerant was challenged by religious tensions, some of which became violent. Similarly, as you will discover in the unit 'Britain and empire, 1839–1886' (Unit 15), global trade and empire, far from delivering peace and tranquillity, drew Britain into a number of wars and conflicts as the century progressed. By the late 1860s and the 1870s equipoise was in decline and optimism in short supply. Writers who were critical of industrialisation, such as Karl Marx (1818–1883), were coming to prominence and, as the unit 'Politics and the people' (Unit 14) explains, working men stepped up their campaign for the vote. The conclusion to this unit will revisit how these issues will be taken up in the rest of Block 2.

8.1 Chartism and the Anti-Corn Law League in the 1840s

In the 1840s many of the social, political and economic problems that had emerged in the early nineteenth century got progressively worse. The sense of a crisis building was fostered by three trends.

First, in the aftermath of a depression from 1837 to 1843, greater publicity was given to the plight of the poor. In the 1830s statistical evidence about the impact and extent of poverty was generated by investigators such as James Kay-Shuttleworth (1804–1877) and circulated in learned societies. In the 1840s the impact of poverty reached the public through the voices of the poor themselves in popular newspapers such as the *Morning Chronicle*. The investigative journalist Henry Mayhew (1812–1887) described the lives of the poor in their own words, giving particular scope to those displaced by modernisation, from the starving navvies employed to build railways, roads and bridges, to the impoverished weavers of Lancashire replaced by factories and machines, and to the **sweated labourers** of London's East End garment and furniture trades. Empathy for the poor was cultivated by sketches in illustrated papers, and poems and fiction dramatised the personal struggle to survive. A poem by Thomas Hood (1799–1845), 'Song of the Shirt', which describes a seamstress working herself to death, was reproduced in many newspapers in 1843 (Boyce, 2012, p. 426).

Second, resentment about the unfair impact of industrialisation on the working classes was sharpened by a hatred of the Corn Laws, which dated from 1815, and the new Poor Law of 1834, which together fuelled claims made by radicals that the British government was corrupt, self-interested and intent on protecting the landed elites at the expense of ordinary working people.

Third, the investment bubble generated by the expansion of the railways in the 1840s was brought to a sudden end in the crash of 1847. In the commercial crisis that followed, businesses collapsed, including a number of provincial savings banks, and many people including ordinary working- and middle-class savers lost a lot of money. Together these events fuelled fears that industrialisation had come to an end and many critics argued that the dominating ideology of the day, laissez-faire political economy, was producing nothing more than poverty and disorder.

The uncertainties and crises of the 1840s fuelled radical politics and provided the basis for two reform movements: Chartism and the Anti-Corn Law League. Both movements coexisted for around ten years until the Corn Laws were repealed in 1846. The Chartist movement and the Anti-Corn Law League kept the plight of the working-class family at the forefront of political debate in the 1840s. On the surface, their solutions looked very different – the extension of the franchise to all adult men and the repeal of the Corn Laws – but there were also grounds for agreement. Understanding 'equipoise' in the mid-century requires an examination of Chartism's aims and its relationship with the Anti-Corn Law League.

Chartism

As you know from Unit 3, the Chartist movement was formed in the late 1830s after disappointment with the Reform Act of 1832. Its primary focus on parliamentary reform – the six points that you studied in the unit '"Bliss was it in that dawn to be alive"?' (Unit 1 in Block 1) – enabled it to draw together men and women from a range of backgrounds, from artisans in well-paid trades to agricultural labourers and factory workers. However, for many Chartists the vote was a means to an end: a fairer society for working people.

Chartism was a national movement organised through local committees and was particularly strong in London, Wales and the manufacturing districts of the north of England and the Midlands. It had a rich and vibrant culture. It made great use of the press – the Chartist newspaper the *Northern Star* was published between 1837 and 1852 – and it used memorabilia, merchandise, fairs and tea parties to inspire loyalty, attract members and raise money. Women were an integral part of Chartism. They rarely gave speeches but they were active in the movement and present on marches and rallies (Chase, 2007).

Exercise 8.1

Turn to Reading 8.1, 'First Chartist petition, 1839', located at the end of the unit. After you have read this, answer the following questions:

- Who do the Chartists blame for their present distress? And who do they not blame?

- What do the Chartists ask for? And why? What do they threaten if they don't get it?

This should take around 30 minutes.

Specimen answer

- The Chartists blame the 'rulers' for their distress. They don't blame God (providence) or nature. They argue that the 'land itself is goodly, the soil rich'. They also don't blame the manufacturers. They note that merchants and manufacturers are enterprising and 'skilful' and the workers are industrious. All the conditions are right for prosperity, but excessive taxation has led to bankruptcy for the capitalists and starvation for workers.

- The Chartists ask for adult male suffrage on the principle that they are freemen. With the vote they can challenge corruption and ensure policies that work in the interests of ordinary people rather than the wealthy. They don't directly threaten violence, but they hint that without social, economic and political changes the 'stability of the throne and the peace of the kingdom' are endangered.

Discussion

There has been extensive debate among historians about whether or not Chartists identified with each other as members of the working class united in opposition to other social groups such as manufacturers and the landed elite. Reading 8.1 shows how complicated this question is. In the extract, Chartists define themselves as 'freemen' and as a part of the state. You can see this when they say they are 'required ... to support and obey the laws'. There is little reference to the Chartists as a group of workers, although there is evidence they are concerned as workers to ensure that taxes are reduced and food and products are made affordable. Instead, they think that 'property' should bear the burden of taxation. However, they also share some interests with their 'masters': they assume that healthy trade is good for all and argue that masters must be allowed to keep their capital. They avoid class language but they do talk of 'the people'. As you saw in Unit 3, this sort of language enabled Chartists to include a vast range of people in the movement.

The Anti-Corn Law League

The Anti-Corn Law League was formed in January 1839 in Manchester by members of the manufacturing middle class who had campaigned successfully for political reform in 1832. Like the Chartists, they were responding to the depression of the late 1830s. They argued that abolishing the Corn Laws would revive industry by bringing cheap corn into the country, leaving working families with more money to spend on other things. They also thought free trade agreements would create a market for British manufactured goods abroad. As one of their members, the businessman and MP for Bolton Dr John Bowring (1792–1872), put it in a speech in 1838 on the need for a national association, 'When I went to Brittany and Normandy, what said the Normans and Bretons? … "we are millions said they, willing to clothe ourselves in the garments you send us, and you have millions of hungry mouths to take our corn"' (quoted in Prentice, 1853, p. 65). For many in the movement, repeal of the Corn Laws was part of a wider vision that saw free trade as the basis for prosperity and peace.

Like the Chartists, the Anti-Corn Law League was formed of local associations that constituted a national body. It raised money through membership subscriptions, bazaars and the sale of souvenirs and memorabilia. It had its own press and used newspapers and pamphlets carried through the post to keep members informed of meetings and rallies. The *Economist* magazine, established to help further the interests of the Anti-Corn Law League, became an outspoken supporter of free trade policies.

The Anti-Corn Law League was well resourced financially and politically. Members paid a subscription, which funded campaigns and which helped get Anti-Corn Law League candidates elected to Parliament. Richard Cobden (1804–1865) and John Bright (1811–1889), both cotton manufacturers, become the most outspoken members of the league in the House of Commons.

Exercise 8.2

Turn to Reading 8.2, 'Resolutions of the Anti-Corn Law League (1853)', located at the end of the unit. These resolutions were agreed at a meeting of the Anti-Corn Law League in Manchester in 1839 and published by Archibald Prentice in his history of the league of 1853.

After you have read this, answer the following questions:

- Considering Resolution 3, how do the members of the Anti-Corn Law League define their interests? Are they separate from the rest of the people?

- Look again at Resolution 4; do you notice any similarities in the argument and language in the Chartist petition?

This should take around 30 minutes.

Specimen answer

- The Anti-Corn Law League members see their interests as the same as those of other productive members of society. The repeal of the Corn Laws would prove a stimulus to trade, which would benefit both capitalists and labourers in agriculture and industry.

- Like the Chartists, the Anti-Corn Law League members argue that there is nothing natural about the present distress. Instead they argue that men are hungry in the 'midst of boundless fields of employment', because of government legislation and taxation. And like the Chartists, they also refer to 'the people' and the 'nation'.

Discussion

The Chartist movement and the Anti-Corn Law League were mass movements organised through local associations (Vernon, 2014). This enabled them to accommodate members from different parts of the British Isles with different kinds of interests and agendas. They each also had a clearly stated aim – the charter and repeal – that was used to argue for a broader set of demands.

They both used similar language and motifs in their literature and articles of association. Both the Anti-Corn Law League and the Chartists referred to shared interests between manufacturers and workers, employers and employees. Both were optimistic that the energy and enterprise of manufacturers, merchants and workers would lead to prosperity if unhindered by taxes and government interference to protect landowners. They both talked about 'the people' and 'the nation', which suggests they imagined a community that shared basic values, one that cut across class differences. They both believed in 'order', but warned that this could be threatened if deprivation continued.

Exercises 8.1 and 8.2 have demonstrated the strong connections between the interests pursued by the Anti-Corn Law League and the Chartist movement. Historians such as Patrick Joyce have argued that the shared interests of Chartists and free traders developed into a broad-based **popular liberalism** in the 1850s and 1860s, which in turn provided the foundations for a mid-Victorian consensus (Joyce, 1991). By talking of 'the people' and 'the nation' these movements cut through class interests. They presented workers and manufacturers as

Figure 8.1 An Anti-Corn Law League membership card for 'John Lomas', no. 1,362, which shows a poor family eating dear bread (representing protection) and a prosperous family eating cheap bread (representing free trade). They are separated by the Anti-Corn Law League symbol of a sheaf of wheat, beneath a banner that says 'He that withholdeth corn, the people shall curse him.' Source: www.chartistancestors.co.uk, used under creativecommons. org/licenses/by-nc/4.0/

'producers', who, unlike landowners, worked together to promote national prosperity.

There were limits to this consensus. Before moving on, let's finish this consideration of Chartism and the Anti-Corn Law League by looking at what happened when the two movements discussed work and wages.

Exercise 8.3

Turn to Reading 8.3, 'Wages and the Corn Laws (1853)', located at the end of the unit, which is an extract from Prentice's *History of the Anti-Corn Law League*. What do Mr Heywood and Mr Cobden say is the cause of low wages?

This should take around 15 minutes.

Specimen answer

Cobden gives a 'a clear explanation of the principles that regulate wages'. These principles are those of political economy, and Mr

Heywood argues that low wages are caused by lack of work and competition for wages. No government intervention can help working men secure better wages. Cheap bread, however, should enable them to spend less on food and make them feel better off.

Discussion

Issues of work and wages threatened to undermine any unity of interest between the Anti-Corn Law League and the Chartists. Most members of the league adhered to the concept of a laissez-faire political economy and believed that government intervention upset the natural harmony of free markets. Many were also manufacturers and members of the middle class. Meanwhile, many Chartists were trade unionists and active in the campaign for factory reform. They argued that government regulation of industry was necessary to prevent over-competition and reduced wages. They also thought that employers deliberately encouraged competition to reduce the wage bill and argued that trade unions should have a say in determining wages. When Thomas Attwood (1783–1856) presented the Chartist petition of 1839 to Parliament he argued that Chartists wanted from it 'a fair day's wages for a fair day's work' (HC Deb, 14 June 1839).

As you saw in the unit 'Managing uncertainty: new forms of "knowledge"' (Unit 4 in Block 1), the campaign for factory reform culminated in the Factory Acts. One of these – the Factory Act of 1847, otherwise known as the Ten Hours Act – limited the working hours of women and children. This Act irritated some manufacturers in the north of England who sharpened their resolve to resist all further intervention in their industries, whether from government or from trade unions. On the other hand, trade unions argued that the Factory Acts showed that regulation of industry could be effective without ruining trade.

Chartists and repealers (supporters of the Anti-Corn Law League) focused on food because it was a powerful symbol of basic needs and basic human rights. Figure 8.1 shows how simple and powerful the symbol was. It also enabled them to avoid talking about things they disagreed on, such as the organisation of work and the protection of wages. Instead, focusing on bread suggested that rather than the reorganisation of production, it was free trade and fair consumption, with better access to food and goods, which provided the answer to poverty and privation. As this suggests, the focus on food and consumption hid fundamental differences in attitudes to work, politics and laissez-faire political economy.

Activity 8.1

Now go to the module website and complete Activity 8.1 'Understanding how historians use sources'. This should take around an hour and a half.

8.2 1848: the year of revolutions

Chartism reached a peak in 1848, a year of revolutions across Europe. These revolutions were orchestrated by a broad alliance of middle- and working-class people with a range of grievances, united by the desire to challenge autocratic leaders. They had varying degrees of success over the long term, but in 1848 the revolutionaries appeared to be in the ascendant and in France and Hungary rulers were toppled.

Thus the Chartist plan to hold a rally on Kennington Common, south London (Figure 8.2) and to present a petition for the vote to Parliament on 10 April 1848 stoked fears of revolution in the British Isles (Quinault, 1988). The British government responded with urgency and the Chartists who turned up on the day were met by a well-organised force. The Duke of Wellington (1769–1852, prime minister 1828–30), hero of the Battle of Waterloo and an active representative of the old regime who had strongly opposed reform in 1832, persuaded the government to deploy large numbers of police, troops and special volunteer forces (Taylor, 1995). The Chartists were hemmed in on Kennington Common and prevented from crossing the River Thames to reach Westminster. A few leaders, including Feargus O'Connor (1794–1855), were eventually escorted to deliver the charter to Lord John Russell (1792–1878, prime minister 1846–52 and 1865–66). The charter was found not to contain the number of signatures expected and was roundly ridiculed in Parliament. The Chartists dissipated and Chartism was widely considered to have failed.

The apparent failure of Chartism, the United Kingdom's first mass working-class political movement, has puzzled generations of historians. Reading 8.1, the Chartist petition of 1839 that you considered in Exercise 8.1, contains the line 'Our slavery has been exchanged for an apprenticeship to liberty …'. This line confronted liberal arguments that the vote was not a right but something that had to be earned through self-help, education, independence and individual improvement. As you will see in Unit 14, for many contemporaries the failure of Chartism and the rise of popular liberalism suggested that a politics of progress through steady improvement rather than rapid change had won.

Figure 8.2 Photograph by William Kilburn of the great Chartist meeting on Kennington Common, south London, 1848. Royal Collection Trust © Her Majesty Queen Elizabeth II, 2016 / Bridgeman Images

Chartism and equipoise: a historical debate

Historians have struggled to explain why Chartism petered out, why the campaign for the vote stalled, and why the working class appeared to align itself with liberal politicians such as Bright and Cobden who argued for gradual political reform, free trade and laissez-faire political economy. To explain this, some historians have returned to the writings of Karl Marx and his ideas about revolution.

Writing in the nineteenth century, Karl Marx argued that economic forces changed history. He thought that social and economic inequalities produced by industrialisation would create a class consciousness among workers, based on an awareness of their shared exploitation by manufacturers supported by politicians. This would, he argued, lead to revolution.

Marxist historians adapted Marx's ideas in the twentieth century and looked at the role of culture in explaining the lack of revolution in the United Kingdom. They argued that the growth of working-class reformism after Chartism was the result of both divisions within the working class and **bourgeois hegemony**. In these accounts a privileged section of the working class, the artisans, craftsmen and those in superintendence roles in factories, formed a 'labour aristocracy' whose values of independence and respectability closely resembled those of the new middle class. This left them open to 'indoctrination' through the churches, charities, town halls, libraries, schools and museums that were built in the mid-century by the middle classes interested in reform (Foster, 1974; Hobsbawm, 1964). These accounts saw the mid-century as producing a break in radicalism until the revival of socialism in the 1870s and 1880s.

Other historians have emphasised the continuities and connections between the working and middle classes in the early and mid-century. Gareth Stedman Jones has argued that the class politics of the early nineteenth century was overstated in Marxist historical accounts. Instead, he holds that the focus on 'old corruption' in early nineteenth-century radicalism provided the basis for a shared politics uniting the working and middle classes against a corrupt aristocracy (Stedman Jones, 1983). James Vernon and Patrick Joyce have argued that middle-class leaders such as Bright and Cobden simply harnessed liberal values of fairness and justice that were already embedded in working-class communities (Vernon, 1993; Joyce, 1991). Miles Taylor contends that the generation of liberal politicians who came to power after the Reform Act of 1832, men such as Cobden and Bright, restored faith in parliamentary democracy and persuaded working people that their interests would be represented despite them not having a vote (Taylor, 1995). Jonathan Parry and Margot Finn have also demonstrated how liberalism provided the basis for a powerful patriotism that was able to cut through class differences to unite people around values such as liberty, the nation and independence (Parry, 2006; Finn, 1993); though, as Finn also notes, laissez-faire political economy was a continued source of tension between working-class and middle-class liberals.

Somewhat differently, Peter Gurney and Martin Hewitt have noted that insecurity and the threat of poverty continued to unite the working classes in the mid-nineteenth century despite improvements in the standard of living. A distinctly working-class radicalism persisted after Chartism, but was channelled into societies and associations such as trade unions, friendly societies and cooperative societies (Gurney, 2009; Hewitt, 1996). It was these collectivised forms of self-help that provided the practical support and stability for working people that informed the sense of well-being and equipoise. As Hewitt has shown,

Chartism was a national movement composed of lots of local organisations, which adapted to the changing conditions in the 1850s by forming new associations. Educational groups, friendly societies, savings banks and cooperatives were not the result of middle-class hegemony, social control or working-class acceptance of liberalism. They were, according to Hewitt, 'a rational response to changes in the environment' (Hewitt, 1996, p. 303). In this analysis Chartism did not fail; it was absorbed into other kinds of working-class movements.

Exercise 8.4

Political cartoons were an important way of presenting political argument and opinion in the nineteenth century and are a good resource for historians. To get the most out of them you need to read and examine them carefully. The cartoon in Figure 8.3 appeared in *Punch* magazine just before Christmas in 1848. Different nations are represented by the people around the table looking at the Christmas pudding.

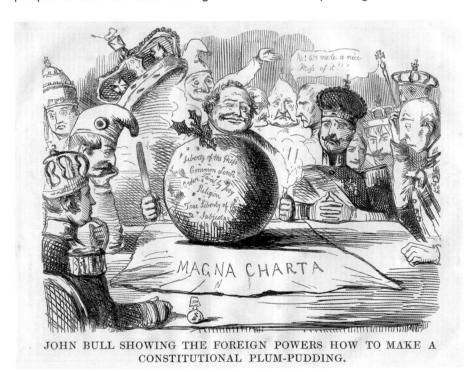

JOHN BULL SHOWING THE FOREIGN POWERS HOW TO MAKE A CONSTITUTIONAL PLUM-PUDDING.

Figure 8.3 Unknown artist, 'John Bull showing the foreign powers how to make a constitutional plum-pudding', Magna Carta cartoon, *Punch*, 23 December 1848. Photo: © Mary Evans Picture Library

Britain is represented here in the character of John Bull with a knife and fork about to tuck into the Christmas pudding. In the eighteenth century

John Bull was seen as the archetypal 'freeborn Englishman' of Anglo-Saxon origins. By the late nineteenth century he came to represent the United Kingdom and was often pictured wearing the Union flag. In the mid-nineteenth century he hovered somewhere between the two – although he represented the United Kingdom, this was really an extension of the values of the 'freeborn Englishman' to Scotland, Ireland and Wales.

Look at both the image and the text. What values are associated with Britain here?

This should take around 10 minutes.

Specimen answer

John Bull is represented in simple attire. He is also plump and content; despite his simplicity he is clearly well fed and prosperous. He appears to have little to worry about. In contrast, the other leaders are adorned with crowns, robes and uniforms (including the French revolutionary with his cap of liberty), but they are puzzled and pensive.

The source of John Bull's contentment is represented in the pudding. You might have noticed that it is resting on the 'Magna Charta' (Magna Carta) – seen as the basis of the British constitution. On the plum pudding are inscribed the key rights associated with the constitution: liberty of the press, common sense, order, trial by jury, religion and true liberty of the subject.

In effect the cartoon is arguing that British contentment lies in a shared respect for liberty and law among all the people, in contrast to the leaders of autocratic regimes.

Discussion

In the aftermath of 1848, commentators such as the Whig historian Thomas Macaulay (1800–1859) argued that the British constitution and the British character saved the nation from the European diseases of over-centralisation, corruption and autocracy. Only the British people really understood liberty to be a combination of pragmatism and principle that required compromise in the interests of all. This view, popularised by Macaulay in his *History of England* (published in 1848–55), became known as **Whig history** (Butterfield, 1931). Macaulay tended to assume that Britain and the United Kingdom were, in effect, England writ large. He argued that progress in England was achieved through gradual improvement and constitutional reform, and that this superior kind of history and progress could be transposed onto others in the British Isles and the empire.

After Chartism a new kind of liberal politics emerged that combined patriotism, respect for British institutions and popular constitutionalism. It provided the foundation for a renewed confidence in progress and industry. It presented the British people as rational and reasonable: they knew when to insist on their rights and when to restrain themselves in the national interest. For working people, this included the right to earn a living. After Chartism, the argument that this right was best served through global free trade gained currency, an argument that had been popularised by the Anti-Corn Law League (Parry, 2006). In this way, character, patriotism and constitutionalism became strongly associated with global trade, industry and empire. Events such as the Great Exhibition were essential in creating this new vision of a United Kingdom as the preeminent nation among nations and the 'workshop of the world'.

8.3 The Great Exhibition

The Great Exhibition of the Works of Industry of All Nations opened on 1 May 1851. The exhibition was huge. It contained 100,000 exhibits, half of which were from around the British Isles and the empire, the other half from the rest of the world. They were housed in the Crystal Palace, designed by Joseph Paxton (1803–1865), a temporary structure of steel and glass that covered almost 950,000 cubic metres in a 7.7-hectare enclosed area of Hyde Park in London. The building was immediately seized on as a symbol of all that the Great Exhibition hoped to achieve. It was built by skilled workmen directed by engineers with material produced by British industrialists, using the latest technology in glass and steel but designed to work with the natural environment. The glass allowed natural light in, was easy to ventilate and could accommodate trees and plants. The structure drew on recent advances in science and incorporated the latest inventions designed to increase personal comfort – flushing toilets, water fountains and refreshment stands were incorporated into the building, additions that were intended to make a day at the exhibition enlightening and enjoyable.

The original idea for the exhibition came from the Royal Society of Arts, which wanted to educate the public in industry and design. It was organised by Henry Cole (1808–1882), a civil servant who had worked with Rowland Hill (1795–1879) in designing the postal service, and Prince Albert (1819–1861), the husband of Queen Victoria (1819–1901, reigned 1837–1901), who helped raise the money for the exhibition through charity events, voluntary contributions and subscriptions. The overarching aim of the exhibition was to demonstrate that a harmony between nature, industry and the arts was possible through manufacturing and that peaceful relations between classes and nations could be achieved through trade and commerce. It also aimed to show that great things could be achieved by individual effort and initiative, and from people working together, rather than through an Act of Parliament.

Plans for the Great Exhibition initially emerged out of concerns about the quality of British manufactured goods and a desire to compare them with those from other countries, particularly those from Germany, France and the USA, which were seen as newly industrialising countries and potential competitors. By the time the exhibition opened it was a celebration of progress in science, art and manufacturing and a demonstration of what could be achieved by cooperation between people, nations and classes. It is no surprise, then, that it has been interpreted by many historians as a turning point in history, as a break with the 'hungry forties' and the radical politics of Chartism and as evidence of a new optimism about industry and progress (Purbrick, 2001). However, the Great Exhibition should also be examined as an event that was intended to *produce* this optimism. It aimed to persuade people that the benefits of industry would be open to all and that Britain would lead the world into a new era of peace and prosperity through manufacturing and trade. Historians need to go beyond the surface presentation of the events to the public, to explore the private interests of the organisers and to distinguish the vision of society the organisers wanted to present from the thoughts and feelings of ordinary people.

The Great Exhibition organisers were conscious of making history and kept careful records of their plans. The Royal Society of Arts built an archive of notes and letters relating to the event and the first historical accounts were produced at the same time as the exhibition itself. Henry Cole's *Official Descriptive and Illustrated Catalogue of the Industry of All Nations* (1851) included a detailed history of the event, and fundraising speeches made much of the historical significance of the exhibition before it had even taken place.

Exercise 8.5

Turn to Reading 8.4, 'Prince Albert, "Mansion House speech" (1849)', located at the end of the unit. This is an extract from a speech given by the prince at Mansion House, London, on 21 March 1849.

After you have read this, answer the following questions:

- In brief, how does Prince Albert describe the age?

- What does he see as leading to the 'unity of mankind'?

This should take around 30 minutes.

Specimen answer

- Prince Albert notes that the 'present era' is a period of 'most wonderful transition' heading towards the 'unity of mankind'.

- The prince sees the division of labour and exchange of knowledge as leading to the unity of mankind. He refers to the division of labour as 'the moving power of civilisation' and he argues that it is being applied to science, industry and art. Rather than knowing and doing everything, men acquire specialist knowledge in small areas, which is then exchanged and shared to the benefit of all or the 'community at large'.

Discussion

You may have noticed something odd about Prince Albert's speech. It is not always clear what he is talking about. He starts off talking about knowledge and science and ends up referring to products, production, competition and capital. This was not an accident. Albert's speech and the Great Exhibition itself were intent on exploring the relationship between industry, science, art and commerce.

Cole and his circle at the Royal Society who organised the exhibition were utilitarians, interested in what kinds of relationships and things created the 'greatest happiness for the greatest number'. You can see the influence of their ideas in Albert's speech. The 'greatest happiness', according to the prince, is produced by the division of labour. For many contemporaries and historians, the division of labour defined industrialisation. It aimed for efficiency by breaking production down into distinct parts, each performed by an individual.

There were many critics of the division of labour: Adam Smith (1723–1790), whom you will recall from Block 1, was concerned it made work boring and repetitive, while Marx argued that it deskilled labour, reduced wages and alienated workers from the products they were producing. However, there were many political economists who admired and idealised the division of labour because it depended on the cooperation of a number of individuals to make it work.

Prince Albert's speech takes this view further. When applied to science, art and commerce, he imagines the division of labour uniting communities and nations, each playing a part in building a better world. Competition drives the process forward, encouraging the development of ideas and products that are produced and exchanged. This process of competition and exchange finds a balance between nature and industry and a balance between science and religion without outside intervention. And it also reveals what or who is superior. As you might have guessed, after the Great Exhibition it was generally assumed by many in Britain that Britain was the greatest power in the world (Parry, 2006).

Alternative perspectives

This patriotic view of Britain's progress fuelled greater optimism about the future. Nevertheless there were notable critics of this vision, including the **Christian Socialists** and the writer Matthew Arnold (1822–1888), who feared that society was becoming materialistic and philistine (Parry, 2006). There were also critics from within the liberal movement. The liberal philosopher John Stuart Mill (1806–1873) was concerned that the kind of individualism promoted by utilitarians was making society narrow, mean and selfish. Instead of helping to soften competitive individualism, religion was making people intolerant and those in authority were becoming snooty and bigoted (Mill, 1869 [1859]). Mill wanted to define an individualism that was more humane and altruistic, one based on open communication and a genuine understanding of each other's interests (Collini, 1991). In a famous essay of 1859, *On Liberty*, he argued that individuals were free to pursue their own interests as long as the pursuit of them did not intrude on the freedom of others. He argued that debate and discussion would help people settle their differences amicably and find solutions that benefited the greatest number. Mill's ideas were very persuasive and much discussed. According to Stefan Collini, this is because he was saying what many people at the time were thinking (Collini, 1991).

Mill's ideas chimed with those of radicals and liberals who viewed the United Kingdom as a progressive, patriotic and pluralistic society founded on an ethical union of people and regions (Parry, 2006). Nevertheless, as you work through Block 2 you will see that this principle was difficult to put into practice and under constant strain. For example, Unit 11 explores fierce debates about religious toleration and the rights of Irish and British Catholics, many of whom were still considered a threat to the British state. And as you will learn in the discussion of parliamentary reform in Unit 14, there were debates about who had the ability to exercise freedom. Women, the poor and the masses were considered too feeble or ignorant to act in their own interests. Similarly, as Unit 15 on empire explains, imperial subjects were seen as not advanced enough to be given political liberty. While British writers justified the empire in terms of liberty and free trade, imperial governance was authoritarian and repressive, given the perceived and actual threats to imperial rule from colonised peoples.

Visiting the Great Exhibition

Regardless of these alternative views and debates about liberalism, the exhibition appeared to capture a more optimistic public mood. The opening was a spectacular event, captured in the commemorative painting by Henry Courtney Selous that you can see in Figure 8.4. Much of this optimism resulted from the events of 1848. The fact that London could host an event in which Queen Victoria could mingle with the masses three years after that revolutionary time was seen as a national triumph, prompting an outpouring of patriotism. As Macaulay wrote on the opening day of the Great Exhibition, 'There is as much chance of a revolution in England as the falling of the moon' (quoted in Parry, 2006, p. 63).

Figure 8.4 Henry Courtney Selous, *Opening of the Great Exhibition*, 1851–52, oil on canvas. Photo: © Bridgeman Images

The Great Exhibition was immensely popular with a broad range of people. Over 6 million visits were made in the six months it was open. These included the great and good of Victorian society: aristocrats and politicians from across the political spectrum, as well as Victorian notables and celebrities such as the writers Charles Dickens (1812–1870) and Charlotte Brontë (1816–1855). Many members of the middle and working classes visited, taking advantage of the 'shilling [5p] days' (Monday to Thursday) introduced from 26 May (depicted in

Figure 8.5). Visitors travelled from around the United Kingdom, Europe and further afield, and much was made of those arriving on the latest contrivances of the industrial age, the steamship and the railway. Many railway companies organised excursions and day trips promoting affordable travel to the working classes. The press made much of the good-natured crowd and appeared to take pleasure in a new phenomenon, the mixing of a diverse group of people in a public space. That the event took place without serious unrest or extensive crime was considered a great success.

Figure 8.5 John Leech, 'The pound and the shilling', cartoon commenting on the 'shilling days' at the Great Exhibition, *Punch*, vol. 20, 1851. Photo: © Mary Evans Picture Library

Exercise 8.6

The opening of the Great Exhibition was covered extensively in newspaper reports. You can find two such descriptions in the next two readings, located at the back of the unit. Reading 8.5, 'The Times report on the opening of the Great Exhibition (2 May 1851)', is from a well-established daily British newspaper. Reading 8.6, 'Scientific American report on the opening of the Great Exhibition (24 May 1851)', is from a weekly newspaper interested in inventions, manufacturing and enterprise (and one of many foreign newspapers that sent a reporter to the Great Exhibition).

After you have read these extracts, answer the following questions:

- Who, according to these descriptions, is at the opening of the Great Exhibition?

- What do you notice about the way the crowds are described?

This should take around 30 minutes.

Specimen answer

- Readings 8.5 and 8.6 suggest that almost everyone is at the Great Exhibition, from the royal family to working men and their families and foreign visitors. The reporter for Scientific American suggests that people have come from near and far (the latter probably on railways and steamships).

- The reports emphasise words such as 'mass' and 'multitude', which could give the impression of a disorderly mob. However, they also describe, with some surprise, that the crowds are happy, playful and peaceful.

Discussion

Three years after 1848, words such as 'mass' and 'multitude' would still have been associated with riot, revolution and disorder. However, the crowds of working people at the Great Exhibition are quite different. The reports are keen to emphasise that these working-class people are eager to participate in the celebrations. This sentence in Reading 8.5 is particularly telling:

'Those honest English workmen, in their round fustian jackets and glazed caps, felt they had a right to take part in the honours of the day, and to have an honest pride in the result of their own and their brethren's labours, and they walked contentedly, and happily, amid prancing horses and gaudy liveries.'

This report shows that the working-class people present are not cowed or deferential. Nor are they disgruntled or disaffected. As you may have noticed, the working classes are included in the crowds *because of* their status as labourers and not *despite* it. According to the reporter, they feel they have a right to be there and they are rightly proud of the labour that has made the exhibition possible.

Work at the Great Exhibition

In the mid-nineteenth century work became idealised as the source of all progress. The Victorian 'gospel of work', as it became known, presented work as noble and liberating, producing men (it was often male artisans who were associated with this idea, despite the fact that many women worked) of great character and helping to build a prosperous society. As Ford Madox Brown's (1821–1893) famous painting called *Work* (Figure 8.6) attempted to demonstrate, society could function only when everybody did their bit, from the navvies laying water pipes to the aristocrats and intellectuals providing leadership. His painting included notable figures who celebrated work, such as the thinker and writer Thomas Carlyle (1795–1881), who argued that all labour was noble and that 'a man perfects himself by working' (Carlyle 1870 [1843], p. 244). It also included those who represented workers, such as the founder and leader of the Christian Socialist movement, Frederick Maurice (1805–1872). The need to work was accepted as a universal condition that applied to everyone throughout history. This idea was the theme of a famous book, *Self Help* (1859), by the writer and reformer Samuel Smiles (1812–1904). It argued that even those born into luxury had a duty to work for the benefit of mankind.

Work was celebrated in the mid-century as a shared practice that built society in the connections it formed between capital and labour, landed aristocracy and farm worker, mistress and servant. Waged work in particular was considered to be the foundation of character, individual liberty and national prosperity. The Great Exhibition was one of many mid-century attempts to celebrate this idea of work. According to Henry Mayhew, it was 'the first public national expression ever made in this country, as to the dignity and artistic quality of labour' (Mayhew, 1851, p. 131). It would improve the self-respect and status of workers and 'inspire them into a sense of their own position in the State'. In

Figure 8.6 Ford Madox Brown, *Work*, 1852–65, oil on canvas, 137 x 197cm. Manchester Art Gallery, Acc. No. 1885.1. Photo: © Manchester Art Gallery / Bridgeman Images

fact, he argued, 'The Great Exhibition is a higher boon to labour than a general advance of wages' (Mayhew, 1851, pp. 131–2).

This vision of work as noble and improving was in sharp contrast to other images of work and workers. Carlyle and Mayhew critiqued political economy for imagining work as a **cash nexus**, a strictly economic phenomenon based on competition between workers for work which, in turn, drove down wages. Instead, in the 'gospel of work', work was well organised by enlightened employers in modern factories or undertaken by educated artisans in workshops. It was morally and spiritually improving as well as economically profitable. As you will see later in Block 2, tensions between these different ideas about work and society shaped responses to the Irish Famine and to the new Poor Law and inspired a revived campaign for the vote in the 1860s. These tensions were also soon exposed during the Great Exhibition.

Exercise 8.7

Look at Figure 8.7. It is taken from the satirical magazine *Punch*. A characterisation of Mr Punch is present in the cartoon to expose the hypocrisy of Victorian society. In this case, he reveals a very different image of work from that on display at the Great Exhibition.

What do you notice about the way work is represented in this cartoon?

This should take around 15 minutes.

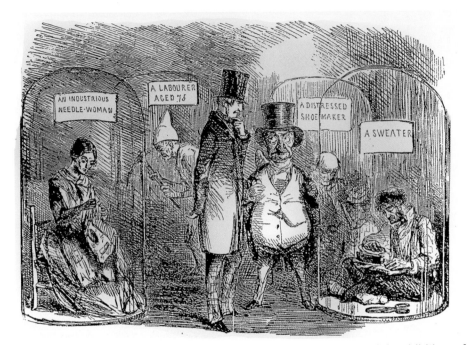

Figure 8.7 John Leech, 'Specimens from Mr Punch's industrial exhibition of 1850', engraving. *Punch*, 13 April 1850. Photo: © Bridgeman Images

Specimen answer

In this cartoon work is not mechanised. It is still being predominantly done by hand. Work is not artistic or improving. Workers are haggard and drawn and clearly starving. As the image of the 'labourer aged 75' shows, people are still having to work to earn a living when old and infirm.

Discussion

This cartoon challenged the 'gospel of work'. It would have chimed with audiences still familiar with the debates about the plight of the poor that you encountered at the start of the unit. Despite industrialisation, a lot of work was still performed by hand in the mid-century and mechanisation increased the need for new kinds of skilled labour (Samuel, 1977). There were many handicraft and artisan trades that were esteemed and well-paid, such as engineering and machine-making. Workers in these trades managed to protect their work and wages by using apprenticeships and trade unions to limit entry.

In other cases, however, artisanal workers were subject to competition from factories. You may remember the handloom weavers in Unit 3. Workers in the shoe trade, for example, such as the 'distressed shoemaker' in the cartoon in Figure 8.7, also had to compete with new mechanised types of production in factories, which could produce more articles for sale quickly and cheaply. Wages in other trades were threatened by sweated workers in an overcrowded labour market. In the textiles and garment trades, tailors and seamstresses had to compete for work with lots of other workers. It was easy to blame migrant workers for cheapening labour. As you will see in Unit 9, migrant workers fleeing the Famine in Ireland in the 1840s were blamed for driving down wages and prices in the industrial districts of England. Similarly, in the East End of London, Jewish migrants from eastern Europe were the targets for complaints about low pay and poor working conditions.

A number of exposés on sweated labour were produced in the mid-nineteenth century. One of these, *Cheap Clothes and Nasty* by the Christian Socialist Charles Kingsley (1819–1875), first published by the *Morning Chronicle* in 1850 under the pseudonym Parson Lot, argued that merchants and middlemen were exploiting this overcrowded labour market to make a quick profit (Kingsley, 1850). However, Kingsley also blamed consumers, including aristocrats, clergymen and government contractors, for demanding cheaper prices in the first place. His investigation showed that sweated workers were found in **slop shops** making uniforms for the navy and clothes for West End shops. He berated the hypocrites who campaigned against slavery in the Caribbean but who bought clothes made by 'white slaves' at home, and argued that ignorance was no excuse. As he said, 'men ought to know the conditions of those by whose labour they live' (Kingsley, 1850, p. 12). He also argued that knowledge of working conditions was a matter of self-interest. In a sensationalist account, Kingsley argued that diseases such as typhoid and smallpox were being passed from the poor sweated labourer to the aristocrat and clergyman through clothes:

> The Rev. D— finds himself suddenly unpresentable from a cutaneous disease ... little dreaming that the shivering dirty being who made his coat has been sitting with his arms in the sleeves

for warmth while he stitched at the tails. The charming Miss C—
is swept off by typhus or scarlatina, and her parents talk about
'God's heavy judgment and visitation' – had they tracked the girl's
new riding-habit back to the stifling undrained hovel where it
served as a blanket to the fever-stricken slopworker, they would
see *why* God had visited them … .

(Kingsley, 1850, p. 22)

As you will see in Unit 13, anxieties about the easy spread of disease
across the classes as a result of the interconnectedness of modern
industrial and urban life began to cut through laissez-faire ideologies
and fuel support for slum clearance and public health reform in
the 1870s. In this case, Kingsley uses the 'gospel of work' and the idea
that the classes are connected through work and consumption to argue
that the plight of the poor sweated worker cannot be ignored.

Activity 8.2

Now go to the module website and complete Activity 8.2 'Responses to
the Great Exhibition'. This should take around an hour.

Slavery at the Great Exhibition

The Great Exhibition was a self-conscious attempt to celebrate work
and free trade as the foundation of peace and prosperity. It does not
take long to see that behind the image the old fault lines were
emerging. As you have already seen, the image of work as noble and
civilising was challenged by troubling associations with 'white slavery'.
Other kinds of associations with slavery were also made. As you know
from the unit 'The British Isles and the Atlantic World' (Unit 7 in
Block 1), the abolition movement was prominent in the early part of
the nineteenth century and had campaigned successfully for the
abolition of slavery in 1833. However, plantation slavery was still a
fundamental part of the economy of the USA and, through the
importation of slave-picked cotton for the cotton industry in
Lancashire, part of Britain's industrial success.

The abolitionist Atlantic networks that you encountered in Unit 7 were
still active in the mid-century: between 1840 and 1865 around 80
abolitionist speakers visited Britain, giving anti-slavery lectures and
raising money to support fugitive and freed slaves (Knadler, 2011).

One group of abolitionists including three fugitive slaves, William Wells Brown (1814–1884), William Craft (1824–1900) and Ellen Craft (1826–1891), performed a protest in the US gallery of the Great Exhibition. They stood next to a famous statue, *The Greek Slave*, by the American sculptor Hiram Powers (1805–1873) – an idealised representation of a white female slave, captured by Turks to be sold at a slave auction – and gave speeches and lectures on the reality of slavery in the present-day USA. They spoke of the effects of the cruelty and brutality of forced labour on generations of plantation labourers. Their intention was to advertise and promote the abolitionist cause, but the effect was to challenge the ideals of British progress and the vision of an international community based on free and fair exchange.

It is difficult for historians to measure the impact of protests such as this. At the very least it shows that not everyone who attended the Great Exhibition was persuaded by its celebration of work and free trade. Some historians have dug deeper among all the celebratory news stories and optimistic outpourings written about the Great Exhibition in the 1850s to trace other kinds of challenges. Laura Kriegel has found that commentators were also worried about Britain's increasing dependence on other countries for raw materials and for trade. Concern was expressed about the 'purity' of tobacco and tea, about the morality of the opium trade and about the way that the trade in sugar cultivated by emancipated slaves in the West Indies was being conducted. However, the question of cotton was the most contentious. The United Kingdom might have been the 'workshop of the world', but its most advanced and modern industry, the cotton industry, whose machinery was proudly on display at the exhibition, was reliant on slavery, which, as *The Illustrated London News* reminded its readers, was 'the worst institution of modern times' (quoted in Kriegel, 2001, p. 154). As you will see in Unit 15, these competing ideas of the United Kingdom as highly civilised, helping to promote free trade and fair exchange around the world and, at the same time, brutal and oppressive in its pursuit of trade, was a feature of the British Empire. It serves as a reminder of how fragile the vision of progress was in the mid-nineteenth century.

The Great Exhibition and progress

Historians now tend to view the Great Exhibition as an event that was trying to bring forth the world it described. It aimed to persuade the public that industrialisation would lead to progress. A trip to the Great Exhibition was supposed to educate the public about the positive effects of manufacturing on the British economy and of self-help on the British character. It was, as one historian has noted, both a 'museum and a market place' (Richards, 1990, p. 19). On the one hand, the exhibition demonstrated the emergence of a commodity culture in which people are persuaded to desire things and want to buy them. It is no surprise that historians have traced the emergence of department stores and the advertising industry to the exhibition (Richards, 1990). On the other hand, historians have also traced back to the exhibition the roots of a didactic national museum culture in which galleries of objects are used to communicate lessons about art, industry and the nation. In this way the Great Exhibition was an example of Victorian 'rational recreation' in which increased leisure time was to be spent on self-improvement activities. The magazine *Art Union* noted that 'The loyalizing effect of such an exhibition is not the least of its moral recommendations. Every man would see in its treasures the result of social order and reverence for the majesty of the law' (quoted in Greenhalgh, 1988, p. 30). The collection from the Great Exhibition was used to establish two London institutions, the Victoria and Albert Museum in 1852 and the Science Museum in 1857, as permanent museums to design, technology and industry.

This culture of visibility and exemplarity, of looking and learning, was also expected to impart good behaviour to those who attended. Organisers hoped that the mixing of people together in a shared space, using maps and catalogues as guides, would help the crowd learn from each other how to behave respectably in public. Some historians have argued that this represented a new, subtle shift in nineteenth-century governance where the crowd was expected to discipline itself. As you read in Unit 4, utilitarians drew up designs for an ideal prison, or 'panopticon', so that every individual could be observed by a regulatory figure. In much the same way, the glass structure of the Crystal Palace and the arrangements of galleries and stalls allowed people to see each other. They might be encouraged to notice habits of dress and the latest fashions but they were also expected to notice patterns of accepted behaviour, something the organisers hoped would ensure the people policed each other and themselves (Purbrick, 2001). Tony Bennett has argued that, in this way, the Great Exhibition and the museum culture of the United Kingdom in the nineteenth century did the work of the state for it (Bennett, 1995). It is no surprise, then, that one historian has called the Great Exhibition a great 'counter-revolutionary measure' and one that normalised a society organised around industry and commerce (Purbrick, 2001, p. 13).

It is difficult to know what the effect of the exhibition was on working-class visitors. Undoubtedly many attended on the 'shilling days', but who they were and where they came from is a matter of some uncertainty. The newspaper descriptions of working-class visitors such as those you read in Exercise 8.6 (Readings 8.5 and 8.6) do not tell us what they thought, and radical movements were largely silent about the exhibition.

Such silence was part of a more general quietude in British working-class politics after 1848. There were occasional strikes and fierce industrial disputes in the mid-century, such as the famous cotton-workers' strike of 1853–54 in Preston, Lancashire, but these were contained. This correlation between the Great Exhibition and the decline of working-class radicalism has been interpreted by some historians as further evidence that 1851 marks a turning point, one that demonstrates the power of popular liberal culture to unite people around patriotism, self-help and work. However, as you have seen, the Great Exhibition was a grand and lavish gesture that sought to create a particular image of the nation at a point in time. We have to be careful to look beyond the 'common narrative' generated by organisers of the exhibition by using a range of sources to interrogate alternative perspectives.

8.4 Budgets, finance and the standard of living

The Great Exhibition attempted to inspire optimism in future progress, but it would only be able to do so if it there were real reasons for confidence.

There was an event that took place soon after the exhibition that might be more useful in explaining the new tenor of politics and the 'social settlement' of the mid-century. In 1852 the Conservative government led by Lord Derby (1799–1869, prime minister 1852, 1858–59 and 1866–68) was forced out of office when the House of Commons failed to pass a budget presented by the chancellor of the Exchequer, Benjamin Disraeli (1804–1881, prime minister 1868 and 1874–80). The budget was highly controversial because it was widely seen as retrograde. In the budget of 1842 the Conservative prime minister, Sir Robert Peel (1788–1850, prime minister 1834–35 and 1841–46), had introduced **income tax** as a way of reducing the national debt without increasing indirect taxes and tariffs on goods and in the hope of laying the foundation for free trade and repeal of the Corn Laws (Matthew, 1997). This appealed to free traders and to the middle and working classes as a fairer way to tax the people. However, in the budget of 1852 Disraeli attempted to compensate landlords for the repeal of the Corn Laws by reducing their taxes and increasing the taxes on ordinary people. The budget revived the passionate debates about class, trade and fairness that had circulated in the campaigns for repeal of these laws. Marx, for example, argued that Disraeli was presenting 'measures for the elevation of the idle classes' (Marx, 1852). Disraeli had misjudged the mood of Parliament and his proposals were rejected. After a new election William Gladstone (1809–1898, prime minister 1868–74, 1880–85, 1886 and 1892–94; portrayed in Figure 8.8) was appointed chancellor of the Exchequer under the Whig–**Peelite** government led by Lord Aberdeen (1784–1860, prime minister 1852–55). Gladstone's budget of 1853 was quite different from Disraeli's. He lowered indirect taxes on food and drink and restricted income tax to those earning over £100 a year (Matthew, 1987). It was the first of Gladstone's 'people's budgets' (Gurney, 2014, p. 258). Others followed in the 1850s and 1860s, which further reduced indirect taxes, lowered levels of income tax and cemented Gladstone's reputation as a man of the people.

M. Gladstone, chancelier de l'échiquier, présentant à la chambre des communes le budget et le traité de commerce.

Figure 8.8 William Gladstone at the House of Commons' dispatch box. *Le Monde Illustré*, 25 February 1860. Photo: © Mary Evans Picture Library

Activity 8.3

Now go to the module website and complete Activity 8.3 'Gladstone's first budget speech'. This should take around 30 minutes.

As you have seen, historians such as Patrick Joyce, Miles Taylor and Margot Finn have argued that the kind of liberal politics Gladstone popularised undermined radicalism by persuading the working classes that mainstream liberalism would represent their cause. As men such as Cobden and Bright took their seats in Parliament in the 1840s, they began to give voice to reform campaigns such as the Anti-Corn Law League and, after repeal of the Corn Laws in 1846, there was a renewed faith in parliamentary politics. The old politics of Whigs and Tories began to crumble and a modern Liberal Party composed of Whigs, Peelites and liberal Tories emerged in the 1850s. Members of the Liberal Party disagreed on many things but were able to agree on the need for cheap, efficient government that was fair and constitutional. This provided the basis for a fragile consensus between the working and middle classes, particularly in the industrial districts. This was fostered by improvements in living standards.

Measuring living standards is fraught with difficulty. However, the evidence suggests that both the middle and the working classes experienced greater prosperity after 1850. As you saw in the unit 'The Industrial Revolution' (Unit 2) and in Unit 3 in Block 1, in the first half of the nineteenth century economic growth increased, as did profits, but wages stalled, leading to increased levels of inequality. After 1850 growth was accompanied by higher wages. Overall, between 1851 and 1873 the economy grew more quickly than before, expanding at a rate of 3 per cent a year on average. The national income rose from £523 million in 1851 to £916 million in 1871 (Steinbach, 2012). Growth in the textiles and metals industries created work, and the expansion of railways and shipping also generated jobs. The rise of the middle class created a market for consumer goods and a demand for servants. The service sector grew rapidly in the mid-century; by 1871, one third of working-class women were servants (Steinbach, 2012). Stability was ensured by the growth of banking and finance. Banks and building societies proliferated and provincial stock exchanges flourished as the number of investors grew (Crouzet, 1982). With the reform of company law and the extension of limited liability, capital was more readily available for those who wanted to start up in business.

That this economic growth was accompanied by population growth was seen by many as a cause for optimism. There was confidence that the dire predictions of Thomas Malthus (1766–1834), discussed in Block 1, had finally been put to rest. Between 1851 and 1871 the population of Britain grew from nearly 21 million to 26 million (although that of Ireland fell from 6.5 million to 5.4 million). Much of this growth was concentrated in cities. In 1851, London had a population of 2,362,000, Liverpool of 376,000, Glasgow of 329,000 and Manchester of 303,000. Twenty years later, these figures had increased to 3,254,000 in London, 493,000 in Liverpool, 477,000 in Glasgow and 358,000 in Manchester (Population Statistics, n.d.).

Exercise 8.8

Read the extract below from a report on the census of 1861. Why is the author positive about population growth?

This should take around 10 minutes.

> The United Kingdom is now covered by *twenty-nine millions of
> people*; and has thrown out towards the West a long line of
> colonies and independent states that speak her language, that
> preserve the purity of the English family, that have lost none
> of the courage or industry of their race – but furnish this
> country with supplies of food, as well as with the materials of
> manufactures, in exchange for wrought produce. ...
>
> There is nothing, therefore, in the past or in the present
> conjugal condition of the population to inspire any
> apprehension of a redundancy or a scarcity of population in
> England; but a great deal to encourage the policy of further
> improvement in this condition – in the training of the young, in
> the circumstances in which children are born and families live;
> so that the English race, growing better and greater, may
> increase in numbers at home, and continue to send out every
> year thousands of new families to the colonies.
>
> (*Parliamentary Papers*, 1863)

Specimen answer

In sharp contrast to Malthus's views, population growth is seen here as a
good thing. This is because the 'English race' can disperse through the
colonies. These new colonial communities can provide the networks for
trade and the materials for British industry, the kind of international
community of exchange that was imagined at the Great Exhibition.

Discussion

We do not know who wrote this report. It was produced by the census
office and presented to the government. We do not know how widely
held the views expressed in it were. However, it strongly suggests that
the optimism on display at the Great Exhibition was still very much in
evidence in the early 1860s. In fact the expansion of the British Empire
through colonies in Australia, Canada, India and Africa gave reason for
greater optimism. You will read more about this in Unit 15. The extract
refers to the population of the United Kingdom but it makes clear that
the English 'race' is superior and capable of further improvement. Such
sentiments about the English were often expressed in contrast both to
the Irish at home and to the indigenous populations of colonies, who
were often presented as incapable of progress. Such views helped
justify colonisation as something that would civilise distant lands.

In the mid-century the expansion of the British Empire was presented as beneficial to all in the United Kingdom through increased trade and through emigration which, it was hoped, would reduce competition in overcrowded labour markets and provide new living spaces for the poor and the unemployed. In the 1850s emigration societies emerged in response to various crises and problems. For example, as a result of failed harvests and the Highland Clearances, the Highlands and Islands Emigration Society helped nearly 5,000 people move from western Scotland to Australia between 1852 and 1857 (Devine, 2011).

The popular liberalism of the mid-century made equilibrium possible by imagining a world of different interests balanced by a minimal state that created the environment for self-help to flourish. Such a vision depended on prosperity and stability. In practice there were booms and busts throughout the mid-century, which threatened different industries at different times. The **cotton famine** caused a widespread depression in Lancashire from 1861 to 1865, while intensive competition in London continued to erode the quality of life of artisans and craftsmen in trades such as furniture making and tailoring. Steady economic growth was over by the 1870s, and the period between 1873 and 1896 is widely considered to have been a depression.

The impact of depression on the poor was made worse by the patchy nature of education, welfare and support across the United Kingdom. The Liberal governments of the mid-century promised a careful balance between tax and spending and assured the public that their money would be spent wisely and with caution. They recognised the need to improve life in the cities and to provide access to education, public health and poor relief, even to emigration, but they insisted this was best paid for and delivered by voluntary groups and local ratepayers in local communities. According to Colin Matthew, 'the classic Victorian scenario was for central government to identify a problem (or to have a problem brought to its attention) and to solve it by setting up a locally accountable, controlled and financed institution, sometimes helped by a grant-in-aid' (Matthew, 1987, p. 44). In this way, as you will see in Unit 13 on health in the city, it was able to minimise the state while advocating social reform though local government and voluntary agencies. This strength was also a weakness. Unit 10 will explore how it resulted in a patchwork of charitable agencies which operated alongside the Poor Law system but which were often unable to provide reliable support for the poor and the sick at times of crisis.

Undoubtedly, increased levels of stability and prosperity in the 1850s helped inspire optimism, but this did not run very deep. The experience of modern life in mid-Victorian Britain and Ireland was often unpredictable and precarious. After Chartism, working people responded to this precariousness with their own organisations and institutions. The cooperative movement, friendly societies and trade unions flourished in the 1860s. Although these were just the sort of collectivised self-help measures that liberals such as Cobden and Gladstone would support, they also became a vehicle for a different kind of politics, one that expressed some of the criticisms of competitive individuals and political economy that you saw in the Chartist movement. In Unit 14 you will learn how these groups helped shape a revived campaign for an extension of the franchise to working men in the late 1860s.

Conclusion

Block 2 asks you to explore the nature of mid-Victorian Britain and Ireland. As you work through Units 9–15, consider whether you think equipoise is a useful concept for explaining the years from 1840 to 1880.

First you will look at two issues that stretched the logic of liberalism to its limits: the Irish Famine and the new Poor Law. As Units 9 and 10 demonstrate, the effects of the Irish Famine and the new Poor Law were felt across the mid-century as stories of hunger and starvation exposed the limits of self-help and the cruelty of laissez-faire political economy. Despite this, as you will go on to see in Unit 11 and Unit 12, the period saw the thriving of a religious pluralism that fuelled networks of charitable agencies and voluntary societies, and the rise of a middle class who promoted Victorian values of individualism, work and thrift. You will explore how these new social forces began to transform the urban landscape and make inroads into local and central government through civic reform and the reform of the civil service. Through an investigation of public health in Unit 13 you will see how the practicalities of reform involved struggles between central and local government and questions over the role of experts and scientists in everyday life.

Despite improvements in social and economic life, the continued precariousness of working-class life started to undermine the sense of equipoise. Critics of capitalism such as Karl Marx pointed out the powerlessness of workers in the face of mechanisation, competition for work, deskilling and low wages but, by the 1860s, liberals such as John Stuart Mill also began to question whether it was fair to subject individuals to the vagaries of the free market. Unit 14 will look at how, by the 1860s, working men were yet again persuaded that ensuring a fairer society depended on them having a vote and a say in government. Finally, as you will see in Unit 15, the idea behind the Great Exhibition, that free trade and non-intervention would unleash enterprise and energy and lead to peace and prosperity, was fundamentally exposed in the British Empire when attempts to secure markets and influence led to conflict and violence.

Now turn to the module website to complete the independent study activities associated with this unit.

References

Bennett, T. (1995) *The Birth of the Museum*, London, Routledge.

Boyce, C. (2012) 'Representing the "hungry forties" in image and verse: the politics of hunger in early-Victorian illustrated periodicals', *Victorian Literature and Culture*, vol. 40, no. 2, pp. 421–49.

Burn, W. L. (1964) *The Age of Equipoise: A Study of the Mid-Victorian Generation*, London, George Allen & Unwin.

Butterfield, H. (1931) *The Whig Interpretation of History*, London, G. Bell.

Carlyle, T. (1870 [1843]) *Past and Present*, London, Chapman and Hall.

Chase, M. (2007) *Chartism: A New History*, Manchester, Manchester University Press.

Collini, S. (1991) *Public Moralists: Political Thought and Intellectual Life in Britain, 1850–1930*, Oxford, Oxford University Press.

Crouzet, F. (1982) *The Victorian Economy*, Abingdon, Routledge.

Devine, T. (2011) *To the Ends of the Earth: Scotland's Global Diaspora, 1750–2010*, London, Penguin.

Finn, M. (1993) *After Chartism: Class and Nation in English Radical Politics, 1848–1874*, Cambridge, Cambridge University Press.

Foster, J. (1974) *Class Struggle and the Industrial Revolution: Early Industrial Capitalism in Three English Towns*, London, Weidenfeld & Nicolson.

Greenhalgh, P. (1988) *Ephemeral Vistas: The Expositions Universelles, Great Exhibitions and the World's Fairs, 1851–1939*, Manchester, Manchester University Press.

Gurney, P. (2009) '"Rejoicing in potatoes": the politics of consumption in England during the "hungry forties"', *Past and Present*, no. 203, pp. 99–136.

Gurney, P. (2014) *Wanting and Having: Popular Politics and Liberal Consumerism in England, 1830–70*, Manchester, Manchester University Press.

HC Deb 14 June 1839, vol. 48, col. 224 [Online]. Available at http://hansard.millbanksystems.com/ (Accessed 21 June 2017).

Hewitt, M. (1996) *The Emergence of Stability in the Industrial City: Manchester, 1832–67*, Farnham, Ashgate.

Hobsbawm, E. (1964) *Labouring Men: Studies in the History of Labour*, London, Weidenfeld & Nicolson.

Joyce, P. (1991) *Visions of the People: Industrial England and the Question of Class*, Cambridge, Cambridge University Press.

Kingsley, C. (1850) *Cheap Clothes and Nasty* [originally published under the pseudonym Parson Lot], London, William Pickering.

Knadler, S. (2011) 'At home in the Crystal Palace: African American transnationalism and the aesthetics of representative democracy', *ESQ: A Journal of the American Renaissance*, vol. 56, no. 4, pp. 328–62.

Kriegel, L. (2001) 'Narrating the subcontinent in 1851: India at the Crystal Palace', in Purbrick, L. (ed.) *The Great Exhibition of 1851: New Interdisciplinary Essays*, Manchester, Manchester University Press, pp. 146–178.

Martin, T. (1876) 'At the Mansion House: Speech by the Prince', *The Life of His Royal Highness The Prince Consort*, vol. 2, London, Smith, Elder & Co.

Marx, K. (1852) 'Parliament. – Vote of November 26. – Disraeli's Budget', *New York Daily Tribune*, 28 December.

Matthew, H. C. G. (1987) 'Gladstonian finance', *History Today*, vol. 37, no. 7, pp. 41–5.

Matthew, H. C. G. (1997) *Gladstone 1809–1898*, Oxford, Oxford University Press.

Mayhew, H. (1851) *1851: or, The Adventures of Mr. and Mrs. Sandboys and Family* …, illus. G. Cruikshank, London, George Newbold.

Mill, J. S. (1869 [1859]) *On Liberty*, London, Longman, Roberts, & Green Co.

Parliamentary Papers (1863) vol. liii: Census of England and Wales 1861, 'General Report; Summary Tables, Abstracts of Ages, Occupations and Birthplaces of People, Division I. to Division III' [Online]. Available at http://parlipapers.proquest.com.libezproxy.open.ac.uk/parlipapers/result/pqpdocumentview?accountid=14697&groupid=95579&pgId=bb74c8ef-fcaf-45a9-b30e-9fdb30d85cca&rsId=15AAADE55A4 (Accessed 12 April 2017).

Parry, J. (2006) *The Politics of Patriotism: English Liberalism, National Identity and Europe, 1830–1886*, Cambridge, Cambridge University Press.

Population Statistics (n.d.) [Online]. Available at www.populstat.info/ (Accessed 12 April 2017).

Postgate, R. W. (ed.) (1921) *Revolution, from 1789 to 1906*, Boston and New York, Houghton Mifflin Company.

Prentice, A. (1853) *History of the Anti-Corn-Law League*, vol. 1, London, W. & F. G. Cash.

Purbrick, L. (2001) 'Introduction', in Purbrick, L. (ed.) *The Great Exhibition of 1851: New Interdisciplinary Essays*, Manchester, Manchester University Press, pp. 1–25.

Quinault, R. (1988) '1848 and parliamentary reform', *The Historical Journal*, vol. 31, no. 4, pp. 831–51.

Richards, T. (1990) *The Commodity Culture of Victorian England: Advertising and Spectacle, 1851–1914*, Stanford, CA, Stanford University Press.

Samuel, R. (1977) 'Workshop of the world: steam power and hand technology in mid-Victorian Britain', *History Workshop*, no. 3, pp. 6–72.

Scientific American (1851) 'Opening of the Great Exhibition – London on the 1st of May', vol. 6, no. 19, p. 282.

Stedman Jones, G. (1983) *Languages of Class: Studies in English Working Class History, 1832–1982*, Cambridge, Cambridge University Press.

Steinbach, S. (2012) *Understanding the Victorians: Politics, Culture and Society in Nineteenth-century Britain*, Abingdon, Routledge.

Taylor, M. (1995) *The Decline of British Radicalism*, 1847–1860, Oxford, Clarendon.

The Times (1851) 'The Opening of the Great Exhibition', 2 May, p. 4.

Vernon, J. (1993) *Politics and the People: A Study in English Political Culture, 1815–1867*, Cambridge, Cambridge University Press.

Vernon, J. (2014) *Distant Strangers: How Britain Became Modern*, Berkeley, CA, University of California Press.

Readings

Reading 8.1 First Chartist petition, 1839

Source: Postgate, R. W. (ed.) (1921) *Revolution, from 1789 to 1906,* **Boston and New York, Houghton Mifflin Company, pp. 127–9.**

Unto the Honourable the Commons of the United Kingdom of Great Britain and Ireland in Parliament assembled, the Petition of the undersigned, their suffering countrymen,

HUMBLY SHEWETH,

That we, your petitioners, dwell in a land where merchants are noted for enterprize, whose manufacturers are very skilful, and whose workmen are proverbial for their industry.

The land itself is goodly, the soil rich, and the temperature wholesome; it is abundantly furnished with the materials of commerce and trade; it has numerous and convenient harbours; in facility of communication it exceeds all others.

For three-and-twenty years we have enjoyed a profound peace.

Yet, with all these elements of national prosperity, and with every disposition and capacity to take advantage of them, we find ourselves overwhelmed with public and private suffering.

We are bowed down under a load of taxes; which, notwithstanding, fall greatly short of the wants of our rulers; our traders are trembling on the verge of bankruptcy; our workmen are starving; capital brings no profit and labour no remuneration; the home of the artificer is desolate, and the warehouse of the pawnbroker is full; the workhouse is crowded and the manufactory is deserted.

We have looked on every side, we have searched diligently in order to find out the causes of a distress so sore and so long continued.

We can discover none in nature, or in Providence.

Heaven has dealt graciously by the people; but the foolishness of our rulers has made the goodness of God of none effect.

The energies of a mighty kingdom have been wasted in building up the power of selfish and ignorant men, and its resources squandered for their aggrandisement.

The good of a party has been advanced to the sacrifice of the good of the nation; the few have governed for the interest of the few, while the interest of the many has been neglected or insolently and tyrannously trampled upon.

It was the fond expectation of the people that a remedy for the greater part, if not for the whole, of their grievances, would be found in the Reform Act of 1832.

They were taught to regard that Act as a wise means to a worthy end; as the machinery of an improved legislation, when the will of the masses would be at length potential.

They have been bitterly deceived.

The fruit which looked so fair to the eye has turned to dust and ashes when gathered.

The Reform Act has effected a transfer of power from one domineering faction to another, and left the people as helpless as before.

Our slavery has been exchanged for an apprenticeship to liberty, which has aggravated the painful feeling of our social degradation, by adding to it the sickening of still deferred hope.

We come before your Honourable House to tell you, with all humility, that this state of things must not be permitted to continue; that it cannot long continue without very seriously endangering the stability of the throne and the peace of the kingdom; and that if by God's help and all lawful and constitutional appliances an end can be put to it, we are fully resolved that it shall speedily come to an end.

We tell your Honourable House that the capital of the master must no longer be deprived of its due reward; that the laws which make food dear, and those which, by making money scarce, make labour cheap, must be abolished; that taxation must be made to fall on property, not on industry; that the good of the many, as it is the only legitimate end, so must it be the sole study of the Government.

As a preliminary essential to these and other requisite changes; as means by which alone the interests of the people can be effectually vindicated and secured, we demand that those interests be confided to the keeping of the people.

When the state calls for defenders, when it calls for money, no consideration of poverty or ignorance can be pleaded in refusal or delay of the call.

Required, as we are universally, to support and obey the laws, nature and reason entitle us to demand that in the making of the laws, the universal voice shall be implicitly listened to.

We perform the duties of freemen; we must have the privileges of freemen.

…

WE DEMAND UNIVERSAL SUFFRAGE.

Reading 8.2 Resolutions of the Anti-Corn Law League (1853)

Source: Prentice, A. (1853) *History of the Anti-Corn Law League*, **London, W. & F. G. Cash, vol. 1, p. 102.**

3   That the agricultural proprietor, capitalist, and labourer are benefited equally with the trader, by the creation and circulation of the wealth of the country …

4   That this meeting cannot separate without expressing its deep sympathy with the present privations of that great and valuable class of their countrymen who earn their daily bread by the sweat of their brow; many of whom are now suffering from hunger in the midst of boundless fields of employment, rendered unproductive solely by those unjust laws which prevent the exchange of the products of their industry for the food of other countries. So long as a plentiful supply of the first necessities of life is denied by acts of the British legislature to the great body of the nation, so long will the government and the country by justly exposed to all the evils resulting from the discontent of the people. With a view to avert so great a danger by an act of universal justice, this meeting pledges itself to a united, energetic, and persevering effort for the total and immediate repeal of all laws affecting the free importation of grain.

Reading 8.3 Wages and the Corn Laws (1853)

Source: Prentice, A. (1853) *History of the Anti-Corn Law League*, **London, W. & F. G. Cash, vol. 1, p. 168–9.**

On the 30th of November, a crowded meeting was held in Warrington, at which were present, as deputies from their respective Anti-Corn-Law Associations, Mr. Cobden, Mr. W. Rawson, and Mr. John Brooks, of Manchester, and Mr. Lawrence Heyworth, of Liverpool. Amongst the audience were a number of chartists ... Mr. Heyworth characterised the Corn Law as operating to make the poor still poorer, and the rich still richer, and said that the remedy lay in making a proper use of the elective franchise. An intelligent-looking man, named Travis, rose and proposed a resolution, uniting opposition to the Corn Laws with the six points of the charter ... Mr. Rawson ably showed the fallacy of Travis' argument, and drew from him the admission that he only opposed repeal as a single measure. Mr. Heyworth said that the manufacturers had no power to prevent the reduction of wages. It was want of work and the consequent competition of unemployed men that reduced wages. Mr. Cobden ... did not skulk the question but vigorously grappled with it at once, and by a clear explanation of the principles which regulate wages, and an appeal to the experience of all present that their condition was better when food was plentiful and cheap, than when it was scarce and dear, carried the whole meeting with him, and when the resolution was put, there was not a single hand held up for it but that of the mover. A motion made by Mr. Eskrigge pledging the electors present to vote for no candidate for the representation of the borough who was not favourable to the repeal of the Corn Law was then put and carried, the only dissentient being the mover of the rejected resolution.

[p. 169]

Reading 8.4 Prince Albert, 'Mansion House speech' (1849)

Source: Martin, T. (1876) 'At the Mansion House: Speech by the Prince', *The Life of His Royal Highness The Prince Consort*, **vol. 2, London, Smith, Elder & Co., p. 247–8.**

I conceive it to be the duty of every educated person closely to watch and study the time in which he lives, and, as far as in him lies, to add his humble mite of individual exertion to further the accomplishment of what he believes Providence to have ordained.

Nobody, however, who has paid any attention to the peculiar features of our present era, will doubt for a moment that we are living at a period of most wonderful transition, which tends rapidly to accomplish that great end, to which, indeed, all history points – *the realisation of the unity of mankind*. Not a unity which breaks down the limits and levels the peculiar characteristics of the different nations of the earth, but rather a unity, the *result and product* of those very national varieties and antagonistic qualities.

The distances which separated the different nations and parts of the globe are rapidly vanishing before the achievements of modern invention, and we can traverse them with incredible ease; the languages of all nations are known, and their acquirement placed within the reach of everybody; thought is communicated with the rapidity, and even by the power, of lightning. On the other hand, the *great principle of division of labour*, which may be called the moving power of civilisation, is being extended to all branches of science, industry, and art.

[p. 248]

Whilst formerly the greatest mental energies strove at universal knowledge, and that knowledge was confined to the few, now they are directed on specialities, and in these, again, even to the minutest points; but the knowledge acquired becomes at once the property of the community at large; for, whilst formerly discovery was wrapped in secrecy, the publicity of the present day causes that no sooner is a discovery or invention made than it is already improved upon and surpassed by competing efforts. The products of all quarters of the globe are placed at our disposal, and we have only to choose which is the best and the cheapest for our purposes, and the powers of production are intrusted to the stimulus of *competition and capital*.

So man is approaching a more complete fulfilment of that great and sacred mission which he has to perform in this world. His reason being created after the image of God, he has to use it to discover the laws by which the Almighty governs His creation, and, by making these laws his standard of action, to conquer nature to his use; himself a divine instrument.

Science discovers these laws of power, motion, and transformation; industry applies them to the raw matter, which the earth yields us in abundance, but which becomes valuable only by knowledge. Art teaches us the immutable laws of beauty and symmetry, and gives to our productions forms in accordance with them.

Reading 8.5 *The Times* report on the opening of the Great Exhibition (2 May 1851)

Source: *The Times* (1851) 'The Opening of the Great Exhibition', 2 May, p. 4.

The arteries of the great city, surcharged with life, beat full and strong under the pressure of a great and hitherto unknown excitement. Never before was so vast a multitude collected together within the memory of man. The struggles of great nations in battle, the levies of whole races, never called forth such an array as thronged the streets of London on the 1st of May ...

Down the cross streets – from Lincoln's-inn-fields, Camden-town, Kensington, Bayswater, Kennington, Islington, the City, Southwark, from the most remote suburb, by train, omnibus, cab, horse, and foot, teemed those crowds some are fond of calling the masses, but in a spirit far different from that which their nomenclatures ascribe to them. ...

The tramp of men, with wives and daughters on their arms, resounded from the pavement as they all trudged westwards with contented and happy faces. Those honest English workmen, in their round fustian jackets and glazed caps, felt they had a right to take part in the honours of the day, and to have an honest pride in the result of their own and their brethren's labours, and they walked, contentedly and happily, amid prancing horses and gaudy liveries.

Reading 8.6 *Scientific American* report on the opening of the Great Exhibition (24 May 1851)

Source: *Scientific American* (1851) 'Opening of the Great Exhibition – London on the 1st of May', vol. 6, no. 19, p. 282.

LONDON, May 2, 1851.

We were on the ground – that is to say, opposite the great building-at 6 o'clock in the morning, when we flattered ourself that, by selecting such an early hour, we should get a desirable standing-place and escape, to some extent, the rude jostling of the leviathan crowd,– but, when we arrived, it seemed that seventy thousand individuals, beside ourself, had conceived the same shrewd idea, and, per consequence, at just past daylight, the throng was most intense; there were acres of human beings from Knightsbridge to the Albert Gate of Hyde Park, and so on to Buckingham Palace, taking in the vast area of the Green Park and all the various thoroughfares leading thereto. We shall never forget the sight; and even at this early hour, an old inhabitant of London remarked to us that he had never witnessed its equal in broad day, much less at a time when it was fair to presume that half the metropolis were in their beds. The crowds kept pouring in the direction of Hyde Park by shoals of hundreds, thousands, and tens of thousands, until about 2 o'clock, when, after the Queen had left the crystal building, the mighty current seemed to turn and disappear in the mazes of London streets. It is calculated that there were over 3,000,000 people in the neighborhood of Hyde Park, among which were natives of various countries, not forgetting the glorious presence of about 600 Americans who contributed, in a small degree, to swell the almost interminable mass of vitality.

Unit 9 Ireland and the Famine

Suzanne Forbes

Contents

Aims

This unit will:

*   evaluate the British government's response to the Irish Famine

*   explore the impact of the Famine on Ireland, Britain and the wider world

*   develop your skills in analysing visual sources

*   develop, through a discussion of the historiography of the Irish Famine, an understanding of how political issues influence the way in which the past is interpreted.

Introduction

This unit will look at the Irish Famine of the 1840s, sometimes called the 'Great Famine' or the 'Great Hunger'. The immediate cause of this famine was a natural disaster: the failure of successive potato crops due to a fungus known as *Phytophthora infestans*, then commonly referred to as 'potato blight'. Once infected, a field of potatoes could be destroyed in a matter of hours. In the following lines, William Steuart Trench (1808–1872), a **land agent** in King's County (now County Offaly), describes the impact of the blight on his crop in 1846:

> I could scarcely bear the fearful and strange smell, which came up so rank from the luxuriant crop then growing all around; no perceptible change, except the smell, had as yet come upon the apparent prosperity of the deceitfully luxuriant stalks … It is enough to say that the luxuriant stalks soon withered, the leaves decayed, the disease extended to the tubers, and the stench from the rotting of such an immense amount of rich vegetable matter became almost intolerable. I saw my splendid crop fast disappearing and melting away under this fatal disease.
>
> (Trench, 1869, pp. 101–2)

The potato blight originated in North America and is thought to have spread to continental Europe as a result of trans-Atlantic trade. Wind, rain and mist spread the fungus further afield and large areas of the continent were affected, notably Belgium, the Netherlands, France and Germany (see Figure 9.1). In 1845, the blight spread to Britain too and had a particularly severe impact in northern Scotland, specifically agricultural communities in the Hebrides and western Scottish Highlands. Although *Phytophthora infestans* caused difficulties for the poor wherever it struck, what made Ireland remarkable was the scale of its impact.

Between 1845 and 1851, it is estimated that over 1 million people died as a result of successive failures of the potato crop in Ireland. This figure represented approximately 12.5 per cent of the population, making the Irish Famine of the 1840s proportionally one of the most destructive in world history. In addition to the multitudes who died from starvation and famine-related diseases, a further million people fled Ireland.

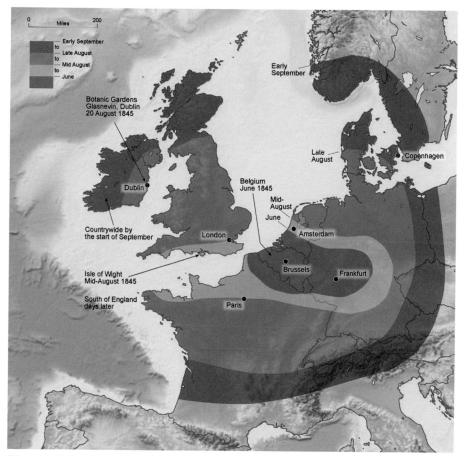

Figure 9.1 Map showing the spread of the potato blight, based on cartographer Mike Murphy's map in Crowley et al. (eds) (2013), p. 31, Figure 2b

Ireland is divided into four provinces (Connaught, Ulster, Leinster and Munster) and 32 counties. As you can see from Figure 9.2 (below), the greatest concentration of famine-induced deaths occurred in the western province of Connaught and the south-western province of Munster. To establish the 'excess death' rate, normal mortality rates (that is, death rates before the emergency) are subtracted from the crude mortality rate during the period under consideration. The resulting figure is a measure of 'excess deaths' only, in other words those deaths specifically related to the emergency. So in County Mayo, for example, out of every 1,000 people, 60 more died during the years 1846–51 than was usual. This may not sound like much, but Mayo had a population of 388,887 in the 1841 census. If you divide 388,887 by 1,000, and multiply it by 60 (the rate of excess deaths per 1,000 people), you can see that you are looking at a figure of over 23,000

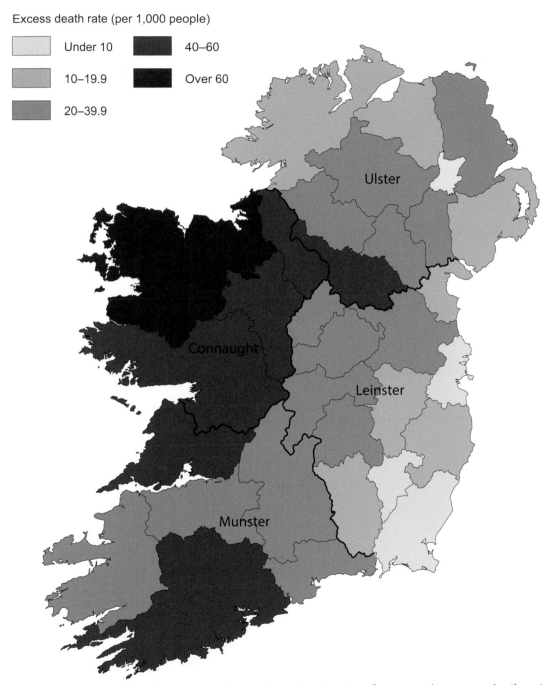

Excess death rate (per 1,000 people)

Under 10

10–19.9

20–39.9

40–60

Over 60

Figure 9.2 Map showing average lower-bound estimates for annual excess death rates per 1,000 population, 1846–51. Based on data compiled by Joel Mokyr. Source: Crowley et al. (eds) (2013), p. 108, Figure 7

excess deaths in Mayo alone for this five-year period, and this figure is based on conservative estimates.

Section 9.1 will consider some of the reasons why the failure of a single crop had such a devastating impact in Ireland. Section 9.2 will consider the course of the Famine, with a particular focus on the British government's response to the crisis. Indeed, the extent to which the British government's actions and inactions served to exacerbate and prolong the Famine has been the subject of intense debate among historians, which you will be introduced to in this section. Finally, Section 9.3 will look at some of the immediate and long-term consequences of the Famine for Ireland, Britain and the wider world.

Clearly this unit deals with an extreme event in one part of the United Kingdom, and an extreme event in global history. It is an event that both challenges and supports the ideas of equipoise and progress in the mid-nineteenth century, especially in the context of the British government's response to the crisis. As you work your way through this unit, you will see that a mid-Victorian sense of confidence, particularly a sense that 'new knowledge' and 'new ideas' could overcome seemingly overwhelming difficulties, was evident at times. These new ideological views, as well as older views about religion and the Irish people, play an important role in explaining the government response. While the Famine was over by 1851, unresolved issues from this time would re-emerge in the late 1860s to challenge the fragile political stability that had prevailed in the mid-nineteenth century.

9.1 The Irish problem

Unravelling the reasons why Ireland was so badly affected by the failure of a single crop in the 1840s is quite a challenge. However, for many people at the time, and historians since, the answers could be found by looking at the existing weaknesses of the pre-Famine economy, specifically the problem of widespread poverty in Ireland. In order to fully understand historical debate about the Famine, we need to begin by taking a look at contemporary attitudes to Irish poverty in the early nineteenth century.

Informed by the ideas of Thomas Malthus, whom you encountered in Block 1, many contemporaries attributed Irish poverty to overpopulation. Malthus argued that as the population grew, pressure on wages and land would increase, thereby causing widespread poverty and population decline. According to Malthus, nature might also step in to repress 'redundant population' through events such as 'sickly seasons, epidemics, pestilence, and plague' or 'gigantic inevitable famine' (Malthus, 1798). Although many contemporaries held that the poor were responsible for their own poverty due to their laziness, indolence and immoral behaviour, by identifying the 'excessive procreation of the lower classes' as the chief reason for their poverty, Malthus absolved the state and wealthier people from any responsibility for ameliorating the conditions of the poor (Malthus, 1798). Indeed, any intervention in this regard would serve only to encourage further procreation and population growth, ultimately bringing about the inevitable destruction of the poor.

Malthus's theory appeared to be particularly applicable to Ireland in the early nineteenth century. The Irish population had certainly grown rapidly from the mid-eighteenth century. Whereas the population is thought to have stood at between 2 and 3 million in 1732, by 1800 it had doubled to approximately 5 million. Growth had continued in the early decades of the nineteenth century and on the eve of the Famine, in 1841, the Irish population stood at 8.2 million. Furthermore, the Irish poor were seen as particularly problematic. As *The Times* newspaper put it in an 1847 article, Ireland was a 'nation of beggars' who were particularly notable for their 'indolence, improvidence, disorder, and consequent destitution' (quoted in Donnelly, 2008). This view was informed in part by the deep-seated anti-Irish and anti-Catholic sentiment in Britain that you have touched on in the unit

'Imagined nations made real?' (Unit 6 in Block 1). However, a number of other additional factors were seen to contribute to Irish poverty at this time.

Most of the land in early nineteenth-century Ireland was owned by the proprietors of vast estates, the majority of which had come into the possession of Protestant families as a result of various land confiscations from 'Old English' Catholics and Gaelic Irish in the seventeenth and eighteenth centuries. As a result, the owners of large estates were widely associated by the Irish with the 'English' or 'British' interest in the country. In Britain, however, this landlord class was widely regarded as 'Irish'. These landed proprietors let part or all of their land to others for use in farming. While some of these landowners lived on their estates and collected rents from tenants themselves, a significant group of **absentee landlords** let their estates to land agents, or 'middlemen', who in turn sublet both large and small tracts of lands to others. As a result, the vast majority of agricultural land was let, or sublet, to small farmers and agricultural labourers, who paid their rent in cash or through labouring for their immediate landlord. On the eve of the Famine, agricultural production in Ireland relied on these self-employed tenant-farmers, the majority of them working tiny plots of land. As landlords could depend on rents from their tenants for income, and there was an abundance of cheap labour in the country, there was little incentive for them to invest in their estates or to introduce new technologies or more efficient agricultural practices. Meanwhile, many small tenant-farmers who were living at subsistence level, and without capital, or protection from rent increases or eviction, had no real incentive to invest in their land.

Aside from hindering agricultural productivity, the proliferation of small farms in Ireland had another important consequence: by the 1840s, approximately one-third of the population had come to be entirely dependent on potatoes for sustenance. This occurred because considerably less land was needed to grow a sufficient quantity of potatoes to feed a family than was needed to obtain the necessary quantities of milk or grain. Potatoes are also a relatively reliable crop, and one that can grow in soil unsuitable for other purposes, including wetter, poor-quality land, such as land in the west of Ireland (Daly, 1986). Furthermore, the potato is now known to be one of the most nutritious sources of food available. Whereas a diet restricted to a single item such as corn would result in a range of diseases related to nutritional deficiencies, the potato satisfies all dietary requirements when eaten in the right quantities and supplemented by a small amount of green vegetables and dairy produce. Indeed, as a result of their potato-based diet, Ireland had 'one of the tallest, healthiest, and most fertile' peasant populations in early nineteenth-century Europe (Kinealy, 1997, p. 6). In many ways, the potato helps to explain continuing Irish population growth in spite of widespread poverty. However, this dependence on a single crop made Ireland particularly susceptible to the impact of the blight.

These interconnected problems of overpopulation, the Irish land tenure system, agricultural 'backwardness', dependence on a single crop and widespread poverty created a particularly sticky mess, and it was difficult for contemporary observers to propose constructive solutions to them. Such difficulty was compounded by new ideas about how to manage the economy that gained ground in the 1830s and 1840s.

Exercise 9.1

Turn to Reading 9.1, 'Robert Torrens, Extract from *Plan of Association in Aid of the Irish Poor Law* (1838)', located at the end of the unit. This is an extract from the writings of a political economist and MP, Robert Torrens (1780?–1864). As you read it, jot down your thoughts on the following two questions:

- What is the main problem that Torrens identifies in Ireland?

- What solutions does Torrens recommend to resolve this problem?

This should take around 15 minutes.

Specimen answer

- Torrens suggests that in England a single farmer can cultivate a large farm with little hired help, whereas in Ireland a single peasant cultivates a small farm alone. He regards this as inefficient, and something that hinders agricultural productivity.

- Torrens recommends two solutions to this scenario. First, he argues that small farms should be brought together into larger units so that far fewer people will be needed to farm them. Second, 'adequate provision' must be made for the people who are to be removed from their land.

Discussion

To improve agricultural production in Ireland, many contemporaries, like Torrens, believed it was necessary to increase the size of Irish farm units in order to reduce costs and maximise profits. However, if farm units were increased in size so fewer people were needed to work the land, what would happen to all of the people who lost their jobs and homes as a result? Although Torrens suggests that 'adequate provision' must be made for them, how could alternative employment and housing be found for so many people?

These questions were even more difficult for contemporaries to answer due to prevailing ideas about the economy and the poor. As you will remember from Block 1 and also from the unit 'The "age of equipoise" and the Great Exhibition of 1851' (Unit 8), political economists, particularly proponents of the doctrine of laissez-faire, held that governments should interfere with trade and industry as little as possible because the market itself was capable of allocating resources with great efficiency. Furthermore, providing overly generous support to the poor would serve only to encourage idleness and contribute to their plight. But how could any reforms in Ireland take place without significant government intervention?

The introduction of a Poor Law system in the 1830s was the most significant attempt undertaken to improve Irish conditions in the early nineteenth century. Initially, however, a government commission appointed in the early 1830s to investigate Irish poverty had rejected the idea of imposing a Poor Law in Ireland along English lines, as nearly 3 million workhouse places would be required if Irish people were to qualify for relief on the same terms as their English counterparts (Crowley et al., 2013, pp. 87–8). Instead, the commission had recommended a radical programme of land reform, economic development projects, assisted emigration, and the introduction of national institutions to provide for the poor and infirm, all to be funded by a national tax. However, for many contemporaries, this would represent unnecessary government intervention, place a burden on taxpayers and, moreover, encourage idleness among the poor, thereby encouraging rather than resolving the root cause of Irish problems: population growth.

Ultimately the majority of the recommendations of the government commission were rejected on this basis, and an Irish Poor Law, modelled on that of England and Wales, was introduced in Ireland in 1838. It provided for the establishment of a Poor Law Commission and the division of the country into Poor Law Unions. By providing limited assistance to the poor in exchange for wages, it was intended that this system would encourage waged labour in Ireland, thereby undermining the attachment of the people to farming. An assisted emigration scheme, actively promoted by Torrens, was also established under the terms of the Act to help tackle the problem of Irish 'overpopulation'. While these initiatives went some way towards tackling Irish poverty, no attempt had been made to reform Irish landholding practices or Irish agriculture on the eve of the Famine.

Irish problems were difficult to resolve; new ideas about how to organise economies came up against a complex land system and ingrained ideas about Ireland and the Irish and who should pay for alleviating poverty. While responses to the Irish Famine were influenced by these contemporary debates about the best ways to deal with poverty and the poor, so too was historical writing.

A 'Malthusian apocalypse'?

Historians of the Famine have paid a great deal of attention to the ideas and writings of Malthus and to contemporary debate about Irish poverty in order to understand why a famine occurred in Ireland in the 1840s. Some historians have accepted uncritically Malthus's theory on population and contemporary arguments about the 'backwardness' of the Irish economy. On this basis, they have concluded that the Famine was the inevitable result of a 'population time bomb' (Ó Gráda, 1993, p. 13).

Indeed, some historians have argued that 1815, the year that marked the conclusion of the Napoleonic Wars and the beginning of an economic downturn in the British Isles, was the point at which the Irish population became unsustainable. Writing in the 1960s, Raymond Crotty argued that a drop in demand for Irish agricultural goods in Britain from 1815 had ushered in a shift from **tillage** farming to less labour-intensive **livestock** farming in Ireland (Crotty, 1966). This meant that there was less work for agricultural labourers and many smallholders were evicted, in turn contributing to poverty and creating unsustainable pressure on the land. This analysis was famously echoed by Roy Foster in the late 1980s. He argued that 'If there is a watershed year in Irish social and economic history it is not 1846, but 1815, with the agricultural disruption following the end of the French wars' (Foster, 1988, p. 318). Foster also characterised what happened in the 1840s as a '**Malthusian** Apocalypse' (Foster, 1989, p. 203; bold added).

By emphasising Irish overpopulation, economic decline and poverty on the eve of the Famine, these historians argue that some kind of dramatic population decrease would have occurred in Ireland whether or not it was triggered by a natural disaster. Since then, however, a number of scholars have definitively challenged this idea. For example, economic historians Peter Solar, Joel Mokyr and Cormac Ó Gráda, among others, have shown that on the eve of the Famine, Irish population growth was showing signs of slowing (due in part to rising emigration) and Irish population density was actually comparable to that of Britain or Belgium (Ó Gráda, 2004). While Irish people could generally be regarded as poor, they were well fed thanks to their monotonous diet of potatoes. They were also relatively healthy and well housed. Furthermore, immediately before the Famine struck there is evidence that the agricultural, industrial and financial sectors of the Irish economy were picking up. Reflecting on these findings, Ó Gráda concludes: 'the pre-Famine economy, for all its problems and injustices, did not contain the seeds of its own inevitable destruction by famine' (Ó Gráda, 1993, p. 40).

While a single 'event', such as the arrival of *Phytophthora infestans*, can trigger a famine, the precise circumstances that transform a food shortage into a scenario in which mass starvation and death occur are more complex. If the state of the Irish economy on the eve of the Famine does not *fully* explain why this occurred in the Irish case, it is useful to evaluate the response of the British government and media to the crisis in Ireland. After all, how could a crop failure in one part of the United Kingdom, one of the wealthiest states in the world, result in such a prolonged and devastating crisis?

9.2 The progress of the Famine

This section provides an account of the British government response to the Famine, and also touches on the role that the media played in shaping public perception of what was happening in Ireland. As you read this section, I'd like you to assess whether or not the government response was adequate. Note down the government actions that are outlined below, and what you think might have been done differently in each case. These issues will be discussed in detail at the end of this section, in the subsection 'A policy of extermination?'.

As you read above, the potato blight first reached Ireland in 1845. In that year, 10 million tonnes of potatoes were produced, compared with 15 million tonnes in 1844. In the months that followed this first, partial, failure of the potato crop in 1845–46, the Tory government led by Prime Minister Sir Robert Peel responded quickly to the crisis. Government funds were made available for Poor Law relief. Indeed, by 1845, 118 out of 130 Poor Law Unions were already operational in Ireland. In addition, a temporary public works scheme was put in place, which provided wages in exchange for labour, typically on road-building projects. Grain exports from Ireland were permitted to continue, but the government purchased and distributed food – imported Indian corn (a type of maize) – at controlled prices. Indeed, along with the pressure exerted by the Anti-Corn Law League, the pressing need for new sources of cheap grain to alleviate the Irish crisis played a role in Peel's decision to support calls to phase out the Corn Laws in 1846. By and large, the relief measures enacted by the government in 1845 proved adequate. However, it is important to remember that the failure of the potato crop was partial and some food reserves were still in place.

A more complete failure of the potato crop occurred in 1846 when less than 3 million tonnes of potatoes were produced, marking the real beginning of the Famine. By the winter months of 1846–47, horrific reports of hunger, disease and death in Ireland were being related to newspaper readers in Britain and around the world (Gray, 2000).

Exercise 9.2

Turn to Reading 9.2, 'Nicholas Cummins, "Letter to the Duke of Wellington" (pub. 24 December 1846)', located at the end of the unit. This is an extract from a letter to the *Times* newspaper from a Justice of the Peace living in County Cork in the south-western province of Munster. Cummins describes the impact of the potato blight in his locality. He also asks his correspondent, the Duke of Wellington, to make both the British government and Queen Victoria aware of what is taking place in Cork.

As you read the letter, try to answer the following two questions:

• How would you describe the tone of this letter?

• Why do you think Cummins wrote in this way?

This should take around 30 minutes.

Specimen answer

• In this letter Cummins provides an emotional response to scenes of disease and death he witnessed in Skibbereen. He uses quite colourful language throughout the letter. For example, he refers to 'scenes of frightful hunger', the 'wretched hamlet' he visited, the 'ghastly skeletons' and the 'demonic yells' of the sick.

• Cummins may have been writing in this way to emphasise, or even exaggerate, the extent of the crisis in Skibbereen in the hope of encouraging his correspondent to secure aid. However, when you consider the subject matter, it is also entirely possible that Cummins was genuinely disturbed by what he had witnessed and his letter reflects that.

Discussion

While the author of this letter wrote with a purpose – to attain relief for people affected by famine in County Cork – there is no particular reason to doubt the veracity of the scenes described. As is the case with all major famines, the crisis in Ireland resulted in many reports of illness and death arising from starvation and disease, anti-social behaviour, and challenges faced by the living in disposing of dead bodies.

Meanwhile, in Scotland approximately three-quarters of the potato crop failed in 1846, leaving around 200,000 people at risk, mostly concentrated in the western Highlands and Hebrides. Poorer tenant-farmers and labourers in Scotland were particularly vulnerable, as they relied heavily on potatoes as a food source. In contrast to Ireland, however, private relief efforts were well coordinated and were quite effective in the Scottish Highlands. In 1847, the blight was less severe and a Central Board of Management was effectively managing relief efforts. Government relief was also provided according to the Scottish Poor Law, and oatmeal and other grains were sold at controlled prices. As was the case in Ireland, grain exports were permitted to continue. Although the scale of the crisis in Scotland was smaller, and relief efforts more effective, the famine in the Highlands caused significant suffering, and news of its impact was also relayed to readers throughout Britain by the press.

These newspaper reports contributed to an outpouring of sympathy for Irish and Scottish famine victims in late 1846 and early 1847. Charitable giving was encouraged in the press, by religious groups (notably the Roman Catholic Church and the Society of Friends, or Quakers) and by various relief associations. With government approval, Queen Victoria also encouraged private giving for famine relief. In January 1847, she wrote a letter to the Archbishop of Canterbury requesting that a collection be made to aid famine victims in Ireland and Scotland. This 'Queen's letter' was reprinted in *The Times* not long thereafter. A special day of prayer and fasting was ordered for 24 March 1847 to implore God to relieve famine victims in Ireland and Scotland. Those attending Anglican church services on the day were encouraged to donate to the cause. All in all, the 'Queen's letter' and fast day in March 1847 helped to raise over £170,000 for famine relief.

Changing attitudes

In June 1846, a Whig (liberal) government had taken office under Prime Minister Sir John Russell. Many leading members of the new ministry felt that Peel's relief efforts had been too generous and hoped to ensure that the cost of famine relief would in future fall more firmly on Irish landlords, those whom they believed to be truly responsible for the crisis. The Russell government continued to purchase and distribute food, but Indian corn was now to be sold at market prices. Irish grain exports were also permitted to continue. Meanwhile the crisis continued to deepen. Employment on the public works increased dramatically, from around 150,000 people in October 1846 to over 700,000 in March 1847 (Crowley et al., 2013, p. 48). With the public works thus at crisis point, their closure was announced in early 1847.

As a temporary expedient, a Soup Kitchen Act was passed in January 1847. This ambitious scheme would see food rations delivered directly to the poor. Alexis Soyer (1810–1858), a flamboyant French chef (widely recognised as one of the first 'celebrity chefs'), also offered his services to the British government to help ease the crisis in Ireland. He created soup recipes, as well as a custom kitchen and distribution system, to ensure relief would be administered in the most cost-effective manner possible. In April 1847, he opened a 'model' soup kitchen at the Royal Barracks in Dublin. The opening (depicted in Figure 9.3) was subject to a great deal of fanfare and the event was attended by the Lord Lieutenant of Ireland, John Ponsonby, fourth Earl of Bessborough (1781–1847), his family and other notables. Although some contemporaries complained that it was distasteful for the wealthy to go to 'see the paupers feed' on this occasion, confidence in the soup relief scheme proved well placed (*Freeman's Journal*, quoted in Cowen, 2007).

Figure 9.3 Unknown artist, 'M. Soyer's Model Soup Kitchen', engraving. *The Illustrated London News*, 17 April 1847. Photo: © Look and Learn / Illustrated Papers Collection / Bridgeman Images

The scheme was both remarkably successful and cost-effective. By the summer of 1847, the government-funded soup kitchens were providing emergency rations to over 3 million people daily, an impressive feat in any era (Crowley et al., 2013, p. 49). However, the switch from public works to soup relief had not been seamless and many areas were left without any relief for a time.

Despite its success, soup relief had been a temporary measure, and was phased out by mid-August to make way for the Poor Law Extension and Amendment Acts of 1847. These Acts would ensure that the full cost of maintaining the Poor Law Unions would now fall entirely on Irish ratepayers. The inclusion of the 'Gregory Clause' meant that tenants who held more than one quarter of an acre (*c*.1,000 square metres) of land were required to give up their holdings before receiving relief.

Although the impact of blight on the 1847 harvest was less severe than it had been the previous year, the cumulative effect of the two previous bad harvests meant that fewer seed potatoes had been planted in Ireland and only 2 million tonnes of potatoes were produced. However, as the situation in Ireland continued to deteriorate, public opinion in Britain had started to shift. Several factors can be seen to have contributed to this development. As you know from Unit 8, hunger had also become an issue throughout Britain at this time as an economic recession took its toll. Physical distance from the consequences of the Famine and the onset of what has been described as 'compassion fatigue' or 'donor fatigue' among sections of the British public have also been identified as factors in this shift in public attitudes. Accounts from Ireland of starvation, suffering and death had simply become so familiar in the media that they no longer elicited a sympathetic response. Indeed, a number of British printed publications, notably the *Economist*, *The Times* and *Punch* magazine, were now openly questioning the wisdom of government spending on Irish relief. Changing opinion about the Famine over the course of 1847 was evident in the response to a second 'Queen's letter' in October 1847, which raised only £27,000 (Gray, 2000).

A deepening crisis

In 1848 and 1849 potato crop yields remained well below pre-Famine levels. The government held fast to its policy that Irish property should pay for Irish poverty, but by now the burden of providing relief was taking its toll on ratepayers at a time when both farming and rental incomes were falling. Furthermore, as rates payable were dependent on the number of tenants one had, it made economic sense for some landlords to remove those who could not pay their rent.

Exercise 9.3

Turn to Reading 9.3, 'James Hack Tuke, Extract from *A Visit to Connaught in the Autumn of 1847* (1848)'. The author, James Hack Tuke (1819–1896), was a Quaker from York who was involved in private relief efforts in County Mayo, located in the western Irish province of Connaught.

As you read this extract, jot down your responses to the following questions:

- In what ways did landlords recoup their losses for unpaid rent? Does the writer approve of these practices?
- What were the prospects for those evicted?

This should take around 15 minutes.

Specimen answer

- Landlords, or agents and bailiffs acting on their behalf, moved to repossess goods and crops in exchange for unpaid rent, including seed or crops distributed by charitable organisations. Evictions were also carried out. Tenant dwellings appear to have been destroyed through the removal of the roof. Tuke is sympathetic to the evicted tenants.

- Tuke suggests that death is the likely outcome for many of those turned out of their homes, although he speculates that some might make it to the nearest workhouse in Westport, some 40 miles (64 km) away.

Discussion

Numerous sources support Tuke's account of evictions, such as the image from *The London Illustrated News* reproduced in Figure 9.4.

Tuke's account also provides insight into a major shortcoming of the Poor Law system in rural Ireland. As you can see from this reading, Tuke was concerned that those evicted were in no condition to undertake the long journey by foot to the Westport workhouse and might die along the way. Again, this observation is supported by numerous reports from all over Ireland of people dying by the roadside in an effort to access relief. This was the result of the large distances between Poor Law Unions in rural Ireland.

It has been estimated that, over the course of the Famine, approximately 70,000 families were legally and permanently ejected from their homes. Irish landlords were condemned by political economists, the press, government officials and Irish nationalists at the time, and by historians since, for contributing to the difficulties faced by the poor and starving. It is, however, important to note (as Tuke does) that there were 'noble exceptions'. Some landlords were actively involved in private relief efforts by lowering rents, providing seed or food to their tenants free of charge, providing financial assistance to emigrate, or organising and contributing to private fundraising campaigns. These efforts were most evident during the early years of the Famine, but by 1849 its impact was being felt at all levels of Irish society. Many landlords were heavily in debt or completely bankrupt.

Figure 9.4 Unknown artist, 'The Ejectment', engraving. *The Illustrated London News*, 16 December 1848. Photo: © Look and Learn / Illustrated Papers Collection / Bridgeman Images

The Encumbered Estates Acts were passed in 1848–49 to facilitate the sale of bankrupt Irish estates. Within a few years, a quarter of the land in Ireland had changed hands as a result of this legislation. The government saw this as an opportunity to attract British investors who would introduce large-scale farming and new agricultural techniques to Ireland, but most of the purchasers were Irish, and mainly from non-farming backgrounds.

Meanwhile, the Poor Law Unions had come under increasing pressure. By 1849 there were in excess of 900,000 people in receipt of relief. The government introduced a controversial 'rate-in-aid' scheme, a property tax, which forced better-off regions to subsidise those in distress. This had sparked numerous complaints, particularly in Ulster, that the English Poor Law Unions should also contribute on the basis that Ireland was a part of the United Kingdom. Eventually the government relented and provided some assistance in 1849 and 1850 for the distressed Irish Poor Law Unions.

After 1849, potato yields improved, but remained lower than pre-Famine levels for quite some time. Overall the British government had spent £8.3 million on famine relief. This equates to 'less than half of one percent of the British gross national product over five years' (Gray, 1995, p. 95). Both contemporaries and historians have asked the question: was this enough?

Activity 9.1

Now go to the module website and complete Activity 9.1 'Images of the Famine'. This should take around an hour.

A policy of extermination?

For many contemporaries, not only was the government response to the Irish crisis inadequate, it had been cruel, cold, and possibly even calculated. In May 1847, George William Frederick Villiers, fourth Earl of Clarendon (1800–1870), had been appointed Lord Lieutenant of Ireland. He had become increasingly critical of government policy during his time in the country, and in 1849 wrote to Russell expressing his view that there was not 'another legislature in Europe that would disregard such suffering as now exists in the west of Ireland, or coldly persist in a policy of extermination' (quoted in Kinealy, 1997, p. 138). Clarendon was not alone in this view. Many contemporaries complained that the government had not been particularly interested in alleviating the impact of the Famine in Ireland. After all, there had long been calls from political economists to reduce the Irish population, which would, in turn, allow for the creation of larger farms and reform of Irish agricultural practices. The devastating consequences of the Famine had helped to achieve all of these aims.

There were certainly some shortcomings in the government response to the Famine. Adhering to policies of laissez-faire political economy and free trade, both the Peel and Russell governments had refused to prohibit Irish grain exports or the use of grain in industry. The Russell government had also refused to regulate the price of imported grain, thereby allowing prices to escalate significantly as demand rose. These inactions have led to charges that the Famine was 'artificial' in nature. In other words, it had resulted not from a genuine shortage of food in the country, but rather from a failure on the part of the government to ensure that food was made available to the people who needed it. Historical research has shown that, in the first years of the Famine, there was a very real shortage of food in Ireland and that government interference in the market for grain would have done little to redress this situation. However, increasing grain imports to Ireland meant that, from the beginning of 1848, there would have been sufficient food to meet demand if it had been adequately distributed to the people. The success of the soup kitchen scheme also suggests that it was well within the government's ability to distribute food effectively.

The public works and the Poor Law system have also been heavily criticised as measures that added to, rather than reduced, the death toll (Crowley et al., 2013, p. 79). Those employed on the public works were expected to engage in hard physical labour and this kind of work exerted a greater toll on a weakened, starving population. The wages provided were also too low to purchase adequate supplies of food at a time when food prices were soaring. Meanwhile, the workhouses were overcrowded and disease spread rapidly in the cramped conditions. However, in many ways the suspension of the public works in 1847 and the introduction of the Poor Law Extension and Amendment Acts of that year made matters worse by making relief harder for many people to access and by shifting its cost onto struggling Irish ratepayers.

It has also been observed that the government might have taken action to prevent mass evictions, which served only to increase the strain on the workhouses and to increase mortality. The 'Gregory Clause' which required tenants to give up their land before receiving relief, a measure that would help make way for the introduction of large-scale farming along English lines, is seen to have exacerbated mortality as many families refused to abandon their holdings. More assistance might also have been provided to those who were willing to emigrate to escape conditions in Ireland.

Strict adherence to the principles of political economy and the doctrine of laissez-faire meant that many leading politicians objected to more invasive interventions, which provides some explanation for the 'minimalist' government response to the Irish crisis. However, religious or 'moral' thinking was also another important factor at play. Many political leaders saw the Famine as an act of providence, or in other words a case of 'divine intervention'. Of course, why, and for what reasons, God had seen fit to intervene in this precise manner was open to interpretation. As the historian Thomas Bartlett succinctly explains, for some people the Famine was

a righteous punishment from God on the Irish for their popery, and that as a nation of incorrigible workshy slackers, they had it coming. Still others, equally devout, welcomed famine as literally a heaven-sent opportunity to solve the Irish problem of gross overpopulation through a thorough-going transformation of Irish society.

(Bartlett, 2010, p. 285)

Although various shortcomings in the relief effort can be identified, and it is possible to see how political ideas and religious beliefs may have influenced government thinking at the time, the question remains: was the government pursuing a *deliberate* policy of extermination in Ireland?

Exercise 9.4

Turn to Reading 9.4, 'Charles Trevelyan, "Letter to Thomas Spring-Rice, Lord Mounteagle" (9 October 1846)', located at the end of the unit. The author of this letter, Charles Trevelyan (1807–1886), was Assistant Secretary to the Treasury and the person responsible for Irish famine relief throughout the 1840s.

Read the extract carefully and jot down your responses to the following two questions:

- As far as Trevelyan is concerned, what responsibilities does the British government have with regard to the crisis in Ireland?

- Does Trevelyan view the Famine as a positive or a negative development?

This should take around 15 minutes.

Specimen answer

- As far as Trevelyan is concerned, the government has limited powers to deal with the situation in Ireland and is doing all it possibly can to ameliorate conditions. For example, he explains to his correspondent that 'It forms no part of the functions of government to provide supplies of food or to increase the productive powers of the land'. He also explains that it is the government's duty to protect the 'merchant and the agriculturist' in the free exercise of their trade.

- In the final paragraph Trevelyan seems to suggest that the Famine is a positive development. He suggests that it is a 'blessing' from God to cure Ireland's 'social evil', the refusal of its people to take responsibility for themselves. Providing aid to Ireland would only serve to turn the 'blessing' of famine into a 'curse' of a dependent nation.

Discussion

This reading is particularly interesting as it shows how a mixture of ideas about the economy, religion and the Irish people influenced the author's thinking. Trevelyan complains that people in Ireland are not taking responsibility for their own welfare. He suggests that such behaviour is some kind of intrinsic characteristic of Irish people, or a 'defective part of the national character', a comment that is directed at the landlord class in particular. This perhaps shows some anti-Irish prejudice on Trevelyan's part, but it is certainly in line with government thinking that 'Irish property must pay for Irish poverty'. A 'providential' interpretation of the Famine is evident here, too, as Trevelyan describes the event as a 'blessing' from God.

After reading a primary source such as this one, it is not particularly difficult to see why some contemporaries and historians might have argued that the British government *wanted* the Famine to run its course, and as such its actions and inactions amounted to a 'policy of extermination'. Of course, this issue has been, and continues to be, the subject of intense historical debate.

Activity 9.2

Now go to the module website and complete Activity 9.2 'Debating the Irish Famine'. This should take around an hour.

9.3 Consequences

Census returns for 1851 clearly showed the devastating impact of the Irish Famine. Whereas the population had stood at 8.2 million in 1841, ten years later it had been reduced to 6.5 million. The primary cause of this reduction had been Famine-related deaths and emigration. While some commentators reflected on the negative impact of depopulation, others focused on the positive and expressed confidence for the future. Indeed, the census report itself concluded that 'the population has been diminished in so remarkable a manner by famine, disease and emigration between 1841 and 1851, and has since been decreasing, the results of the Irish census of 1851 are, on the whole, satisfactory, demonstrating as they do, the general advancement of the country' (quoted in Kinealy, 2002, p. 211).

In the two decades after the Famine, agricultural production in Ireland shifted from an emphasis on tillage to livestock, particularly cattle. Livestock were reared for export and the sector benefited from high food prices in the last quarter of the century. Irish farm incomes rose by almost one-third during this time. However, tillage was more labour-intensive than livestock and this reorganisation of Irish agriculture limited employment opportunities in rural areas. While those who did find work benefited from increased wages, many thousands of poorer Irish people opted for emigration (Bartlett, 2010, p. 288).

Figure 9.5 reproduces an image from the *Weekly Freeman* of 2 July 1881, showing Erin – a female personification of Ireland – looking at census returns since 1841. The caption states: 'In forty years I have lost, through the operation of no *natural* law, more than Three Millions of my Sons and Daughters, and they, the Young and the Strong, leaving behind the Old and the Infirm to weep and die. *Where is this to end?*'

You might be able to make out from the image (especially if you view it in the web gallery) that the 1881 census revealed a further drop in population, to 5.1 million. The background of the image points to some of the reasons for this decline. To the left you can see a ship taking emigrants overseas. To the right you can see an eviction taking place – an indication of continuing challenges for the poor who remained at home. An old man and woman sit on either side of Erin,

Figure 9.5 J. F. O'Hea, 'A Terrible Record', chromolithograph, supplement to the *Weekly Freeman*, 2 July 1881. National Library of Ireland, Dublin. This image is reproduced courtesy of the National Library of Ireland, call number: PD Weekly Freeman 1881 July

lamenting the loss of the younger people who made up the bulk of emigrants.

In the rest of this section, you will consider the emigration that occurred during and after the Famine years, its impact on Britain and the wider world, and some of its longer-term political consequences.

The 'scattering'

The main destination of Irish Famine emigrants was North America. As you can see very clearly from Figure 9.6, this destination continued to be favoured by emigrants as the nineteenth century progressed.

Undertaking the voyage across the Atlantic in cramped sailing ships was often fatal, as food shortages and disease remained a threat. It has been estimated that mortality rates of 30 per cent were common on such vessels. Indeed, the term 'coffin ship' is often used today to refer to the vessels that carried both Irish and Scottish people fleeing famine across the Atlantic.

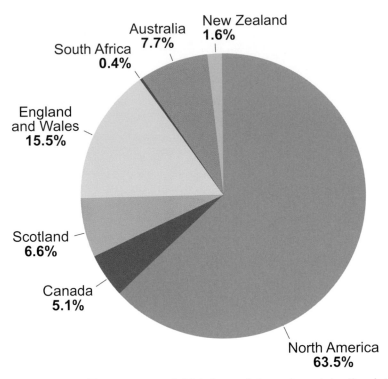

Figure 9.6 'Percentage of Irish-born living abroad in the late nineteenth century', from Crowley et al. (eds) (2013), p. 11

The impact of the Irish emigrants was significant in towns such as Boston and New York. Indeed, by 1855 Irish-born people made up one-third of the population of the latter city. Irish emigrants also travelled even further afield. For instance, approximately 70,000 Irish Famine victims migrated to the British colony of Australia between 1845 and 1855, followed by a further 175,000 Irish immigrants in the decade that followed, significantly increasing the colony's small population of European settlers and, as the bulk of Irish emigrants were Roman Catholic, altering its religious profile (Crowley et al., 2013, p. 550).

Many more Irish people moved to other parts of the United Kingdom. Between a quarter and a third of a million Irish people ended up in Liverpool, Glasgow, London and other British cities (Crowley et al., 2013, p. 11). Even the short trip to Britain had its perils, particularly for those who could afford only passage on deck. One eyewitness, Julius Besnard, gave an account of immigrants arriving in Liverpool:

[N]o language at my command can describe the scenes I have witnessed there; the people were positively prostrated … from the inclemency of the weather … seasick all the way … drenched from the sea and rain … suffering from cold at night … debilitated … scarcely able to walk after they got out of the steamers. In fact, I consider the manner in which passengers are conveyed from Irish to English ports disgraceful, dangerous, and inhuman.

(Quoted in Scally, 1995, p. 181)

Figure 9.7 Unknown artist, 'Irish Emigrants, the Recent Collision on the Mersey', engraving. *The Pictorial Times*, 6 June 1846. Photo: © Look and Learn / Illustrated Papers Collection / Bridgeman Images. Emigrants faced all sorts of difficulties in their journeys. This engraving depicts Irish passengers on board a ship, but delayed in their departure for America from Liverpool following a collision on the River Mersey with another ship.

For many passengers, Liverpool was merely a stop on a longer journey to North America by sailing ship (although even this might not be straightforward, as Figure 9.7 shows). However, plenty of Irish people remained in the city. Pre-Famine Irish immigration to Liverpool meant that in 1841 Irish-born people accounted for some 17 per cent of the population, but by 1851 this figure stood at over 22 per cent. The sudden surge of Famine immigrants to Liverpool in the 1840s, destitute and in very poor condition, put a strain on the city's resources.

Exercise 9.5

Turn to Reading 9.5, 'Extract from *The Times* (2 April 1847)'; Reading 9.6, 'Extract from the *Liverpool Mail* (6 November 1847)'; Reading 9.7, 'Extract from the *Liverpool Mercury* (1 August 1848)'; and Reading 9.8, 'Extract from the *Liverpool Herald* (17 November 1855)'. These are located at the end of the unit. The extracts are drawn from a variety of contemporary newspapers, and all of them address the issue of Irish immigration to Liverpool.

As you read through these brief extracts, try to identify some of the main complaints made against, and some of the key characteristics attributed to, the Irish immigrants.

This should take around 20 minutes.

Specimen answer

Various complaints are made about the Irish: specifically that they are making Liverpool 'unhealthy' and bringing disease, they are putting a strain on services and inhabitants due to the cost of caring for them, they are poor and impoverished, and they are beggars. Some of the complaints address what were thought to be inherent Irish characteristics. Aside from being associated with disease, death and dirt, the Irish are described as 'inferior', 'slothful', 'improvident', 'reckless', 'drunken', 'obscene', 'savages' and 'criminals'. They are also described as 'Celts'.

Discussion

Irish Famine immigrants did put a strain on Liverpool's resources. They crowded into poor accommodation close to the docks. Disease spread as quarantine stations and fever sheds were put in place along the River Mersey. Those who did not find employment placed an increased burden on the public works. The cost of these measures was reflected in increased levies on ratepayers. It is notable here, however, that negative responses to the Irish immigrants were also informed by longstanding stereotypes that held the Irish were uncivilised, lazy, indigent, drunkards. The extent to which racial prejudice influenced anti-Irish sentiment in Britain is an issue debated by historians (Paz, 1992). However, there is a hint in these extracts that emerging new ideas about 'race', and specifically the idea that certain races of people were more advanced and therefore superior to others, were influencing attitudes to the Irish.

Terms such as 'Celt' were sometimes used by contemporaries to distinguish the 'inferior' Irish from the 'superior' English or 'Saxons'. In the case of Liverpool these negative attitudes had significant consequences. Some 15,000 people were deported back to Ireland in 1847, the point at which, as one historian has put it, 'sympathy in Liverpool for these people had effectively run out' (Crowley et al., 2013, p. 505).

Liverpool was not the only British city impacted by Famine immigration. Irish immigrants settled in South Wales, in London and in the industrial towns of the north of England, including the infamous 'Little Ireland' ghetto in Manchester. Scotland was also a popular destination for Irish Famine victims. For instance, approximately 100,000 Irish people arrived in the Glasgow area during the Famine years. By 1851 almost 20 per cent of the city's population was Irish-born (Crowley et al., 2013, p. 516). Of course, famine in the Scottish Highlands had also seen significant migration to lowland areas of the country. As was the experience in Liverpool, new arrivals from Ireland and the Highlands were in poor condition and placed a strain on medical and welfare systems.

In the years that followed the Famine, the Irish tended to be perceived as a 'social problem' wherever they settled in Britain. This was due in large part to their low social status. Figure 9.8, showing an Irish pauper family on an English roadside, typifies this – one man is shown asleep and another drunk, while the children beg an indifferent passer-by for alms. The vast majority of Irish Famine refugees to Britain had come from rural areas, were illiterate and had few skills suitable for finding employment in Britain's industrial cities. The work that they did find tended to be low-paid and unskilled. For this reason the Irish were seen to lower wages and pose a threat to British jobs. Some, with the necessary skills, worked as artisans, some as servants, and many joined the army (by the mid-Victorian period some 30 per cent of the army were Irish). A small minority of immigrants even successfully assimilated into the ranks of the middle classes. Overall, the status of Irish immigrants in Britain improved only very gradually over the remainder of the century (Swift, 1987).

Figure 9.8 Walter Howell Deverell, *The Irish Vagrants*, *c.*1853–54, oil on canvas, 63 x 72cm, Johannesburg Art Gallery. Photo: © Johannesburg Art Gallery / Bridgeman Images

Political implications

Assessing the political impact of the Famine is a difficult task. When Queen Victoria conducted her first official visit to Ireland in 1849, when the effects of the Famine were still very much being felt, she received a rapturous welcome. She landed at Cobh in County Cork, promptly renamed Queenstown in her honour, and thereafter visited Cork city, Waterford and Dublin. As she noted in her diary at Dublin:

> It was a wonderful, striking scene, such masses of human beings so enthusiastic, so excited, & yet such perfect order maintained then, the numbers of troops, the different Bands stationed at certain distances, – the waving of hats & handkerchiefs, – the bursts of welcome that rent the air, *all* of which made it a never

to be forgotten scene, particularly when one reflects on what state the country was in, quite lately.

(Victoria, 1849)

Whether these scenes were evidence of Irish loyalty to the British monarch or simply the response of curious crowds to the pageantry of a royal visit is open to debate. The future relationship between Britain and Ireland was certainly not clear to contemporaries at this time.

As you will know from your work in Unit 6, Irish nationalist sentiment had already been evident in the 1820s and 1830s in the mass political movements led by Daniel O'Connell (1775–1847) calling for Catholic emancipation and the repeal of the Act of Union. In the years that followed, repeal remained high on the political agenda, while other movements such as trade unionism and Chartism made little headway in the country. Electoral support for the repeal movement had dipped somewhat in the years before the Famine, as O'Connell reined in political agitation in order to cooperate with the Whig Party in the British Parliament. However, while the Famine can be seen to have temporarily bolstered support for the cause of repeal, by 1847 a significant split in the movement had emerged.

Growing increasingly impatient with the Repeal Association's progress, a group of Romantic nationalists known as the 'Young Irelanders' had come to advocate an 'all-embracing, non-denominational nationalism', a concept articulated to the public through their organ, *The Nation* newspaper (Jackson, 2014, p. 541). By the summer of 1847, O'Connell was growing fearful that the Young Irelanders had come to advocate military conflict to achieve self-rule for Ireland and he pressed for the Repeal Association to adopt a set of 'Peace Resolutions' precluding the organisation's involvement in any form of armed conflict.

Thomas Francis Meagher (1823–1867), one of the founders of *The Nation* and a prominent Young Irelander, gave a speech on 28 July 1846 at Conciliation Hall, headquarters of the Repeal Association, explaining his reasons for dissenting from the Peace Resolutions. Once Meagher had delivered his speech, he and the Young Irelanders departed the hall and left the Repeal Association permanently.

Exercise 9.6

Turn to Reading 9.9, 'Extract from the speech of Thomas Francis Meagher at Conciliation Hall (28 July 1846)', located at the end of the unit. After you have read this, answer the questions below.

It will be helpful for you to know that towards the end of the reading Meagher makes reference to several 'democratic' revolutions, the Tyrolean Rebellion (1809), the American Revolution (1765–83) and the Belgian Revolution (1830–31).

- Does Meagher advocate Irish people taking to arms in order to bring about repeal of the Act of Union? What are his reasons for this stance?
- Why does he refuse to endorse the Peace Resolutions?

This should take around 15 minutes.

Specimen answer

- No. He says that taking to arms would be 'senseless' and 'wicked', and the attempt would be 'a decided failure'. He argues that organising and voting are the 'only weapons' that they can employ to achieve repeal, and the methods most likely to succeed.
- Meagher refuses to endorse the Peace Resolutions because he does not repudiate the use of physical force in all circumstances and countries. He argues that violence is warranted for 'the defence' and 'assertion of a nation's liberty', and he cites America and Belgium as examples of this.

Discussion

Not long after the incident at Conciliation Hall, O'Connell died while on a pilgrimage to Rome, leaving the Repeal Association in disarray. Meanwhile, the Young Irelanders had formed a new organisation – the Irish Confederation – with the aim of attaining a national parliament for Ireland. While the group initially sought to pursue this agenda through peaceful means, as Meagher suggests here, ultimately the 1848 republican revolutions in Paris, Berlin, Vienna, Rome, Prague and Budapest inspired the Young Irelanders to take a more revolutionary, republican stance.

Just as the Chartist movement split into 'moral' and 'physical' force factions, so too did the Irish nationalist movement. This division between those who sought to further the cause of liberty or the 'nation' through peaceful, constitutional means and those willing to pursue a more radical, revolutionary, republican agenda would endure throughout the period you will study in the rest of this module.

In September 1848, the Young Irelanders staged a short-lived and unpopular rebellion against British rule. Afterwards, some of their leaders were arrested and sentenced to deportation. Other Young Irelanders, notably James Stephens (1824–1901) and John O'Mahony (1815–1877), fled to Europe. In Paris, both men made plans to further the cause of an independent democratic Irish republic. O'Mahony travelled to North America and founded the Fenian Brotherhood and Stephens went back to Ireland to organise support for its sister organisation, the Irish Republican Brotherhood (IRB).

Irish emigrants in North America joined the Fenians (and other Irish fraternal organisations) in significant numbers. Many had already been politicised before leaving their homeland, due to their exposure to the campaigns for Catholic emancipation and repeal of the Act of Union. Furthermore, as the historian Kerby Miller has observed, many Irish emigrants saw their situation in terms of an involuntary exile, brought about as a result of the actions and inactions of the British government (Miller, 2008). Other common emigrant experiences may also have had a role to play in the decision to join the Fenians, including homesickness, linguistic barriers, and difficulties adapting to work in cities and factories. Indeed, it has been suggested that organisations such as the Fenians may have helped emigrants to acclimatise to their new circumstances, to form a coherent community and to improve their status in society (Lynch, 2009).

Whatever the reasons for their interest in the Fenians, the financial support that Irish emigrants in North America provided for the organisation was of great significance to the nationalist movement in Ireland in the years that followed. In contrast to the Fenians in North America who openly advertised their activities, the IRB (typically also referred to by contemporaries as 'Fenians') remained a relatively small, secret, oath-bound body, organised along military lines and led by an 11-man 'supreme council'. The organisation came to have a membership of over 60,000 people throughout its seven 'districts': the four provinces of Ireland, as well as Scotland, North England and South England (Bartlett, 2010).

Overall, the Fenian movement gave a focus to the new, more violent form of Irish nationalism that emerged in the decades after the Famine. In March 1867, with the assistance of funds gathered in North America, IRB members staged an ill-fated rebellion against British rule in the area around Dublin (known as the 1867 Fenian Rising). In the months that followed, the IRB was also active in Britain. Notably, in September 1867 a police van in Manchester was attacked in order to free two IRB members, and in the process a police officer was killed. As a result, three of the Fenians involved were executed by hanging. While the 'Manchester Outrages' caused a wave of anti-Irish hysteria in Britain, the conduct of the trial and the execution of the three 'Manchester Martyrs' (depicted in Figure 9.9) caused outrage in Irish communities around the world.

Figure 9.9 Unknown artist, *The Three Martyrs Executed at Manchester, England*. Library of Congress, Washington D. C. Photo: Chronicle / Alamy

IRB violence in Britain continued in the months that followed the events of September 1867. Although the IRB was not acting on behalf of the majority of people living in Ireland, its campaign of violence had some important repercussions in the longer term.

Isaac Butt (1813–1879), a Protestant, Conservative MP and barrister who had defended the Fenian leaders of the 1867 Rising in Dublin, was motivated by the violence to create a moderate nationalist movement. To this end, in 1870 he founded the Home Government Association, later to become known as the Home Rule League and Irish Parliamentary Party. The aim of these organisations was to attain a parliament for Ireland, or 'Home Rule', by constitutional means. At the same time some Liberal politicians, most notably perhaps William Gladstone, became convinced that in order to prevent further nationalist violence it was necessary to undermine the use of physical force as a means to redress Irish grievances (Lynch, 2009). After becoming prime minister in 1868, Gladstone famously declared: 'My mission is to pacify Ireland' (Matthew, 2004). Ultimately, Gladstone would preside over the introduction of legislation that attempted to address many Irish grievances, including an Act to disestablish the Church of Ireland (1869), the first Irish Land Act (1870) and the first Home Rule Bill (1886). Meanwhile, the Home Rule movement had a significant impact on British parliamentary politics. You will examine both of these issues in more detail in Block 3.

Activity 9.3

Now go to the module website and complete Activity 9.3 'Remembering the Famine'. This should take around an hour.

Conclusion

As you have seen, the reasons why the Irish Famine was so devastating and went on for so long were quite complex. They included a natural disaster, existing economic weaknesses, and a slow and inadequate government response. The reasons for the latter issue are also complex. Confidence in the natural laws of the market and in the doctrine of laissez-faire, and a prevailing view that the poor were responsible for their own poverty can all be seen as factors that contributed to government thinking at the time. A sense that the Irish were not truly part of the British nation and the idea that the Famine was an act of 'divine providence' are also evident at times.

By 1851, there was a sense that the 'Irish problem' had been resolved. Now that the evils of Irish overpopulation had been overcome, Ireland would become a more productive and prosperous part of the United Kingdom, feeding into that mid-Victorian sense of confidence and optimism that you considered in Unit 8. However, the Famine had a long-lasting legacy. It changed the profile of Irish society, and that of many cities in Britain, the British Empire and the USA. A substantial Irish **diaspora** had been created, with many of its members coming to support a new, more violent form of Irish nationalism that would make itself felt in the late 1860s.

Meanwhile, the Famine had also raised important questions about the Irish land-tenure system, landlords, tenant rights and landownership in Ireland. Significantly, the Encumbered Estates Acts had seen the government intervene in the land market for the first time. This encouraged Ulster tenants to call for further state intervention to ensure that their customary right of **free sale** was enshrined in law. In the years that followed, calls grew for this right to be extended throughout Ireland, with the addition of **fair rent** and **fixity of tenure**. These 'three Fs' became the primary political aims of the Land League, a mass political movement that emerged in the decades that followed the Famine. You will learn more about the Land League and ensuing Land Wars of the later nineteenth century in Block 3.

Now turn to the module website to complete the independent study activities associated with this unit.

References

Bartlett, T. (2010) *Ireland: A History*, Cambridge, Cambridge University Press.

Cowen, R. (2007) *Relish: The Extraordinary Life of Alexis Soyer, Victorian Celebrity Chef* [Online], London, Phoenix. Available at Google Books (Accessed 15 March 2017).

Crotty, R. D. (1966) *Irish Agricultural Production: Its Volume and Structure*, Cork, Cork University Press.

Crowley, J., Smyth, W. and Murphy, M. (eds) (2013) *Atlas of the Great Irish Famine*, Cork, Cork University Press.

Daly, M. (1986) *The Famine in Ireland*, Dundalk, Dublin Historical Association.

Donnelly, J. S. (2008) *The Great Irish Potato Famine* [Online], Stroud, The History Press. Available at Google Books (Accessed 11 April 2017).

Foster, R. (1988) *Modern Ireland, 1600–1972*, London, Penguin.

Foster, R. (1989) *The Oxford Illustrated History of Ireland*, Oxford, Oxford University Press.

Gray, P. (1995) *The Irish Famine (New Horizons)*, London, Thames & Hudson.

Gray, P. (2000) 'National humiliation and the Great Hunger: fast and famine in 1847', *Irish Historical Studies*, vol. 32, no. 126, pp. 193–216.

Griffith, A. ed. (1916) *Meagher of the Sword: Speeches of Thomas Francis Meagher in Ireland 1846–1848*, Dublin, M. H. Gill & Son, Ltd.

Jackson, A. (2014) *The Oxford Handbook of Modern Irish History*, Oxford, Oxford University Press.

Kinealy, C. (1997) *A Death-dealing Famine: The Great Hunger in Ireland*, London, Pluto Press.

Kinealy, C. (2002) *The Great Irish Famine: Impact, Ideology and Rebellion*, Basingstoke, Palgrave MacMillan.

Kinsella, J. (2017) *Polysituatedness: A Poetics of Displacement*, Manchester, Manchester University Press.

Liverpool Mail (1847) 6 November.

Liverpool Mercury (1848) 1 August.

Lynch, T. G. (2009) 'A kindred and congenial element': Irish-American nationalism's embrace of republican rhetoric', *New Hibernia Review*, vol. 13, no. 2, pp. 77–91.

Malthus, T. R. (1798) *An Essay on the Principle of Population* [Online]. Available from Library of Economics and Liberty at http://www.econlib.org/library/Malthus/malPop1.html (Accessed 22 March 2017).

Matthew, H. C. G. (2004) 'Gladstone, William Ewart (1809–1898)', in *Oxford Dictionary of National Biography*, Oxford, Oxford University Press [Online]. Available at http://www.oxforddnb.com.libezproxy.open.ac.uk/view/article/10787?docPos=1 (Accessed 11 April 2017).

Miller, K. (2008) *Ireland and Irish America: Culture, Class, and Transatlantic Migration*, Dublin, Field Day Publications.

Neal, F. (1988) *Sectarian Violence: The Liverpool Experience, 1819–1914: An Aspect of Anglo-Irish History*, Manchester, Manchester University Press.

Ó Gráda, C. (1993) *Ireland Before and After the Famine: Explorations in Economic History, 1800–1925*, 2nd edn, Manchester, Manchester University Press.

Ó Gráda, C. (2004) *Ireland's Great Famine: An Overview*, UCD Centre for Economic Research Working Paper Series, 1–26.

Paz, D. G. (1992) *Popular Anti-Catholicism in Mid-Victorian England*, Stanford, CA, Stanford University Press.

Scally, R. (1995) *The End of Hidden Ireland: Rebellion, Famine, and Emigration*, Oxford, Oxford University Press.

Swift, R. (1987) 'The outcast Irish in the British Victorian city: problems and perspectives', *Irish Historical Studies*, vol. 25, no. 99, pp. 264–76.

The Times (1846) 24 December.

The Times (1847) 2 April.

Torrens, R. (1838) *Plan of Association in Aid of the Irish Poor Law*, London, Longman, Orme, Brown, and Green.

Trench, W. S. (1869) *Realities of Irish Life* [Online], London, Longmans, Green, and Co. Available at Google Books (Accessed 11 April 2017).

Tuke, J. H. (1848) *A Visit to Connaught in the Autumn of 1847: A Letter Addressed to the Central Relief Committee of the Society of Friends, Dublin*, 2nd edn, London, Charles Gilpin.

Victoria (1849) *Queen Victoria's Journals* (Princess Beatrice's copies), 6 August 1849, vol. 27, f.281 [Online]. Available at www.queenvictoriasjournals.org/search/displayItemFromId.do?FormatType=fulltextimgsrc&QueryType=articles&ResultsID=2962146376335&filterSequence=0&PageNumber=2&ItemID=qvj06100&volumeType=PSBEA (Accessed 9 March 2017).

Readings

Reading 9.1 Robert Torrens, Extract from *Plan of Association in Aid of the Irish Poor Law* (1838)

Source: Torrens, R. (1838) *Plan of An Association in Aid of The Irish Poor Law,* **London, Longman, Orme, Brown and Green, pp. 6–8.**

Industry performs her miracles only when many hands are employed at the same time upon the same work. In England a farmer possessing adequate capital, cultivates 500 acres with the combined labour of fifteen hired labourers; and therefore the produce is large in proportion to the number of hands employed in raising it. In Ireland, a peasant, nearly destitute of capital, cultivates ten acres by means of his own isolated and unassisted exertions; and therefore the quantity of produce is small, in proportion to the quantity of labour employed in raising it.

We have now arrived at the root of the disease. The want of combined labour and capital upon the soil is the cause of the defective agriculture of Ireland; and the defective agriculture is the cause of the poverty of the people. No measure for relieving the distress of the Irish people can have a chance of success, unless it be calculated to augment the productive powers of agriculture in that country, and to enable a given quantity of labour to extract from the soil a greater quantity of produce.

...

When the cause of the poverty in Ireland is placed in the proper point of view, we see at once the nature of the remedies which ought to be applied, and the extent of the difficulties which are opposed to their application. Two objects must be accomplished. In the first place, farms must be consolidated, until the agricultural labour of Ireland can be performed by two-fifths of the labourers now employed in performing it; and in the second place, adequate provision must be made for maintaining the other three-fifths of the present agricultural population, which the consolidation of farms must displace from their small holdings.

Reading 9.2 Nicholas Cummins, 'Letter to the Duke of Wellington' (pub. 24 December 1846)

Source: *The Times* (1846) 24 December.

Having for many years been intimately connected with the western portion of the county of Cork, and possessing some small property there, I thought it right personally to investigate the truth of the several lamentable accounts which had reached me, of the appalling state of misery to which that part of the country was reduced.

I accordingly went on the 15th inst. to Skibbereen, and to give the instance of one townland which I visited, as an example of the state of the entire coast district, I shall state simply what I there saw. … Being aware that I should have to witness scenes of frightful hunger, I provided myself with as much bread as five men could carry, and on reaching the spot I was surprised to find the wretched hamlet apparently deserted. I entered some of the hovels to ascertain the cause, and the scenes that presented themselves were such as no tongue or pen can convey the slightest idea of. In the first, six famished and ghastly skeletons, to all appearance dead, were huddled in a corner on some filthy straw, their sole covering what seemed a ragged horsecloth, their wretched legs hanging about, naked above the knees. I approached with horror, and found by a low moaning they were alive – they were in fever, four children, a woman, and what had once been a man. It is impossible to go through the details. Suffice it to say, that in a few minutes I was surrounded by at least 200 of such phantoms, such frightful spectres as no words can describe. By far the greater number were delirious, either from famine or fever. Their demoniac yells are still ringing in my ears, and their horrible images are fixed upon my brain. My heart sickens at the recital, but I must go on.

In another case, decency would forbid what follows, but it must be told. My clothes were nearly torn off in my endeavour to escape from the throng of pestilence around, when my neckcloth was seized from behind by a grip which compelled me to turn. I found myself grasped by a woman with an infant just born in her arms, and the remains of a filthy sack across her loins – the sole covering of herself and babe. The same morning the police opened a house on the adjoining lands, which was observed shut for many days, and two frozen corpses were found, lying upon the mud floor, half devoured by the rats.

... They will soon be few indeed in the district I speak of, if help be longer withheld.

Once more, my Lord Duke, in the name of starving thousands, I implore you to break the frigid and flimsy chain of official etiquette, and save the land of your birth, the kindred of that gallant Irish blood which you have so often seen lavished to support the honour of the British name, and let there be inscribed upon your tomb 'Servata Hibernia'.

Reading 9.3 James Hack Tuke, Extract from *A Visit to Connaught in the Autumn of 1847* (1848)

Source: Tuke, J. H. (1848) *A Visit to Connaught in the Autumn of 1847: A Letter Addressed to the Central Relief Committee of the Society of Friends, Dublin,* **2nd edn, London, Charles Gilpin.**

The landlords of Mayo, as well as of many other portions of Connaught, as a class (there are many noble exceptions who feel and see the impolicy and evil of such proceedings), are pursuing a course which cannot fail to add to the universal wretchedness and poverty which exist. The corn crops, bountiful as they may be, are not sufficient to meet the landlords' claim for rent and arrears contracted during the last two years of famine ... In every direction, the agents of the landlords, armed with the full powers of the law, are at work – everywhere one sees the driver or bailiff 'canting' the small patches of oats or potatoes – or keepers placed over the crop, whose charges, in some cases amounting to as much as the rent distrained for, must be paid by the unfortunate tenant. Even the produce of seed, distributed through the agency of benevolent associations, has been totally swept away. To add to the universal distress ... eviction is in many cases practised, and not a few of the roofless dwellings which meet the eye have been destroyed at the instance of the landlords, after turning adrift the miserable inmates ... Here, a few days previous to my visit, a driver of Sir R. O'Donnells, whose property it is, had ejected some twenty families, making, as I was informed, with a previous recent eviction, about forty. A crowd of these miserable ejected creatures collected around us, bewailing, with bitter lamentations, their hard fate. ... What prospects are there for these miserable outcasts? Death indeed must be the portion of some, for their neighbours, hardly richer than themselves, were principally subsisting upon turnip-tops; whilst the poor-house of the Union at Westport is nearly forty miles distant.

Turnips taken – can we say stolen? – from the fields, as they wearily walked thither, would be their only chance of support.

Reading 9.4 Charles Trevelyan, 'Letter to Thomas Spring-Rice, Lord Mounteagle' (9 October 1846)

Source: Kinsella, J. (2017) *Polysituatedness: A Poetics of Displacement*, Manchester, Manchester University Press, pp. 318–9.

To the Right Hon. Lord Mounteagle

My Dear Lord,

I have had the pleasure of receiving your letter dated 1 inst., and before proceeding to the subjects more particularly treated in it, I must beg of you to dismiss all doubt from your mind of the magnitude of the existing calamity and its danger not being fully known and appreciated in Downing Street.

The government establishments are strained to the utmost to alleviate this great calamity and avert this danger, as far as it is in the power of government to do so …

My purchases are carried to the utmost point short of transferring the famine from Ireland to England and giving rise to a counter popular pressure here, which it would be the more difficult to resist because it would be founded on strong considerations of justice. But I need not remind your lordship that the ability even of the most powerful government is extremely limited in dealing with a social evil of this description. It forms no part of the functions of government to provide supplies of food or to increase the productive powers of the land. In the great institutions of the business of society, it falls to the share of government to protect the merchant and the agriculturist in the free exercise of their respective employments, but not itself to carry on these employments; and the condition of a community depends upon the result of the efforts which each member of it makes in his private and individual capacity. …

In Ireland the habit has proverbially been to follow a precisely opposite course, and the events of the last six weeks furnish a remarkable illustration of what I do not hesitate to call this defective part of the national character. The nobility and the gentry have met in their respective baronies, and beyond making presentments required by law, they have, with rare exceptions, confined themselves to memorials and deputations calling upon the government to do everything, as if they have themselves no part to perform in this great crisis of the country.

The government is expected to open shops for the sale of food in every part of Ireland, to make all the railroads in Ireland, and to drain and improve the whole of the land of Ireland, to the extent of superseding the proprietor in the management of his own estate, and arranging with his tenants the terms on which the rent etc. is to be adjusted. ...

... I see a bright light shining in the distance through the dark cloud which at present hangs over Ireland. ... The deep and inveterate root of social evil remains, and I hope I am not guilty of irreverence in thinking that, this being altogether beyond the power of man, the cure has been applied by the direct stroke of an all-wise Providence in a manner as unexpected and unthought as it is likely to be effectual. God grant that we may rightly perform our part, and not turn into a curse what was intended for a blessing.

Reading 9.5 Extract from *The Times* (2 April 1847)

Source: *The Times* (1847) 2 April.

Ireland is pouring into the cities, and even into the villages of this island, a fetid torrent of famine, nakedness, dirt, and fever. Liverpool, whose proximity to Ireland has already procured for it the unhappy distinction of being the most unhealthy town in this island, seems destined to become one mass of disease.

Reading 9.6 Extract from the *Liverpool Mail* (6 November 1847)

Source: *Liverpool Mail* (1847) 6 November.

That the scum of Ireland come to Liverpool and die in thousands is true. But whose fault is that? Misgovernment in Ireland – idleness on the part of the peasantry, and ignorance and extravagance on the part of the 'gentry'. The people of Liverpool are taxed to a degree almost beyond endurance to support these swarms of starved and diseased peasants ... The people that come here from the sister island are not labourers ... They are beggars and paupers. They never were labourers.

They never did an honest day's work in their lives. They lived by begging, as the Roman Catholic prelates *regret* to say they cannot do now, for the potato crop has failed, and when they arrive here begging is their profession, the workhouse their retreat, the fourpenny loaf per day a certainty, and medical aid, port wine, soup, a coffin, and Christian burial the last resort. ... We have clearly shown that we are not the creators but the victims – not the nurserymen of infectious fever, but the sufferers from an inundation of wretched, starved, and diseased beggars from Ireland.

Reading 9.7 Extract from the *Liverpool Mercury* (1 August 1848)

Source: *Liverpool Mercury* (1848) 1 August.

It is not to be forgotten, too, that much, very much of Irish misery lies quite beyond the reach of any 'remedial measures' of a Government, being seated in the character of the Irish people. No Government, except by a very indirect and gradual process, can change the idiosyncrasies and habitudes of a nation, and convert a slothful, improvident, and reckless race into an industrious, thrifty, and peaceful people. ... We may see of what stuff the 'finest peasantry in the world' are made, by visiting the 'Irish quarter' in any of the large towns of England or America. There is a taint of inferiority in the character of the pure Celt which has more to do with his present degradation than Saxon domination.

Reading 9.8 Extract from the *Liverpool Herald* (17 November 1855)

Source: Neal, F. (1988) *Sectarian Violence: The Liverpool Experience, 1819–1914: An aspect of Anglo-Irish History*, Manchester, Manchester University Press, pp. 114–5.

Let a stranger to Liverpool be taken through the streets that branch off from the Vauxhall Road, Marylebone, Whitechapel and the North End of the docks, and he will witness a scene of filth and vice, as we defy any person to parallel in any part of the world. The numberless whiskey shops crowded with drunken half clad women, some with infants in their arms, from early dawn till midnight – thousands of children in rags ... the stench of filth in every direction, – men and

[p. 115]

women fighting, the most horrible execrations and obscenity, with oaths and curses that make the heart shudder; all these things would lead the spectator to suppose he was in a land of savages where God was unknown and man was uncared for. And who are these wretches? Not English but Irish papists [...] the filthiest beings in the habitable globe, they abound in dirt and vermin and have no care for anything but self gratification that would degrade the brute creation ... Look at our police reports, three fourths of the crime perpetrated in this large town is by Irish papists. They are the very dregs of society ...

Reading 9.9 Extract from the speech of Thomas Francis Meagher at Conciliation Hall (28 July 1846)

Source: Griffith, A. ed. (1916) *Meagher of the Sword: Speeches of Thomas Francis Meagher in Ireland 1846-1848*, **Dublin, M. H. Gill & Son, Ltd, pp. 34–7.**

[p. 35]

In the existing circumstances of the country an incitement to arms would be senseless, and, therefore, wicked. To talk, now-a-days, of repealing the Act of Union by the force of arms, would be to rhapsodise. If the attempt were made, it would be a decided failure. There might be riot in the street – there would be no revolution in the country. ... The registry club, the reading-room, the hustings, these are the only positions in the country we can occupy. Voters' certificates, books, reports, these are the only weapons we can employ. Therefore, my lord, I do advocate the peaceful policy of this Association. It is the only policy we can adopt. If that policy be pursued with truth, with courage, with fixed determination of purpose, I firmly believe it will succeed. But, my lord, I dissented from the resolutions before us, for other reasons. ... I felt that, by assenting to them, I should have pledged myself to the unqualified repudiation of physical force in all countries, at all times, and in every circumstance. This I could not do; for, my lord, I do not abhor the use of arms in the vindication of national rights. There are times when arms will alone suffice, and when political ameliorations call for a drop of blood, and many thousand

[p. 36]

drops of blood. ... Abhor the sword? Stigmatise the sword? No, my lord, for at its blow, and in the quivering of its crimson light a giant nation sprang up from the waters of the Atlantic, and by its redeeming magic the fettered colony became a daring, free Republic. Abhor the sword? Stigmatise the sword? No, my lord, for it swept the Dutch marauders out of the fine old towns of Belgium – swept them back to their phlegmatic swamps, and knocked their flag and sceptre, their laws and bayonets, into the sluggish waters of the Scheldt. My lord, I learned that it was the right of a nation to govern itself – not in this Hall, but upon the ramparts of Antwerp. [p. 37]

Unit 10 Work, poverty and the new Poor Law

Donna Loftus and Samantha Shave

Contents

Aims

This unit will:

- investigate the causes of poverty in England and Wales in the nineteenth century

- evaluate the impacts of different policies under the new Poor Law

- explore some of the controversies and tensions surrounding the new Poor Law and its implementation.

Introduction

The Poor Law Amendment Act, passed in 1834, was one of the most divisive pieces of English legislation enacted by Parliament in the nineteenth century. As you know from Block 1, it was meant to overhaul what many believed to be a too-generous system of relief, the old Poor Law. Under the old Poor Law, **outdoor relief** was common. This gave assistance to the poor in their own homes. In the early nineteenth century, as living standards declined, more people needed relief and the poor rates increased. In response, the new Poor Law was intended to bring about a modern, efficient and national system of poor relief in which a central Poor Law body made the rules for local boards of guardians to impose on the local population.

Much of the controversy surrounding the new Poor Law emerged out of the principle of 'less eligibility'. This aimed to discourage able-bodied claimants by insisting that those in receipt of relief 'on the whole shall not be made really or apparently as eligible as the independent labourer of the lowest class' (Senior, 1905 [1834]). In practice this meant that relief offered under the new Poor Law could not provide a standard of living better than subsistence: outdoor relief was to be limited and many claimants were forced to enter the workhouse, in which they were separated according to gender and, for able-bodied adults at least, required to work for their keep.

Controversy also emerged out of differences in perceptions of poverty and its causes. As you know from the unit 'Managing uncertainty: new forms of "knowledge"' (Unit 4 in Block 1), in the early part of the century poverty was widely felt to be a normal condition of life, an inevitable result of overpopulation and low wages, meaning that incomes were sometimes unable to sustain individuals and families. Pauperism was the legal status of those whose income was so low that they chose to apply to the Poor Law authorities for relief. The Poor Law Amendment Act of 1834 signalled a shift in this definition (Harris, 2004). While it was accepted that disabled and elderly people might genuinely fall on hard times, poverty and pauperism among the able-bodied was seen as a result of laziness and improvidence in claimants who assumed relief from the Poor Law authorities was easier than working and saving for unforeseen events such as sickness or unemployment. However, a number of crises in the mid-century challenged assumptions about the causes of poverty and the efficacy of the new Poor Law. In turn, the response from the central authorities was to reform the system but, at the same time, to restate the principles of 1834 and to further limit outdoor relief.

This unit explores the new Poor Law in England and Wales. Section 10.1 examines attitudes to poverty in the mid-nineteenth century and explains why poverty was a frequent feature of working people's lives. It also considers what, if anything, the new Poor Law can tell us about the 'age of equipoise'. As you may remember from the unit 'The "age of equipoise" and the Great Exhibition of 1851' (Unit 8), 'equipoise' was the term used to describe the optimism that the economic difficulties and social unrest of the early century could be resolved through a shared culture built around work and self-help. As you will see in this unit, the Poor Law threatened such optimism. Section 10.2 describes how the Poor Law came under strain in the 'hungry forties', a period of high unemployment and widespread poverty. Section 10.3 looks at the workhouse and explores why it was such a central feature of poor relief. Section 10.4 examines how a scandal about starvation in a workhouse in Andover, Hampshire provoked widespread outrage. Section 10.5 explores problems associated with the new Poor Law that emerged during the depression of the 1860s. Section 10.6 shows how one particular controversy emerged over the treatment of the poor in 'casual wards', spaces in the workhouse reserved for tramps. Section 10.7 considers how these crises began to challenge the principles of the new Poor Law and how the Poor Law authorities responded by restating these principles with what became known as a 'crusade against outdoor relief'. Section 10.8 examines how new understandings of the causes of poverty in the late nineteenth century began to undermine the new Poor Law by questioning the assumptions made about the causes of poverty.

As you will see, the history of the Poor Law illustrates many of the topics of the module and of Block 2 in particular. Perhaps more than any other subject, it shows the paradoxes and contradictions of the age: how optimism about the economic future of the nation existed alongside evidence of widespread poverty, and why the principles of the new Poor Law were constantly restated despite numerous questions over its efficacy. It also shows how the great ambition to produce a centralised system of poor relief organised around local boards of guardians and uniform workhouses nevertheless produced significant regional variations in practice.

The new Poor Law and the British Isles

The new Poor Law was implemented in England and Wales from 1834, and later variants of the law were devised, passed and implemented in Ireland (from 1838) and Scotland (from 1845). The new Poor Laws in Ireland and Scotland were different in their application and operation from those in England and Wales. In Ireland, for instance, the workhouse did not necessarily serve a union of parishes, as one workhouse was placed in each town and served electoral divisions instead. In rural Scotland, the poor received outdoor relief, as it was impractical to build large workhouses (called poorhouses in Scotland) to serve a thinly spread population. This unit focuses on the new Poor Law in England and Wales, but it is worth bearing in mind that the workhouse and the attempt to stigmatise poverty became common throughout all countries of the Victorian British Isles.

10.1 The new Poor Law in the 'age of equipoise'

Poor Law reform was born out of the frustration of local ratepayers, who were increasingly concerned about the rising cost of relief in the late eighteenth and early nineteenth centuries. The £2 million spent on relief in England and Wales in 1783–85 had doubled by 1802–03 and quadrupled by 1818. The population grew during these years too, so if we take that into account by looking at the costs per head, these had risen from 4 shillings in 1776 to 13 shillings in 1818 (Harris, 2004, p. 43). Under pressure from ratepayers, a Royal Commission on the Poor Laws was set up by the government in 1832 with the task of investigating the rising costs of poor relief. Its report suggested that the best way to reduce poverty and the poor rate would be by deterring the poor from claiming relief through the threat of the workhouse and by enforcing the principle of less eligibility. The aim was to discourage the able-bodied, those who could make a living from their own labour, from entering the workhouse, and to encourage more deserving groups, such as elderly people, to seek help from family or local charities. Such a strategy could work only if outdoor relief delivered by the Poor Law authorities to claimants in their own homes came to an end, forcing people to rely on themselves, their family or local charity, and, if absolutely desperate, on the workhouse. The commission gradually issued 'General Orders' prohibiting the delivery of outdoor relief to able-bodied men and their families; eligibility was restricted to widows with children, or to cases of emergency.

A Poor Law Commission, formed after the end of the royal commission, was headed by three commissioners who would direct the implementation of the new Poor Law. They sent out assistant commissioners to encourage parishes to unite to form new Poor Law unions with a central workhouse. By 1838, 573 new Poor Law unions had formed in England and Wales. These covered 80 per cent of parishes. Within a further 30 years, after laws were passed that dismantled all remaining systems associated with the old Poor Law, the whole of England and Wales operated according to the new Poor Law system.

By the 1840s the new Poor Law was well established but no less controversial than the old system had been. It had a 'reputation for meanness and uncaring dictation from the centre' (Parry, 2006, p. 93).

Anti-Poor Law riots took place in northern manufacturing towns in the late 1830s and resistance was particularly fierce in Wales. In the Rebecca Riots of 1843–44, workhouses were specifically targeted (Englander, 1998). Just over a decade after its introduction, the new Poor Law was held in disrepute and it remained controversial for the rest of the century and into the next. How, then, did it endure for so long and what, if anything, can it tell us about the so-called age of equipoise?

Answering these questions requires an understanding of what those who supported the new Poor Law thought it would achieve. As you know from Unit 4, the new Poor Law was passed by a reformed Parliament influenced by new ideas of political economy and utilitarianism. It put in place a national system of relief for the poor, the sick, orphans and **lunatics**, organised by an ambitious state confident it could deal with social and economic problems without raising rates or taxes. More than this, it was consciously devised to reform society and to modernise the economy. Supporters thought that the old Poor Law had helped cause poverty through overly generous systems of outdoor relief that interfered with the free market. They thought that the new Poor Law would help restore the proper balance. This conviction was strong enough for many politicians, ratepayers and Poor Law guardians to maintain faith in the new system through the mid-century despite frequent scandal and constant controversy. As Jose Harris has argued, 'The spectre of the so-called Speenhamland system – the belief that lax Poor law administration before 1834 had brought the nation to the brink of bankruptcy, over-population, and moral ruin – was a living object-lesson in official Poor law thinking right down to 1914' (Harris, 1993, p. 238).

Exercise 10.1

Read the extract below from the Poor Law Commissioners' report of 1834. The author, Nassau Senior (1790–1864, pictured in Figure 10.1), was an influential economist and lawyer in the 1830s and 1840s, interested in how political economy could be used to shape government policy. He was a member of the royal commission of 1832 and, along with Edwin Chadwick (1800–1890), whom you encountered in Unit 4, one of the chief architects of the Poor Law Amendment Act of 1834. In this extract he describes how the poor received cash in exchange for work under the old Poor Law.

Figure 10.1 After Henry Wyndham Phillips, *Nassau William Senior*, 1855, stipple engraving, 22 x 15cm plate size. National Portrait Collection, London, Reference Collection, NPG D5014. Photo: © National Portrait Gallery, London

How does Senior characterise the impact of the old Poor Law on the people?

This should take around 10 minutes.

> The labourer feels that the existing system, though it generally gives him low wages, always gives him easy work. It gives him also, strange as it may appear, what he values more, a sort of independence. He need not bestir himself to seek work; he need not study to please his master; he need not put any restraint upon his temper; he need not ask relief as a favour. He has all a slave's security for subsistence, without his liability to punishment. As a single man, indeed, his income does not exceed a bare subsistence; but he has only to marry, and it increases. Even then it is unequal to the support of a family; but it rises on the birth of every child. If his family is numerous, the parish becomes his principal paymaster; for, small as the usual allowance of 2 s. a head

may be, yet, when there are more than three children, it generally exceeds the average wages given in a pauperized district. A man with a wife and six children, entitled, according to the scale, to have his wages made up to 16 s. a week, in a parish where the wages paid by individuals do not exceed 10 s. or 12 s., is almost an irresponsible being. All the other classes of society are exposed to the vicissitudes of hope and fear; he alone has nothing to lose or to gain.

(Senior, 1905 [1834])

Specimen answer

Senior argues that the old Poor Law gives the working man low wages for easy work but, worse, the guarantee of wages and the promise of relief if he cannot support his family means that he has no need to exercise discipline over his conduct. This arrangement ruins the character of the working man by making him irresponsible.

Discussion

Like many political economists, Senior thought that progress depended on the evolution of society from one based on dependence and obligation to one based on individually negotiated contracts for work. He believed that working men (but not women) were capable of exercising freedom in the marketplace and thought the new Poor Law was an important step in emancipating them from dependence on the charity of their wealthier neighbours.

The utilitarian promoters of Poor Law reform blamed poverty on an economy that had become corrupt and inefficient – as seen in the Corn Laws – and on a system of poor relief that encouraged dependence and mendacity and that supported the poor to have children they could not afford, further swelling the number of labourers and driving wages down. As Steven King notes, the commission set out to show how 'Generous allowances encouraged idleness and immorality, undermining the desirable self-help ethic which should have lain at the heart of welfare' (King, 2000, p. 227).

In contrast, politicians, both Tory and Liberal, and many members of the liberal middle classes thought reform of the Poor Laws would help to produce a virtuous, energetic and entrepreneurial nation. The new

Poor Law would force the poor to become more self-reliant through the principle of less eligibility. At the same time, the popular press was used to convince the public of the need for self-help. Didactic books on political economy and self-help by writers such as Harriet Martineau (1802–1876) and Samuel Smiles aimed to persuade the middle and working classes of the benefits of independence, work and saving, with stories of individuals and communities transformed from rags to riches through work and thrift. For those who could not achieve riches, the modest benefits of self-help were to be found in 'A healthy home, presided over by a thrifty cleanly woman [which] may be the abode of comfort, of virtue, and of happiness. It may be the scene of every ennobling relation in family life' (Smiles, 2006 [1876], p. 188). According to Smiles, the new Poor Law legislation was 'one of the most valuable that has been placed on the statute-book in modern times' (Smiles, 2006 [1876], p. 190). It taught the working man the value of independence and self-reliance, though, as he acknowledged, 'no law proved more unpopular than this was, for years after it had been enacted' (Smiles, 2006 [1876], p. 190).

The unpopularity of the new Poor Law hinged on the fact that many people's experience of work and hardship bore little resemblance to the theories and ideas about the causes of poverty promoted by supporters of the new law. It did not take long for the first crisis to emerge. From early in the 1840s and throughout the mid-century, the principles behind the new Poor Law were challenged by depressions in trades and by scandals that revealed the complex causes of poverty caused by an overcrowded labour market, low wages and under- or unemployment.

Activity 10.1

Now go to the module website and complete Activity 10.1 'Mayhew, social investigation and the causes of poverty'. This should take around an hour.

10.2 The 'hungry forties'

The 'hungry forties' were the first time the new Poor Law had to cope with mass unemployment. A slump between 1837 and 1839 had affected trade in most key industrial sectors, including textiles. To make matters worse, there were poor harvests between 1839 and 1841. The Corn Laws, yet to be repealed, kept the price of wheat high and meant that both rural and urban populations suffered intense poverty.

The problem was particularly acute in the north of England. Factory inspectors in Lancashire found a 15 per cent unemployment rate near cotton mills in the last three months of 1841, but even higher unemployment rates were found among certain trades in some towns and cities. Table 10.1 shows statistics for Bolton collected by the local cotton employer Henry Ashworth (1794–1880) for the Statistical Society of London.

Table 10.1 Unemployment in Bolton, 1842

Trade	Total employed in 1836	Total employed whole or part time in 1842	Percentage unemployed
Mills	8,124	3,063 (full time)	60
Ironworkers	2,110	1,325 (short time)	36
Carpenters	150	24	84
Bricklayers	120	16	87
Stonemasons	150	50	66
Tailors	500	250	50
Shoemakers	80	40	50

The percentages do not allow for the possible increases in the labour force since 1836, and thus overstate unemployment. But they may serve as an order of magnitude.

Source: Hobsbawm, 1957, p. 53, Table 1

Unemployment figures, however, obscured as much as they revealed at this time. This is because many employers put their staff on 'short time', which allowed workers to keep their jobs but reduced their hours. Their wages fell as a result (Boyer, 1990).

Exercise 10.2

Table 10.2 reproduces figures on poor relief provision to able-bodied men in Lancashire from 1840 to 1845; these figures come from the Poor Law Commission's annual reports.

Compare the number of those relieved (receiving relief) on account of 'want of work' with those relieved because of 'insufficiency of earnings'. What do these figures show?

This should take around 10 minutes.

Table 10.2 Poor relief provision to able-bodied men in Lancashire, 1840-1845

Quarter (three months) ending Lady Day (April)	Number relieved on account of		Total
	Want of work	Insufficiency of earnings	
1840	883	2,632	3,515
1841	978	2,904	3,882
1842	3,841	4,597	8,438
1843	5,213	5,058	10,271
1844	2,031	3,416	5,447
1845	1,041	2,402	3,443

Source: Seventh to Twelfth Annual Reports of the Poor Law Commission, adapted from Boyer, 1990, p. 236, Table 8.1

Specimen answer

These are the key points that struck me:

- In Lancashire the number of able-bodied men receiving relief on account of low or insufficient earnings was higher than those who were unemployed, except in 1843.

- The number of able-bodied men who received relief was at its highest in the quarter ending in April 1843.

- Between 1840 and 1843, the number of men in Lancashire who needed relief because of unemployment or insufficiency of earnings in the three months ending in April increased significantly.

Discussion

The principle of less eligibility compelled Poor Law guardians to limit outdoor relief but, as these figures show, at times of crisis local boards of guardians felt there was little option but to allow it. Local boards of guardians were often fully aware of local labour markets and the genuine difficulties the poor had with finding work. In the 1840s they frequently wrote to the Poor Law Commission asking it to relax the prohibition of outdoor relief. There were some concessions. Hundreds of 'Special Orders' were sent to individual unions throughout the country permitting relief to particular families, all of whom had to be named for the commission. This allowed immediate relief to destitute families for the duration of the crisis.

Despite the exceptions made in times of crisis, the central Poor Law authorities still sought to preserve the principle of less eligibility. As early as 1842 the commission created the 'outdoor labour test'. This measure asked Poor Law unions to assign recipients of outdoor relief to hard work without them having to enter the workhouse. They would undertake similar work to the poor in workhouses, such as stone-breaking in labour yards attached to the workhouse. This was cheap for the unions to implement, and making relief contingent on claimants undertaking some of the hardest and most unpleasant work available made them earn their keep through stigmatising labour.

The economic causes of poverty remained unaddressed by the new Poor Law – instead, when crises occurred, as they did in the 1840s and again in the 1860s, temporary concessions were made allowing local authorities to provide outdoor relief, though this was usually accompanied by a restatement of the principle of less eligibility and of the importance of the workhouse.

10.3 The nineteenth-century workhouse

The Poor Law authorities maintained that the best way to prevent dependence on welfare, and to deter individuals from receiving poor relief, was to make any receipt of assistance conditional on entry to a workhouse. Offering claimants a place in a workhouse acted as a 'self-acting test of the claim of the applicant', otherwise known as the 'workhouse test' (Driver, 1993, p. 24). Put simply, you would enter a workhouse only if you *really* needed help. To accord with the principle of less eligibility, life in the workhouse was meant to be harsh. Nevertheless, the workhouse still had a duty to provide for those who were unable to support themselves through no fault of their own: sick, 'insane' or elderly people, and children. As a result, classification and discipline were core features of life in the workhouse.

After the passing of the 1834 Act there was a vast programme of workhouse construction. The commission intended that these buildings would reflect the deterrent function of the new Poor Law (Englander, 1998). The commission paid several architects to create plans for workhouses, which local boards of guardians could choose between and adapt, depending on the number of people they would accommodate, as well as their budget. A model plan was drawn up by architect Samuel Kempthorne (1809–1873).

Exercise 10.3

Look at Kempthorne's design for a 'square workhouse for 300 paupers' (Figure 10.2, which shows the exterior, and Figure 10.3, a ground-floor plan).

Then answer the following questions:

- What do you notice about the design of the workhouse?
- Why do you think it is designed like this? (Think back to your study of 'sites of knowledge' in Unit 4.)

This should take around 15 minutes.

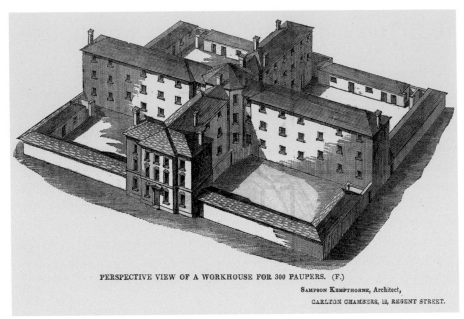

PERSPECTIVE VIEW OF A WORKHOUSE FOR 300 PAUPERS. (F.)

Sampson Kempthorne, Architect,
CARLTON CHAMBERS, 12, REGENT STREET.

Figure 10.2 Samuel Kempthorne, 'Perspective view of a workhouse for 300 paupers', *First Annual Report of the Poor Law Commission*, 1835, London. Photo: © Mary Evans / Peter Higginbotham Collection

Specimen answer

- Kempthorne's workhouse is enclosed by high walls and entrances are limited. The inside is arranged around a central parlour for the 'master'. The ground plan shows separate spaces for women and men, girls and boys. The men's space is surrounded by workrooms, the women's spaces by the laundry and the kitchen.

- Kempthorne's design encompasses the principles of the new Poor Law. The deterrent effect of the workhouse is demonstrated in its external appearance. It looks like a prison. Inside, discipline and order are reflected in the separation of men and women, girls and boys, in spaces for work and in the central position of the 'master', modelled on the 'panopticon' – which you may remember from Unit 4 – proposed by Jeremy Bentham (1748–1832) and intended to give a central authority figure a view of the whole institution.

Discussion

Kempthorne was praised in the *Architectural Magazine* for the way he could incorporate into the designs 'the principles of separation and classification' (quoted in Green, 2010, pp. 107–8). As you can see from Figures 10.2 and 10.3, women, men, young girls and boys were placed in different segments of the workhouse, and would live for most of the time without contact with each other. They would be expected to work,

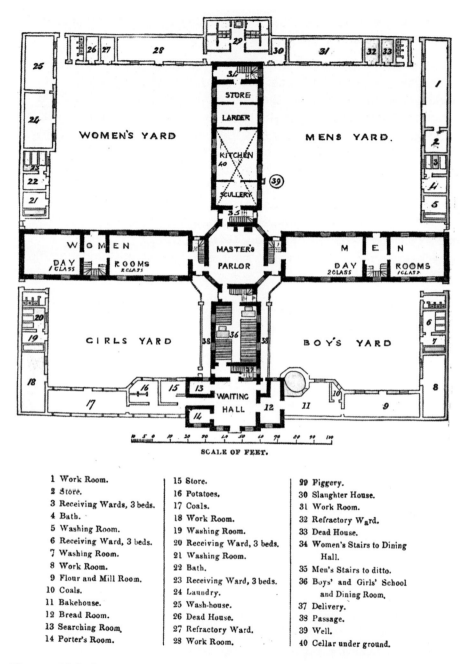

Figure 10.3 Samuel Kempthorne, 'Workhouse for 300 paupers – ground plan, no. 1', *First Annual Report of the Poor Law Commission*, 1835, London. Photo: © Mary Evans / Peter Higginbotham Collection

1 Work Room.
2 Store.
3 Receiving Wards, 3 beds.
4 Bath.
5 Washing Room.
6 Receiving Ward, 3 beds.
7 Washing Room.
8 Work Room.
9 Flour and Mill Room.
10 Coals.
11 Bakehouse.
12 Bread Room.
13 Searching Room.
14 Porter's Room.
15 Store.
16 Potatoes.
17 Coals.
18 Work Room.
19 Washing Room.
20 Receiving Ward, 3 beds.
21 Washing Room.
22 Bath.
23 Receiving Ward, 3 beds.
24 Laundry.
25 Wash-house.
26 Dead House.
27 Refractory Ward.
28 Work Room.
29 Piggery.
30 Slaughter House.
31 Work Room.
32 Refractory Ward.
33 Dead House.
34 Women's Stairs to Dining Hall.
35 Men's Stairs to ditto.
36 Boys' and Girls' School and Dining Room.
37 Delivery.
38 Passage.
39 Well.
40 Cellar under ground.

with men typically breaking stones that would be sold for road making, or crushing bones for fertiliser, and women employed in domestic tasks that helped to run the workhouse. The precise nature of the work differed according to locality but the principle was the same: inmates had to contribute towards their own keep.

The association with prison was intended. As Kathryn Morrison, a senior investigator at English Heritage, has noted, the appearance of workhouses 'made an unmistakable statement about the culpability of pauperism, and warned would-be paupers to expect no comforts within' (Morrison, 1999, p. 53). As the *Poor-Law Sonnets*, published in 1841, described it, people 'Without a crime' were nevertheless 'condemned – imprisoned' (quoted in Fowler, 2007, p. 103). The masters and matrons of workhouses were deliberately chosen to maintain control. In a directive offered by the commission on the topic are these words: 'The habits of firmness, self-control, and coolness, combined with attention and exactitude, imparted by military services, have been found peculiarly to fit them for the performance of the duties' (quoted in Brundage, 2002, p. 78).

The design, layout and organisation of the workhouse were intended to help produce order and discipline. The reality was a little different for two reasons. First, the programme of workhouse construction that took place between 1834 and 1870 often involved adapting or extended the buildings that already existed (Englander, 1998). In most areas with existing workhouses, the fabric remained largely unchanged, but the ethos and rules changed to fit with the new system. Second, the workhouse had to provide a deterrent for the able-bodied poor but it also had to provide a home for other kinds of helpless poor, such as orphans and those deemed to be sick, 'insane' or elderly. According to David Englander, the workhouse had to be a 'general hospital, almshouse, foundling hospital, maternity home, school house, lunatic asylum, blind home, deaf and dumb asylum, [and] home for mental defectives' (Englander, 1998, p. 35). Adapting to these different needs, and in old buildings, often frustrated any attempts at order, discipline and control from the centre. Nevertheless, by 1870 most Poor Law unions had a workhouse which, as one historian argues, existed as an 'enormous monument' to the principles of the new Poor Law (Williams, 1981, p. 81).

Activity 10.2

Now go to the module website and complete Activity 10.2 'Pauper palaces: Bridge Street Workhouse, Manchester'. This should take around an hour.

10.4 The new Poor Law: reputation and controversy

Despite the ideals and principles of the Poor Law authorities, by the mid-1840s the Poor Law Commission was ridiculed as chaotic and disorganised. It was, as you have already seen, shown to be incapable of dealing with the mass unemployment of the early 1840s. Also, the workhouse system gained a reputation for being unnecessarily cruel and unfeeling, and overseers and guardians were accused of profiting from the Poor Law system, as Figure 10.4 illustrates. Problems, such as delays in building works, the corruption of guardians and the abuses experienced by the poor, were quickly reported in local and national newspapers. As you might expect, Chartist newspapers regularly reported scandals and abuses. More surprisingly, so did the establishment newspaper *The Times*. Its editor, John Walter (1776– 1847), had opposed the 1834 Act and was keen to publicise the new Poor Law's failings. In 1841, the Welsh Nonconformist George Robert Wythen Baxter (1815–1854) published *Book of the Bastiles*, which reprinted almost every possible abuse that could be found from these newspaper and pamphlet sources. Some of the cases were exaggerated, but others were – on inspection by the Poor Law Commission – found to be true (Roberts, 1963). All in all, the new Poor Law was exposed in a number of reports as very different in practice from the high ideals and aspirations of the utilitarianist visionaries who had designed the workhouse system.

Reports of one such abuse reached Parliament in August 1845. It began when the radical MP for Finsbury, Thomas Wakley (1795–1862), posed a question in the House of Commons: he asked the home secretary, Sir James Graham (1792–1861), whether he had heard from the Poor Law Commission of the 'practice which he understood to prevail in the Union of Andover' in Hampshire, where the poor had been 'quarrelling with each other about the bones' from which they foraged meat to eat? (HC Deb 1 August 1845). The Poor Law Commission was immediately instructed to investigate by sending the region's assistant commissioner, Henry Parker, to Andover to interview the inmates and staff of the workhouse. The scandal that followed 'triggered public outcry and parliamentary investigation, which in turn led to the first major overhaul of the administrative structure of the New Poor Law' (Brundage, 2002, p. 87).

Figure 10.4 Isaac Robert Cruikshank, the front page of 'Just Starve Us', a comic song about workhouse life by Auber, adapted by T. C. Lewis, c.1843. British Library, London, h.1260.(1.). Photo: © British Library Board. All Rights Reserved / Bridgeman Images

Parker's investigation showed that Andover workhouse inmates were eating the flesh from the bones they were supposed to be crushing. In a bid to contain the scandal, an immediate ban on bone-crushing work in workhouses was imposed (Shave, 2017, p. 227). But media interest escalated. Numerous sensationalist stories circulated, including the claim that inmates' faces were scarred by fragments of bones flying out of the grinding boxes, and an (unfounded) account of cannibalism after human bones from a local graveyard were added to the bones to be pounded by the inmates. In January 1846, the local Whig MP, Ralph Etwall (1804–1882), called for a parliamentary select committee investigation into the events at Andover. The investigation took over three and a half months and witnesses from the Andover Poor Law Union were interviewed, including inmates. The hearings revealed that the master and matron were guilty of significant misconduct. They had siphoned off food from the prescribed diets, leaving the inmates hungry, and abused the poor, including women and children, physically and psychologically (Anstruther, 1984). The committee proved 'that some inmates of the workhouse were in the habit of eating raw potatoes and grain and refuse food which has been thrown to the hogs and fowls … Instances occurred in which inmates of the workhouse, employed in bone-crushing, ate the gristle and marrow of the bones which they were set to break' (Longmate, 2003 [1974], p. 133).

The select committee inquiry into Andover, like all government inquiries of this nature, was supposed to disabuse the public about the sensationalist horror stories emerging about the workhouse and, using the methods of official inquiry, gain control of the scandal and identify the real problem to be remedied. In this case, the public might have been reassured that cannibalism was not taking place in workhouses, but nevertheless the brutality and corruption of the workhouse system were powerfully exposed.

The Andover inquiry, as Felix Driver notes, became 'a trial of the central authorities rather than of the Guardians at Andover' (Driver, 1993, p. 35). The master and matron, Mr and Mrs M'Dougal, resigned and Parker was dismissed for showing an 'unlimited confidence' in the Andover board of guardians (Longmate, 2003 [1974], p. 133). However, the inquiry revealed that the commission had sanctioned an insufficient dietary table for use in the Andover Union workhouse: the diet of the inhabitants was found to be inadequate even before it had been further reduced by the master and matron. The system of regulation from the centre was also criticised. The select committee inquiry revealed the discord among the Poor Law Commissioners and between the commissioners and their secretary, Edwin Chadwick, as well as the inability of the Poor Law Commission to acknowledge the deplorable work given to inmates in the workhouses. The system of inspection was also deemed to be inadequate. Cuts in previous years meant that the number of assistant commissioners had been reduced from 21 to just nine. As a result, the assistant commissioner responsible for Andover had a huge region to check on and consequently was unable to pick up on the problems in his brief and infrequent inspections (Longmate, 2003 [1974], pp. 133–5; Brundage, 2002, p. 88).

Commentators at the time, as well as historians, agree that the select committee's findings had a large part to play in the decline of the commission's reputation. Yet the new Poor Law itself was not scrapped. After lengthy debates in both houses of parliament, the Poor Relief Administration Bill – a measure to reorganise the Poor Law administration – was passed in July 1847 by a Liberal government that included many of the original architects of the new Poor Law. The Poor Law Commission had come to an end. The bill introduced a new administrative structure, allowing the relief of poverty to be even more centrally controlled by the government. A 'new' Poor Law Board was created, and was notably less autonomous than the commission it replaced. Government had taken a closer grip on poor relief.

Like many scandals in public life, the Andover case was the tipping point for a system and an authority already in crisis. The abuses at Andover came to the public's knowledge through the actions of protestors and the campaigning of gentlemen in power, such as the editor of *The Times*, who were against the new Poor Law. They used print media to spread knowledge about the abuses and to campaign for reform. Supporters hoped that the Act of 1847 would restore legitimacy to the new Poor Law, but the new administrative structure did nothing to tackle the fundamental problem: ideas about the causes of poverty and the need for less eligibility bore little resemblance to the everyday life of the poor. As such, as you will see, scandals and controversies reoccurred.

10.5 The Poor Law in the 1860s

Following the reform of 1847 there were no major incidents associated with poor relief until a series of economic downturns in the 1860s produced the same cycle of scandal, debate and reform that you saw in relation to Andover. However, in the 1860s these problems went further in challenging the fundamental principle underlying the Poor Law: that poverty for the able-bodied was a choice, one that could be discouraged through the deterrent effect of the workhouse. The challenge to the Poor Law was particularly acute in London and Lancashire because of the large number of workers who had moved there for work. At times of depression there were a lot of unemployed workers and the Poor Law system struggled to cope.

In the 1840s the journalist Henry Mayhew had exposed the plight of workers in London's craft and artisanal industries who were forced into poverty through too much competition in an overcrowded labour market. Things were no better in the 1860s when Mayhew published another edition of his study of *London Labour and the London Poor* (1861–2). Mayhew's inquiries found artisans and craftworkers complaining that the market was flooded with cheap, foreign-made goods. The immigration of workers from rural areas, from provincial towns and from further afield was also blamed for the state of the labour market. The Irish had been blamed for undercutting wages in the 1840s. In the 1860s Jewish immigrants were blamed for causing too much competition in the garment and tailoring trades in London (Englander, 1994). On top of this, London experienced several extraordinary events. There was a harsh freeze in the winter of 1860–61, which led to the mass unemployment of dock-workers, and a cholera epidemic in the east of the city in 1866, killing 4,000 people in a little over three months. Pauperism was rising, leading to increasing demand for welfare. It was in this context that poor relief was sought by a family in the parish of St Pancras.

Exercise 10.4

Turn to Reading 10.1, '"Starvation before the workhouse" (6 March 1868)', located at the end of the unit. This is an extract from an article that was published in *The Daily News*.

As you read this, think about the following questions:

- What happened to the two youngest children of Eliza and John Tullet?

- Why did this family experience poverty?

- Why did John Tullet not want to enter the local workhouse?

- What judgements are implied about the family, especially Eliza Tullet, in this newspaper report?

- What did the coroner, Dr Slater, think of poor relief and John Tullet's ability to work, and how did the jury treat the family?

This should take around 30 minutes.

Specimen answer

- The coroner found that the two children, Charles Arthur Tullet and Fredrick John Tullet, aged 7 and 5 years old, respectively, died from starvation. The newspaper reports that they were 'emaciated' and the coroner found both of the boys' intestines were empty.

- It seems that this family relied heavily on one main, male breadwinner. The husband and father, John Tullet, was a whitesmith, someone who worked with tin. When he was in good health his earnings were 30 to 36 shillings per week. However, he had been out of whitesmith work for the last 12 months. He was sometimes able to pick up bits of work, earning just 10 shillings per week from this. Two of the eldest boys were at work, but the family's total income was not enough to sustain them all. After paying rent, only 3 shillings were left in the household budget each week. The parish offered John Tullet work breaking stones that was usually paid at 9 pence per day, but his ill health meant he was unable to work very hard and could earn only up to 6 pence per day.

- John Tullet said that he had asked for relief, but 'they would not relieve me unless the whole of my family, including myself, went into the workhouse'. He refused to do this as he did not want to 'break up my home' by seeing his family divided up in the workhouse.

- The newspaper report states that the mother of the children, Eliza Tullet, had a 'clean and neat' appearance and that the coroner remarked the floor was so clean food could be eaten off it. Both of these statements suggest that the family looked after themselves well, indicating they were not intentionally neglectful.

- The coroner suggested that the relief system was not necessarily relieving poverty, and that John Tullet was 'unfitted for further work for his family'. The jury allowed for a collection of over 1 shilling – an act that suggests they sympathised with the family.

Discussion

Eliza Tullet asked for some outdoor relief from a relieving officer, but was denied on the basis that her husband should have enough work. He discounted the fact John Tullet had been unwell. In these circumstances the officer should have asked the board of guardians for emergency outdoor relief and informed the central Poor Law authorities of this decision in a letter. Either the Tullets did not know their rights, or were too scared to ask for such emergency assistance. It would seem the principle of less eligibility worked: John Tullet did not want to split up the family by entering the workhouse and forcing them to endure its bleak uniformity, as illustrated in Figure 10.5.

Figure 10.5 Dinner-time in St Pancras workhouse, London. Photograph from *The Queen's Empire*, 1899, London, Cassell. The crowded, bleak discipline and uniformity of workhouse life extended to mealtimes. Photo: © Look and Learn / Bridgeman Images

You may have noticed that the coroner went to great lengths to emphasise the cleanliness of the Tullet family home, the sobriety of John Tullet and the fact that they were only one week in debt. Contemporaries would have recognised these statements as an indication of the family's respectability. The Poor Law was supposed to be able to distinguish between the rough and the respectable, the deserving and the undeserving poor. However, cases such as this demonstrated that, in practice, these distinctions were difficult to make and often meaningless. Whether rough or respectable, destitute families were equally reliant on the Poor Law and, through sickness and depressions in trade, could suffer privation in much the same way. Cases such as this undermined faith in the new Poor Law. The coroner asked whether parish relief was a 'misnomer' and questioned whether it was right to let children starve in a Christian land.

10.6 Casual wards

As you have already seen, newspapers and social inquiry played an important role in publicising the plight of the poor. However, even writers such as Mayhew, who allowed the poor to speak for themselves, were otherwise removed from the experience of poverty. In the later nineteenth century, a new kind of undercover reportage became popular in sensational circumstances. At a time of increasing pauperism in London, James Greenwood (*c*.1835–1927), a journalist working for the *Pall Mall Gazette,* decided to go incognito and enter the Lambeth workhouse as a vagrant. His aim was to experience the workhouse as a 'casual' during the very cold January of 1866. His experiences were serialised in the *Pall Mall Gazette* and then published in a stand-alone pamphlet.

Tramps

One group of poor people who were treated very differently from the others in the workhouse were the homeless, often called casuals because of their temporary residence there. Throughout the mid-nineteenth century many workhouses, especially those along routes between major towns or cities, built separate casual or 'vagrant' wards, where the homeless roaming poor would lodge temporarily for the night. The rationale behind having separate vagrant wards was to prevent these poor from disturbing the other, longer-term, inmates, in particular sick or elderly residents, and to set them to work in labour yards before their breakfasts, as illustrated in Figure 10.6. Casuals were allowed to stay only three nights in a workhouse before moving on, creating a class of mobile paupers otherwise known as tramps.

Greenwood's exposé, like the revelations about the Andover workhouse, captured a growing unease about the working of the new Poor Law. In the summer of 1865, the results of an investigation into conditions in the infirmaries in London's workhouses had been published in a series of articles in the *Lancet*, later reprinted in a pamphlet, *Report of the Sanitary Commission for Investigating the State of the Infirmaries of Workhouses, 1866* (Koven, 2004, p. 25). The report revealed how unnecessary deaths had been caused by leaving the sick

Figure 10.6 Labour yard, Bethnal Green Employment Association, 1868.
Photo: © Mary Evans / Peter Higginbotham Collection

on dirty wards to be tended by untrained nurses who were themselves
paupers. As the title indicates, the report was not sensationalist. It
focused on the medical and administrative details of Poor Law care,
such as the right diet and the amount of space needed for patients and
the requisite qualifications for nurses and doctors. The report received
support from well-known campaigners for reform in medical care,
people such as Florence Nightingale (1820–1910). However, the report
failed to capture the public imagination. In contrast, Greenwood's
eyewitness account caused a sensation. His reports were reprinted as a
pamphlet called 'A night in a workhouse' (see Figure 10.7), which sold
in its thousands and was read throughout the United Kingdom and
further afield (Koven, 2004, p. 26).

Exercise 10.5

Turn to Reading 10.2, 'James Greenwood, Extract from *A Night in a
Workhouse* (1866)', located at the end of the unit, which is taken from
Greenwood's pamphlet.

As you read, consider the following questions:

- What were conditions like in the Lambeth workhouse?

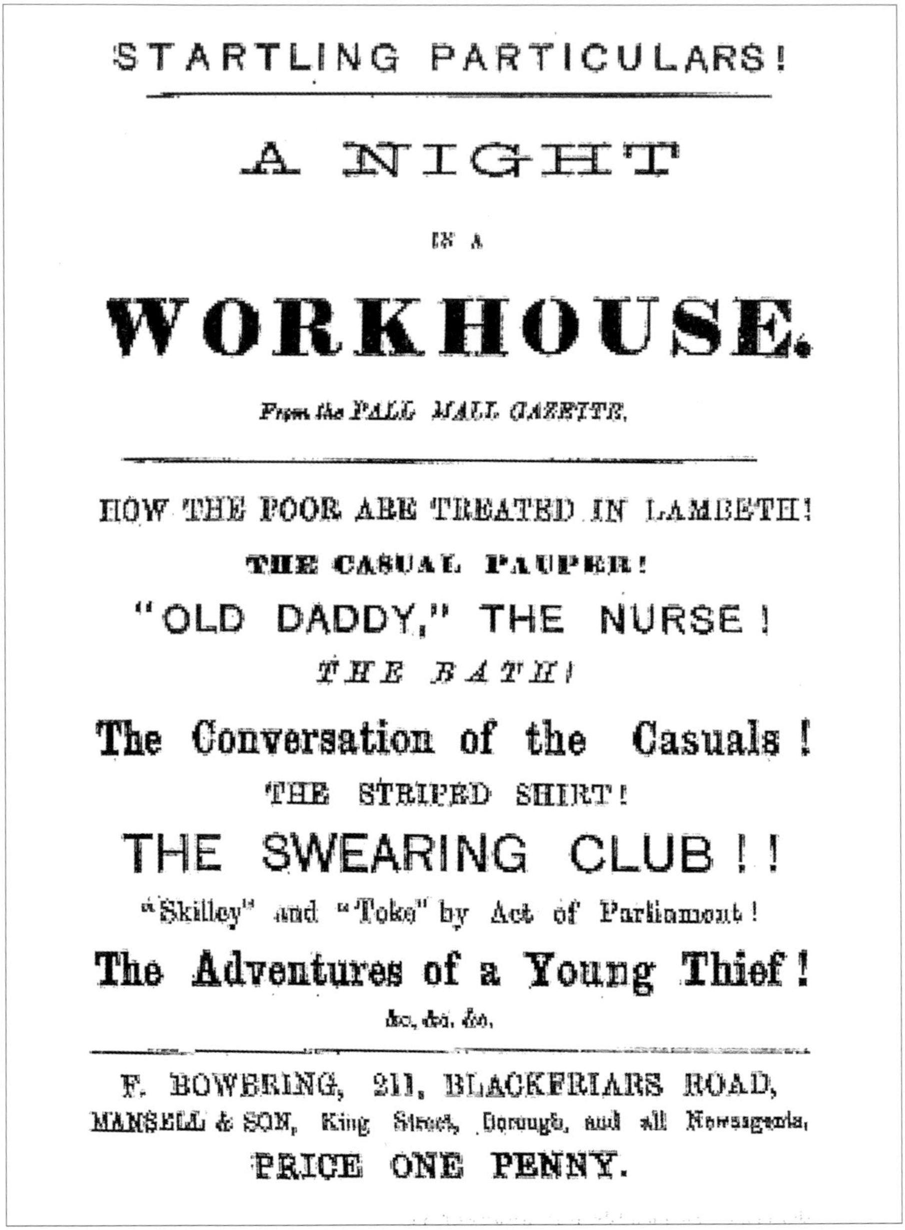

STARTLING PARTICULARS!

A NIGHT

IN A

WORKHOUSE.

From the PALL MALL GAZETTE,

HOW THE POOR ARE TREATED IN LAMBETH!

THE CASUAL PAUPER!

"OLD DADDY," THE NURSE!

THE BATH!

The Conversation of the Casuals!

THE STRIPED SHIRT!

THE SWEARING CLUB!!

"Skilley" and "Toke" by Act of Parliament!

The Adventures of a Young Thief!

&c., &c., &c.

F. BOWERING, 211, BLACKFRIARS ROAD,

MANSELL & SON, King Street, Borough, and all Newsagents,

PRICE ONE PENNY.

Figure 10.7 Cover page of the pamphlet 'A night in a workhouse', written by James Greenwood and originally published in the *Pall Mall Gazette*, 1866. Photo: © Mary Evans / Peter Higginbotham Collection

- Why do you think Greenwood's account was so compelling to contemporary readers?
- Do you think this is a reliable source for information on life inside new Poor Law workhouses?

This should take around 30 minutes.

Specimen answer

- The conditions in the workhouse were grim. Greenwood slept in a cold room, alongside 30 other men, and his bed was a rug and a bag of straw stained with blood. He was forced to strip naked and bathe in dirty water and the floor was so filthy that it was like standing on the bare earth. The room for sleeping in was freezing cold and windy and you could see through the roof. Casual inmates slept together for warmth.

- Greenwood's account is written from an undercover eyewitness's perspective. Moving between the dialogue with 'Daddy' and descriptions of the surroundings makes the account seem real and immediate. His descriptions of the room and the men are emotive – for example, when he writes that the sleeping men are 'like the result of a railway accident'. His account describes his vulnerability – he is, at moments, naked and cold – and, at the same time, there is the threat that he might be exposed as a journalist. This gives the account dramatic tension.

- Greenwood was a journalist and he may have embellished the truth in order to entertain readers and sell copies of the newspaper.

Discussion

We have to be careful with this source. But some elements of Greenwood's account can be verified. For example, historians know from Poor Law records that the sleeping conditions and food in casual wards were not as good as those for long-term residents. Despite problems of reliability, accounts such as Greenwood's are often the closest we can get to the experience of vagrants. Very few vagrants had the opportunity to record their experiences. And, as evidence of how crises emerge, the source is very useful. It reveals what kinds of stories attracted the public's attention and helps historians to understand how scandals developed.

Greenwood's writing, like that of Mayhew earlier in the century, is an example of a new form of investigative journalism that highlighted the everyday plight of the poor through close descriptive accounts, drawn from direct observation and sometimes stated in the pauper's own words. These inquiries shifted the focus of contemporary debate about the Poor Law to the experience of poverty rather than administration and policy. The personal view was calculated, according to Englander, to 'engage their readers' sympathies, disturb their equipoise and make the case for Poor Law reform suddenly seem more urgent' (Englander, 1998, p. 62).

One historian, Seth Koven, has argued that Greenwood used unspoken references to sexual danger to emphasise the threat to the social order from the mixing of young and old, rough and respectable, together in the casual ward. According to Koven, Greenwood's image of naked, impoverished boys and men would have resonated with Victorians who were already primed to see the sexual dangers of overcrowding. As Koven points out, the philanthropist reformer Anthony Ashley Cooper, Lord Shaftesbury (1801–1885), famous for campaigning for the Factory Acts of 1833 and 1847, also campaigned for the inspection of mixed-sex lodging houses – which, he argued, had become 'the deepest dens of vice, filth and misery' (quoted in Koven, 2004, p. 42). The Victorians were also familiar with the 1842 inquiry into the employment of women and children down the mines, which emphasised the threat to the social order from unrestrained sexuality underground (Koven, 2004). Greenwood may have been attempting to revive an established narrative in which the unregulated mixing of people was linked to moral degeneration and social disorder, but we do not know with certainty if readers read his account in this way. Our attempts to understand are made harder by the 'calculated ambiguities of Greenwood's prose [which] makes it easy to miss them if we choose' (Koven, 2004, p. 46). Like contemporary readers, we do not know what really happened in the Lambeth casual ward on the night that Greenwood wrote about, but we can perhaps see why his account created such a sensation.

10.7 Crisis, charity and the 'crusade' against outdoor relief

The continued downturn in the London trades stretched the metropolitan Poor Law to its limits in the 1860s. However, contemporaries were inclined to see London's situation as unusual, a product of its atypical labour market and no indication of what was going on in the rest of the country. But when a severe depression hit the cotton industry in the north of England the fundamental efficacy of the Poor Law system was brought into question. The cotton famine, mentioned in Unit 8, raised public awareness of the difficulties of dealing with poverty caused by mass unemployment within the terms of the new Poor Law.

THE COTTON FAMINE : DISTRIBUTING TICKETS FOR BREAD, SOUP, MEAT, MEAL, COAL, ETC, AT THE OFFICE OF A DISTRICT PROVIDENT SOCIETY, MANCHESTER.

Figure 10.8 Unknown artist, 'The Cotton Famine: Distributing Tickets for Bread, Soup, Meat, Meal, Coal, etc, at the Office of a District Provident Society, Manchester', 1862, engraving. *The Illustrated London News*, 22 November 1862. Photo: © Look and Learn / Illustrated Papers Collection / Bridgeman Images

The cotton famine in Lancashire in 1861–65 was, according to one of the first historians of the Poor Law, 'the most serious crisis with which the English Poor Law has ever been called on to grapple' (MacKay, 1904, p. 388). The depression started when the American Civil War (1861–65) interrupted supplies of raw cotton to Lancashire. Factories began to stop work or to impose short-time hours and thousands of workers were left under- or unemployed. In January 1862 applications for poor relief were up by 70 per cent, and they continued to increase. By November 1862, the Poor Law system in Lancashire was relieving over a quarter of a million people (Henderson, 1969, p. 53). Very soon, the crisis in Lancashire was beyond the scope of the local Poor Law authorities to deal with. The Union Relief Aid Act of August 1862 allowed the government to assist a Poor Law union in distress with rates raised from other local parishes. This emergency measure was later extended across the whole country under the Union Chargeability Act of 1865. But the huge numbers of people requiring relief could still not be accommodated and, as the crisis went on, more help was needed. The answer was a scheme of public works and the mass mobilisation of charity: controversial solutions that many advocates of the new Poor Law feared would undermine its principles.

In 1863 a Public Works Act was passed, allowing local authorities to borrow money to fund schemes to build roads, sewers and parks. The intention was that these works would employ paupers. Still, there was nothing in the Act to say who should be employed and, as such, the Act was presented as a measure for sanitary improvement rather than relief for the able-bodied poor (MacKay, 1904, p. 399). Manchester town council, desperate to help distressed cotton-workers but keen to maintain the principle of freedom of contract at the heart of laissez-faire political economy, gave contracts for the building of reservoirs, parks, sewers and roads to businesses that agreed to engage unemployed operatives at typical labourers' rates of pay. The Public Works Act was a modest success. It protected the middle classes from having to pay more in rates to support the distressed cotton operatives, enabled up to 4,000 paupers to earn wages, helped improve the sanitary state of Lancashire and just about managed to maintain the fiction of laissez-faire. But more help was needed, and appeals were made to charities. Local landowners, churches and the middle classes took the initiative by setting up schemes to feed and clothe distressed cotton operatives. As Figure 10.8 illustrates, charities and cooperatives issued tickets for food and fuel that operatives could use in local shops. Money was even raised outside the region. The Lord Mayor of London, William Cubbitt (1791–1863), persuaded that the local funds in Lancashire were exhausted, raised £528,336 9s. 9d. through the **Mansion House Fund** (Henderson, 1969).

Most cotton-workers survived the crisis as a result of the mobilisation of Poor Law, charities and voluntary agencies. As a result, defenders of the new Poor Law were concerned that its principles had been undermined. The civil servant Charles Trevelyan, whom you encountered in the unit 'Ireland and the Famine' (Unit 9), thought that the cotton famine, like the Irish Famine, had done serious damage to the principles of the new Poor Law. In an article in *The Times* he claimed that 'when ... labour and charity are mixed together, great abuse and demoralisation are always engendered ... It was so in the Irish Famine. It was so in the Cotton Famine' (quoted in Henderson, 1969, p. 66). As Thomas MacKay noted in his history, supporters of the new Poor Law felt that the benefits of 1834 were just beginning to bear fruit in the 1860s, evidenced in the 'successful practice of the arts of independence, and by greater thrift among the poor, supplemented by a better discharge of family duty' (MacKay, 1904, p. 389). They were keen that this good work should not be undone. After the cotton famine and the Poor Law crisis in London in 1867–68, there was a concerted effort to restate the principles of the new Poor Law of 1834 by attempting to rein in charities and limiting outdoor relief.

Charities existed alongside the new Poor Law. Their functions were wide-ranging and some organisations enabled the poor to avoid the workhouse by providing specialist assistance, dole money and items of food and clothing. Crises such as the harsh winters in London and the cotton famine in Lancashire revealed just how important charities were in supporting the poor in exceptional times of distress. For Poor Law advocates, this raised a problem: did the indiscriminate provision of private charity to those who were regarded as undeserving undermine the principles of the new Poor Law and ultimately lead to an increase in Poor Law expenditure? After the problems of the 1860s, defenders of the new Poor Law thought that a response was needed and, in 1869, a memorandum was issued by George Goshcen (1831–1907), a banker, businessman and politician and, at this time, president of the Poor Law Board (Brundage, 2002, p. 103).

Exercise 10.6

Turn to Reading 10.3, 'George Goschen, "The Goschen minute" (1869)', located at the end of the unit.

This reading is difficult to follow because the original was aimed at an informed audience. The language is dense and technical. The following questions will help you pull out the main points:

- What does Goschen think is the problem with the combination of charity and Poor Law relief?

- What does he think should happen instead?

This should take around 30 minutes.

Specimen answer

- Goshcen thinks that charity in London (or the metropolis, as he calls it) is producing a vicious cycle. Paupers are attracted to areas where charity is given out – in this case, the East End of London. This fuels alarm about the extent of poverty, which, in turn, encourages more charity giving and more poverty. He also thinks that the poor could come to expect relief in times of crisis and, as a result, forget 'the necessity for self-reliance and thrift' – in other words, to save for unforeseen misfortune.

- Goschen argues that the Poor Law and charities should work together to avoid the 'indiscriminate distribution of charitable funds' and the 'double distribution of relief to the same persons'.

Discussion

Underlying Goschen's memorandum was the worry that charities were undermining the principles of the new Poor Law. Goschen was concerned to establish a 'proper balance' to ensure that these principles were maintained. He wanted the Poor Law authorities and charities to work together, with the former providing relief for the destitute and the latter helping those on the verge of claiming relief. However, to ensure the principle of less eligibility was maintained, he wanted charities to provide only clothes and bedding and not food and money.

Around the same time as the 'Goschen minute' was issued in 1869, the Society for Organising Charitable Relief and Repressing Mendacity, or COS (Charity Organisation Society), was formed in London. It was managed by politicians, experts and organisers of large charitable organisations, such as Octavia Hill (1838–1912), known for her pioneering social housing schemes. Goschen became vice-president of the COS.

The COS revived the ideas of Thomas Chambers (1780–1847), an influential Scottish minister, writer and social reformer who thought that poverty was caused by poor character. Charles S. Loch (1849–1923), the secretary of the COS from 1875 to 1913, was directly influenced by Chambers. He argued that the morals of both the donor and the receiver of charity needed to be assessed, and that the relaxed approach to the provision of charity which had crept in as a result of recent crises needed redressing. Loch and the COS encouraged charitable donors and organisations to scrutinise the lives of each individual person or family involved, making sure the giver was aware of a potential recipient's character, circumstances and alternative options for assistance – and would discriminate accordingly. The COS worked with and within local Poor Law boards of guardians. Branch agencies were formed throughout the country with the aim, in the words of one historian, 'to restrain and control the charitable gift; to reduce the total amount of charitable giving and to direct the remainder only to those they considered deserving' (Kidd, 1999, p. 97).

The COS typically advocated a more intrusive assessment of individuals and families asking for poor relief than had been previously practised. The society asked for detailed information about applicants' character and conduct, inquiring as to why they had ended up in need of help. This had direct influence on the Local Government Board, which took over the functions of the Poor Law Board in 1871. In a circular of the same year issued by the new board, Poor Law unions were instructed to restrict outdoor relief.

Exercise 10.7

Turn to Reading 10.4, 'Manchester guardians' regulations on outdoor relief (1875)', located at the end of the unit. Who was able to apply for outdoor relief?

This should take around 15 minutes.

Specimen answer

Unless they were sick, not many people could apply. According to these criteria, the only 'able-bodied' people who could apply for outdoor relief were widows with more than one child to support.

Discussion

These rules on outdoor relief were particularly harsh on women, who were the principal recipients. Able-bodied widows supporting just one child were now disallowed relief. Widows with more than one child could apply for relief, but guardians were encouraged to make them enter the workhouse instead. Relieving officers were also mandated to inspect the poor, investigating their character and conduct, while ensuring that they did not receive help for more than three months (Harris, 2004).

The influence of the COS in what historians have called this 'crusade against outdoor relief' is clear. However, the success of the society in reforming relief practices under the Poor Law depended on the willingness of boards to direct their relieving officers accordingly, and then on the willingness of the relieving officer who issued outdoor relief to apply the new practices. As Anthony Brundage notes, relieving officers were already overworked and at times just too busy to interview everyone applying for outdoor relief (Brundage, 2002).

Activity 10.3

Now go to the module website and complete Activity 10.3 'Women and the Poor Law'. This should take around an hour.

The campaign against outdoor relief was seen by its promoters as a way to return to the original principles that underpinned the Poor Law Amendment Act of 1834. It was intended to encourage self-reliance. However, as with the original Act, the ideals that informed the campaign failed to take account of the experience of work and the causes of poverty.

Exercise 10.8

Bearing this in mind, look at Table 10.3, compiled using the Local Government Board's official statistics on people in England and Wales receiving outdoor relief from 1871 to 1877.

From what you see here, how successful do you think was the 'crusade' against outdoor relief?

This should take around 10 minutes.

Table 10.3 Number of paupers relieved outside of the workhouse on the 1 January, 1871–77

Year	Able-bodied			Not able-bodied		
	Adults		Children	Adults		Children
	Males	Females		Males	Females	
1871	44,102	106,407	282,087	107,681	265,638	54,784
1872	29,793	98,925	238,683	101,098	257,535	51,385
1873	22,044	83,600	204,683	100,662	242,605	45,523
1874	18,245	75,486	187,798	92,241	228,557	40,290
1875	20,166	73,847	182,055	88,949	221,010	37,318
1876	14,940	64,070	161,942	80,686	206,099	33,610
1877	13,680	60,133	153,798	75,607	195,979	31,726

Year	Lunatics, insane persons and idiots			Vagrants	Total
	Adults		Children		
	Males	Females			
1871	15,952	19,772	506	951	917,890
1872	15,895	19,936	534	816	824,600
1873	16,068	20,338	461	462	736,446
1874	16,426	20,656	422	368	680,489
1875	17,122	21,370	429	291	662,557
1876	17,424	22,017	336	295	601,419
1877	17,874	22,482	360	343	571,982

Source: First Annual Report of the Local Government Board; cited and adapted by Harris, 2004, pp. 54–5

Specimen answer

These are the key points that struck me:

- The figures show a significant reduction in outdoor relief given to both able-bodied and non-able-bodied adults and children from 1871 to 1877. There was also a dramatic decrease in the number of vagrants given outdoor relief over this period.

- There was an increase in both adult male and female 'lunatics, insane persons and idiots' given outdoor relief over the seven years. This was the only group that increased in number over this period.

- Overall, the total number of poor given outdoor relief decreased from 917,890 to 571,982.

From this table, it appears that the 'crusade' was a success in England and Wales.

Discussion

When we look beyond 1877, the picture of poor relief is more mixed. There were reductions in the numbers of people receiving outdoor relief, but these were small. There were also several notable peaks in the numbers of the outdoor poor during recessions, such as 1879–80. These temporary spikes occurred approximately once every decade into the early 1900s. More noteworthy, perhaps, than the occasional spike in outdoor relief are the indoor relief figures, covering those being accommodated in the workhouse. Indeed, the numbers of the indoor poor increased dramatically, from a mean of 103,507 in 1860 to 192,105 in 1889 (Kidd, 1999, p. 169). The indoor poor represented between 6 and 8 people per 1,000 of the population between 1870 and 1914, not including vagrants in casual wards or pauper lunatics in asylums (Crowther, 1981, p. 59).

Based on this evidence, it is actually fairly hard to assess the success of the 'crusade'. While it did achieve an overall reduction in outdoor relief, the result was to force people into workhouses, which did not necessarily reduce poor relief costs.

Historians and the Poor Law

The first histories of the Poor Law were written in the nineteenth century. For example, the *History of England 1830–1874* by William Nassau Molesworth (1816–1890), written in the Whig history tradition of the time, presented the new Poor Law as a progressive measure that saved the country from corruption by encouraging the virtues of individualism, work and self-help. But in the early twentieth century new histories emerged that were critical of the new Poor Law. The **Fabian socialists** Sidney Webb (1859–1947) and Beatrice Webb (1858–1943), who wanted to promote **collectivist** responses to poverty, published the *English Poor Law History*, Part 2: *The Last Hundred Years* in 1929. Despite their differences, both works – that of Molesworth and that of the Webbs – focused attention on ideologies, politics and the national system of poor relief. They influenced subsequent histories, many of which sought to investigate the roots of the national welfare state in the administrative functions and the centralising ambitions of the new Poor Law.

Later in the twentieth century, historians turned their attention to looking at how the Poor Law worked in practice. Pioneering work by Peter Dunkley and Anthony Brundage showed that local boards were staffed by guardians drawn from the local landed elite and the local middle classes. As such, they varied considerably in their outlook and in the way they applied the statutes and orders that came from the centre (Dunkley, 1974; Brundage, 1972). Numerous local studies have confirmed that the local working of the Poor Law was much more varied than traditional histories accounted for. As David Green has argued, 'there is no single history of the New Poor law but instead several different histories of distinctive institutional and regional practices' (Green, 1995, p. 210). Historians have also become interested in the experience of the poor. They have used letters and autobiographies to argue that the poor were not passive recipients of relief, but active agents for whom the workhouse was part of an 'economy of makeshift' (King and Tomkins, 2003, p. 1).

These local studies have enriched understandings of the new Poor Law, but they can also create a problem for historians. The sheer volume of local studies makes it difficult to say anything certain about the new Poor Law. However, new directions of research are attempting to link local studies and administrative histories with histories of law, culture and political ideas to produce an enlarged understanding of a dynamic system of poor relief (Jones and King, 2015).

10.8 New debates on poverty

Local Poor Law studies show that, despite the best intentions of the central authorities, local guardians used their discretion and continued to provide outdoor relief in times of crisis. In response, as you read above, defenders of the new Poor Law restated the principles of 1834 with evangelical vigour, invoking the memory of an overpopulated, immoral, corrupt and poverty-stricken country before reform. As late as 1879, William Gladstone felt the need to restate the principle of less eligibility at a meeting of workmen in St Pancras:

> It is necessary that the independent labourer of this country should not be solicited and tempted to forego his duty to his wife, his children, and the community by thinking that he could do better for himself by making himself a charge upon that community. There is no more subtle poison that could be infused into the nation at large than a system of that kind. We were in danger of it some 50 or 60 years ago, but the spirit and the courage of the Parliament of 1834 and of the Government of that day introduced a sounder and a wiser system.
>
> (*The Times*, 22 August 1879, quoted in Hilton, 1988, p. 359)

Gladstone's sentiments echoed those of Senior, whom you encountered at the start of this unit. Both feared that a too generous system of relief would undermine self-help, which they believed was essential in building the character of the working man and, by extension, the prosperity of the country.

The promotion of self-help in the mid-century was a great success. It resulted in the proliferation of burial societies, insurance schemes, savings banks, building societies, cooperatives and friendly societies and enabled working people to save for the future. According to one study, by 1905 some 5.8 million Englishmen (61 per cent of the adult male population) belonged to a friendly society paying sickness benefits (Prom, 2010).

Table 10.4 Occupations of men joining the Ancient Order of Foresters 'Court of Three Marys' in Halifax (percentages of total membership)

	1861–1870	1891–1900
Middle class (clerks, grocers, commercial travellers)	12.3	6.4
Artisans (boilermakers, shoemakers, plumbers, tailors)	20.0	11.5
Skilled labour (overlookers, moulders, weavers, warehousemen)	43.1	51.1
Unskilled or low-skilled labour (labourer, carter, lamplighter)	24.6	31.1

Source: Prom, 2010, p. 890

Table 10.4 gives membership details of a local branch of one such friendly society. At a local level, as the table shows, members were drawn from both the working and the lower middle classes. Friendly societies performed a social function as well as providing economic benefits, as places where people could get together for 'good fellowship and mutual insurance', as one historian has put it (Gosden, 1973, p. 2). This combination of social, economic and moral good and the cross-class connections that friendly societies supposedly fostered cultivated the spirit of collaboration and compromise that gave the 'age of equipoise' its name. However, many working people found that their savings were modest while their work was unstable and insecure. As a result, even the most independent of skilled workers could find themselves requiring poor relief. Geoffrey Crossick's study of the occupational status of all men over the age of 22 admitted to the Greenwich workhouse in south London in 1864 due to sickness and poverty confirms that the majority (70 per cent) were unskilled, but a significant number (27.5 per cent) were skilled men who had fallen on hard times (Crossick, 1978).

Towards the end of the nineteenth century and at the start of the twentieth, new kinds of social investigation combined interviews with the poor with the collection of statistics on incomes and expenditure in households over time to produce a better understanding of poverty. Inquiries by Charles Booth (1840–1916), Joseph Rowntree (1836–1925) and Benjamin Seebohm Rowntree (1871–1954) showed just how easy it was for the respectable working classes to fall into poverty, using charts and diagrams to represent poverty in new ways (see, for example, Figure 10.9).

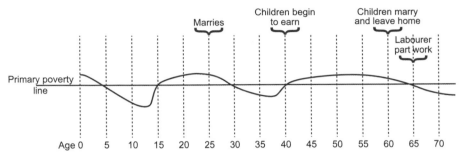

Figure 10.9 Rowntree's diagram of labourers' life-cycle poverty. Source: Rowntree, 1908, p. 137

Exercise 10.9

To end this unit, read B. S. Rowntree's description of life for a family in poverty below. This is taken from his 1901 study of poverty in York in which social investigators visited families in their own homes.

What do you think is the implication for the principles of the new Poor Law and the ethos of self-help in this description of poverty?

This should take around 10 minutes.

> A family living upon the scale allowed for in this estimate [of poverty] must never spend a penny on railway fare or omnibus. They must never go into the country unless they walk. They must never purchase a halfpenny newspaper or spend a penny to buy a ticket for a popular concert. ... They must never contribute anything to their church or chapel, or give any help to a neighbour which costs them money. They cannot save, nor can they join [the] sick club or [a] Trade Union, because they cannot pay the necessary subscriptions. The children must have no pocket money for dolls, marbles, or sweets. The father must smoke no tobacco, and must drink no beer. The mother must never buy any pretty clothes for herself or for her children, the character of the family wardrobe as for the family diet governed by the regulation, 'Nothing must be bought but that which is absolutely necessary for the maintenance of physical health, and what is bought must be of the plainest and most economical description.' Should a child fall ill, it must be attended by the parish doctor; should it

die, it must be buried by the parish. Finally, the wage-earner must never be absent from his work for a single day.

If any of these conditions are broken, the extra expenditure involved is met, *and can only be met*, by limiting the diet; or, in other words, by sacrificing physical efficiency.

(Rowntree, 1908, pp. 133–4)

Specimen answer

Rowntree's description of poverty suggests that it is not a choice. Even when life is stripped down to its absolute basics, to subsistence level, with nothing spent on luxuries, working people still cannot save money to plan for any future crises and cannot survive without help when these crises occur.

Discussion

The social investigations of the late nineteenth century began to challenge the principles of the Poor Law and the belief that self-help was enough to prevent poverty. But they did not really say anything new. In fact one historian has argued that these studies came 'surprisingly late', given that many people in the mid-century had already made the point that the respectable hard-working poor could easily slip into poverty (Hoppen, 1998, p. 61). However, their rigour and statistical method meant it was now impossible for the government to ignore the problem of poverty and the inadequacies of the Poor Law system. In the late nineteenth century the efficacy of the Poor Law and the culture of self-help in a world of uncertain employment began to come into question.

Conclusion

The new Poor Law in the mid-century demonstrates the contradictions and paradoxes of the 'age of equipoise'. It was, and still is, characterised as brutal and harsh, but it was passed by a reformed Parliament which was confident that the workhouse system and the principle of less eligibility would transform the country from one mired in poverty, overpopulation and corruption to one defined by the energy and independence of its people.

The architects of reform, men such as Nassau Senior and Edwin Chadwick, were influenced by political economy and utilitarianism. They argued that restricting outdoor relief would enable laissez-faire political economy to flourish: no longer would poor rates be used to subsidise low wages. Instead, the market would find the right balance. They also thought that less eligibility would encourage individualism and entrepreneurialism and lead to growth. At the same time, the encouragement of self-help and thrift would transform working-class families and their communities by requiring them to look after each other. To ensure these ends were met, the reformers devised a national system of poor relief organised through local boards of guardians working under instruction from the centre.

But the working of the new Poor Law in practice was quite different. As numerous crises demonstrated, the causes of poverty were complex and could not be tackled by the principle of less eligibility. In times of great need, for example during the depressions of the 1840s and the 1860s, the limits of the Poor Law were exposed. Nevertheless, support for the principles of 1834 remained remarkably strong among politicians; momentary crises in the operation of the new Poor Law were followed by reform and a reassertion of less eligibility, which led to the 'crusade' against outdoor relief and the push for further centralisation.

The optimism that sustained the new Poor Law was beginning to fade in the late 1870s as new understandings of poverty emerged. Social investigations in the mid-century went some way towards exposing the failings of the Poor Law and, by highlighting the experiences of the poor, elicited the sympathy of the public. The new Poor Law was further undermined by proliferating evidence on the incomes and expenditure of the poor. Data on poverty produced by Booth and the Rowntrees, and also in the culture of accounting encouraged by the

COS, revealed the reality of the cycle of poverty in some working-class households and so the efficacy of the Poor Law was brought into question.

> Now turn to the module website to complete the independent study activities associated with this unit.

References

Anstruther, I. (1984) *The Scandal of the Andover Workhouse*, Gloucester, Geoffrey Bles.

Baxter, G. R. W. (1841) *The Book of the Bastiles; or, The History of the Working of the New Poor Law*, London, J. Stephens.

Boyer, G. (1990) *An Economic History of the Poor Law, 1750–1850*, Cambridge, Cambridge University Press.

Brundage, A. (1972) 'The landed interest and the new Poor Law: a reappraisal of the revolution in government', *English Historical Review*, vol. 87 no. 342, pp. 27–48.

Brundage, A. (2002) *The English Poor Laws, 1700–1930,* Basingstoke, Palgrave.

Crossick, G. (1978) *An Artisan Elite in Victorian Society: Kentish London 1840–1880*, London, Croom Helm.

Crowther, M. A. (1981) *The Workhouse System 1834–1929*, Athens, GA, University of Georgia Press.

Driver, F. (1993) *Power and Pauperism: The Workhouse System 1834–1884*, Cambridge, Cambridge University Press.

Dunkley, P. (1974) 'The "hungry forties" and the new Poor Law: a case study', *The Historical Journal*, vol. 17, no. 2, pp. 329–46.

Englander, D. (1994) *A Documentary History of Jewish Immigrants in Britain, 1840–1920*, Leicester, Leicester University Press.

Englander, D. (1998) *Poverty and Poor Law Reform in Nineteenth-Century Britain, 1834–1914: From Chadwick to Booth*, London, Longman.

Fowler, S. (2007) *Workhouse: The People, The Places, The Life behind Doors*, Kew, The National Archives.

Goschen, G. J. (1869) *Letter of the Rt. Hon. G. J. Goschen, President of the Poor Law Board. On the Relief to the Poor in the Metropolis*, 20 November, London, Shaw and Sons.

Gosden, P. H. (1973) *Self-help: Voluntary Associations in the 19th Century*, London, B. T. Batsford.

Green, D. (1995) *From Artisans to Paupers: Economic Change and Poverty in London, 1790–1870*, London, Scolar Press.

Green, D. (2010) *Pauper Capital: London and the Poor Law, 1790–1870*, Farnham, Ashgate.

Greenwood, J. (1866) *A Night in a Workhouse*, London, Office of the Pall Mall Gazette.

Harris, B. (2004) *The Origins of the British Welfare State: Social Welfare in England and Wales, 1800–1945*, Basingstoke, Palgrave Macmillan.

Harris, J. (1993) *Private Lives, Public Spirit: Britain 1870–1914*, London, Penguin.

HC Deb 1 August 1845, vol. 82, cols. 1320–1 [Online]. Available at http://hansard.millbanksystems.com/ (Accessed 4 July 2017).

Henderson, W. O. (1969) *The Lancashire Cotton Famine*, Manchester, Manchester University Press.

Hilton, B. (1988) *The Age of Atonement. The Influence of Evangelicalism on Social and Economic Thought 1785 to 1865*, Oxford, Oxford University Press.

Hobsbawm, E. (1957) 'The British standard of living 1790–1850', *Economic History Review*, vol. 10, no. 1, pp. 46–68.

Hoppen, T. (1998) *The Mid-Victorian Generation 1846–1886*, Oxford, Oxford University Press.

Jones, P. and King, S. A. (eds) (2015) *Obligation, Entitlement and Dispute under the English Poor Laws, 1600–1900,* Newcastle, Cambridge Scholars.

Kidd, A. (1999) *State, Society and the Poor in Nineteenth Century England*, Basingstoke, Macmillan.

King, S. (2000) *Poverty and Welfare in England 1700–1850: A Regional Perspective*, Manchester, Manchester University Press.

King, S. and Tomkins, A. (eds) (2003) *The Poor in England, 1700–1850: An Economy of Makeshifts*, Manchester, Manchester University Press.

Koven, S. (2004) *Slumming: Sexual and Social Politics in Victorian London*, Princeton, NJ, Princeton University Press.

Longmate, N. (2003 [1974]) *The Workhouse: A Social History*, London, Pimlico.

MacKay, T. (1904) *A History of the English Poor Law*, vol. III, London, King and Son.

Morrison, K. (1999) *The Workhouse: A Study of Poor-Law Buildings in England*, Swindon, English Heritage.

Parry, J. (2006) *The Politics of Patriotism. English Liberalism, National Identity and Europe, 1830–1886*, Cambridge, Cambridge University Press.

Prom, C. (2010) 'Friendly society: discipline and charity in late-Victorian and Edwardian England', *The Historian*, vol. 72, no. 4, pp. 888–908.

Roberts, D. (1963) 'How cruel was the Victorian Poor Law?', *The Historical Journal*, vol. 6, no. 1, pp. 97–107.

Rowntree, B. S. (1908) *Poverty: A Study of Town Life*, London, Macmillan and Co.

Senior, N. (1905 [1834]) 'Poor Law Commissioners' report of 1834' [Online], London, HM Stationery Office. Available at http://www.econlib.org/library/YPDBooks/Reports/rptPLC.html (Accessed 19 April 2017).

Shave, S. (2017) *Pauper Policies: Poor Law Practice in England, 1780–1850*, Manchester, Manchester University Press.

Smiles, S. (2006 [1876]) *Thrift*, Teddington, The Echo Library.

The Daily News (1868) 'Starvation before the workhouse', 6 March.

Williams, K. (1981) *From Pauperism to Poverty*, London, Routledge.

Readings

Reading 10.1 'Starvation before the workhouse' (6 March 1868)

Source: *The Daily News* (1868) 'Starvation before the workhouse', 6 March.

Yesterday an inquiry was held by Dr. Lankester, the coroner for the central division of Middlesex, at the Lord Nelson Tavern, Holloway-road, on the bodies of two boys, named respectively Charles Arthur Tullet, aged seven, and Frederick John Tullet, aged five, two of a family, who died under very painful circumstances.

Eliza Tullet, whose appearance was very clean and neat, said she was the mother of the deceased boys, and lived at 15, Clayton-street, Caledonian-road. … They were very poor, as her husband a year ago had suffered from a severe illness. Since Christmas he had been out of work, and at the present time he was a dying man. Two of their eldest boys were out at work, and brought in a little money, leaving 3s. after the rent for their home was paid. She and her husband also got little odd jobs, but the whole receipts afforded them little beyond starvation.

…

Dr. J. T. Slater, parish surgeon, was next examined, and deposed to being called to the deceased at four o'clock in the afternoon of Saturday last. He found the elder boy insensible and convulsed. The younger boy was simply insensible, and both died shortly after his attendance.

Dr. Edward Ballard, medical officer of health to the parish of Islington, said he had made a *post-mortem* examination of the bodies of the two boys. The eldest was very puny for a child of seven years of age, and was ricketty, also very much emaciated. The intestines were completely empty from one end to the other. The cause of death in this case was convulsions from starvation. The child had been starved for some time past. The second child was also ricketty and very small for its age, and emaciated. The small intestines were entirely empty, but in the larger there was something of a fluid or semi-fluid character. In this case also it was a death from starvation.

The Coroner advised that the father of the deceased children should be called.

John Tullet said he was the father of the deceased. He was a whitesmith. When in health he earned from 30s. to 36s. a week, but he had been out of work for twelve months. Sometimes he got a job, and might earn 10s. a week. He did not see the children until after they were found dead.

By the Coroner – Have you applied to the parish, under your distressed circumstances, for relief?

Witness – I did once, but they would not relieve me unless the whole of my family, including myself, went into the workhouse. I felt that I could not break up my home, and tried to struggle on.

The Coroner – There must be something wrong in workhouse relief, either one way or the other.

Mr. Stanwell, the coroner's officer, said the father of the deceased was a most respectable man, and was very sober.

In answer to the foreman the father of the deceased said that work in the stone yard had been offered to him by the parish at 9d. a day, but he was unable to do it.

Mr. Stanwell said from his knowledge of the father that if he were put to break stones he would not earn 6d. a day.

The mother of the deceased said she had applied for an order from the relieving officer of St. Pancras Workhouse, and was told that as her husband was a whitesmith he should not ask for relief, and that was after he had been out of work for six months, and ill.

Dr. Slater said the room in which the family lived was most cleanly. It was poorly furnished, but literally speaking, 'you might have taken your food from the boards of the floor,' and everything was very clean.

The landlady of the house said it was almost heart-breaking to know the condition of the family who resided in her house. Under starvation their honour was extreme, and they only owed one week's rent. She knew they wanted 'bread,' and she had exerted herself to obtain relief from the religious visitors.

The Coroner said it was a very melancholy case, and raised the question as to whether the parish relief was a misnomer, or one of truth. The present case was one that might have been relieved by the parish without its penalty – stone-breaking, and not allowed starvation of children in a Christian land.

A combined verdict of 'Death from convulsions by starvation,' and 'Starvation' in the second case, was returned.

The jury were so impressed with the case that a collection was made, and more than 1*l*. was given into the hands of the father of the deceased, who was stated by the coroner to be entirely unfitted for further work for his family.

Reading 10.2 James Greenwood, 'Extract from *A Night in a Workhouse*' (1866)

Source: Greenwood, J. (1866) *A Night in a Workhouse*, London, Office of the Pall Mall Gazette, pp. 8–14, 18.

'Come in,' said Daddy, very hospitably. 'There's enough of you to-night, anyhow! What made you so late?'

'I didn't like to come in earlier.'

'Ah! that's a pity now, because you've missed your skilley (gruel). It's the first night of skilley, don't you know, under the new Act.'

'Just like my luck!' I muttered dolefully.

The porter went his way, and I followed Daddy into another apartment where were ranged three great baths, each one containing a liquid so disgustingly like weak mutton broth that my worst apprehensions crowded back.

'Come on, there's a dry place to stand on up at this end,' said Daddy kindly. 'Take off your clothes, tie 'em up in your hank'sher, and I'll lock 'em up till the morning.'

Accordingly, I took off my coat and waistcoat, and was about to tie them together when Daddy cried, [p. 9]

'That ain't enough, I mean *everything*.'

'Not my shirt, sir, I suppose?'

'Yes, shirt and all; but there, I'll lend you a shirt,' said Daddy. 'Whatever you take in of your own will be nailed, you know. You might take in your boots, though – they'd be handy if you happened to want to leave the shed for anything; but don't blame me if you lose 'em.'

With fortitude for which I hope some day to be rewarded, I made up my bundle (boots and all), and the moment Daddy's face was turned away shut my eyes and plunged desperately into the mutton broth.

....

[p. 10]

'Where am I to sleep, please, sir?'

'I'll show you.'

And so he did. With no other rag but the checked shirt to cover me, and with my rug over my shoulders, he accompanied me to the door at which I had entered, and, opening it, kept me standing with naked feet on the stone threshold, full in the draught of the frosty air, while he pointed out the way I should go. ...

[p. 11]

No language with which I am acquainted is capable of conveying an adequate conception of the spectacle I then encountered. Imagine a space of about thirty feet by thirty enclosed on three sides by a dingy white-washed wall, and roofed with naked tiles which were furred with the damp and filth that reeked within. As for the fourth side of the shed, it was boarded in for (say) a third of its breadth; the remaining space being hung with flimsy canvas, in which was a gap two feet wide at top, widening to at least four feet at bottom. This far too airy shed was paved with stone, the flags so thickly encrusted with filth that I mistook it at first for a floor of natural earth. ... My bed-fellows lay...

[p. 12]

distributed over the flagstones in a double row, on narrow bags scantily stuffed with hay. At one glance my appalled vision took in thirty of them – thirty men and boys stretched upon shallow pallets which put only six inches of comfortable hay between them and the stony floor. These beds were placed close together, every occupant being provided with a rug like that which I was fain to hug across my shoulders. In not a few cases two gentlemen had clubbed beds and rugs and slept together. ...

the practised and well-seasoned casual seems to have a peculiar way of putting himself to bed. He rolls himself in his rug, tucking himself in, head and feet, so that he is completely enveloped; and, lying quite still on his pallet, he looks precisely like a corpse covered because of its hideousness. Some were stretched out at full length; some lay nose and knees together; some with an arm or a leg showing crooked through [p. 13] the coverlet. It was like the result of a railway accident: these ghastly figures were awaiting the coroner.

…

…In the middle of the bed I had selected was a stain of blood bigger [p. 14] than a man's hand! I did not know what to do now. To lie on such a horrid thing seemed impossible; yet to carry back the bed and exchange it for another might betray a degree of fastidiousness repugnant to the feelings of my fellow lodgers and possibly excite suspicions that I was not what I seemed. Just in the nick of time in came that good man Daddy.

'What! not pitched yet?' he exclaimed; 'here, I'll show you. Hallo! somebody's been a-bleedin'! Never mind; let's turn him over. There you are, you see! Now lay down, and cover your rug over you.'

…

For several minutes there was such a storm of oaths, threats, and [p. 18] taunts – such a deluge of foul words raged in the room – that I could not help thinking of the fate of Sodom; as, indeed, I did several times during the night.

Reading 10.3 George Goschen, 'The Goschen minute' (1869)

Goschen, G. J. (1869) *Letter of the Rt. Hon. G. J. Goschen, President of the Poor Law Board. On the Relief to the Poor in the Metropolis*, **20 November, London, Shaw and Sons, pp. 3–5.**

RELIEF TO THE POOR IN THE METROPOLIS.

The published statements of metropolitan pauperism have for some weeks past shown a considerable increase in the number of the out-door poor, not only as compared with previous weeks, but as compared with the high totals of 1867 and 1868. At the same time it has come to the knowledge of the Board that many persons (especially in the East-end of London) who two winters ago were most eager in soliciting charitable contributions, have now expressed the opinion that the large sums spent then in charity tended to attract pauperism to those districts where money flowed most freely, and that they

[p. 4]

deprecate a repetition of the system then pursued. Under these circumstances, the Board consider it equally important to guard on the one hand against any alarm which might arise on the part of the public, and result in an indiscriminate distribution of charitable funds, and on the other hand to take such precautions and make such preparations as may enable Boards of Guardians and charitable agencies to work with effect and rapidity, if any emergency should arise. And, indeed ... it appears to be a matter of essential importance that an attempt should be made to bring the authorities administering the poor laws and those who administer charitable funds to as clear an understanding as possible, so as to avoid the double distribution of relief to the same persons ...

[p. 5]

The fundamental doctrine of the English poor laws, in which they differ from those of most other countries, is that relief is given, not as a matter of charity but of legal obligation, and to extend this legal obligation beyond the class to which it now applies, namely, the actually destitute, to a further and much larger class, namely, those in receipt of insufficient wages, would be not only to increase to an unlimited extent the present enormous expenditure, but to allow the belief in a legal claim to public money in every emergency to supplant, in a further portion of the population, the full recognition of the necessity for self-reliance and thrift.

Reading 10.4 Manchester guardians' regulations on outdoor relief (1875)

Source: Englander, D. (1998) *Poverty and Poor Law Reform in Nineteenth-Century Britain, 1834–1914: From Chadwick to Booth*, London, Longman, p. 107.

1   Out-door relief shall not be granted or allowed by the Relief Committees, except in case of sickness, to applicants of any of the following classes:–

(a) Single able-bodied men.

(b) Single able-bodied women.

(c) Able-bodied widows without children, or having only one child to support.

(d) Married women (with or without families) whose husbands, having been convicted of crime, are undergoing a term of imprisonment.

(e) Married women (with or without families) deserted by their husbands.

(f) Married women (with or without families) left destitute through their husbands having joined the militia, and being called up for training.

(g) Persons residing with relatives, where the united income of the family is sufficient for the support of all its members, whether such relatives are liable by law to support the applicant or not.

Unit 11 Religion, revival and reform

Janice Holmes

Contents

Aims

This unit will:

- develop your understanding of the religious landscape in Britain and Ireland in the period 1840–80 and how it was changing

- examine the tensions that existed within mid-Victorian religion, which was experiencing both revitalisation and marginalisation at the same time

- give you practice in reviewing and assessing contrasting interpretations of the same event.

Introduction

It can be hard to imagine from a modern perspective just how important religion was to the people who lived in Britain and Ireland in the nineteenth century. Religion really mattered. And when I say 'religion', I mean both the private, internal beliefs people had about God, heaven and sin, and the public, external ways in which they demonstrated those beliefs, such as attending church on Sunday or choosing to abstain from drinking alcohol. Promoting religion and morality was seen to be an obligation of the state, which had set up official, or 'established', church systems for that purpose. Religious attitudes underpinned debates about poverty, working conditions, the economy and imperial expansion. Throughout the nineteenth century, then, religion was something that occupied a large space within both public and private spheres.

In the past, historians have argued that, as the nineteenth century progressed, British society became increasingly secularised (Bruce, 1992). As new scientific knowledge emerged, religion and belief in God were no longer seen to be necessary. It is easy to find evidence for this position, and you will explore some of it in this unit. However, historians today are much less convinced by this 'secularisation' narrative, mainly because it does not explain the evidence for the continued religious vitality and belief that exists in the modern world. Today's religious practice has obliged historians to look again at the nineteenth century. What they have found is a much more complicated picture. Alongside the evidence of disbelief and religious decline they have also discovered renewal, reform and revitalisation.

This unit will explore the religious world of mid-nineteenth century Britain and Ireland from this new perspective. Section 11.1 starts with a survey of the Victorian religious 'landscape'. Here you will look at the 1851 census of religion and identify the size and character of Britain and Ireland's main religious denominations. Section 11.2 will examine 'everyday' religion – that is, religion as average people would have experienced it. There was a common set of religious values and a shared religious culture that everyone would have recognised. You will also learn about three movements of religious vitality that dominated the mid-nineteenth century and that provoked considerable conflict and debate: Evangelicalism, Catholicism and liberal theology or 'scepticism'. Section 11.3 takes these three religious movements and explores in more detail the public controversy which each created. The Papal Aggression of 1850, the Ulster Revival of 1859 and the debate over the publication of *Essays and Reviews* in 1860 show how changes to the religious status quo could be deeply resisted, but that ultimately they were incorporated into an ever-widening acceptance of religious differences and diversity. Section 11.4 will consider the changing legal relationship between the church and the state to show how British society was becoming, despite opposition and resistance, more tolerant and pluralist. As you will see, this pluralism reflected the sense of 'equipoise' you studied in the unit 'The "age of equipoise" and the Great Exhibition of 1851' (Unit 8). At the same time, the conflicts it provoked showed the limits of toleration at the mid-century.

11.1 The Victorian religious landscape

The inhabitants of England and Wales, Scotland and Ireland converted to Christianity from the fifth century onwards. Until the Reformation they were Catholic and part of a denominational network that extended across Europe and was based in Rome. As you may remember from your reading in the unit 'Imagined nations made real?' (Unit 6 in Block 1), except for some small and isolated groups of Catholics in England and Scotland, and almost all of Ireland, by the late 1500s the rest of Britain had become Protestant.

The way the state promoted Protestantism and ensured everyone had access to religious services was through the mechanism of an established church. Several of the units you have already read have referred to this institution. It was, in fact, three separate organisations. The biggest was the Church of England, which was responsible for the people of England and Wales. The other two were the Church of Ireland and the Church of Scotland. The Church of England and the Church of Ireland were 'episcopal' in organisation, with territorial divisions called dioceses and parishes and leadership provided by bishops and priests. In 1801, as part of the Act of Union between Great Britain and Ireland, the two churches were merged, but in practice they continued to be largely separate entities. Each had had a regional representative body, called a 'convocation', for the administration of business, but these had been greatly diminished in the eighteenth century. Only in the 1850s did a newly resurrected and now 'united' convocation begin to exercise any significant authority on behalf of both churches (see Figure 11.1).

The Church of Scotland, by contrast, was 'presbyterian' in organisation. Each congregation was governed by a 'kirk session' comprised of the minister and local lay leaders called elders. Sessions then sent representatives to their district 'presbytery', and so on up a chain of regional and then national governance committees. Despite the union of Scotland and England in 1707, the Scottish Church operated with considerable autonomy.

In the years after the Reformation the British state passed laws that required everyone to be a member of their local state church. Everybody was expected to attend its services and to celebrate communion (a ceremony that commemorates the death and resurrection of Jesus through a ritual of eating bread and drinking wine) according to its particular rites. Everybody was also required to pay taxes and rates towards the upkeep of church buildings and the payment of clergymen's salaries. Because clergymen were, in essence, local government officials, they were also responsible for local governance and administration. Clergymen in the established church were responsible for administering and recording the rites of passage (births, marriages and deaths) and, as you know from the unit 'The birth of the modern state' (Unit 5 in Block 1), contributed to local law enforcement and poor relief. Their duty of care was intended to include everyone who lived in their designated parish. In the early nineteenth century, most people in Britain (but not Ireland) were members of these established churches.

Figure 11.1 Unknown artist, 'Convocation of the Clergy, Sitting of the Lower House in the Jerusalem Chamber', engraving. *The Illustrated London News*, 27 November 1852. Photo: © Look and Learn / Illustrated Papers Collection / Bridgeman Images

Your reading so far should have made you aware of the fact that there were also some people who had, for reasons of conscience, rejected the established church systems and had chosen to worship according to some other form. During the sixteenth and seventeenth centuries, these groups included Baptists and Independents (or Congregationalists), English and Irish Presbyterians, Quakers and

Unitarians. Methodists emerged in the eighteenth century and many other groups were set up in the nineteenth century. Originally called 'dissenters', because they dissented from the established church, they were increasingly referred to as 'Nonconformists'. While technically Catholics were dissenters too, the term Nonconformist was reserved for Protestants. All of these non-Anglicans were subject to a variety of legal disadvantages, such as exclusion from civic office, fines for failing to take communion in an Anglican church and other indignities around rites of passage and access to university education. In early nineteenth-century England and Wales, however, these minority communities were very small. Historians suggest they amounted to no more than 10 per cent of the total population (Currie et al., 1977).

By the 1850s, certain aspects of this landscape had changed. Britain and Ireland were still overwhelmingly Christian, with only a small community of Jews, based largely in London, and only tiny numbers of individual Hindus and Muslims, living mostly in port towns and urban centres (Census of Great Britain, 1851, p. clxxviii). The country was still strongly Protestant, but there were now large Catholic populations not just in Ireland (where they numbered roughly 78 per cent of the total population) but also in England and Scotland, where Irish migrants fleeing the Famine in the 1840s had formed sizeable communities in cities such as Manchester, Liverpool and Glasgow (as described in the unit 'Ireland and the Famine': Unit 9). Most significant, however, was the emergence of a large and vocal dissenting community. It had grown in size, because of the rapid growth of Methodism between 1780 and 1830, and in political influence, because of the expansion of the franchise. As you saw in Block 1, the Reform Act of 1832 extended the right to vote to middle-class men. Many of these were dissenters.

The religious census of 1851

Up until the 1850s no one was really sure how many people belonged to each denomination. There had been some small, informal surveys in the eighteenth and early nineteenth centuries (Field, 2010), but the first major attempt to provide a comprehensive, statistical analysis of denominational affiliation was the religious census of England, Wales and Scotland in 1851. This was, in part, an extension of the state's drive to collect statistics about everyday life that you read about in Block 1. The 1851 census provided a snapshot of the number of churches in Britain, the number of people they could hold and how many actually did attend on Sunday 30 March. It was not a survey of personal belief, but an attempt to use a measurable indicator – attendance – as a way to gauge the religious health of the nation as a whole. It was very controversial at the time, and was never repeated. The Irish religious census, which ran from 1861 to 1921, asked respondents to state their own perceived religious affiliation: a very different approach.

The 1851 religious census was directed by the civil servant and statistician Horace Mann (1823–1917). It was the first government-sponsored census of religion and it attracted considerable attention, with the published report from the census selling over 21,000 copies. It produced two headline conclusions that shocked Victorian society. The first was the size of the dissenting community. Mann and others had not expected it to be so big and were startled at its collective size. It made the established church's claim to represent the religious beliefs of the nation a mockery. Dissenters used this finding to press their existing demands for equality of treatment still further. The second headline was that only 47 per cent of the population attended church. While this may seem like a large proportion to us, for Mann and his associates it was a worrying outcome. Church attendance was considered to be an important part of Britain's understanding of itself as a Christian (even Protestant) country. Anything less than full attendance suggested that a process of secularisation was occurring.

In his introductory report, Mann included a lengthy discussion about the factors affecting church attendance. He expressed grave concerns about the state of Victorian religion, the low attendance of working-class people and the high number of Nonconformist worshippers. His ideas were important in shaping wider attitudes and perceptions.

Mann was particularly worried about working-class non-attendance. He and many others felt that this rejection of what was meant to be a religious duty could have disastrous social and moral results. Going to church indicated that people knew about and accepted the existing social order. Low attendance could suggest an impending moral crisis or a breakdown in traditional social norms, particularly in the cities, where traditional authority was less secure. This pessimistic view of the religious state of society was widely shared and prompted many churches and their members to attempt to **evangelise** the working classes. Much of this attention was focused on the urban poor, because cities were believed to have a particularly negative impact on religious belief. While the new cities did undermine traditional habits of religious affiliation, they also presented opportunities for groups, such as the Methodists, to start new religious endeavours. Historians have generally seen these efforts as heroic but only partly successful (McLeod, 1997). While some members of the working classes found church affiliation to be meaningful, many others were happy to stay away and practise a more 'diffusive' Christianity of mutual help, fair dealing and love for one's fellow man (Cox, 1982).

Activity 11.1

Now go to the module website and complete Activity 11.1 'The religious census of 1851'. This should take around an hour.

11.2 Everyday religion

When the 1851 religious census was published, many people were
critical of the way it had been organised and how the data had been
collected. There was confusion over what constituted a 'place of
worship', accusations that attendance figures had been falsified and a
feeling that the decision to measure attendance, rather than profession
of faith, had been a grave error. Historians now agree that the data
collection process was fairly robust, but are critical of Mann's attempt
to use this data to measure the actual size of denominations (Snell and
Ell, 2000, pp. 35–46). Since the 1960s they have used more modern
methods to test census data in local areas, such as the East Midlands
(Thompson, 2014), Yorkshire (Wolffe, 2008) and Oxfordshire
(Tiller, 1987). They have discovered a much more complex picture of
mid-century religious practice, one that challenges ideas of
secularisation. In some places working-class attendance was very low.
But in other places there was a range of popular religious practices.
People might attend church, but only at certain times of the year.
People sometimes attended Anglican services, and at other times would
go to dissenter meetings. In some parts of Yorkshire, in the years
leading up to the census, John Wolffe has found that many new
churches had been built and church attendance had steadily increased
(Wolffe, 2008). Mann's negative perceptions of the census results has
probably masked a more vibrant, and diverse, reality.

For there is no getting away from the fact that, at mid-century, almost
half of the population of England and Wales still attended church on
Sundays. This was a substantial figure. It meant that many people knew
and understood basic religious ideas. They would have been familiar
with the rituals and customs surrounding church services, and religion
would have had a prominent position in everyday life. Some of the
most popular 'celebrities' of the mid-Victorian period were religious
figures. The Rev. Charles Spurgeon (1834–1892, depicted in
Figure 11.2), Rev. Newman Hall (1816–1902) and the American
revivalists Dwight L. Moody (1837–1899) and Ira D. Sankey (1840–
1908) each attracted tens of thousands of people to their religious
meetings. Religious personalities, themes and issues inevitably made
their way into popular print and visual culture. Books, pamphlets,
tracts, illustrations, pottery, art and sculpture all reflected a widespread
preoccupation with religious matters.

THE REV. MR. "SPURGEON PREACHING HIS "HUMILIATION DAY" SERMON IN THE CRYSTAL PALACE.

Figure 11.2 Unknown artist, 'The Rev. Charles Haddon Spurgeon Preaching His 'Humiliation Day' Sermon in the Crystal Palace', 1857, engraving from unknown publication. Photo: © Look and Learn / Peter Jackson Collection / Bridgeman Images. Spurgeon held religious services here while his permanent church, the Metropolitan Tabernacle, was being built and he routinely attracted crowds of between 4,000 and 5,000 people.

This religious culture, while sharing many common elements, was divided between 'church', a term used to denote the Church of England, and 'chapel', a collective word used to describe the Nonconformist groups. Each had their own particular rituals and practices and provided a range of distinct services for their respective communities.

Exercise 11.1

To get a sense of the division between church and chapel culture in mid nineteenth-century Britain, I would like you to examine Figure 11.3. This was originally a small, fold-up card illustrated by George Cruikshank (1797–1878). Cruikshank was a well-known cartoonist and illustrator and this piece likely dates from the mid-1870s. It depicts, in stereotypical form, 12 figures associated with different roles within church and chapel. Of these 12, nine represent Anglicans, two (the Wesleyan Minister and the Salvation Army officer) represent non-Conformists and one (the 'Lady Sunday School teacher') could be either.

Figure 11.3 George Cruikshank, *[C]hurch and Chapel*, c.1865–75, 6 x 32cm. John Johnson Collection, scraps II (60c), Bodleian Library, University of Oxford

The reproduction here is quite small, so for convenience I have reproduced below the text underneath each person. From left to right, the figures are labelled: 'Pet Parson. The Ladies Own Minister'; 'Vicar. Not of Bray'; 'Mrs Vicar. Charity and Clothing'; 'Chorister. Music Hath Charms etc'; 'Lady Sunday School Teacher. The Girls I Instruct/The Boys I Conduct'; 'Wesleyan Minister. Preacher and Teacher'; 'The Dean. A Very Prime Minister'; 'Salvation for All'; 'Mrs Pet Parson'; 'Churchwarden. Pork and Piety'; 'Verger. The Guardian of the Church'; 'Clerk. Amen'.

If you would like to take a closer look, a zoomable version of the image is available on the module website.

After studying the image, answer the following questions:

- How does Cruikshank depict the different individuals associated with the Church of England? In particular, what differences in appearance and characterisation can you discern between the different figures? (If you are not sure what the occupations mean, you can look them up in the *Oxford Dictionary of the Christian Church*, available through the OU Library.)

- How do the two Nonconformist characters differ from their Anglican counterparts?

This should take around 15 minutes.

Specimen answer

- The illustrations depict the clergymen (the Dean, the Vicar and the Parson) as affluent and respectable, with elaborate clerical dress. The characters of Churchwarden, Verger and Clerk are portrayed as slightly lower down the social scale. The women are shown as occupying supporting roles, such as charity work and Sunday school teaching. The younger figures, especially 'Pet Parson' and his wife and the 'Chorister', are highly romanticised, if not effeminate.

- The Wesleyan minister is portrayed in plain dress and in a way that suggests he lives an ascetic life. The Salvation Army officer is shown in his uniform, with his hand in the air, as if demonstrating enthusiasm in his preaching.

Discussion

This illustration is a satirical, or mocking, portrayal of the social and cultural divisions within the broad categories of 'church' and 'chapel'. Cruickshank has depicted what he thinks are widely held views about Anglican and Nonconformist characters and is exaggerating them for comic effect. That said, his depiction reflects a broadly accurate view of the two groups. The Church of England did tend to represent the more affluent section of society but its more secular positions, such as churchwarden, were often occupied by local working men. The portrayal of 'Pet Parson' reflects the widespread impression that Anglican clergy were becoming increasingly 'feminised'. Nonconformist clergymen did wear plainer dress, although it became more elaborate as the century progressed. The Salvation Army was founded in 1865 as a breakaway Methodist group and did represent a more enthusiastic brand of religious practice. The 'Lady Sunday school teacher', however, demonstrates an aspect of shared religious culture. Sunday schools, and the middle-class ladies who taught at them, were a common feature of religious life within all mid-century denominations.

The idea of a basic division in British society between church and chapel is a very important one, but it needs to be qualified in two respects. First, this division only really operated in England and Wales. In Scotland and Ireland, religion divided along very different lines. In Scotland the fracture points were between different types of Presbyterians, while in Ireland it was the Protestant–Catholic relationship that caused religious conflict. Although there were Irish 'dissenters' (Presbyterians mostly, but also Baptists and Congregationalists) who objected to the established Church of Ireland, as Unit 6 has shown, they increasingly united under a shared Protestant and anti-Catholic banner.

Second, the mid-nineteenth century witnessed the growing influence of three distinct theological ideas, or movements: Evangelicalism, Catholicism and liberal theology. Each cut across the church–chapel divide and blurred these traditional religious allegiances. Each was dynamic and expansionist and contributed to the religious conflicts that you will study later on in this unit.

Three religious ideas

Evangelicalism was a set of religious ideas that emerged in central Europe in the late seventeenth century and spread to Britain and Ireland in the 1740s, where it was most clearly seen in the emergence of Methodism. Evangelicals sought, through prayer, Bible reading and collective discussion, to live a committed life of faith. An essential part of this commitment was the experience of 'conversion', an emotional transformation when the individual, realising their sinfulness, accepted the power of Christ to enable them to live according to biblical principles. Evangelicals believed that this transformation could happen to anyone, if they would but accept it, and that no one was excluded from the peace and joy it could bring.

Those who adopted Evangelical principles, therefore, pursued a life of both personal and active piety. Reading the Bible and attending church were key priorities, as was prayer, performed both as an individual and with family members, and other supplementary religious meetings, such as Sunday school and mid-week Bible classes. Evangelicals were prompted by their interpretation of the Bible to seek the conversion of others and so they were keen supporters of outdoor preaching, 'revival' meetings, tract and Bible distribution and missionary activity (such as the exhibition shown in Figure 11.4). Evangelicals were also driven by their principles to care for the poor and to work for the wider reformation of society. William Wilberforce (1759–1833), a key figure in the campaign to abolish slavery, whom you encountered in Block 1, and Lord Shaftesbury, who spearheaded the factory reforms of the 1840s, were both committed Evangelicals. However, Evangelicals' emphasis on the Bible – that it was inspired by God, that it was 'inerrant' and that it should be read literally – made it difficult for them to accommodate alternative perspectives. Evangelicals were particularly hostile to Catholicism and to any challenge to orthodox Christian doctrines, such as the Trinity, the divinity of Christ and the existence and character of Satan and hell. While Evangelicals were synonymous with Methodism, they were also increasingly influential within the Church of England and in the older dissenting denominations. These changes did much to bring Methodism and old dissenters together; Evangelicalism was an important source of Nonconformist unity. Attracting as it did the emerging middle classes, it became the most influential of all of these new religious movements.

EXHIBITION AND SALE AT THE WESLEYAN CENTENARY HALL, BISHOPSGATE-STREET WITHIN; FOR THE WESLEYAN MISSIONARY SOCIETY,—(SEE NEXT PAGE.)

Figure 11.4 Unknown artist, 'Exhibition and Sale at the Wesleyan Centenary Hall, Bishopsgate-Street Within; for the Wesleyan Missionary Society', engraving. *The Illustrated London News*, 21 June 1851. Photo: © Look and Learn / Illustrated Papers Collection / Bridgeman Images

The second set of religious ideas to expand during this time was Catholicism. As you have already seen in Unit 6, many of the legal disabilities against Catholics had been removed in the eighteenth and early nineteenth centuries. Catholic emancipation, passed in 1829, enabled Catholics to sit as members of the Westminster Parliament. With these new rights, Catholics were able to adopt a greater public presence and, both in Ireland and in Britain, the Catholic community began to grow in confidence, size and status. The rapid influx of Irish migrants in the late 1840s put considerable pressure on what had been, up until then, a very small, elite English Catholic community. Grassroots Catholic clergymen worked heroically, especially in working-class urban areas, to resource and support these emergent Catholic communities (Parsons, 1988a).

Catholic beliefs and practices were given a significant boost by the emergence of the Oxford Movement within the Church of England. Led by the clergymen John Keble (1792–1866) and John Henry

Newman (1801–1890), it sought to return the Church of England to its pre-Reformation roots and to emphasise the Catholic origins of its doctrines and practices. In 1833, prompted by the Whig government's proposal to reform the Church of Ireland, they started to publish *Tracts for Our Times*, a series of books and pamphlets that articulated their reformist agenda. 'Tractarians', as they became known, were behind the widespread shift within Victorian religion towards more 'Catholic' styles of practice which were often termed 'High Church'. This was seen most clearly in the architectural shift towards the Gothic, which influenced the construction of almost all Anglican (and even Nonconformist) buildings in the nineteenth century (see Figure 11.5). The Oxford Movement initiated the widespread reconfiguration of Anglican church interiors, the adoption of more elaborate clerical vestments and the return to abandoned 'Catholic' rituals such as incense and plainchant.

The third movement of religious ideas was the growth of sceptical or critical attitudes towards religion. Inspired by the secularist ideas of Thomas Paine (1737–1809) and the French Revolution, and coming out of the radical politics of the early nineteenth century, new secular societies were formed. Their working-class members were atheists, arguing that there could be no god if there was poverty and hunger and that the churches were agents of hypocrisy and oppression. Instead, they advocated a new creed, with faith based on humanity in the here and now. Such ideas were deemed to be dangerous, and were illegal. In the 1840s, working-class secularists, such as Charles Southwell (1814–1860) and George Holyoake (1817–1906), were arrested and imprisoned for blasphemy.

Public expressions of disbelief became acceptable only in the late nineteenth century. This was because many middle-class people also started to have doubts about their religion. Starting in the 1830s, a number of intellectuals, such as George Eliot (1819–1880), Charles Darwin (1809–1882), Alfred Tennyson (1809–1892) and Harriet Martineau, began to articulate their objections to traditional Christianity. They were uncomfortable with the idea of hell and the doctrine of everlasting punishment. They struggled with the notion of 'substitutionary atonement', which holds that salvation comes only through the sacrificial death of an innocent Jesus. This so-called 'crisis of faith' was driven by moral objections. It was also driven by the emergence of biblical criticism, a new field of scholarly research that studied the Bible like any other text. New scientific ideas (such as the

Figure 11.5 All Saints Church, Margaret Street, London (1850–59), designed by William Butterfield, is one of the finest examples of an Anglican nineteenth-century Gothic church interior. Photo: Arcaid Images / Alamy

notion of 'natural selection', first published by Darwin in 1859) were of limited influence at this time. For the middle-class writers, lawyers, doctors, engineers and politicians, it was their high moral sensibilities that provoked these doubts and encouraged them to explore new thinking and adopt a 'liberal' theological position.

This middle-class 'honest doubt', as it is sometimes called, added to the pre-existing liberal trend within the Church of England known as the Broad Church movement, and found common cause with the long-standing Nonconformist tradition of Unitarianism, a theological position that rejects the divinity of Christ and, thereby, the doctrine of the Trinity. Unitarians, although always small in number, became a significant intellectual and social movement from the 1840s onwards. You will learn more about them at the end of the unit.

Starting in the mid-nineteenth century, then, growing numbers of middle-class liberals began to express their doubts about traditional points of Christian theology and the Bible. These were extremely controversial views at the time but they were the start of a growing acceptance on the part of the state, and the wider public, of religious diversity.

Shared aspects of everyday religion

Despite the very obvious divisions within the mid-Victorian religious landscape, there were many areas of everyday religious practice that were common to everyone. One was the Bible. According to Timothy Larsen, the Bible was 'the strongest and deepest cultural resource that people had in common across society' (Larsen, 2013, p. 153). It was a basic school text and used to teach reading and literacy in Sunday and other schools. New printing processes increased the range of bibles available to purchase, and reduced their cost. Cheap bibles, New Testaments and extracts were produced and freely distributed by the many Bible and tract societies as a work of evangelisation. The Bible was read aloud in church and it formed the central core of 'family worship', a devotional practice whereby the male head of the house would gather all members of the household together (including servants) to listen to the Bible and take part in collective prayer (as depicted in Figure 11.6). The Bible would also have been read alone, as part of personal religious study. This exposure to the Bible meant it came to provide an 'essential set of metaphors and symbols' that everyone recognised (Larsen, 2011, p. 4).

The translation of the Bible that everyone read was the King James Version, originally produced in 1611 and modified in the eighteenth century. Its age, along with its archaic yet poetic language, appealed to the romantic sensibility of the time, with poets, writers and intellectuals embedding biblical metaphors into their own creative outputs. By the end of the nineteenth century, this 'Authorised' version was venerated as a literary and cultural touchstone, cited and referenced by sceptics as much as by the devout (Bebbington, 2011).

Figure 11.6 An idealised portrayal of morning worship in a middle-class Victorian home. Note the women in the corner, who are probably servants. Photo: North Wind Picture Archives / Alamy

Another aspect of shared religious practice was the experience of Sunday. By the mid-nineteenth century, changes to legislation meant that most people had Sunday off and could stay away from church if they wanted to. At this time, though, Sunday leisure opportunities were limited. Non-churchgoers could relax at home, visit friends, or do limited shopping, although many of them continued to send their children to church, mainly to Sunday school. Sunday schools were started in the late eighteenth century in order to provide free education to poor children. Volunteer teachers taught reading and literacy alongside a limited range of 'secular' subjects. This model was widely adopted across all Victorian churches and by the mid-nineteenth century had become one of the most popular educational movements in the country. In 1851, there were over 300,000 volunteer teachers and over 2.6 million children attending Sunday schools. This represented three-quarters of all working-class children in England and Wales and, by extension, gave the majority of the population a rudimentary understanding of basic religious principles (Snell, 1999).

For those who were religious, Sunday was defined by going to church. As the 1851 census showed, religious services were held in the morning, afternoon or evening. While church and chapel services had their own distinctive features, the general contours of worship were very similar. In the early nineteenth century, church services were dominated by lengthy sermons and, apart from the singing of metrical psalms, there would have been little opportunity for congregational participation. As the century progressed, however, worship became more elaborate and participative. Church buildings and their interiors became more formal and elaborate. Services and sermons became shorter and service books and set prayers became common. As Charles Cashdollar points out in his study of nineteenth-century British and American Nonconformist congregations, worship became less focused on preaching and more focused on providing a colourful experience for those in the pews (Cashdollar, 2000).

Exercise 11.2

Turn to Reading 11.1, 'William Hale White, "A Nonconformist Sunday"
(1881)', located at the end of the unit. This is an extract from *The
Autobiography of Mark Rutherford*. Rutherford was the pseudonym of the
Congregationalist minister William Hale White (1831–1918) who, in the
1880s, wrote a number of books that were broadly critical of the
Nonconformist tradition. Here, White describes his memory of a typical
Nonconformist Sunday, probably dating from the 1830s.

What did White find so unpleasant about the Sundays of his childhood?

This should take around 20 minutes.

Specimen answer

White seems to have disliked how rigid and austere the day was. The
food was always cold, the reading material was restricted and even
letters were not to be opened. He resented how much time was spent in
church and how boring the services were. He points out that the Bible
was always read, but never explained, and that the prayers were 'a
horrible hypocrisy'. He was also critical of the sermons, saying they all
followed the same format and harped on the same gloomy themes.

Discussion

White's comments touch on the frequent characterisation of the Victorian
Sunday as restricted and dull. It is true that there were significant
constraints on leisure opportunities and that religious families, such as
White's, did restrict reading and leisure options for their children. This
private trend was mirrored in the public sphere when, starting in the
1830s, influential campaigns to restrict Sunday trading and the sale and

consumption of alcohol achieved some measure of legislative success. There was, however, always public resistance to this. In 1855 working people in London rioted against trading restrictions and the more extreme temperance legislation proposed in Parliament was never successful.

White's criticisms can, however, be read in a different way. His hostility to the way the Sunday service was conducted suggests that he felt worship could have been done better, with more care and attention to the needs of the congregation. This objection reflects the attitude of many 'honest doubters' who, as we saw earlier and as we shall see later, were repelled by conventional faith because of their moral objections to Victorian religion and the hypocritical way it was often practised.

Another aspect of religious practice that was widely shared across class and denomination was the experience of hymn singing. Since the eighteenth century, Nonconformists had started to experiment with new types of religious singing. The custom of singing the psalms to very basic tunes gave way to the adoption of hymns with original lyrics and tunes that reflected greater musical complexity. The publication in 1861 of the Anglican hymn book *Hymns Ancient and Modern* provided a whole new canon of songs for Victorian congregations to learn. While each denomination had its own favourites, some hymns became popular with everyone. They became, in the words of John Wolffe, 'an almost universal expression of Christian worship' (Wolffe, 1997, p. 65).

One final shared aspect of religious life was the experience of being part of a local congregation. For those who attended their local church regularly, the relationships they forged and the activities they took part in could be an important source of identity, community and belonging. Congregational membership, then, was not only a way to demonstrate religious commitment. It was also an opportunity for leadership, education and sociability. Congregational affiliations could shape an individual's choice of friendships, marriage partners and job opportunities.

Nonconformists, who did not receive any financial support from the state, relied on the voluntary contributions of their members to build a church and pay their minister's salary. Unlike Anglican churches, where local rates went to pay churchwardens and clerks, Nonconformist congregations relied on volunteers fulfilling many different roles. This gave them a particular investment in their congregation and a significant say in the way it was run. For men, chapel leadership positions, such as treasurer, elder, deacon or local preacher, could often prove a stepping stone to political office or trade union activism. For women, charitable work, Sunday school teaching and, in some denominations, **revival preaching** provided opportunities for the exercise of limited leadership roles.

It can be hard to find first-hand descriptions of congregational life. Fictional accounts can fill this gap, if they are used carefully. As many novelists and writers noted, congregational life set the scene for many local dramas and, in the nineteenth century, many novels and short stories used congregations as their setting.

Exercise 11.3

Turn to Readings 11.2, 'George Eliot, "Janet's Repentance" (1858)' and 11.3, 'Margaret Oliphant, "Salem Chapel" (1863)', located at the end of the unit. These are short extracts from works by George Eliot and Margaret Oliphant (1828–1897), respectively. In Reading 11.2, Eliot is describing the fictional Anglican parish of Milby and the changes being implemented as a result of the appointment in the 1830s of its first Evangelical clergyman, Edward Tryan, to the **chapel of ease** located near the working-class neighbourhood of Paddiford Common. In Reading 11.3, Oliphant is describing a dissenting congregation in the 1860s in the fictional town of Carlingford, which is about to receive a new minister, Mr Vincent.

How does the religious activity taking place in 'Milby parish' differ from that associated with 'Salem Chapel'? Are there any similarities between them?

This should take around 20 minutes.

Specimen answer

In 'Milby', the middle-class, mostly single, women of the parish are covering books for the newly established lending library. Eliot's description highlights the prominent role that women played in congregational life. In 'Salem Chapel', a much wider range of activity is described – tea meetings, singing groups, charitable and missionary societies are all mentioned. Both passages suggest that religious activity was closely caught up with sociability and, in some cases, with opportunities to meet the opposite sex.

Discussion

Eliot's description of religious life in 'Milby' in the rest of 'Janet's Repentance' reflects the more limited range of activities that were on offer in the churches of the 1830s. Charitable work is undertaken by Mr Tryan and other pious individuals, not by organised societies, and the introduction of a lending library is an exciting innovation. As Oliphant's description of 'Salem Chapel' makes clear, by the 1860s churches had diversified and expanded their offerings considerably. In particular, churches had introduced a much wider range of 'fellowship' activities, such as soirées, tea meetings and bazaars. Youth groups and sporting clubs were still in the future, but there were signs of a growing awareness of the need to compete with emerging leisure opportunities.

The descriptions of congregational life presented by Eliot and Oliphant in Readings 11.2 and 11.3 might give you the (mistaken) impression that congregational life was always peaceful and agreeable – mistaken because, as with any family, congregations experienced differences of opinion. Local disagreements, conflicts with denominational leadership, or the emergence of theological differences could all be motives behind schism and separation. Methodists were particularly prone to internal division, producing no fewer than five significant breakaway groups by the 1850s. But, as Cashdollar points out, most congregations spent very little time arguing over points of principle. For the most part they focused on the practical issues of fabric and finance, and sought, where possible, to avoid conflict and encourage fellowship (Cashdollar, 2000).

So far, this study of religious ideas and practices has shown the 'equipoise' of mid-nineteenth-century British society. Although the Church of England was the established church, there were many people who practised their religious beliefs in other ways. While many people did not go to church at all, for others it was a significant part of their spiritual lives. Denominational differences could be very deep, but Bible reading and hymn singing were practices that everyone shared. Religious life had a basic coherence and promoted a shared Christian ethos. However, the new theological movements you have just considered, combined with a changing attitude towards the role of religion in public life, could also provoke challenges to this mid-century consensus. The result was a series of intense, short-term conflicts that exposed deep-seated tensions that ultimately took British society in a more modern, tolerant and pluralist direction.

Activity 11.2

Now go to the module website and complete Activity 11.2 'Community and congregational life: the Victorian hymn'. This should take around an hour.

11.3 Revival, reform and conflict

As the previous section showed, the practice of religion was a visible and widely accepted part of everyday life and many features of this religious culture were shared across theological and denominational boundaries. But the mid-nineteenth century was also a time when religious conflicts came to the fore, when emerging attitudes and practices clashed with older, 'traditional' structures and beliefs. In this section I would like to examine three religious controversies and use them to illustrate wider changes taking place during this period. The Papal Aggression of 1850 was the last sustained public manifestation of popular anti-Catholicism in Britain. The Ulster Revival of 1859 was an outburst of unconventional religious enthusiasm in the north of Ireland. *Essays and Reviews* was a controversial collection of liberal theological essays published in 1860. The outcomes of each conflict, although highly contested, reflect the growing influence of religious toleration and a more 'modern' understanding of 'appropriate' religious behaviour.

The Papal Aggression of 1850

You learned in Block 1 that British and Irish Protestants have had a long association with anti-Catholicism. As Linda Colley has demonstrated, Catholicism was believed to be incompatible with the liberties and freedoms of the British state (Colley, 2003). In the years after Catholic emancipation, a number of events contributed to popular anti-Catholic attitudes: the Oxford Movement, the government's decision to fund a Catholic seminary in Ireland, the growing confidence of the Irish Catholic hierarchy, the influx of poor Irish Catholics into British cities and the political activity of Pope Pius IX (1792–1878, pope 1846–78). As a result, starting in the 1830s, anti-Catholic organisations such as the Evangelical Alliance and the Reformation Society were formed in an attempt to promote Protestant unity and 'defence'.

It was against this historical backdrop that the Papal Aggression took place. Since the seventeenth century, the Catholic Church in England had been administered not by a local hierarchy of bishops, as was the case with the Church of England, but by a group of four, later eight, 'Vicars Apostolic' managed from Rome. Throughout the 1830s and 1840s the Vicars called for a local hierarchy to be put in place. In 1847

Pius IX agreed and in October 1850 the **papal rescript** *Universalia Ecclesia* was issued. One archbishopric, titled 'Westminster', and 12 dioceses were re-established. Although 'Westminster' and other titles were deliberately chosen so they did not replicate any Anglican titles, the choice of terminology, and the whole restoration process itself, prompted a widespread public controversy.

The controversy began when, on 14 October 1850, the leading newspaper of the British establishment, *The Times*, published an editorial that was scathing in its denunciation of a restored Catholic hierarchy. It then published an open letter that Cardinal Nicholas Wiseman (1802–1865), an Anglican convert and the newly appointed archbishop of Westminster, had written to all of the Catholics in England. Wiseman had been out of the country and was unaware of the mounting controversy when he directed his personal secretary to agree to its publication. Several days later, with the public debate reaching crisis point, the Whig prime minister, Lord John Russell, a well-known advocate of religious toleration, was obliged to publish his own response in the form of a letter to his friend, the bishop of Durham. It too appeared in *The Times*, although it and the other sources were widely reprinted in newspapers across the country.

Exercise 11.4

Turn to Reading 11.4, 'Excerpts from *The Times* relating to the Papal Aggression (1850)', located at the end of the unit, which comprises three extracts from *The Times* newspaper. The first is from the editorial of 14 October 1850. The second, dated 29 October 1850, quotes from Wiseman's letter. The third comes from Russell's letter to the bishop of Durham and is dated 4 November 1850.

As you read, jot down your responses to the following questions:

- What are the objections in *The Times* editorial to a restored Catholic hierarchy?

- How does Wiseman unintentionally exacerbate these concerns?

- How does Russell seek to calm things down?

- Describe the tone and language that these writers are using. Can you see why they have chosen such words and expressions?

This should take around 30 minutes.

Specimen answer

- *The Times* editorial objects to the fact that the restored hierarchy is using the name 'Westminster' to describe its archbishopric. The newspaper sees this as an 'impertinence' and an unwarranted assumption of a national title.

- Wiseman doesn't mention Rome by name but, as his audience would have understood, his address assumes there will be a strengthened connection to Rome after the 'restoration'. He describes Rome as 'the centre of unity' and 'the source of jurisdiction'. This must have sounded very worrying to Protestants and the British state.

- Russell restates his support for the civil rights of Catholics and he argues that the Catholic Church has an important role to play in guiding Irish immigrants. He also expresses concern at Catholic impertinence, but he thinks the Protestant nation is too well established to fall victim to 'foreign' forces.

All of the writers are using highly emotional and inflammatory language. They employ familiar metaphors and insider language to evoke a sympathetic reaction from their readers. The issue at stake seems a relatively minor one, but the rhetoric of these writers seems to reflect deep anxieties (or triumphalist gloating) about the proposed restoration and fundamentally different views about the relationship between religion, identity and the British state.

What was the public reaction to this religious wrangling? Letters of protest were sent to Queen Victoria. Public meetings were organised, like the one at the Guildhall in London on 25 November (see Figure 11.7). The unfortunate timing of Guy Fawkes night (5 November) only exacerbated the situation, prompting anti-Catholic graffiti, mock processions and the burning of Wiseman in effigy in London and elsewhere. More substantial riots broke out in Cheltenham, Liverpool, London and Birkenhead where people were killed and Catholic property damaged (Paz, 1969, pp. 35–48). Wiseman's efforts to calm the situation came too late. In order to address the outcry, the government introduced, and subsequently passed, the Ecclesiastical Titles Act, forbidding Catholic bishops from using geographical place names in their titles.

Figure 11.7 A public meeting, held at the Guildhall, London, to protest against the Papal Aggression. Page from *The Illustrated London News*, 30 November 1850. Photo: © Look and Learn / Illustrated Papers Collection / Bridgeman Images

What is interesting about this controversy is that the forces of Protestant conservatism did not win. Yes, the government was obliged to pass some restrictive legislation, but the Papal Aggression did not lead to a systematic attempt to control the Catholic population or to implement sustained anti-Catholic legislation. Such a response, often described as a **Kulturkampf**, was adopted in several European countries at this time, especially Germany. In Britain, however, there was no Kulturkampf (Barr, 2005). Instead, the Ecclesiastical Titles Act quickly became an aberration. Its terms were never implemented and it was repealed within 20 years. Within Britain and Ireland as a whole, anti-Catholicism was on the decline, although it remained a potent force for conflict in areas such as Ulster and in cities such as Belfast, Glasgow and Liverpool. For the most part, the Papal Aggression became a 'stark and incongruous contrast to the steady constitutional trend towards a tolerant religious pluralism' that had been set in motion since the eighteenth century. 'The clear trend was towards the acceptance of Catholicism and Catholics as firmly within the fabric of national life' (Parsons, 1988a, p. 176).

The Ulster Revival of 1859

A revival is a short-lived burst of religious enthusiasm, frequently associated with the Evangelical movement, that is characterised by crowded meetings, numerous conversions and, sometimes, physical manifestations of intense religious feeling. Participants can tremble, jerk or convulse; they can shout out loud, or even collapse into a trance. This is what sociologists and historians call 'charismatic' behaviour and individuals throughout the history of Christianity have experienced it. Charismatic manifestations have always been controversial. When they appeared in a revival that had started in Ulster in March 1859, they provoked considerable debate. Professional opinion was divided between newspapers, clergymen and doctors who supported the revival and those who felt it was not an acceptable or respectable display of faith.

Most accounts of the revival agree that it began in the rural settlements around the mid-Antrim town of Ballymena in 1858. Here a group of young working men, mostly weavers by trade, had started a Sunday school and weekly prayer meeting. Several local people were converted and in early 1859 meetings were organised to hear their experiences. At some of these meetings, participants displayed charismatic forms of religious behaviour.

A number of people experienced sudden conversions: their bodies started to shake and they began to pray obsessively. Throughout the summer of 1859, revival meetings spread across the north of Ireland. Converts from Ballymena began to travel to other towns and tell of their experiences. By the beginning of September, the revival had spread throughout much of Ulster, including the city of Belfast. News had spread to Scotland, England and Wales, where there was considerable interest expressed in many quarters but not the same manifestation of religious enthusiasm.

As the revival spread, the physical manifestations of conversion continued to occur and, if anything, grew more extreme. People were reported as falling into trances, experiencing visions, or having marks placed on their bodies by the Holy Spirit. Many educated people were convinced this was a genuine work of God and that this enthusiasm would be channelled into the existing churches. Newspapers, such as the influential *Belfast News-Letter*, published glowing accounts of revival meetings and accepted the charismatic displays uncritically. Many Presbyterian clergy did likewise. In his positive account of the revival, titled *The Year of Grace* and published in 1860, the Presbyterian minister William Gibson (1808–1867) concluded: '[i]ts origin and progress unequivocally attest it as divine … *Within* the Church, a cold formality, an apathetic and unimpressible decorum were exchanged for a living and vigorous piety; *without*, the ignorant and unreclaimed were seized as by a resistless power' (Gibson, 1859, p. 370). His colleague, the Rev. William Magill (1816–1886), likened events in Ulster to the miraculous display of God's power witnessed after Jesus had ascended into heaven that gave authority to the early Christian Church. 'No event since **Pentecost**', enthused Magill, 'has so signally displayed the Divine sovereignty, and so illustrated and established the doctrine of the free grace of God' as the present revival (quoted in Gibson, 1859, p. 141; bold added). Even some medical doctors were convinced. According to Dr J. C. L. Carson (d.*c.*1880) of Coleraine, the revival could not be explained using scientific measures. The physical manifestations looked like hysteria, a common diagnosis at the time for excessive or uncontrollable emotionalism that was believed to affect women; but because they affected men, Carson argued, they had to be a work of God.

Much other educated opinion was not so sure. Some newspapers were openly sceptical about the revival and gleefully reported cases of fraudulent manifestations. Many clergymen were distressed by the physical manifestations and disliked the way the revival seemed to subvert what they felt were divinely ordained church structures. London-based medical opinion was especially critical, arguing that the physical manifestations were a disease (hysteria) and that they could lead to permanent insanity. Indeed, many members of the medical and religious professions thought the revival was a dangerous delusion and worried about the impact it would have on the religious and social order.

Activity 11.3

Now go to the module website and complete Activity 11.3 'The Ulster Revival of 1859 and its critics'. This should take around an hour.

While it is not up to historians to decide which interpretation of the revival is right, it is important to remember that for many people in mid-nineteenth-century Ulster the revival and its physical features were a popular, if temporary, way for them to express their religious feelings. As the late Victorian obsession with seances and spiritualism showed, and as the early twentieth-century explosion in Pentecostal Christianity demonstrated, people in so-called 'modern' and 'rational' societies still seek genuine spiritual experiences.

The problem in the mid-nineteenth century was how this new religious enthusiasm could be accommodated within existing denominational structures. Converts were keen to prioritise the growth aspects of congregational membership, such as evangelism, Sunday schools and philanthropy. But there were others who, in the spirit of Isaac Nelson (1809–1888), a Belfast-based Presbyterian minister who was publicly critical of the revival, felt that their faith was best demonstrated by a quiet commitment to the traditions of their church. At times, schism was the result. Two groups seeking a deeper spiritual life splintered off from the Church of England, and Methodism fractured more than seven times, unable to manage the tension between religious vitality and denominational control. By the end of the century, however, Victorian religious life had become increasingly formal. With church attendance on the decline and secularisation blunting the hard edges of theological differences, the new watchwords for British denominations became reunion and reunification.

The publication of *Essays and Reviews* in 1860

If we consider the Papal Aggression to be an example of sectarian controversy, and the Ulster Revival to be a controversy over method and style, then the debate that arose over the publication of *Essays and Reviews* in 1860 should be considered a controversy over theology. In particular, it should be seen as a controversy over theology in the Church of England. *Essays and Reviews* provoked an extensive public discussion about the Bible and how it could be studied and understood. It also reflected changing ideas about the role of the state church and the beliefs it should, or should not, represent.

Essays and Reviews was a work of seven authors: six clergymen, one layman and all Anglicans. They were all Broad Church intellectuals and scholars who had been influenced by German biblical scholarship and by liberal theological ideas and wanted to bring these new interpretations to a wider audience. It is hard to see, from an examination of the book's table of contents, just what all the fuss was about (see Figure 11.8). But the articles were deeply controversial. Rowland Williams (1817–1870) critiqued the prophecies in the Old Testament. Baden Powell (1796–1860) denied the possibility of miracles. Henry Wilson (1803–1888) questioned the doctrine of eternal punishment. Benjamin Jowett (1817–1893) argued that the Bible should be subject to literary and critical analysis and should be read 'like any other book'.

These ideas, although arguably not new, caused an enormous furore. Coming off the back of the controversial publication of Darwin's *On the Origin of Species* (1859), the collection went through 13 editions in under five years and provoked at least 400 published responses, most of them negative (Parsons, 1988b, p. 41). The book was condemned by the Anglican Church hierarchy and two of the authors, Williams and Wilson, were charged with heresy because of their views. In 1862 the highest 'court' in the Anglican Church found them guilty, but in 1864 they appealed for their case to be heard by the Privy Council, a secular court that had the authority to rule on religious cases. The Privy Council interpreted its role as not to decide which position was 'right' but to decide whether or not the views of the essayists had stepped beyond a reasonable interpretation of the Anglican Church's doctrinal statement, the Thirty-Nine Articles. After some consideration, it agreed that they had not, and overturned Williams' and Wilson's convictions.

CONTENTS.

———

<table>
<tr><td></td><td>PAGE</td></tr>
<tr><td>The Education of the World. By FREDERICK TEMPLE, D.D., Chaplain in Ordinary to the Queen ; Head Master of Rugby School ; Chaplain to the Earl of Denbigh . .</td><td>I</td></tr>
<tr><td>Bunsen's Biblical Researches. By ROWLAND WILLIAMS, D.D., Vice-Principal and Professor of Hebrew, St. David's College, Lampeter ; Vicar of Broad Chalke, Wilts . .</td><td>50</td></tr>
<tr><td>On the Study of the Evidences of Christianity. By BADEN POWELL, M.A., F.R.S., &c. &c., Savilian Professor of Geometry in the University of Oxford . . . . .</td><td>94</td></tr>
<tr><td>Séances Historiques de Genève. The National Church. By HENRY BRISTOW WILSON, B.D., Vicar of Great Staughton, Hunts . . . .</td><td>145</td></tr>
<tr><td>On the Mosaic Cosmogony. By C. W. GOODWIN, M.A. . .</td><td>207</td></tr>
<tr><td>Tendencies of Religious Thought in England, 1688—1750. By MARK PATTISON, B.D. . . . .</td><td>254</td></tr>
<tr><td>On the Interpretation of Scripture. By BENJAMIN JOWETT M.A., Regius Professor of Greek in the University o Oxford . . . .</td><td>330</td></tr>
<tr><td>Note on Bunsen's Biblical Researches . . . . . .</td><td>434</td></tr>
</table>

Figure 11.8 The table of contents from the controversial publication *Essays and Reviews*, 1860. British Library, London, General Reference Collection 4373.cc.14. Photo: © British Library Board / Bridgeman Images

Exercise 11.5

Turn to Readings 11.5, 'Benjamin Jowett, "On the interpretation of Scripture" (1860)' and 11.6, 'Frederic Harrison, "Neo-Christianity" (1860)', located at the end of the unit. Reading 11.5 is an extract from the cleric and academic Jowett's contribution to *Essays and Reviews*. Reading 11.6 is a critical response by the writer and philosopher Frederic Harrison (1831–1923), first published in the *Westminster Review*.

Complex theological issues are discussed in these extracts, so just try to get a general impression of the arguments and then try to answer the following two questions:

- What is Jowett suggesting is wrong with the way the Bible is currently interpreted?

- What does Harrison find so objectionable about *Essays and Reviews*?

This should take around 30 minutes.

Specimen answer

- He does not say it very clearly, but Jowett suggests that bad arguments, failed prophecies and other inconsistencies in names and dates are simply ignored by contemporary biblical scholars. He suggests that this is because it is seen to be a 'holy' book and it is not treated as rigorously as other academic texts or subjects, such as mathematics.

- Harrison argues that the essayists are trying to graft a new 'reasoning' (a philosophy of rationalism) on to the foundations of popular Christianity, and that this is not workable. If the public accept that the Bible is full of errors, they will never continue to venerate it as 'the Book of Life'.

Discussion

Harrison feared that any critique of the Bible would stop people reading it altogether, thus bringing Christianity into disrepute. The essayists, however, claimed that a more critical approach to the Bible would make it more credible and authoritative. Jowett argued that the failure to discuss contradictions and fallacies in the Bible meant ordinary people no longer saw it as a credible text. This controversy reveals the challenge that liberal theology was starting to present to traditional orthodoxy. Opponents objected not only to the collection's liberal theology; they also disliked its tone, which they found unnecessarily negative, and the fact that it seemed to be directed towards the general public, with a view to publicising these ideas more widely. Nevertheless, by the 1880s and 1890s the biblical-critical methods that the essayists endorsed had been, in a more moderate form, quietly integrated into the orthodox position.

The *Essays and Reviews* controversy also revealed the changing attitudes of the secular state to the Church of England. The Privy Council decision made clear that the state was not willing to endorse one theological party within the church at the expense of another. As Anthony Lentin points out, it was 'reluctant to penalize intellectual integrity and honest difference of opinion' (Lentin, 1988, p. 100). Instead, by its rulings over *Essays and Reviews* and other disputes, it forced the church to tolerate the existence of different theological opinions within its ranks. For Gerald Parsons, the church's position at this stage was 'at best ambiguous, at worst, a downright muddle' (Parsons, 1988b, p. 47).

That religious issues should have provoked such intense public debate is a sign that religion was important and how it was practised really mattered. It is also a sign that, despite a shared Christian heritage, there were strong, and growing, differences between denominations and theological world-views. The Papal Aggression and the *Essays and Reviews* controversies are fairly clear-cut cases where the forces of tradition and orthodoxy (although partly successful) were obliged to give way to new ideas of toleration and inclusivity. The Ulster Revival is a more complicated case, but it too can be interpreted as a clash between old and new world-views, and between authoritarian and more democratic visions of religion. Opponents of the revival, including representatives of the new science, articulated what we might call a more 'modern' antipathy towards emotional excess and the growing Victorian fashion for more formal, liturgical and restrained forms of religious expression.

11.4 Toleration, pluralism and the state

As you have seen in Unit 6, in the early nineteenth century the British government had already begun to adjust its relationship to the Church of England and started to extend a measure of toleration towards its religious minorities. In Scotland, where over 90 per cent of the population was Presbyterian, toleration was not really an issue. In Ireland, toleration for Presbyterian and Catholic communities had long been a source of contention. Starting in the eighteenth century, a series of Catholic Relief Acts were passed and Catholic emancipation was granted in 1829. Catholic demands for reform in the years thereafter, and as a result of a popular 'tithe war', when Irish Catholics refused to pay their church rates, meant that the government was obliged to substantially reduce the size and scale of the Church of Ireland and eventually to abolish tithe payments. In 1869, further pressure from Irish nationalists forced the government to disestablish the Church of Ireland, passing laws which removed its privileged status and placed it on the same footing as all other Irish denominations.

In England and Wales, Nonconformists were also making demands for the reform of their grievances. Since the 1660s they too had been subject to a range of discriminatory legislation, in particular the Test and Corporation Acts, which restricted civil and government jobs to members of the Anglican Church. Starting in the early nineteenth century, the government also began to grant them a measure of toleration. In 1812 a new Toleration Act was passed that confirmed Nonconformists' freedom of worship and laid out new rules for the regulation of their ministers and meeting houses; in 1828 the Test and Corporation Acts were repealed. Historians agree that these legislative decisions were highly significant. They showed that the government was willing to adjust its relationship to the Church of England in order to accommodate new ideas and circumstances. For David Thompson, this represented 'a vital breach in the principle of the "Anglican constitution"' (Thompson, 1972, p. 22). For Gerald Parsons, it was 'a constitutional recognition of religious pluralism' (Parsons, 1988b, p. 57). Now, Catholics and Nonconformists, as well as Anglicans, could participate fully in the life of the British state. I would like to spend the rest of this unit looking at how, in the mid-nineteenth century, it was Nonconformists who made the strongest case for further reform.

Nonconformists believed that the state should not interfere with religion and there should be no state church. Religious practice should be 'voluntary'. Everyone was agreed that the established churches no longer represented the entire population, and accepted that they never would do so. How, therefore, could the reality of religious diversity be accommodated? This was a question that was much debated in the middle years of the nineteenth century. Nonconformists were some of the leading voices raised in opposition to the current system. While they were obviously motivated by their own interests, they based their arguments on wider notions of what they called 'religious equality'. This meant 'the equal treatment by the state of all citizens irrespective of their religious convictions' (Larsen, 1999, p. 110). Their actions brought about significant changes to the constitutional basis of British society and contributed to its emergence as a modern, pluralist state.

The Whig reforms of the 1830s – the Reform Act of 1832 and the Municipal Corporations Act of 1835, which enabled Nonconformists to take up positions in local government – gave Nonconformists a new degree of political power, especially in new urban centres such as Birmingham, Manchester and Sheffield. They used this influence to address what they called 'practical grievances': the many small laws that were still in force and that discriminated against those outside the Anglican Church.

Exercise 11.6

Read the six 'practical grievances' of the Protestant Dissenting Deputies, drafted in 1833 and set out below. The Deputies were a group of leading Nonconformists set up in 1732 to protect Nonconformist religious rights in and around London. They were highly respectable and had done much to protect Nonconformists from unwarranted infringements on their religious freedom.

The 'practical grievances' of the Protestant Dissenting Deputies, 15 March 1833

1 compulsory conformity to the Prayer Book in Marriage
2 the want of a legal registration of Dissenters' births and deaths
3 liability to Church Rates and other ecclesiastical demands
4 alleged liability of places of worship to poor rates

5   denial of the right of burial by their own ministers in parochial churchyards

6   virtual exclusion from the benefits of Oxford and Cambridge

(Source: Manning, 1952, p. 274)

Now consider the following questions:

• What do these grievances tell us about the Church of England and its existing relationship with the state?

• Why do you think these practices were seen as 'grievances' by Nonconformists?

(Note that in point 6, 'the benefits of Oxford and Cambridge' refers to being eligible to attend those universities.)

This should take around 15 minutes.

Specimen answer

• The Church of England was closely caught up in the workings of the state at a local and personal level. All life events, such as births and marriages, were regulated by them. The church was financially privileged. Everyone had to pay for its upkeep. Membership of the church conveyed special privileges, such as being able to attend university.

• I think Nonconformists must have felt very frustrated by these requirements to use the Anglican Church or support it financially. They must have felt excluded from activities that were reserved only for Anglicans. They may have felt angry at being forced to conduct important life events, such as burials, using a form of religion that they did not accept.

Even though many of these grievances were quite small and had only a minimal impact on Nonconformists' everyday lives, Larsen has shown it was the social stigma attached to them that really rankled. They obliged Nonconformists to subject themselves to rituals and forms of words to which they did not subscribe. And they had to do this at sensitive, and significant, points in their lives, such as when they were getting married, or on the death of a loved one. Over the course of the 1830s and 1840s these grievances became a focal point for Nonconformist political agitation. Nonconformists argued that these laws were unfair and that they obliged people to act against their consciences. Some of these grievances were quickly addressed. Most political opinion was agreed that there ought to be a civil registration process for births and marriages, and this was introduced by Parliament in 1836 in England and Wales (1845 in Ireland and 1853 in Scotland). The religious tests that had prevented non-Anglicans from attending Oxford and Cambridge universities were repealed in 1854 and 1856, respectively. Other grievances struck closer at the heart of the church–state relationship and were fiercely contested for many decades. Church rates, for example, were abolished only in 1868, after almost a decade of intense political action.

The most contentious of all of these grievances was the issue of burial. According to the common law of England, everyone had a right to be buried in their local parish churchyard, the burial ground attached to the parish church. The only exceptions to this were those who had died unbaptised, who had committed suicide or who had been excommunicated from the church. Ecclesiastical law stated that this ground was **consecrated** and that only an Anglican clergyman using the Anglican burial service could perform the funeral. In the eighteenth century there had been cases of Anglican clergy refusing to bury Nonconformists, claiming that their baptisms were not valid. But the courts in the early nineteenth century had confirmed that Nonconformist baptisms were indeed 'Christian' and were therefore valid. Anglican clergy who refused to bury properly baptised Nonconformists in the early nineteenth century were routinely reprimanded by their bishops.

Part of the reason for this debate was the general lack of suitable burying grounds. By the 1850s, this situation had reached crisis point and new legislation was passed that forced old churchyards to close and enabled new public and private cemeteries to be opened. These were obliged to contain consecrated ground for Anglicans and unconsecrated ground for everyone else. These new burial grounds made it possible for Nonconformists to be buried there. And in the cities, where these cemeteries were located, church–chapel conflict over burial largely ceased. But in rural areas, where the only legal place of burial was the churchyard, conflicts between Anglicans and Nonconformists continued.

Exercise 11.7

Turn to Reading 11.7, 'The Colyton burial case (1864)', located at the end of the unit. This is an account of the burial of John Pavey, a Unitarian living in the parish of Colyton, Devon, published in a national newspaper, the *Daily News*, on 3 November 1864. (Note that this article is reproduced from another newspaper, *The Nonconformist*, the leading voice for political Nonconformity.)

As you read, consider the following questions:

- How does this burial demonstrate the grievances that Nonconformists were complaining about?

- What does the Anglican clergyman, the Rev. Gueritz, say in his defence?

This should take around 20 minutes.

Specimen answer

- John Pavey is described as a respectable, godly man, yet the Rev. Gueritz's actions seem offensive and disrespectful. He makes the family provide him with documentary evidence of Pavey's baptism. Gueritz's refusal to conduct the burial meant the Rev. McCombe had to do it, but standing in the lane outside the churchyard itself. This must have been hurtful and distressing to the family, their friends and the wider Nonconformist community.

- Gueritz acknowledges that the Pavey family had the right to bury their relative in the Colyton churchyard. However, because of Pavey's Unitarian beliefs Gueritz says he could not 'conscientiously' read the burial service over him.

The Colyton burial case illustrates quite neatly the rival issues at stake. Reading 11.7 makes it clear that Nonconformists expected Anglican clergy to fulfil their legal duty and bury a person as long as they had been legitimately baptised. Gueritz's actions, which were probably motivated by his High Church views, demonstrate the difficulties clergymen with sensitive consciences could have in effecting their duty as, in essence, officers of the state. No one was really happy with the way this aspect of the church–state relationship was working. Starting in 1861, Nonconformists began to mount a sustained campaign for the reform of the burial laws. Although they had considerable support from a wide range of political opinion, their proposals were regularly defeated in Parliament by a vociferous group of conservatives, who felt that any changes would be a terrible assault on the church's position. It was only in 1880 that a Burial Act was passed that allowed clergymen of any Christian faith to conduct a burial using their own services in Anglican churchyards.

The campaign to redress practical grievances was coordinated by a group called the Liberation Society. It had been formed in 1844 as the Anti-State Church Society, which reflected Nonconformist commitment to another aspect of religious equality: the complete separation of church and state, or complete disestablishment of the Church of England. Nonconformists were religious 'voluntaryists'. They believed that churches should not be supported by the state, but by voluntary, or private, effort. They admired the example of the USA, where each denomination had to support itself. Their campaign for 'liberation' was led by Edward Miall (1809–1881), a former Congregationalist minister turned journalist and politician. While a consistently militant voice, Miall highlighted the injustice of a 'national' church, with its wealth and resources benefiting only a proportion of the population, and how this relationship prevented the church itself from exercising its theological freedom. However, public support for disestablishment fluctuated. It was strong in the 1830s and rose again in the late 1860s when the Liberals disestablished the Church of Ireland. While Nonconformist grievances led to the eventual disestablishment of the Church of Wales in 1914, the status of the Church of England was never under serious threat. As Deborah Wiggins points out in her study of the Burial Act of 1880, by giving way on practical grievances, 'the Anglican Church may well have saved itself. It certainly silenced its most powerful and vociferous enemies' (Wiggins, 1996, p. 188). In this way, a delicate 'equipoise' was just about maintained.

Conclusion

I hope you can see now how important religion was in mid-nineteenth-century Britain and Ireland. At least half of the population attended a place of worship on Sunday and religious ideas and practices were widely debated and discussed. Expansionist movements of religious vitality – Evangelicalism, Catholicism and 'honest doubt' – generated considerable activity and reform. This enthusiasm, however, also provoked conflict with older, traditional interests. And while these seemed to prevail, at least in part, it is possible to see the signs of new and different ideas coming through. Throughout this period the British state implemented laws that laid the foundations of modern religious equality. Sometimes this was forced on them by political necessity, as was the case often in Ireland. But at other times it was because it was less and less willing to govern in the area of individual belief and conscience. As the century progressed, the challenge would be for all denominations, including the Church of England, to function within this new tolerant environment and to stave off what many saw as the corrosive influence of 'modernity' and 'secularisation'.

Now turn to the module website to complete the independent study activities associated with this unit.

References

Barr, C. (2005) 'An Irish dimension to a British *Kulturkampf*?', *Journal of Ecclesiastical History*, vol. 56, no. 3, pp. 473–95.

Bebbington, D. (2011) 'The King James Bible in Britain from the late eighteenth century', in Jeffrey, D. (ed.) *The King James Bible and the World It Made*, Waco, TX, Baylor University Press, pp. 49–69.

Bruce, S. (ed.) (1992) *Religion and Modernization: Sociologists and Historians Debate the Secularization Thesis*, Oxford, Clarendon.

Cashdollar, C. (2000) *A Spiritual Home: Life in British and American Reformed Congregations, 1830–1915*, University Park, PA, Pennsylvania State University Press.

Census of Great Britain, 1851. Religious Worship. England and Wales. Report and Tables. Cmd 1690, vol. 89, 1852–3.

Colley, L. (2003) *Britons: Forging the Nation 1707–1837*, London, Pimlico.

Cox, J. (1982) *The English Churches in a Secular Society: Lambeth, 1870–1930*, Oxford, Oxford University Press.

Currie, R., Gilbert, A. and Horsley, L. (1977) *Churches and Churchgoers: Patterns of Church Growth in the British Isles since 1700*, Oxford, Clarendon.

Eliot, G. (1985 [1858]) 'Janet's Repentance', in *Scenes of Clerical Life*, Oxford, Oxford University Press.

Field, C. (2010) *Religious Statistics in Great Britain: An Historical Introduction* [Online], Manchester, University of Manchester. Available at http://www.brin.ac.uk/wp-content/uploads/2011/12/development-of-religious-statistics.pdf (Accessed 2 January 2016).

Gibson, W. (1859) *The Year of Grace*, Edinburgh, A. Elliot.

Golby, J. M. (ed.) (1986) *Culture and Society in Britain: A Source Book of Contemporary Writings*, Oxford, Oxford University Press in association with The Open University.

Jowett, B. (1860) 'On the interpretation of Scripture', *Essays and Reviews*, London, John W. Parker and Son.

Larsen, T. (1999) *Friends of Religious Equality: Nonconformist Politics in Mid-Victorian England*, Woodbridge, Boydell.

Larsen, T. (2011) *The People of One Book: The Bible and the Victorians*, Oxford, Oxford University Press.

Larsen, T. (2013) 'The Bible and varieties of nineteenth-century dissent: Elizabeth Fry, Mary Carpenter and Catherine Booth', in Mandelbrote, S. and Ledger-Lomas, M. (eds) *Dissent and the Bible in Britain, c. 1650–1950*, Oxford, Oxford University Press, pp. 153–74.

Lentin, A. (1988) 'Anglicanism, Parliament and the courts', in Parsons, G. (ed.) *Religion in Victorian Britain*, vol. II: *Controversies*, Manchester, Manchester University Press, pp. 88–106.

London Daily News (1864) 'The Colyton burial case', 3 November.

McLeod, H. (1997) *Religion and the People of Western Europe, 1789–1989*, Oxford, Oxford University Press.

Manning, B. (1952) *The Protestant Dissenting Deputies*, Cambridge, Cambridge University Press.

Oliphant, M. (1870 [1863]) *Chronicles of Carlingford: Salem Chapel*, vol. 1, Leipzig, Bernhard Tauchniz.

Parsons, G. (1988a) 'Victorian Roman Catholicism: emancipation, expansion and achievement', in Parsons, G. (ed.) *Religion in Victorian Britain*, vol. I: *Traditions*, Manchester, Manchester University Press, pp. 146–83.

Parsons, G. (1988b) 'Reform, revival and realignment: the experience of Victorian Anglicanism', in Parsons, G. (ed.) *Religion in Victorian Britain*, vol. I: *Traditions*, Manchester, Manchester University Press, pp. 14–66.

Paz, D. (1969) 'The Papal Aggression: creation of the Roman Catholic hierarchy in England, 1850', unpublished MA thesis, Denton, TX, North Texas State University.

Shapcott, R. (ed.) (n.d.) *The Autobiography of Mark Rutherford*, 15th edn, London, T. Fisher Unwin.

Snell, K. D. M. (1999) 'The Sunday-school movement in England and Wales: child labour, denominational control and working-class culture', *Past and Present*, no. 164, pp. 122–68.

Snell, K. D. M. and Ell, P. (2000) *Rival Jerusalems: The Geography of Victorian Religion*, New York, Cambridge University Press.

The Times (1850) 'Editorial', 14 October.

The Times (1850) 'Cardinal Wiseman', 29 October.

The Times (1850) 'Lord John Russell and the Papal Aggression', 7 November.

Thompson, D. M. (ed.) (1972) *Nonconformity in the Nineteenth Century*, London, Routledge & Kegan Paul.

Thompson, D. M. (2014) *Religious Life in Mid-nineteenth Century Cambridgeshire and Huntingdonshire: The Returns of the 1851 Census of Religious Worship*, Cambridge, Cambridgeshire Records Society.

Tiller, K. (ed.) (1987) *Church and Chapel in Oxfordshire 1851: The Return of the Census of Religious Worship*, Oxford, Oxfordshire Record Society.

Wiggins, D. (1996) 'The Burial Act of 1880, the Liberation Society and George Osborne Morgan', *Parliamentary History*, vol. 15, no. 2, pp. 173–89.

Wolffe, J. (1997) '"Praise to the holiest in the height": hymns and church music', in Wolffe, J. (ed.) *Religion in Victorian Britain*, vol. V: *Culture and Empire*, Manchester, Manchester University Press, pp. 59–99.

Wolffe, J. (2008) 'The 1851 census and religious change in nineteenth-century Yorkshire', *Northern History*, vol. 45, no. 1, pp. 71–86.

Readings

Reading 11.1 William Hale White, 'A Nonconformist Sunday' (1881)

Source: Shapcott, R. (ed.) (n.d.) *The Autobiography of Mark Rutherford*, **15th edn, London, T. Fisher Unwin, pp. 5–7.**

… On the Sundays, however, the compensation came. It was a season of unmixed gloom. My father and mother were rigid Calvinistic Independents, and on that day no newspaper nor any book more secular than the Evangelical Magazine was tolerated. Every preparation for the Sabbath had been made on the Saturday, to avoid as much as possible any work. The meat was cooked beforehand, so that we never had a hot dinner even in the coldest weather; the only thing hot which was permitted was a boiled suet pudding, which cooked itself while we were at chapel, and some potatoes which were prepared after we came [p. 77] home. Not a letter was opened unless it was clearly evident that it was not on business, and for opening these an apology was always offered that it was possible they might contain some announcement of sickness. … After family prayer and breakfast the business of the day began with the Sunday-school at nine o'clock. We were taught our Catechism and Bible there till a quarter past ten. We were then marched across the road into the chapel, a large old-fashioned building dating from the time of Charles II. … There were three services every Sunday, besides intermitting prayer-meetings, but these I did not as yet attend. Each service consisted of a hymn, reading the Bible, another hymn, a prayer, the sermon, a third hymn, and a short final prayer. The reading of the Bible was unaccompanied with any observations or explanations, and I do not remember that I ever once heard a mistranslation corrected. The first, or long prayer, as it was called, was a horrible hypocrisy, and it was a sore tax on the preacher to get through it. … Nobody ever listened to this performance. … The sermon was not much better. It generally consisted of a text, which was a mere peg for a discourse, that was pretty much the same from January to December. The minister invariably began with the fall of man; propounded the scheme of redemption, and ended by depicting in the morning the blessedness of the saints, and in the evening the doom of the lost.

Reading 11.2 George Eliot, 'Janet's Repentance' (1858)

Source: Eliot, G. (1985 [1858]) 'Janet's Repentance', in *Scenes of Clerical Life*, Oxford, Oxford University Press, pp. 181-91.

But the inhabitants became more intensely conscious of the value they set upon all their advantages, when innovation made its appearance in the person of the Rev. Mr Tryan, the new curate at the chapel-of-ease on Paddiford Common. It was soon notorious in Milby that Mr Tryan held peculiar opinions; that he preached extempore; that he was founding a religious lending library in his remote corner of the parish; that he expounded the Scriptures in cottages; and that his preaching was attracting the Dissenters, and filling the very aisles of his church. The rumour sprang up that Evangelicalism had invaded Milby parish; ...

[p. 183]

No sugar-basin was visible in Mrs Linnet's parlour, for the time of tea was not yet, and the round table was littered with books which the ladies were covering with black canvas as a reinforcement of the new Paddiford Lending Library. Miss Linnet, whose manuscript was the neatest type of zigzag, was seated at a small table apart, writing on green paper tickets, which were to be pasted on the covers. ... The

[p. 186]

silent handsome girl of two-and-twenty, who is covering the *Memoirs of Felix Neff*, is Miss Eliza Pratt; and the small elderly lady in dowdy clothing, who is also working diligently, is Mrs Pettifer, a superior-minded widow, much valued in Milby, being such a very respectable person to have in the house in case of illness. ...

[p. 191]

The gate of the little garden opened, and Miss Linnet, seated at her small table near the window, saw Mr Tryan enter.

'There is Mr Tryan,' she said, and her pale cheek was lighted up with a little blush that would have made her look more attractive to almost any one except Miss Eliza Pratt, whose fine grey eyes allowed few things to escape her silent observation. 'Mary Linnet gets more and more in love with Mr Tryan,' thought Miss Eliza; 'it is really pitiable to see such feelings in a woman of her age, with those old-maidish little ringlets. I dare say she flatters herself Mr Tryan may fall in love with her, because he makes her useful among the poor.'

Reading 11.3 Margaret Oliphant, 'Salem Chapel' (1863)

Source: Oliphant, M. (1870 [1863]) *Chronicles of Carlingford: Salem Chapel*, **vol. 1, Leipzig, Bernhard Tauchniz, pp. 5–7.**

SALEM CHAPEL

Towards the west end of Grove Street, in Carlingford, on the shabby side of the street, stood a red brick building, presenting a pinched gable terminated by a curious little belfry, not intended for any bell, and looking not unlike a handle to lift up the edifice by to the public observation. This was Salem Chapel, the only Dissenting place of worship in Carlingford. ... On either side of this little tabernacle were the humble houses – little detached boxes, each two storeys high, each fronted by a little flower-plot – clean, respectable, meagre, little habitations, which contributed most largely to the ranks of the congregation in the Chapel. The big houses opposite, which turned their backs and staircase windows to the street, took little notice of the humble Dissenting community. ... It is not to be supposed, however, [p. 6] on this account, that a prevailing aspect of shabbiness was upon this little community; on the contrary, the grim pews of Salem Chapel blushed with bright colours, and contained both dresses and faces on the summer Sundays which the Church itself could scarcely have surpassed. Nor did those unadorned walls form a centre of asceticism and gloomy religiousness in the cheerful little town. Tea-meetings were not uncommon occurrences in Salem – tea-meetings which made the little tabernacle festive, in which cakes and oranges were diffused among the pews, and funny speeches made from the little platform underneath the pulpit, which woke the unconsecrated echoes with hearty outbreaks of laughter. Then the young people had their singing-class, at which they practised hymns, and did not despise a little [p. 7] flirtation; and charitable societies and missionary auxiliaries diversified the congregational routine, and kept up a brisk succession of 'Chapel business,' ...

Reading 11.4 Excerpts from *The Times* relating to the Papal Aggression (1850)

Source: *The Times* (1850) 'Editorial', 14 October.

But this nomination [of Nicholas Wiseman as a Cardinal in Rome] has been accompanied by one other circumstance which has a very different and a very peculiar character. We are informed by the official gazette of Rome that His Holiness the Pope having recently been pleased to erect the city of Westminster into an Archbishopric, and to appoint Dr. Wiseman to that see, it was on this newfangled Archbishop of Westminster so appointed that the rank of Cardinal has been conferred. … But if this appointment be not intended as a clumsy joke, we confess that we can only regard it as one of the grossest acts of folly and impertinence which the Court of Rome has ventured to commit since the Crown and the people of England threw off its yoke. … the appropriation by a foreign priest or potentate of the time-honoured name which is most identified with the glories of our history and even with the tombs of our statesmen, our soldiers, and our kings, is a most ostentatious interference with those rights and associations to which we, as a nation, are most unanimously and devotedly attached.

Source: *The Times* (1850) 'Cardinal Wiseman', 29 October, p. 5.

To our dearly beloved in Christ, the clergy, secular and regular, and the faithful of the said archdiocese and diocese, health and benediction in the Lord. …

Catholic England has been restored to its orbit in the ecclesiastical firmament from which its light had long vanished, and begins now anew its course of regularly adjusted action round the centre of unity, the source of jurisdiction, of light, and of vigour. …

How must the saints of our country, whether Roman or British, Saxon or Norman, look down from their seats of bliss with beaming glance upon this new evidence of the faith and church which led them to glory, sympathizing with those who have faithfully adhered to them through centuries of ill repute, for the truth's sake, and now reap the fruit of their patience and long suffering! … [Wiseman].

Source: *The Times* **(1850) 'Lord John Russell and the Papal Aggression', 7 November.**

TO THE RIGHT REV. THE BISHOP OF DURHAM.

My dear Lord, – I agree with you in considering 'the late aggression of the Pope upon our Protestantism' as 'insolent and insidious' and I therefore feel as indignant as you can do upon the subject.

I not only promoted to the utmost of my power the claims of the Roman Catholics to all civil rights, but I thought it right, and even desirable, that the ecclesiastical system of the Roman Catholics should be the means of giving instruction to the numerous Irish immigrants in London and elsewhere, who without such help would have been left in heathen ignorance.

This might have been done, however, without any such innovation as that which we have now seen.

…

There is an assumption of power in all the documents which have come from Rome – a pretension to supremacy over the realm of England, and a claim to sole and undivided sway, which is inconsistent with the Queen's supremacy, with the rights of our bishops and clergy, and with the spiritual independence of the nation, as asserted even in Roman Catholic times.

I confess, however, that my alarm is not equal to my indignation.

Even if it shall appear that the ministers and servants of the Pope in this country have not transgressed the law, I feel persuaded that we are strong enough to repel any outward attacks. The liberty of Protestantism has been enjoyed too long in England to allow of any successful attempt to impose a foreign yoke upon our minds and consciences. … [Russell].

Reading 11.5 Benjamin Jowett, 'On the interpretation of Scripture' (1860)

Source: Jowett, B. (1860) 'On the interpretation of Scripture', *Essays and Reviews***, London, John W. Parker and Son, pp. 330, 342–3, 374–5.**

It is a strange, though familiar fact, that great differences of opinion exist respecting the Interpretation of Scripture. All Christians receive the Old and New Testament as sacred writings, but they are not agreed about the meaning which they attribute to them. ...

[p. 342]

Much of the uncertainty which prevails in the interpretation of Scripture arises out of party efforts to wrest its meaning to different sides. There are, however, deeper reasons which have hindered the natural meaning of the text from ... prevailing. One of these is the unsettlement of many questions which have an important ... bearing on this subject. ... [I]n mathematics, when a step is wrong, we pull the house down until we reach the point at which the error is discovered. But in theology it is otherwise; there the tendency has been to conceal the unsoundness of the foundation under the fairness and loftiness of the superstructure. It has been thought safer to allow arguments to stand which, although fallacious, have been on the right side, than to point out their defect. ... For a like reason the failure of a prophecy is never admitted, in spite of Scripture and of history ... it becomes a point of honour or of faith to defend every name, date, place which occurs [in the Bible].

[p. 343]

[p. 374]

...[A]s the time has come when it is no longer possible to ignore the results of criticism, it is of importance that Christianity should be seen to be in harmony with them. ... When interpreted like any other book by the same rules of evidence and the same canons of criticism, the Bible will still remain unlike any other book; its beauty will be freshly seen as of a picture which is restored after many ages to its original state; it will create a new interest and make for itself a new kind of authority by the life which is in it.

[p. 375]

Reading 11.6 Frederic Harrison, 'Neo-Christianity' (1860)

Source: Golby, J. M. (ed.) (1986) *Culture and Society in Britain: A Source Book of Contemporary Writings*, **Oxford, Oxford University Press in association with The Open University, p. 47.**

No fair mind can close this volume [*Essays and Reviews*] without feeling it to be at bottom in direct antagonism to the whole system of popular belief. ... In object, in spirit, and in method, in details no less than on general design – this book is incompatible with the religious belief of the mass of the Christian public, and the broad principles on which the Protestantism of Englishmen rests. The most elaborate reasoning to prove that they are in harmony can never be anything but futile and ends in becoming insincere. ... Such reasoning may ease the conscience of troubled inquirers; but is powerless to persuade the mass that *that* is after all the true meaning of that which they have been taught and have believed.

They [the public], at any rate, will never be brought to believe that the Bible is full of errors, or rather untruths; that it does not contain authentic or even contemporary records of facts, and is a medley of late compliers; and yet withal remains the Book of Life, the great source of revealed truth, the standard of holiness, purity, and wisdom.

Reading 11.7 The Colyton burial case (1864)

Source: *London Daily News* **(1864) 'The Colyton burial case', 3 November, p. 6, quoting** *The Nonconformist.*

About the beginning of September last, John Pavey, a parishioner of Colyton, Devon, died. According to the testimony of his pastor, he had been 'an exceedingly worthy man – humble, diffident, and tender-hearted.' Whether he was visited during his last illness by the vicar of the parish to whom the law had assigned the 'cure of his soul,' we have no positive information; but soon after his death, the vicar, the Rev. Mr. Gueritz, called upon the bereaved family, and told the daughter of the deceased that 'as he might probably be expected to bury her father, he felt very uneasy, and hoped she might be able to tell him anything of his faith which might take away his scruples.' To his inquiries the only answer was that John Pavey had died a decided Unitarian – a fact which the vicar regarded as imposing upon himself 'a very difficult and unpleasant' duty. The friends of the departed, however, do not appear to have thought that Mr. Gueritz's private feelings were to be set up as the rule of his official conduct as a public officer, and hence on their behalf he was requested by the Rev. A. M'Combe, Unitarian minister at Colyton, to state whether they might expect him to perform the last sacred offices of the church over the remains of their relative on the following Saturday. The vicar replied that it would be necessary for him to be furnished with legal proofs of his (Pavey's) baptism, but that under any circumstances the notice given would be insufficient, as not allowing him time to receive an answer from the bishop, to whom he had written by that day's post. ...

The vicar acknowledged receipt of the certificate, confessed that it gave the deceased a right to a place in the churchyard, and stated that he should not object to his interment therein at the appointed time, but declined giving him 'a Christian burial, by using the burial office of the church,' ... Mr. M'Combe then formally claimed ... that 'the free use of the church, and of all its services, is the common right of every parishioner, and this right does not depend upon the contingency of a letter from the bishop, nor upon any other contingency.' This elicited the following final reply from the incumbent:– 'The late John Pavey having died a unitarian, denying the divinity of our Lord, and the Atonement, I cannot conscientiously read over him the burial service of the church. His right of interment in his parish burial ground I do not deny, and his friends may exercise that right, if they please, by interring him in the consecrated portion of the cemetery.'

Unit 12 The making of the British middle class

Bob Morris and Donna Loftus

Contents

Aims

This unit will:

- help you to understand who the nineteenth-century middle class was and what role it played in shaping the 'age of equipoise'

- use a range of sources, both economic and cultural, to explain the rise of the middle class

- explore why languages of class emerged as a way of describing socicty

- examine the impact of the middle class on mid-nineteenth-century culture.

Introduction

The mid-nineteenth century is associated with the rise of the middle class. A 'middling sort', a group of people that fits somewhere between the landed elites and the working class, neither rich nor poor, can be identified in most earlier periods of history. As the term 'middling sort' suggests, this group included a diverse range of people, from those with small family businesses working alongside manual labourers, to those with well-paid professional roles that required regular contact with the aristocracy. However, in the British Isles in the mid-nineteenth century a series of economic, cultural and political changes created a new and distinct middle class. This group made their livelihoods from the expansion of trade and industry that accompanied industrialisation and urbanisation and helped reshape an economy around business and service. They took on the governance of new urban centres and filled new professional and administrative roles as state bureaucracy expanded.

The middle class also became associated with liberal politics and culture in the mid-century. It emerged as a political force in the campaign for the extension of the franchise in 1832 and extended this influence in the Anti-Corn Law League, leading to repeal of the Corn Laws in 1846. This liberalism was part of a wider value system that promoted the virtues of individual hard work and self-help as essential to economic growth and the moral regeneration of society. In urban centres, the middle class established institutions and networks to promote this vision. In many respects, as you will see, the 'Victorian values' that have come to characterise the mid-nineteenth century and the 'age of equipoise' are overwhelmingly those associated with the middle class.

This unit considers who middle-class people were and what role they played in shaping the 'age of equipoise'. Section 12.1 starts by looking at the emergence of new ways of describing the inequalities of a rapidly changing society. A language of class emerged to explain such inequalities but it was accompanied by ideas of self-help and respectability, which suggested that every individual could improve themselves through hard work to become part of the middle class. Section 12.2 examines the material structures of income, wealth and property that were related to the language of class, and the range of occupations that made up the middle class.

Section 12.3 considers whether a middle-class value system and culture was strong enough to hold such a diverse group together. This section shows how an ideology of separate spheres between the private life of family and the public world of work and politics helped to create a middle-class world. Family and the different roles of men and women within it were considered an essential part of being middle class and were highly idealised in Victorian culture. However, closer examination will show that the relationships between men and women in the middle-class family were by no means simple and were often organised to help sustain class privilege.

Finally, Section 12.4 looks at how a growing middle class shaped the world around it. The home was considered essential to the reproduction of middle-class life and numerous guides emerged showing middle-class people where to live and how to live. Public political space was also reshaped by the middle class to reflect its interests and build its authority. For example, town halls (see Figure 12.1), improvement societies and self-help organisations were built to host meetings and events designed to promote middle-class values. You will examine some of these spaces and consider what they tell us about the middle class.

Figure 12.1 After R. P. Leitch, 'The New Town-Hall, Leeds – Opened by Her Majesty', engraving, from *The Illustrated London News*, September 1858. Photo: © Illustrated London News Ltd / Mary Evans Picture Library

12.1 The language lesson

Somewhere between the late eighteenth and the mid-nineteenth centuries an increasing number of British people began to discuss inequalities of power and wealth in a new language, the language of class.

Inequalities were not new in this period, but the emergence of a new language for describing them reflected changes in how they were perceived to be produced. In the eighteenth century inequalities were, on the whole, accepted as a product of birth. In the nineteenth century inequalities were increasingly understood to be a result of the rapid economic and social developments of the period. The speed of technological change, fluctuations in markets and the rise of new knowledge and ideas disrupted familiar social and economic relationships and created new ones. Established forms of social description that focused on rank, inheritance, birth and status were too rigid and too static to describe a society in which one's power and wealth were predicated on one's place in the new capitalist economy and in which, in principle at least, some mobility was possible.

Languages of class

Writing in the 1960s and 1970s, Asa Briggs pioneered a new form of social history, which saw the language of class as emerging out of the changed social and economic relationships produced by industrialisation. The language of ranks and orders related to a view of society as a God-given or natural hierarchy, characterised by stability. Groups had different roles in society, but were connected through strong social bonds and ideas of mutual dependence and duties that came with one's rank. The upper ranks, whose wealth was often inherited, were obliged to look after the welfare of the lower, a responsibility often referred to as the 'moral economy'. Briggs argued that the language of duty and dependence no longer made sense after industrialisation. It was replaced by the language of class (Briggs, 1960). A class society was based on markets, work, contract and negotiation and could therefore be changed or challenged. Many who used the language of class wanted to think about the way wealth and political power were distributed and inequalities organised in a rapidly changing world.

This view was challenged by the 'linguistic turn' of the 1980s. Historians such as Gareth Stedman Jones argued that language was not a simple reflection of economic and social reality. Rather, class languages were used strategically to create a group identity among a range of different people (Stedman Jones, 1983). In a development of this argument, the historian Dror Wahrman claimed that the middle class was a product of the political campaign for the vote in the 1820s and 1830s. In this campaign the middling sort argued that there was a middle class with distinct interests resulting from its place in society as employers, businessmen and traders, interests that could not be represented by the landed elite in Parliament. However, in practice the middle class was too diverse to have much in common and was interconnected in everyday life, through work, religion and social life, with the working class and the aristocracy (Wahrman, 1995).

Exercise 12.1

Turn to Reading 12.1, 'John Stuart Mill, "Class and political economy" (1834)' and Reading 12.2, 'Karl Marx and Friedrich Engels, "The Communist manifesto" (1848)', located at the end of the unit. (You encountered Mill, a liberal philosopher and reformer, and Marx, a socialist philosopher and revolutionary, in the unit 'The "age of equipoise" and the Great Exhibition of 1851' (Unit 8); Engels (1820–1895) was a businessman and revolutionary thinker.)

What do you notice about the way society is described?

This should take around 20 minutes.

Specimen answer

Despite the political differences of their authors, both readings present society as divided into classes. A person's class depends on their place in the economy and how they earn a living. In Mill's analysis the world is structured into three classes, 'landlords, capitalists and labourers'. For Marx and Engels it is increasingly divided into two, the '**bourgeoisie** and **proletariat**'.

Discussion

Class is a tricky concept for historians because it is both a historical phenomenon, used to describe people and groups, and also a political concept, used to explain inequality and to suggest remedies.

Mill was critical of political economists for being too rigid in their definition of class. He thought that they imposed class terminology on old ideas of society that saw distinctions of rank as natural and permanent. Instead, he thought that social mobility was essential to stability and he was fairly optimistic that social and economic reforms, including education reforms and saving schemes, could help give members of the working class opportunities to rise above their station.

Marx and Engels were less optimistic. They thought the industrial middle class had replaced feudal ties of obligation with 'cash payment'. They believed this class, the bourgeoisie, would gradually accumulate more and more wealth and power by exploiting the labour of the workers, those they called the proletariat. They argued that these tensions would eventually lead to revolution.

Historians writing about class have to distinguish the way it was understood by people at the time from the debates about inequality that dominated twentieth-century politics. In the twenty-first century, those who think and argue about inequality and power are as likely to refer to race, ethnicity, gender, religion and sexual orientation as they are to class. Nevertheless, in the mid-nineteenth century the language of class was primarily used to describe social relationships in the British Isles.

Marx and Engels weren't alone in thinking that the antagonism between the bourgeoisie and the proletariat would lead to unrest and revolution. In the 1830s and 1840s it was common for writers to comment on the emergence of class society riven with division and constantly under threat of breakdown.

Class in the 1830s

In the 1830s the Edinburgh doctor-in-training James Kay-Shuttleworth (whom you may recall from Unit 8) came to work in Manchester as physician to the Ardwick and Ancoats Dispensary. Rapid industrialisation and urbanisation created social problems that appeared insurmountable and mortality was high. Kay-Shuttleworth was greatly affected by what he experienced. During the cholera epidemic that hit Manchester in 1832, the disease killed 874 people in the town, out of a population of 142,000. On top of this there was hostility and violence arising from political campaigns for parliamentary reform. In 1832 Kay-Shuttleworth published an influential pamphlet called *The Moral and Physical Condition of the Working Classes Employed in the Cotton Manufacture in Manchester*. That account was written before the period covered by Block 2, but it is worth considering briefly here because it shows how the rise of the middle class in the mid-century was shaped by the experiences of men such as Kay-Shuttleworth in the 1830s.

Exercise 12.2

Read Kay-Shuttleworth's account of Manchester below. How many classes does he describe? What is the source of their conflict?

This should take around 10 minutes.

> Between the manufacturers of the country, staggering under the burdens of an enormous taxation and a restricted commerce; between them and the laboring classes subjects of controversy have arisen, and consequent animosity too generally exists. The burdens of trade diminish the profits of capital and the wages of labour: but bitter debate arises between the manufacturers and those in their employ, concerning the proper division of that fund, from which these are derived. The bargain for the wages of labour develops organized associations of the working classes, for the purpose of carrying on the contest with the capitalist ... a gloomy spirit of discontent is engendered, and the public are not unfrequently alarmed by the wild outbreak of popular violence.
>
> (Kay-Shuttleworth, 1832, pp. 9–10)

Specimen answer

Kay's account of Manchester describes two classes, the 'manufacturers' and the 'labouring classes'. The two are bound together through work, but their relationship is not easy. Differences and discontent emerge about how much of a share each should have of the profits from manufacturing; this discontent spills over into violence as the working classes organise themselves to campaign for better wages and conditions.

Discussion

Like Marx, Kay-Shuttleworth anticipated revolution but, like Mill, this motivated him to seek to reform society to try to make it more stable.

As you may remember from Block 1, the Marxist historian E. P. Thompson argued that class is not a thing but a relationship that, as such, can change (Thompson, 1963, pp. 8–9). This is just how Kay-Shuttleworth saw it. Class was a relationship between manufacturers and workers resulting from the way manufacturing was organised and how much of a share of profits each group was entitled to. Kay-Shuttleworth argued that this relationship was conflictual, but he was hopeful that things could change. Kay-Shuttleworth became one of those seeking a more stable set of class relationships, in other words a viable class society. He was sympathetic to both groups and argued that things would get better only if the middle and working classes were better informed of each other's opinion. This required social reform and spaces for cross-class communication. In particular, Kay-Shuttleworth wanted a universal secular education system providing literacy and numeracy for working-class children. He argued this would help them to understand the 'natural laws' of laissez-faire political economy.

Kay-Shuttleworth was part of a generation of men who helped create the middle class. These men were professionals, experts and manufacturers drawn to the new industrial cities for work and business. They argued that they needed greater representation in Parliament because it was they who created the nation's wealth and because they understood better than anyone else the problems of industrialisation, urbanisation and managing a class society. They campaigned for the vote in 1832 and for the Municipal Corporations Act in 1835. In the 1840s they campaigned for things they thought would help produce a viable class society: free trade, repeal of the Corn Laws and social reform to improve life for the working class and to allow self-help to flourish. These ideas were considered radical at the time and reformers established newspapers and voluntary associations to help promote them. According to the historian Miles Taylor, this group was influential in promoting **parliamentary radicalism** in the late 1840s and 1850s, and helped pave the way for the Gladstonian liberalism you read about in Unit 8. Their activities also created a middle-class identity around a disparate group of people (Taylor, 1995).

Activity 12.1

Now go to the module website and complete Activity 12.1 'Looking for the middle class'. This should take around an hour.

Identifying the middle class

Newspaper readers in the 1840s increasingly came across the use of the phrase 'middle class'. Richard Cobden argued that the Reform Act of 1832 and the repeal of the Corn Laws in 1846 demonstrated that the country was run through 'the bonâ fide representatives of the middle class' (quoted in Briggs, 1956, p. 65; see also Wahrman, 1995, p. 410). These campaigns presented the middle class as a group with a shared set of interests emerging out of its experience of trade, industry and manufacturing, interests that could not be represented by the traditional ruling elite.

Middle-class identity was then about one's place in the economy, but it was also about the virtues that were associated with that. The campaigns for the franchise in the 1830s and for repeal of the Corn Laws in the 1840s presented the middle class as improving the nation as it pursued its own self-interest. In particular, in political campaigns, middle-class members argued that they were generating the nation's prosperity through their work in trade and industry and through their investments in business. In 1845 *The Times* claimed that 'A substantial middle class is said to be a sign of the prosperity of the state' (15 July 1845). The claim was based on a list of those who had subscribed £2,000 or more to railway shares, for 'the patriotic purpose of perfecting the railway communication of their native land'. As the article pointed out, the aristocracy, the Sutherlands, Westminsters and Devonshires, were all but absent from the list of investors. Instead, money came from 'worthy capitalists' and members of the ordinary middle class. For example, there were 40 Browns, 28 Joneses and a page and a half of Smiths among the subscribers.

Middle-class investors were promoted as cautious and careful men of character who would provide stable growth because they needed to develop and protect the modest capital they had accumulated through hard work and steady industry. This was in contrast to a dissolute aristocracy who could squander their inherited wealth, and the majority of the working class who were too lazy and intemperate to save

(Taylor, 2006, p. 33). During the financial crisis of 1841, *The Times* pleaded on behalf 'of the middle class of manufacturers among whom industry and character usually constitute credit ... Such men are frequently less liable to overtrading and speculation than their more wealthy competitors' (14 January 1841). Articles such as this presented the middle class as patriotic and virtuous, helping to build economic growth and promote character formation from the way its members had acquired capital in the first place: self-help, thrift and perseverance. They were distinguished from the aristocracy and from the working class because they had earned their place in society and the privileges, such as the vote, that came with it.

Exercise 12.3

Read the account below, written in 1840 by Edward Baines junior (1800–1890), about why the franchise should not be extended to the working class. Baines was editor of the *Leeds Mercury*, a leading Whig newspaper targeted at the middle class.

What do you notice about Baines's argument?

This should take around 10 minutes.

> [W]e do not believe there is in the world a community so virtuous, so religious and so sober-minded as the *middle classes* of England. ... few who do not regularly attend a place of worship. ... We respect highly the steady, reading, moral part of the workmen, many of whom are quite fit for the franchise. But for a safe, intelligent, independent constituency, the substance and staple must be found in the middle classes; ... the lower class of Householders notoriously comprises not only the honest and sober workmen, but also an immense number of persons whose own vices have sunk them into poverty ...
>
> (Quoted in Morris, 1990a, p. 10)

Specimen answer

Baines argues that the virtues of the 'middle classes of England', their sobriety and religiosity, enable them to succeed, make money and acquire property to qualify for the vote. This logic means that the virtues of the poor cannot be guaranteed. Baines implies that those of good character would distinguish themselves from other members of their class through hard work, sobriety and thrift which would, in turn, lead to social mobility.

Discussion

Baines's letter shows how languages of class that started with one's economic role quickly became overlain with moral overtones and associated with respectable behaviours. This combination of economics and morality was a core part of mid-Victorian middle-class culture.

Middle-class education

Baines was, like many of the Leeds middle class, a dissenter and Evangelical in religion. Like many, he used the virtues of the middle class and its distinct position to argue for reforms that would further its interests. In particular, as a Nonconformist he wanted education independent of the state, led by people like him. Linking the virtues of the middle class to the progress of the nation helped further his cause.

The need for an education system that allowed them to progress to British universities and into professional and public life was a key concern of middle-class men. Until the passing of the University Test Act in 1871, every student going to Oxford or Cambridge had to be a member of the Anglican Church. These universities were dominated by the members of the landed aristocracy who attended the great private schools such as Eton and Harrow. From there they went into top jobs in the army, government and civil service. In the mid-century, the middle class argued for a more open education system that promoted people on merit. This was given further impetus by the **Crimean War** (1853–56), which exposed the failings of the British Army, blamed on an incompetent aristocracy who were promoted into positions of power through networks, nepotism and the purchase of commissions rather than ability.

William Gladstone's government reformed the civil service and the army in the 1870s to ensure appointment and promotion based on merit. These reforms were seen as important in opening up military and public life to the middle class.

The nineteenth-century language of class provided a new way of describing society that started with one's place in the economy but which explained differences in terms of morality and behaviour rather than material privileges. Terms such as respectability, character and self-help emerged as ways of explaining social differences. In popular manuals and guides such as Samuel Smiles's *Self-help* (1859), these qualities, rather than inherited wealth, were presented as the source of success and social mobility. They also helped associate the middle class with virtues such as industry, work and thrift.

12.2 Occupation, income and property

Occupation was the starting point for thinking about class in the mid-nineteenth century. Simon Gunn has argued that the middle class was defined as 'comprising property owning groups which engaged in active occupations, usually connected with manufacturing, trade and the professions' (Gunn, 2000, p. 14). However, as you will see in this section, there was considerable porosity between occupations and a vast range of income and status differentials associated with occupations undertaken by the middle class.

Historians have adopted a variety of approaches in recreating a picture of the middle class as a whole. They have used parliamentary poll books drawn from the borough franchise created by the parliamentary reforms of 1832 and published before the Secret Ballot Act of 1872. Equally valuable are the trade and postal directories published for most towns from the later eighteenth century onwards. Many studies have used these sources to get a snapshot of society in the 1830s. They have focused on the 1830s because, as you read above, this decade set the conditions for the growth of the middle class as a social and economic force.

Exercise 12.4

Look at Figure 12.2, a chart of the occupation structure of the middle class in five British towns, complied by Robert Morris from a number of studies. What does it tell you about the nature of the middle class in the 1830s?

This should take around 10 minutes.

Answer

The substantial number of shopkeepers and the small number of professional men are immediately obvious. Another feature is the varying importance of merchants and manufacturers. This suggests that each town has its special character. Glasgow was a merchant city and Manchester dominated by manufacturers. Leeds was somewhere in between. The West Midlands towns had few merchants.

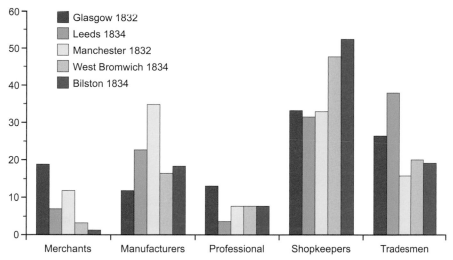

Figure 12.2 Occupational structure of five British towns, 1832–34. Source: Morris, 1990b, p. 22

The middle class was expanding rapidly in the 1830s and by the mid-century was composed of people with a range of occupations. We can explore this in more detail through a study conducted on the Glasgow middle class by Stana Nenadic. Using trade directories and rent books, Nenadic's study shows that, by 1861, 23 per cent of the population of Glasgow was middle class. This figure had grown from 18 per cent at the beginning of the century and 15 per cent in the mid-eighteenth century. Table 12.1 shows that, within this middle class of the 1860s, 73 per cent earned their income from business. Within that group, 45 per cent derived their income from small business.

Table 12.1 The Glasgow middle class in 1861 (n = 894)

	per cent
Businessmen Of whom:	73
merchants/commercial	*18*
manufacture	*10*
small business	*45*
Professionals	10
Employees	8
Independent	9

Source: Adapted from Nenadic, 1991, p. 69

In the 1861 census 52 per cent of the working population were engaged in manufacturing industries. However, only 14 per cent of the middle-class population involved in business were manufacturers and industrialists. Another 25 per cent were involved in commerce as wholesalers and merchants, 27 per cent were shopkeepers and 34 per cent were in craft or artisan trades (Nenadic, 1991, pp. 69–70).

Local studies such as Nenadic's on Glasgow, together with others, provide important insights into the diversity of income and status among the middle class (Koditschek, 1990; Howe, 1984). They show that, in most industrial towns and cities, there were large employers in the industrial trades who were very wealthy and influential. There were also elite groups of bankers, merchants and professional men. There were a small number of women keeping shops or involved in small trades, especially in dressmaking, and in many cases living on independent incomes. Alongside them was another group who owned and ran smaller manufacturing businesses, many of whom lived and worked alongside members of the working class. As Nenadic argues, some of these combined being a manual labourer with being an employer of other labour (Nenadic, 1991, p. 67).

Despite the emphasis given to large-scale manufacturing in accounts of industrialisation, businesses in mid-century Britain were overwhelmingly small. Some sectors such as cotton were associated with mechanisation, factories and large workforces but these were exceptional (Samuel, 1977). Most towns and cities had huge number of small manufacturing businesses, shops and services with few workers. For most, the middle-class experience of being an employer was about small establishments.

Exercise 12.5

The 1851 census collected information on apprentices, journeymen and masters. The sample shown in Table 12.2 enables us to look at the age distribution of each category in Britain in 1851.

What do you notice about the distribution of employment status and age in manual trades? What does this suggest about class and age?

This should take around 10 minutes.

Table 12.2 Employment status and age in Britain in 1851 (male)

% in each age group	under 20	20–25	25–35	35–45	45–55	55 and over	n
Masters and employers	0	3	22	22	21	32	256
Journeymen	7	24	35	16	12	6	214
Apprentices	87	8	2	1	0	0	183
All manual occupations in sample	24	14	21	16	13	14	2569

Note: The figures are taken from a 2 per cent sample of the census enumerators' schedules and have been rounded up or down to produce whole numbers. As a result, not all rows add up to 100 per cent.

Source: Morris, 2005, p. 55

Specimen answer

Table 12.2 suggests that young men start out as apprentices, then work as journeymen before becoming masters and employers. This implies that you could begin life as a member of the working class and later become a master and employer, which could put you into the category of the middle class.

Discussion

The boundaries of social class had considerable porosity. As Table 12.2 shows, for many, progress from journeyman to master equated to stages in their life cycle. However, becoming a small master and employer did not necessarily take people away from their communities. Many lived and worked alongside their employees, did not earn much more money than them and would still have considered themselves part of the working class. As this suggests, we have to be careful when using terms such as class to consider people's own sense of identity as well as their occupation, wealth and status.

The occupational status of members of the middle class varied considerably. Many of the occupations they undertook were continuations of older forms of work, including shopkeepers, small manufacturers and merchants. As the century went on, new middle-class occupations emerged, such as clerks, administrators and civil servants. However, when discussing the mid-century middle class, contemporaries and historians have tended to focus on large manufacturers associated with industry, who were in fact a minority within the middle class. In the following subsection, you will consider why this was.

Manufacturers, merchants and industrialists

Histories of the middle class have focused undue attention on a small number of large manufacturers and merchants because their story fits with traditional accounts of the Industrial Revolution (Rubenstein, 1977). The rise of 'great men of industry' in the early century is related to the rapid pace of economic and technological change. Many were recruited from the ranks of tradesmen and artisans. Those who were enterprising, fortunate and often ruthless could make massive profits in the early days of industrialisation before competition caught up with them. They became notable figures in their locality; this group included people such as the Gotts and Marshalls (textile manufacturers in Leeds), the Bolkows and Vaughans (iron and steel pioneers in Middlesbrough), the Chambers and Nelsons (printer-publishers in Edinburgh), the Stephensons, Hawthornes and Armstrongs (engineering and armaments manufacturers along the River Tyne) and the Guests and Crawshays (ironwork owners in Merthyr Tydfil). Their stories of self-making were used as evidence of the great opportunities for social mobility that came with industrialisation (Smiles, 1968 [1859]).

Exercise 12.6

Turn to Reading 12.3, 'Samuel Smiles, "Self-help" (1859)', located at the end of the unit. This an extract from a short biography of the pottery manufacturer Josiah Wedgwood (1730–1795).

After you have read this, answer the following questions:

- What sort of qualities does Smiles associate with Wedgwood's success?

- How does Smiles's biography of Wedgwood fit with the image of the middle class you have encountered so far in this unit?

This should take around 20 minutes.

Specimen answer

- Smiles describes how Wedgwood emerged out of the ranks of the working class. He was able to distinguish himself by his diligence, dedication and hard work, which enabled him to identify new opportunities arising out of the concurrence of science and manufacture. He even used his leisure time to study chemistry to help improve methods of production.

- Smiles's biography of Wedgwood's rise reproduces many of the ideas about the middle class that were in circulation in the mid-century. For example, it suggests that economic success for men like Wedgwood is the product of their moral virtue, and that it improves localities and the nation by providing both work for others and a better environment through the building of an infrastructure that is essential to business.

Discussion

The rise of large-scale manufacturers from the ranks of labour was possible in the early years of the Industrial Revolution, but it was still exceptional. Smiles used the biographies of self-made businessmen to produce didactic accounts of 'how to succeed' for every man. In these accounts, great emphasis was placed on the moral virtues of successful businessmen, suggesting that individuals could succeed if they had the right characteristics and attitude.

As you know from the unit 'The Industrial Revolution'(Unit 2 in Block 1), historians have now nuanced their understanding of the Industrial Revolution and have put much greater emphasis on continuities with the past, gradual change and uneven development. At the same time, they have developed new understandings of why, given the continuities with the past and the continuing importance of small business, the heroes of industry attracted so much attention in the mid-nineteenth century.

Large-scale manufacturers were a small minority, but they played a substantial part in the way the middle class and others imagined themselves and their society (MacLeod, 2007). They were, perhaps more than anything else, visible agents of change. They signalled the shift in power away from the landed elite towards trade and industry, and they challenged established hierarchies. The wealthiest adopted the lifestyle of the gentry, buying landed property and building country mansions. Some adopted paternalist regimes which imagined the employer as having a duty to look after the welfare of his workers, much like the landed aristocracy of the earlier era (Joyce, 1980).

NEW IRON AND GLASS WAREHOUSE AT GLASGOW.

Figure 12.3 Unknown artist, 'New Iron and Glass Warehouse at Glasgow', engraving, from *The Illustrated London News*, March 1856. Photo: © Illustrated London News Ltd / Mary Evans Picture Library

These 'great' manufacturers attracted attention because large-scale production was new and, as Figure 12.3 demonstrates, factories and warehouses were changing the local landscape. People were impressed with technology, science and industry. They wrote about technology and visited factories to see machinery and people at work. There was a great interest in patents and inventions. Some of the most popular exhibits in the Great Exhibition were machines such as the printing press and the cotton-weaving frames. By the 1850s stories of invention and industry, told in biographical accounts of well-known manufacturers such as Wedgwood in Reading 12.3, were popular. By the 1860s and 1870s local communities were putting up statues to the 'heroes of invention' (MacLeod, 2007), such as the one of Samuel Crompton (1753–1827), inventor of the spinning mule, in Bolton, Lancashire (Figure 12.4).

Large manufacturers also attracted interest locally and nationally because their role gave them considerable power. They were often

Figure 12.4 Maclure, Macdonald and Macgregor, 'Samuel Crompton, Inventor of the Spinning Mule …', lithograph; insert presented with the *Bolton Chronicle*, September 1862. Photo: © Mary Evans Picture Library / Library of Congress

employers of large numbers of people, and their businesses and workforces could promote and sustain wider business development. In short, through their employment of local labour, their need for professional services, accountants, suppliers and lawyers, and their control of capital, manufacturers had the ability to shape the local economy. Above all, manufacturers were involved in the direct confrontation of labour and capital with little intervention from merchants or sub-contractors. The management of this relationship was felt to be of wider significance to the peace and prosperity of the nation. The size of some businesses meant that strikes and industrial unrest could threaten the wider economy, and had the potential to bring down smaller businesses and shopkeepers in the vicinity. It is no surprise that strikes were a central part of mid-century novels such as

Hard Times (1854) by Charles Dickens and *North and South* (1855) by Elizabeth Gaskell (1810–1865).

Activity 12.2

Now go to the module website and complete Activity 12.2 'Using novels as evidence'. This should take around an hour.

Middle-class people were diverse in terms of occupation and income and their status range was considerable, but they all, to some extent, managed capital and depended on credit and many also employed labour. Even the growing minority of professional people – lawyers, clergymen and ministers, medical men, accountants, architects and teachers – depended on selling their services to the growing middle class. Their fortunes were exposed to the economy and, like shopkeepers, to their ability to attract customers. In this respect the middle class shared the experience of business and commerce and its members were often tied together through business networks and other associations of trade. They also shared the experience of opportunity and insecurity that went with commerce.

As the middle class grew it established social networks that helped it manage insecurity and protect its position. Smaller businesses and individual professionals depended on other middle-class men for work. Connections made through business, clubs, church and voluntary societies provided access to wider networks of support (Loftus, 2017). Support from family was also important to security and success. The **joint stock company** had little significance in manufacturing until the twentieth century; whether a small business or a large industrial concern, it was the family firm that was typical in the mid-century. Family loans provided initial capital and credit for suppliers, and kin networks were essential in providing personnel and partners. All this required trust built on family knowledge, extended through social networks. Business success also depended on reputation. Hence supporting all members of the family, choosing marriage partners carefully and mixing in the right circles were all vital to the business.

12.3 Family and gender

The middle class was associated with self-help and social mobility. However, in the turbulent economy of the nineteenth century, this mobility could mean moving down as well as up. Protests and strikes could damage businesses; fears of disorder were stoked in the Chartist era and as campaigns for parliamentary reform re-emerged in the 1860s. There were other, more everyday threats to stability too. Structural changes in the economy and fluctuations in trade could threaten livelihoods. Speculation and fraud were rife, and poor investments could and did lead to bankruptcy. Premature death and chronic ill health could also threaten bankruptcy and throw a middle-class family into poverty. New kinds of professions, experts and services were emerging to provide greater protection for the middle class. Even for those who could afford the best doctors, the knowledge of medical men and the availability of medicines were still limited. Checks on banks, merchant houses, stockbrokers and accountants were also imperfect. As a result, insecurity and anxiety were a part of middle-class life and the middle class often looked to the family to provide security.

The family provided a way for the middle class to secure investment and circulate property and capital, and a place where middle-class values and culture could be nurtured. **Domestic ideology** held these two aspects of middle-class family life together – family capital and family values – but not, as you will see, without some tension.

The nineteenth-century middle class distinguished itself from the working and upper classes by its adoption and adaptation of an earlier eighteenth-century domestic ideology infused by Evangelical religion. This domestic ideology preached the separate roles of men and women in the separate spheres of the public and the private. Men were required to work to protect and provide for their family. Women were responsible for the home and for the spiritual and moral rejuvenation of society by nurturing and nourishing their husbands and children. These roles were perceived to be natural and God-given. Thus the man's duty as breadwinner and patriarch was to be complimented by female service and submission, roles that could be justified through suitable selective quotations from the ever-present Bible on the family table. As you will see in this section, domestic ideology operated to create an ideal type of middle-class family life, though, as you will also see, things were rarely so simple in practice.

Exercise 12.7

In 1839 Sarah Stickney Ellis (1812–1872) published a popular conduct book for middle-class women, *The Women of England, Their Social Duties, and Domestic Habits.* Ellis was a Nonconformist writer from a rural background; her father was a Quaker farmer. Yet she perceived that the growing middle class needed some help finding its place in the urban industrial economy. She argued that 'The middle class must include so vast a portion of the intelligence and moral power of the country at large, that it may not improperly be designated the pillar of our nation's strength' (Ellis, 1839, p. 14). She argued that women had a particular and important part to play in maintaining the virtues of the new middle class.

Turn to Reading 12.4, 'Sarah Stickney Ellis, "The women of England" (1839)', located at the end of the unit.

What does Ellis think the role of English middle-class women should be in the modern industrial city? Why does she think this is more important than ever?

This should take around 30 minutes.

Specimen answer

Ellis thinks that women should stay at home and cultivate domestic life. She thinks this is more important than ever because modern urban life distracts people from the 'laws of nature'. Modern life requires men to spend more and more time in the public world, often in 'degrading' occupations. As a consequence, women are required to spend more time at home compensating for the corrupting effects of public life on men. However, as you may also have noticed, Ellis acknowledges that supporting fathers and husbands may require women helping out in the family business.

Discussion

In many ways the middle-class embrace of domestic ideology in the mid-nineteenth century is a contradiction. As Eric Hobsbawm has argued, middle-class society was premised on the 'cash nexus', freedom, contract and individualism, yet the family was based on reciprocity and collective interests (Hobsbawm, 1975, pp. 278–80). However, John Tosh has argued that 'these very contradictions hold the clue to the mystery' (Tosh, 1999, p. 6). Domesticity was supposed to counter the brutality of the highly competitive and corrupting environment in which men worked.

Ellis's conservatism is also an example of what James Vernon has called 'the dialectic of modernity', where modernisation and new ways of living provoked a defence of habits that some people thought of as 'natural' and 'normal', in this case 'nurturing the family' (Vernon, 2014, pp. 14–15).

Behind the idealised and sentimental images of middle-class domestic life, which you can see in Figure 12.5, lay complex economic negotiations and relationships in which both men and women played their part.

"HE THAT EATETH, EATETH TO THE LORD, FOR HE GIVETH GOD THANKS."

Figure 12.5 George Measom, 'He that Eateth, Eateth to the Lord, for He Giveth God Thanks', engraving, from *The Sunday at Home*, 1858. Photo: © Mary Evans Picture Library

Domestic ideology corresponded with the separation of home and work. At the start of the nineteenth century, family and business were closely intertwined and household and business accounts were often blended. Shops, workplaces and offices were near to the home, if not directly connected, and warehouses and finishing shops occupied the backyards of urban houses. For example, in the households of the yeoman clothiers of northern England the male heads of household dealt with their tradesmen in the front parlour while wives managed servants and apprentices in the back. They would be familiar with each other's work and women might be called on to help out in busy periods. As the century progressed, there was a tendency to adopt more formal accounting procedures which separated home and business budgets and, if possible, separated spaces of work and domestic life entirely. This separation made it harder for women to be involved in business.

Despite this, women still provided a 'hidden investment', giving their labour and capital to ensure business success. In an important study, Leonore Davidoff and Catherine Hall have demonstrated that women's labour was essential to the success of many small businesses in the nineteenth century. The retail trade in particular depended on women running shops, often selling products manufactured or acquired by their husbands. In fact, Davidoff and Hall have found numerous examples of women's contribution to business, from support in times of crisis to everyday help with routine tasks and administration. For example, there were solicitors and estate agents who depended on wives and daughters to arrange meetings, write letters and copy correspondence (Davidoff and Hall, 2002 [1987], p. 283). Women also brought capital to businesses. In a famous example, George Courtauld (1761–1823) borrowed money from his sister and a female friend to help start his silk mill. When Courtauld married, he and his wife lived off her money so that the profits of the silk mill could be reinvested in the business (Davidoff and Hall, 2002 [1987], p. 280).

Women were essential to success in other ways. The middle-class home was important in preparing the next generation for achievement. In general, girls were trained for domestic life. Childhood for boys was a period of dependence on parents, but early teens saw a period of training, perhaps education in a grammar school, preparing for further medical or clerical education, perhaps time in one of the modern commercial schools, learning German and bookkeeping. Others would be apprenticed, perhaps in a mercantile or legal business, or in one of many manufacturing trades in businesses large and small. Mothers would help oversee this early training and provide the regularity of routine that allowed 'character' to flourish (Davidoff and Hall, 2002 [1987], p. 281). A man's early twenties was a time for important decisions. Most middle-class men would enter some form of partnership with a family member, or with friends or contacts who could use or invest in their skills. By their later twenties, once the ability to be independent seemed viable, many men would consider marriage. As the economy of family and firm was so closely linked, marriage was an important step. As the example of Courtauld above illustrates, family was often the source of the initial capital of many firms in the form of loans or credit, and marriage could be used to access extended networks of support. Romantic love was increasingly celebrated in nineteenth-century Britain, but middle-class people were strongly encouraged to fall in love with the right sort of person – one who had family capital, brothers and extended networks that could be trusted.

Middle-class people supported the family through wills and inheritance. Although an extended family of cousins, nephews and nieces may have been useful in establishing business networks, when it came to inheritance the middle class prioritised the nuclear family. Laws of inheritance in England favoured the eldest son, but the middle class typically used wills to protect other members of the family and ensure a degree of control over their future. Provision was also made for a widow and for daughters, usually by investing a share of the estate in a trust. Such trusts were invested in government stock, railway and other joint stock shares, in mortgage bonds or in the purchase of property. In this way, female capital was an important source of finance for much urban property, for the family business and for other businesses in the locality and beyond.

In most cases trust conditions specified that a woman's income was independent of the control of any husband. However, the law of England and Wales meant that a married woman had no legal existence in terms of property, separately from her husband. As one campaigner for a reform of the law, Frances Power Cobbe (1822–1904), stated:

> The husband and wife are assumed to be one person, and that person is the husband. The wife can make no contract, and can neither sue or be sued. Whatever she possess of personal property

at the time of her marriage, or whatever she may afterwards earn or inherit, belongs to her husband, without control on her part.

(Cobbe, 1869 [1868], pp. 6–7)

Exercise 12.8

Turn to Reading 12.5, 'Frances Power Cobbe, "Criminals, idiots, women, and minors" (1869 [1868])', located at the end of the unit.

In this extract Cobbe imagines explaining the concept of marriage to an alien. What impression does she create of what marriage means for women in the mid-nineteenth century?

This should take around 30 minutes.

Specimen answer

Cobbe uses dialogue to expose the unequal state of marriage for women. She contrasts the idealised image of marriage in mid-Victorian culture with the reality in which the 'sweet young woman in white' has no more rights than a criminal or a minor. Cobbe argues that this model of marriage is out of date: women are more active and useful in the modern age, where force and violence are no longer required for conducting one's business. As such, women can play a part in managing their affairs, and that part should be recognised.

Discussion

Unlike Ellis, Cobbe did not argue for a return to a 'natural' balance between the genders, with defined roles of active authority on behalf of men and submission for women. Instead she argued that the law and human relationships needed to modernise to catch up with wider changes in society.

In her extended argument, she referred to new scientific discoveries such as Charles Darwin's *Origin of Species* (1859) to argue that as nature had evolved to fit with a changed environment, so too should human society.

Cobbe was writing as the **Married Women's Property Act** was being discussed in Parliament. The Act was intended to allow women the right to own and control their property after marriage. It was passed in 1870, allowing women to keep the money they earned and to inherit property.

Domestic ideology was an important part of middle-class culture in which the separation of spheres was presented as essential in balancing the economic and moral aspects of life. The family was the site where the corrupting aspects of public activity were neutralised through the cultivation of manners, spirituality and affection. However, historians need to get beyond the ideals of middle-class family life that were discussed in domestic manuals and prescriptive literature, and popularised in sentimentalised scenes of domestic life. Middle-class men were actively involved in family life and even if domestic ideology made middle-class women's work less respectable, it was still accepted as necessary by even the most strident promoters of separate spheres such as Ellis (Tosh, 1999). Detailed local studies have shown that women made up a sizeable chunk of entrepreneurs running successful businesses in the mid-century (Aston, 2016). Economic historians have shown that middle-class women were active investors of their own capital. Moreover, middle-class women were able to reinterpret domestic ideology and their role as carers and educators in the home to carve out a public role. As the urban middle class began to campaign for social reform, the opportunities for middle-class women's work increased through charities, Poor Law boards and, after the passing of the Elementary Education Act of 1870, local school boards.

Domestic ideology can obscure the many complex ways that public and private and work and family were intertwined in the period. As detailed empirical studies of wills and inheritance have shown, the family was the primary mechanism for transferring wealth, and marriage and the extended family were used to develop the networks of support that helped secure business success (Owens, 2001). It was also the site where the next generation were groomed and the appearances of respectability cultivated. Image and materiality combined in middle-class family life. Behind sentimental images of respectability lay complex strategies for securing class privilege into the next generation.

12.4 Middle-class spaces

By the mid-nineteenth century, as the middle class was growing in influence, its members began to shape the world around them to reflect their interests and identity and to help them protect the wealth and status they had acquired. A middle class could be found in most communities. However, their impact was most noticeable in urban industrial towns and cities. Here middle-class culture could be seen in housing developments, in civic buildings such as town halls and libraries, and in clubs and voluntary associations formed to promote self-help and social reform. Such spaces were created by the middle class, but they also helped create the middle-class sense of the world.

Home and work

As you discovered in Section 12.3, the idea of separate spheres was an important part of middle-class culture, albeit one that was difficult to maintain in practice. Nevertheless, in the mid-century new villas were built in leafy suburbs a short distance from places of work. Edgbaston in Birmingham, Victoria Park in Manchester and Headingly in Leeds were all built for the new middle class. They were intended to be close enough to work to allow the breadwinner an easy commute at a time when quick transport links were yet to be established, but far enough away to allow for a genuine separation.

Many different types of houses were built in these suburbs to accommodate the varying economic and social status of middle-class families. Many were bespoke-designed by architects for the upper ranks of the middle class. Others were speculations built in anticipation of a growing market. Builders who undertook these relied on a variety of pattern books produced in the mid-century in response to the sharp increase in demand for more houses. These books demonstrate how houses were constructed to reflect the way that middle-class people thought about themselves in terms of social status.

In 1860 the architect Samuel H. Brooks published his *Rudimentary Treatise on the Erection of Dwelling-houses*. His book was a guide to builders on how to erect a 'pair of semi-detached villas'. The villas would be four storeys high and contain four bedrooms. The guide contained advice on the layout, drainage, brickwork and even decoration of a new house. It included floor plans with measurements and diagrams to help builders with drains and sewage systems (see Figure 12.6).

Figure 12.6 Unknown artist, 'Villa', from Samuel H. Brooks, *Rudimentary Treatise on the Erection of Dwelling-houses,* 1882, London, Crosby Lockwood and Co. Wellcome Library, shelfmark, K54290. Photo: Wellcome Library

---

Exercise 12.9

Turn to Reading 12.6, 'Samuel H. Brooks, "Rudimentary treatise" (1860)', located at the end of the unit.

What do you notice about the way Brooks describes streets and buildings?

This should take around 20 minutes.

Specimen answer

Brooks thinks that streets and buildings reflect what people think and feel and can, in turn, shape the way that people think and feel. As such, he advises builders to reflect the values and identity of the people they are building for. He also thinks that buildings represent the nation and its history. He claims that the middle class is the heart of the nation. As he says, the British are a 'commercial people' and a 'common-sense trading race' and buildings need to reflect that.

Discussion

Brooks was keen to show that design and architecture were linked to higher ideals than mere appearance and could transform and improve everyday life. Features of order, specialisation, knowledge, division and morality were for him a part of middle-class identity and essential to good design.

The growing middle class, anxious about its place in a rapidly changing environment, created a market for guides to modern life. There were guides to building, to business and on how to behave in public and private. Knowing appropriate manners and etiquette was essential to acceptance into middle-class society. As you know, the home was the place where good habits were inculcated. Isabella Beeton (1836–1865) published her *Mrs Beeton's Book of Household Management* in 1861. It was an incredible success and sold over 60,000 copies in its first year.

Activity 12.3

Now go to the module website and complete Activity 12.3 'Order and space in the middle-class home'. This should take around an hour.

Brooks recognised a need for buildings that projected a positive image of the middle class by balancing commercial and aesthetic concerns. Characters such as Mr Gradgrind, the utilitarian employer in Dickens's *Hard Times*, reflected the unflattering stereotypes of the mid-century industrial middle class that were popular at the time. These included being associated with facts, thrift and the cash nexus rather than with culture and refinement. When the middle class did consume, according to contemporary stereotypes, it did so with very poor taste. The critic John Ruskin (1819–1900) saw the Great Exhibition as evidence of the vulgarity of the middle class. In response he presented secular sermons that lauded the success of the Italians in combining trade and artistic achievement and appealed for the middle class in the United Kingdom to do the same. (You may have noticed references to Italy in Reading 12.6.)

In many respects Ruskin and Brooks were preaching to the converted. As Gunn has demonstrated, the design of many of Manchester's cotton warehouses was intended to present the city as the Venice of the north (Gunn, 2000). Even those most utilitarian of buildings, the factory and the warehouse, were built to reflect the high ideals and aspirations of business (see Figure 12.1). For example, as Figure 12.7 illustrates, Temple Works in Leeds was built in the style of an Egyptian temple. In Bradford warehouses became Renaissance palaces with row upon row of Venetian Gothic windows. Some factories had gates which would have suited many a classic country house. Such flourishes were no doubt intended to challenge the view prevailing among the educated elites that the industrial middle class was formed of uncouth philistines simply interested in making money. Instead, these building were intended to show commerce 'as glorious, honorable and noble, and as inextricably linked with magnificent and lasting architecture and civic virtue' (Hill, 1999, p. 102). These buildings were also intended to make a political statement and show that trade and commerce were ancient and enduring, and would, like the middle class, shape the future of the nation.

Figure 12.7 Temple Works, Leeds, built between 1836 and 1840. Photo: Rob Ford / Alamy

Civic spaces

In towns and cities new buildings appeared, representing middle-class ambitions for commerce, leisure, local government and social reform. Areas for shopping emerged to accommodate the expansion of consumption and a growing number of arcades and department stores were built. Shopping and department stores provided a way for respectable middle-class women to transcend the private sphere and be seen in public (Nead, 2011). And, as you can see in Figure 12.8, art galleries provided space for the family to enjoy educational recreation. However, many other urban spaces were given over to politics and masculine pursuits. The specialist office block and the gentlemen's club provided spaces for middle-class men's work and leisure. Other spaces were intended as shared spaces for governance and social reform.

A SUNDAY AFTERNOON IN A PICTURE GALLERY
DRAWN FROM LIFE

Figure 12.8 Unknown artist, 'A Sunday Afternoon in a Picture Gallery', engraving, from the *Graphic*, February 1879. Photo: © Illustrated London News Ltd / Mary Evans Picture Library

The most prominent spaces presenting the rise of the middle class were provincial town halls (as you saw in Figure 12.1), many of which were rebuilt to reflect the increased business of municipal governance in the mid-century. Despite the impact of 'Manchester men', Liberal MPs such as Richard Cobden and John Bright, national politics was dominated by the landed elite well into the late nineteenth century. However, the middle class became increasingly influential in local politics after the passing of the Municipal Corporations Act in 1835. In Lancashire towns, men put themselves forward for election to the municipal council on the basis of their role as cotton manufacturers. They argued that they were the new wealthy elite who should take responsibility for leadership in the locality and that their knowledge of local business and local people made them best placed to represent the people. They also argued that, if they could run a business, juggling competing interests of capital and labour and balancing aspirations and resources, they were fit to run the municipal council (Howe, 1984).

The building of civic spaces in industrial towns and cities is seen by historians as evidence of the growing influence of a middle class. However, in these spaces differences and distinctions within the middle class became apparent. There were bitter disputes about the influence of the established church in local politics, especially in places dominated by Nonconformity. In matters of formal constitutional power and politics, the middle class was also bitterly divided according to politics and social status. These divisions could surface in disputes over local policy and improvement schemes. In Leeds, rival water company schemes competed for municipal sanction and support to secure the parliamentary legislation needed for their adoption. Expensive improvement schemes for drainage and the clearance of unhealthy housing gained support from the merchant elites, major manufacturers and professional men. But shopkeepers, manufacturers of lesser capital and traders were opposed to such schemes because of the increase in local taxation involved.

Middle-class civic politics attempted to address political and religious divisions by fostering networks of middle-class men through voluntary associational culture (Loftus, 2017). Spaces appeared in towns and cities where people could get together for specific purposes, such as meeting halls and assembly rooms for clubs, groups and organisations. Voluntary associations were not new in the nineteenth century, but their progress was marked by a massive increase in their number, by the variety of such organisations in the mid-century and by the dominance of a particular form, the subscriber democracy. This required only the payment of a subscription and the willingness to support the stated aims of the association. As such, some historians have seen it as an extension of the market economy into associational life (Gunn, 2000).

Subscriber democracies were powerful ways of overcoming the sectarian, political and status divisions of the middle class. They were spaces where differences could be broken down and compromise reached to ensure the interests of the middle class as a whole. Literary and philosophical societies drew people together by promoting debate and discussion of topical subjects. Local business groups such as the Chamber of Commerce and local employer organisations would pool their knowledge about trade and work together to promote their mutual interests regardless of their political and religious differences. However, there were other associations that were intended to open up civic life to the working class.

The Woodhouse Temperance Hall and Mechanics Institution, Leeds, was a typical mid-century voluntary association intended to build connections across classes and 'improve' the working class through education and moral instruction. The building was funded through subscriptions from members. The classical front was designed to announce that this was an important building. The plaque across the front included the clasped hands of friendship, a symbol often used to denote cooperation. Inside, it provided a simple associational space. There was a stage for speakers, a committee room and spaces for instruction and education. The balcony provided a flexible space for the higher classes to withdraw from more general educational activities aimed at the working class. It was also a space for 'the ladies' to sit and watch the activities below.

The hall was also the place where Smiles first gave his lecture on 'self-help', at its opening in January 1851. On the surface, the opening of the hall appeared to demonstrate the 'age of equipoise' in the building of spaces for cross-class communication, self-help and voluntarism. However, if you dig a little deeper you can detect the limits to this view.

Exercise 12.10

Turn to Reading 12.7, 'Opening of the Woodhouse Temperance Hall and Mechanics' Institution (1851)', located at the end of the unit. This is an extract from a report in the *Leeds Mercury* on 4 January 1851.

What do you think these speeches by members of the local middle class say about class society in Leeds?

This should take around 20 minutes.

Specimen answer

The fact that notable members of the local middle class are keen to support the Mechanics Institution suggests that the social improvement of the working class is a key concern. Improvement of the working class required adopting the supposed habits and attitudes of the respectable middle class, such as self-reliance and temperance. However, the middle-class members appear to be thwarted in their attempts at reform because the majority of working-class men are not interested in these kinds of associations.

Discussion

Middle-class reformers provided outlets for **rational recreation** by building libraries, museums and educational institutes. 'Respectable' working-class people were implored to use these facilities to distinguish themselves from their 'rougher' counterparts. Henry Solly (1813–1903), a Nonconformist reformer and the founder of working men's clubs, appealed to the 'more prudent, worthier members of the working class' to attend his clubs as a way of distinguishing themselves from 'their reckless, drinking, cowardly, or dishonest neighbours' (quoted in Bailey, 1979, p. 338). The extent to which membership of self-help associations increased the 'respectability' of the working class is open to question. First, as Peter Bailey has argued in an influential article, members of the working class were able to play the role of respectable citizen when it suited them without fully adopting middle-class values (Bailey, 1979). Second, as historians such as Martin Hewitt and Peter Gurney have argued, the working class built its own institutions, which promoted its own versions of respectability, and its own forms of collectivised self-help, such as cooperatives, trade unions and friendly societies (Hewitt, 1996; Gurney, 1994).

The middle class often expressed the optimistic view that social improvement and social mobility would result from self-help fostered through voluntary associations. In the mid-century, through their experience of these associations, members of the middle class began to realise that this voluntarism was not enough to transform society. As you saw in the unit 'Work, poverty and the new Poor Law' (Unit 10) and as you will see in the unit 'Cities, disease and health' (Unit 13), experts and professionals acknowledged that improvement schemes could benefit from government intervention to coordinate provision and set standards for local authorities. The limits of voluntarism and the increasing support for state intervention were most obvious in education.

The need for working-class education was seen as essential to a viable class society, one that shared basic values and could guarantee a capable workforce. Kay-Shuttleworth made this argument in the 1830s. As you may have noticed in Reading 12.7, the Rev. George Conder (1821–1874) argued that real improvements in the working class were limited by 'want of early education'. In the mid-century, a belief in laissez-faire and strong suspicion about the role of the established church meant that there was little support for state education. Instead, a number of charities and agencies organised by the local middle class offered education to the masses. In the 1860s leaders of the voluntary movement in education admitted that they needed the state if they were to help extend education provision to the working class. In 1870 an Elementary Education Act was passed, creating school boards with the ability to raise rates to build schools. In 1880 another Elementary Education Act, known as Mundella's Act, made schooling compulsory for children up till the age of 10.

The need of middle-class people both to justify their own class position through ideas of self-help and to ensure a stable society into the future explains why a period that was so strongly associated with laissez-faire and voluntarism resulted in the expansion of the state. The middle class began to accept that, to ensure both needs were met, it would need state-supported social reform to work alongside the voluntary sector. Greater support for the role of government also demonstrates how the suspicion of the state that lay behind laissez-faire ideas began to evaporate as the middle-class view of the world was increasingly represented in Parliament and as the middle class took on roles in national political life.

Conclusion

The cultural, economic and political changes of the mid-nineteenth century are often presented as 'the rise of the middle class'. The transformation of urban space to reflect middle-class values and the emergence of organisations such as the Anti-Corn Law League support such a view. The middle class was diverse in occupation and outlook: some members worked and lived alongside the working class; others associated with members of the aristocracy and gentry. Nevertheless, most were involved in some sort of commercial activity, and even the growing numbers of professional men were used to selling their services. Most were involved in managing capital and property, using the family and extended networks to help secure middle-class status and privileges for the next generation.

The middle class was also diverse in its religious and political views. However, members were conscious of such differences and often took steps to build spaces that would help them find areas of shared interests and networks of support. They were also interested in building a viable class society through the promotion of self-help. Local space was designed to promote these values through the building of civic institutions and voluntary associations intended to encourage social reform through individual improvement in well-ordered civic space. However, as the mid-century progressed, the limits of this kind of activity to provide opportunities for improvement were exposed and increasing support was found for state intervention. This support coincided with the opening up of public life to Nonconformists and to the wider middle class through the reform of the civil service and the growth of state bureaucracy.

> Now turn to the module website to complete the independent study activities associated with this unit.

References

Aston, J. (2016) *Female Entrepreneurship in Nineteenth-century England*, London, Palgrave.

Bailey, P. (1979) '"Will the real Bill Banks please stand up?" Towards a role analysis of mid-Victorian working class respectability', *Journal of Social History*, vol. 12, no. 3, pp. 336–53.

Briggs, A. (1956) 'Middle-class consciousness in English politics, 1780–1846', *Past and Present*, no. 9, pp. 65–74.

Briggs, A. (1960) 'The language of "class" in early nineteenth century England', in Briggs, A. and Saville, J. (eds) *Essays in Labour History*, London, Macmillan, pp. 43–73.

Brooks, S. H. (1860) *Rudimentary Treatise on the Erection of Dwelling-houses*, London, John Weale.

Cobbe, F. P. (1869 [1868]) *Criminals, Idiots, Women, and Minors, Is the Classification Sound? A Discussion of the Laws Concerning the Property of Married Women*, Manchester, A. Ireland and Co.

Davidoff, L. and Hall, C. (2002 [1987]) *Family Fortunes: Men and Women of the English Middle Class, 1780–1850*, London, Routledge.

Ellis, S. S. (1839) *The Women of England, Their Social Duties, and Domestic Habits*, New York, D. Appleton & Co.

Gunn, S. (2000) *The Public Culture of the Victorian Middle Class: Ritual and Authority and the English Industrial City*, Manchester, Manchester University Press.

Gurney, P. (1994) 'The middle class embrace: language, representation and the contest over co-operative forms in Britain, 1860–1914', *Victorian Studies*, vol. 37, no. 2, pp. 253–86.

Hewitt, M. (1996) *The Emergence of Stability in the Industrial City*, Aldershot, Scolar.

Hill, K. (1999) '"Thoroughly embued with the spirit of ancient Greece": symbolism and space in Victorian civic culture', in Kidd, A. and Nicolls, D. (eds) *Gender, Civic Culture and Consumerism: Middle-class Identity in Britain, 1800–1940*, Manchester, Manchester University Press, pp. 99–111.

Hobsbawm, E. (1975) *The Age of Capital 1848 to 1875*, London, Weidenfeld & Nicolson.

Howe, A. (1984) *The Cotton Masters*, Oxford, Clarendon.

Joyce, P. (1980) *Work, Society and Politics: The Culture of the Factory in Later Victorian England*, Brighton, Harvester.

Kay-Shuttleworth, J. P. (1832) *The Moral and Physical Condition of the Working Classes Employed in the Cotton Manufacture in Manchester*, 2nd edn, London, James Ridgeway.

Koditschek, T. (1990) *Class Formation and Urban Industrial Society: Bradford, 1750–1850*, Cambridge, Cambridge University Press.

Leeds Mercury (1851) 'Opening of the Woodhouse Temperance Hall and Mechanics' Institution', 4 January.

Loftus, D. (2017) 'Time, history and the making of the industrial middle class: the story of Samuel Smith', *Social History*, vol. 42, no. 1, pp. 29–51.

MacLeod, C. (2007) *Heroes of Invention: Technology, Liberalism and British Identity, 1750–1914*, Cambridge, Cambridge University Press.

Marx, K. and Engels, F. (1969 [1848]) 'Manifesto of the Communist Party', *Marx/Engels Selected Works*, Vol. 1, Progress Publishers, Moscow.

Mill, J. S. (1834) 'On Miss Martineau's summary of political economy', in Fox, W. J. (ed.) *The Monthly Repository for 1834*, vol. 8, London, Charles Fox, pp. 318–22.

Morris, R. J. (1990a) *Class, Sect and Party: The Making of the British Middle Class, Leeds, 1820–1850*, Manchester, Manchester University Press.

Morris, R. J. (1990b) 'Occupational coding: principles and examples', *Historical Social Research/Historische Sozialforschung*, vol. 15, no. 1, pp. 3–29.

Morris, R. J. (2005) *Men, Women and Property in England, 1780–1870: A Social History of Family Strategies amongst the Leeds Middle Classes*, Cambridge, Cambridge University Press.

Nead, L. (2011) '"Many little harmless and interesting adventures": gender and the Victorian city', in Hewitt, M. (ed.) *The Victorian World*, London, Routledge, pp. 291–307.

Nenadic, S. (1991) 'Businessmen, the urban middle classes, and the "dominance" of manufacturers in nineteenth-century Britain', *Economic History Review*, vol. 44, no. 1, pp. 66–85.

Owens, A. (2001) 'Property, gender and the life course: inheritance and family welfare provision in early nineteenth-century England', *Social History*, vol. 26, no. 3, pp. 297–315.

Rubinstein, W. D. (1977) 'The Victorian middle classes: wealth, occupation and geography', *Economic History Review*, vol. 30, no. 4, pp. 602–23.

Samuel, R. (1977) 'Workshop of the world: steam power and hand technology in mid-Victorian Britain', *History Workshop*, no. 3 (Spring), pp. 6–72.

Smiles, S. (1968 [1859]) *Self-help*, London, Sphere Books.

Stedman Jones, G. (1983) *Languages of Class: Studies in English Working Class History 1832–1982*, Cambridge, Cambridge University Press.

Taylor, J. (2006) *Creating Capitalism: Joint-stock Enterprise in British Politics and Culture 1800 to 1870*, Woodbridge, Boydell and Brewer.

Taylor, M. (1995) *The Decline of British Radicalism, 1847–1860*, Oxford, Clarendon.

Thompson, E. P. (1963) *The Making of the English Working Class*, London, Penguin.

Tosh, J. (1999) *A Man's Place: Masculinity and the Middle-class Home in Victorian England*, New Haven, CT, Yale University Press.

Vernon, J. (2014) *Distant Strangers. How Britain Became Modern*, Berkeley, CA, University of California Press.

Wahrman, D. (1995) *Imagining the Middle Class: The Political Representation of Class in Britain 1780–1840*, Cambridge, Cambridge University Press.

Readings

Reading 12.1 John Stuart Mill, 'Class and political economy' (1834)

Source: Mill, J. S. (1834) 'On Miss Martineau's summary of political economy', in Fox, W. J. (ed.) *The Monthly Repository for 1834*, vol. 8, London, Charles Fox, p. 320.

They [political economists] revolve in their eternal circle of landlords, capitalists, and labourers, until they seem to think of the distinction of society into those three classes, as if it were one of God's ordinances, not man's, and as little under human control as the division of day and night. Scarcely any one of them seems to have proposed to himself as a subject of inquiry, what changes the relations of those classes to one another are likely to undergo in the progress of society; to what extent the distinction itself admits of being beneficially modified, and if it does not even, in a certain sense, tend gradually to disappear.

Reading 12.2 Karl Marx and Friedrich Engels, 'The Communist manifesto' (1848)

Source: Marx, K. and Engels, F. (1969 [1848]) 'Manifesto of the Communist Party', *Marx/Engels Selected Works*, Vol. 1, Progress Publishers, Moscow.

The history of all hitherto existing society is the history of class struggles.

…

Our epoch, the epoch of the bourgeoisie, possesses, however, this distinct feature: it has simplified the class antagonisms. Society as a whole is more and more splitting up into two great hostile camps, into two great classes directly facing each other – Bourgeoisie and Proletariat.

…

The bourgeoisie, wherever it has got the upper hand, has put an end to all feudal, patriarchal idyllic relations. It has pitilessly torn asunder the motley feudal ties that bound man to his 'natural superiors', and has left the remaining no other nexus between man and man than naked self-interest than callous 'cash payment'.

Reading 12.3 Samuel Smiles, 'Self-help' (1859)

Source: Smiles, S. (1968 [1859]) *Self-help*, London, Sphere Books, pp. 64–6.

Josiah Wedgwood was one of those indefatigable men who from time to time spring from the ranks of the common people, and by their energetic character not only practically educate the working population in habits of industry, but by the example of diligence and perseverance which they set before them, largely influence the public activity in all directions, and contribute in a great degree to form the national character. ...

[p. 65]

When he had completed his apprenticeship with his brother, Josiah joined the partnership with another workman, and carried on a small business in making knife-hafts, boxes, and sundry articles for domestic use. Another partnership followed ... but he made comparatively little progress until he began business on his own account at Burslcm in the year 1759. There he diligently pursued his calling ...

What he chiefly aimed at was to manufacture cream-coloured ware of a better quality than was then produced in Staffordshire as regarded shape, colour, glaze, and durability. To understand the subject thoroughly, he devoted his leisure to the study of chemistry; and he made numerous experiments on fluxes, glazes, and various sorts of clay. ...

Even when he had mastered his difficulties, and become a prosperous man ... he went forward perfecting his manufactures, until his example extending in all directions, the action of the entire district was stimulated, and a great branch of British industry was eventually established on firm foundations. ...

[p. 66]

He was an indefatigable supporter of all measures of public utility ... he planned and executed a turnpike-road through the Potteries, ten miles in length. The reputation he achieved was such that his works at Burslem, and subsequently those at Etruria, which he founded and built, became a point of attraction to distinguished visitors from all parts of Europe.

Reading 12.4 Sarah Stickney Ellis, 'The women of England' (1839)

Source: Ellis, S. S. (1839) *The Women of England, Their Social Duties, and Domestic Habits,* **New York, D. Appleton & Co., pp. 338–53.**

It may be said, that we dwell too much in cities, and lead too artificial a life, to be able to perceive the instrumentality of Divine Wisdom in all the events that pass beneath our observation. If this be the case, there is the more need that we should rouse ourselves by fresh efforts, to penetrate beyond the polished surface of the world in which we live, [p. 339] into the deeper mysteries that lie beyond – there is the more need that we should endeavour to perceive, in the practical affairs of busy life, those great principles by which the laws of nature are governed, and the system of the universe upheld.

…

It is a curious anomaly in the structure of modern society, that [p. 344] gentlemen may employ their hours of business in almost any degrading occupation, and, if they have but the means of supporting a respectable establishment at home, may be gentlemen still; while, if a [p. 345] lady does but touch any article, no matter how delicate, in the way of trade, she loses caste and ceases to be a lady.

I say this with all possible respect for those who have the good sense and the moral courage to employ themselves in the business of their fathers and their husbands, rather than to remain idle and dependent …

I have before remarked, that there is now, more than ever, a demand [p. 352] for the exercise of their [women's] highest powers, and their noblest energies, to counteract the effects of unremitting toil in obtaining the perishing things of this life. There is a greater demand than ever upon [p. 353] their capabilities of enhancing social and domestic happiness …

It may be said, that English women in the present day are, in this respect at least, superior to the generation before them. But granting that they are so, the necessity for further improvement remains the same, because the habits of men are progressively involving them more deeply in the interests of public life; so that unless some strenuous efforts are made on the part of women, the far-famed homes of England will lose their boasted happiness, and with their happiness, their value in the scale of their country's moral worth.

Reading 12.5 Frances Power Cobbe, 'Criminals, idiots, women, and minors' (1869 [1868])

Source: Cobbe, F. P. (1869 [1868]) *Criminals, Idiots, Women, and Minors, Is the Classification Sound? A Discussion of the Laws Concerning the Property of Married Women*, **Manchester, A. Ireland and Co., pp. 3–6, 23.**

'Ah', we can hear him say to his guide, as they pass into a village church, 'What a pretty sight is this! What is happening to that sweet young woman in white, who is giving her hand to the good-looking

[p. 4]

fellow beside her; all the company decked in holliday attire, and the joy-bells shaking the old tower overhead? She is receiving some great honour is she not? The Prize of Virtue, perhaps?' …

'… I notice her husband has just said, "With all my wordly goods I thee endow." Does that mean that she will henceforth have the control of his money altogether, or only that he takes her into partnership?'

'… By our law it is *her* goods and earnings, present and future, which belong to him from this moment.'

'You don't say so? But then, of course, his goods are hers also?'

'Oh dear, no! not at all. He is only bound to find her food; and, truth to tell, not very strictly or efficaciously bound to do that.'

…

'One question still further – your criminals? Do they always forfeit their entire property on conviction?'

'Only for the most heinous crimes; felony and murder, for example.'

[p. 5]

'Pardon me; I must seem to you so stupid! Why is the property of the woman who commits Murder, and the property of the woman who commits Matrimony, dealt with alike by your law?'

…

To a woman herself who is aware that she has never committed a crime; who fondly believes that she is not an idiot; and who is alas! only too sure she is no longer a minor, – there naturally appears some incongruity in placing her, for such important purposes, in an association wherein otherwise she would scarcely be likely to find herself. But the question for men to answer is: Ought Englishwomen of full age, in the present state of affairs, to be considered as having legally attained majority? or ought they permanently to be dealt with, for all civic and political purposes, as minors? This, we venture to think, is the real point at issue between the friends and opponents of 'women's rights,' and it would save, perhaps, not a little angry feeling and aimless discussion, were we to keep it well in view, and not allow [p. 6] ourselves to be drawn off into collateral debates about equality and abstract rights.

...

It is clear enough that we have come to one of those stages in human [p. 23] history which, like a youth's attainment of majority, makes some change in the arrangements of past time desirable, if not imperative. ... In Feudal times, also, the blended chivalry and tyranny of men towards women was rather to be admired, for the chivalry then condemned for a tyranny which probably fell more lightly on women than on any inferior class of men in the social scale. But all these things are changed for us. ... As the ages of force and violence have passed away, and as more and more room has been left for the growth of gentler powers, women (especially in England) have gradually and slowly risen to a higher place.

Reading 12.6 Samuel H. Brooks, 'Rudimentary treatise' (1860)

Source: Brooks, S. H. (1860) *Rudimentary Treatise on the Erection of Dwelling-houses*, **London, John Weale, pp. v–viii.**

There is such correspondence between outward forms and shows, and [p. vi] inner feelings and emotions, in all truthful matters, that it is far from an affair of indifference in what manner of form we transact our commerce, with what impress of form we endow our churches, or in what fashion of apartments we meet our friends and children.

...

We are a commercial people, and a common-sense trading race; he who can find a brotherhood in architecture with the great republics of mediaeval Italy, the commercial communities of Florence, Genoa, Sienna, will perceive nothing but a source for the highest gratulations.

[p. vii]

… We must develop and not conceal our nationality, in arts as in all things else. From the streets of our cities and manufacturing towns, our wealth and power proceed. Let these become the stepping-stones to our temples; as they must do, if our temples and our worship are to be sincere. It is not by forgetting, but remembering, our commercial street-life that we shall become a people great in wisdom as in wealth. …

[p. viii]

Let us then look upon those buildings and streets in their proper light, and build as if building for honourable men: to give our minds tone, let us discipline them to see in this shop-keeping what promise of greatness it encloses; and, recognising this nature of the times, perceive that it is in these very streets that the way is opened for us to commence our stone daguerreotype of the nineteenth century.

Reading 12.7 Opening of the Woodhouse Temperance Hall and Mechanics' Institution (1851)

Source: *Leeds Mercury* (1851) 'Opening of the Woodhouse Temperance Hall and Mechanics' Institution', 4 January.

The MAYOR, in opening the proceedings … [stated that] it afforded him the greatest pleasure to see so large and commodious a building erected for such important purposes in that locality, and he trusted that it would tend to their [the working classes] happiness, in the promotion of their knowledge, and the increase among them of all those virtues and habits of life which adorned the citizen, and made him a valuable member of society …

They must not rely on what others should do, but they were each called upon to do his or her own business, and the more they did this, carrying out fully the principles of self-reliance, and the nobler creatures they would make themselves. …

Dr. SMILES was received with loud cheers on rising. … The bulk of Mechanics' Institutions were composed of the best educated and most respectable members of the middle classes, and comparatively few mechanics belonged to them. But here was a genuine working-men's institution, started, worked, and in a great measure supported by themselves – (hear) – and to their spirit of self-help and self-reliance was its great success mainly to be attributed.

...

The Rev. G. W. CONDER, of Belgrave chapel Leeds, next addressed the meeting ... It was very justly observed by some speakers at the late soirée of the Leeds Institute, that many of them were not really so, but that their members were found chiefly amongst the middle classes. He believed this was but too true. ...thus it was in great part the fault of the working classes themselves; and that a great many of them not only had no taste or desire for such advantages, but had tastes and desires of so opposite a character, that a positive effort would be needed to bring them into connection with these institutes. Not that sin and low animalism were confined to any class, there being cock-fighting and drinking lords, as well as tinkers and tailors, but among the other (the middle and upper) classes influences had been at work which had diminished the number of such grievous degradations of our nature in a much greater ratio than among the working classes. Into the reason of this fact he would not then enter, whilst he fully believed that one cause had been the want of early education ... He believed that the redemption of the working classes must be achieved by themselves; the wealthy might help with subscriptions, but the workers must keep the machine going ...

Unit 13 Cities, disease and health

Deborah Brunton

Contents

Aims

This unit will:

- explore some of the problems associated with rapid urban growth, especially the prevalence of disease

- help you to understand the different roles of local and central government, and some of the factors shaping public health policy and practice

- use a variety of nineteenth-century records to analyse concerns about disease and public health practice.

Introduction

Cities loomed large in the Victorian consciousness. This reflected high levels of urban growth: for much of the nineteenth century, huge numbers of people were moving away from the countryside. As a result, existing cities were becoming larger and towns were transformed into cities. Contemporary views of the city exemplified the tensions that underlay the 'age of equipoise'. On the one hand, cities were seen in a positive light: they were associated with modernity, economic growth, new industry, new technology and new lifestyles. On the other, they were full of negative connotations: unfamiliar, dirty and possibly dangerous. The air of cities was filled with smoke and the streets and watercourses with industrial and domestic wastes. They were crowded with people and animals, and full of noise. They were places of disorder; of crime, poverty, prostitution and unrest. They were also very unhealthy: life expectancy (the number of years on average that a person can expect to live) was less than 30 years in rapidly growing cities in the late 1830s – around ten years less than the national average.

Bringing order to the city was one of the great Victorian projects. Over the second half of the century, urban environments were improved by better street lighting, paving and drainage, the clearance of slums and the building of new streets. New facilities such as libraries, parks, shops and theatres were created. Urban crime was brought under control by new police forces, and industries and trades were subjected to greater regulation by local government.

This unit will explore these programmes of civic improvement by looking at one major strand – the efforts to control disease. This too was fraught with tensions: while there was general agreement that cities should become healthier, there were conflicts over how to achieve this goal. Section 13.1 will explore Victorian attitudes to cities, both positive and negative. Sections 13.2 and 13.3 will examine the debates around what role central government was to play in the process of disease control. Section 13.4 will analyse the role of local authorities in this. While local government supported the drive for improvements, there were often long debates about how best to proceed. For historians too, Victorian public health has generated debates, and Sections 13.5 and 13.6 will explore judgements on the contribution of central and local government to public health and on the impact of reforms on levels of disease. As you will see, although there were great improvements in the health of cities from the mid-nineteenth century, this is no simple history of progress.

13.1 The Victorian city – prosperity, danger, disease

Urbanisation – the movement of people from the countryside into towns, usually in pursuit of work – was not a new phenomenon in the nineteenth century. Towns and cities, especially London, had grown substantially in the seventeenth and eighteenth centuries. However, as you discovered in the unit 'The Industrial Revolution' (Unit 2 in Block 1), the rate of growth, and the number of towns that grew into major centres, accelerated in the nineteenth century. London was by far the largest city in Britain. It had just under a million inhabitants in 1801; by 1861 this had more than trebled to over 3 million. However, rapid growth in other centres, especially in the 1820s and 1830s, meant that there were a number of cities with around half a million inhabitants by the end of the century. The population of Glasgow was approximately 77,000 in 1801, but had more than quadrupled to 400,000 by 1861. Manchester was slightly larger in 1801, with around 100,000 people, and by 1861 the number had grown to over 350,000. Some smaller towns grew even more rapidly; the fastest-growing towns were seaside resorts. Ports and county towns, which acted as centres for administration, and legal and commercial activities, also expanded at this time.

It is often stated that Britain moved from being a predominantly rural to an urban society in the mid-nineteenth century, with the majority of the population living in towns and cities from 1851 onwards. This is true – but only if a 'town' can have as few as 2,500 inhabitants, a population that would now be regarded as that of a large village. It might be more accurate to say that Britain was urbanised by 1871, when over 50 per cent of the population lived in towns of over 10,000 people (Gunn, 2004). Of course, many more people visited towns and cities and so experienced something of city life.

The growth in the urban population was the result of an influx of migrants. Most came from the surrounding countryside but, as you discovered in the unit 'Ireland and the Famine' (Unit 9), from the late 1840s many cities had a significant population of Irish people, driven out of their homeland by the impact of the Famine. Whatever their origins, most of these new urban dwellers were young: nineteenth-century cities were full of young adults and children. They were attracted to towns and cities by new forms of employment. As you read in Unit 2, urbanisation was often linked to industrialisation, as new factory-based industries created a demand for labour. Many of the rapidly growing cities were the bases for particular industries – Manchester grew on the back of textile manufacture and Sheffield was a centre for metal and cutlery production. However, a mixture of industries was more common: Glasgow, for example, had a mix of heavy industries including shipbuilding and chemical production. Industrial production was not confined to cities; many towns had a few small factories or mills.

Cities of delight

Nineteenth-century cities were places of opportunity. Their industries fuelled economic growth – the pall of smoke generated by steam engines was, ironically, a sign of prosperity – and the sheer scale of commerce was a cause of wonder. In 1844 the political philosopher Friedrich Engels wrote:

> This colossal centralisation ... has raised London to the commercial capital of the world, created the giant docks and assembled the thousand vessels that continually cover the Thames. I know nothing more imposing than the view which the Thames offers during the ascent from the sea to London Bridge. The masses of buildings, the wharves on both sides ... the countless ships along both shores, crowding ever closer and closer together, until, at last, only a narrow passage remains in the middle of the river, a passage through which hundreds of steamers shoot by one another; all this is so vast, so impressive, that a man cannot collect himself, but is lost in the marvel of England's greatness.

(Engels, 1968 [1844], p. 23)

From the middle of the century, cities were associated with modernity – in the city you could find new styles in dress and in buildings, and new spaces for culture. They were centres for new technologies. Factories powered by steam contained the most up-to-date machinery, producing an ever-wider range of goods (the best of which were displayed in the Great Exhibition). Cities were hubs for transport, with railways allowing travel to the rest of the country. Their streets displayed other new technologies. From the 1850s, the occasional street lamps gave way to the gas lighting of whole streets, allowing pedestrians to walk around after dark. Gas lighting and plate glass were also used to illuminate displays in shop windows.

The wealth and influence of cities were displayed in civic building. From the late 1850s, there was a boom in the building of grand town halls in the latest architectural styles (such as the one in Leeds depicted in Figure 13.1), epitomising the pride and wealth of the town. The equally grand offices of private firms were intended to illustrate economic and industrial progress. Libraries, concert halls and exhibitions offered the chance for residents to improve their minds, while theatres, musical halls and gentlemen's clubs provided venues for relaxation from the stresses of business.

Figure 13.1 Unknown artist, 'Arrival of Her Majesty at the Town Hall, Leeds', 1858, engraving, from *Illustrated Times*, 18 September 1858. Photo: © Look and Learn/Illustrated Papers Collection / Bridgeman Images. Major civic events such as this – the opening of Leeds Town Hall by Queen Victoria – were occasions for towns and cities to display their wealth and pride in their community.

Not everyone approved of the new cityscapes. A gazetteer – a guide for travellers – published in the early 1870s defended Liverpool's new buildings against such criticism.

Fault has been found with the ornamental architecture of Liverpool, that it is too pretentious, too grandiose, too destitute of a blending of utility with ornament; but this is simply a matter of taste; and what one man, in respect to it, regards as a blemish, another regards as an excellence. ... Even the merchants' offices, as well as the buildings of a less or more public kind – for example, the elegant and lofty piles of offices along both sides of Fenwick-street, and three great groups side-by-side, erected in 1865–6, at the corner of Tithebarn street – vie with one another, and compare victoriously with the best buildings of the same class anywhere in the world, in at once variety, ornature [*sic*], and splendour.

(Wilson, 1870–2)

While the grand buildings of the city were often for the exclusive use of middle- and upper-class residents, all classes used the streets as venues for entertainment: as well as the attractions of window shopping and simply strolling, there were street musicians and entertainers. For working-class families, streets were spaces for their children to play and venues for commerce – food and small goods were sold from barrows and carts.

Cities of danger

Gazetteers emphasised the grandeur of the city in their guides, but many middle-class commentators found a darker side there. It was a place of conflict and disorder: strange, unstable, and even dangerous. The fears of the city were expressed in descriptions of urban poverty in newspapers and pamphlets, intended to shock and inform their middle-class readership. They began to associate the city with 'slums', overcrowded and squalid places in the city where the poor converged (see Figure 13.2).

Exercise 13.1

Turn to Reading 13.1, 'A Medical Gentleman, "Low life in Victorian Edinburgh", Extract 1 (1850)' and Reading 13.2, 'George Bell, "Blackfriar's Wynd analysed" (1850)', located at the end of the unit. These are extracts taken from writings on slums in Edinburgh in 1850. Very similar descriptions of other cities were published around the same time. 'A Medical Gentleman' was an anonymous medical practitioner.

After you have read the extracts, answer the following questions:

- How are slum dwellers presented in these extracts?
- What is their relationship to the middle classes?

This should take around 20 minutes.

Specimen answer

- In these extracts, the slum dwellers are depicted as people to be pitied by their social betters. They are ignorant, short of food and addicted to alcohol, live in dirty and dilapidated houses, are uneducated and have no knowledge of religion. They are forced to beg or steal – although the 'cinder woman' makes money by selling paper and the prostitutes work by selling sex.

- The poor are presented as very different from the middle classes: in some ways they are not even human. The extracts portray the poor behaving like animals, or living in the sort of conditions that animals would experience. The poor are criminals, with the wealthier classes their victims, and are therefore to be feared. The middle classes know little of the poor or their lives and yet they live in close proximity to them.

Discussion

The life of the poorest was believed to make them different from the respectable residents of the city. Living in slum conditions blunted the physical senses – the poor could no longer detect the terrible smell of filthy conditions and preferred the darkness of unlit, broken-down housing to the light and air of respectable dwellings. This sort of life also damaged their moral sensibilities – slum dwellers lost their sense of respectability and any desire to find honest work and therefore turned to crime as a way of life (Hamlin, 1998). The prostitutes, thieves, drunkards and beggars were therefore a product of the slum and the city. In the minds of middle-class commentators they formed a separate class of people. Jelinger Symons (1809–1860), a barrister with an interest in crime and its remedies, declared in 1849:

> Every country has its dangerous class. It consists not only of criminals, paupers and persons whose conduct is obnoxious to the interests of society, but of that proximate body of people who are within reach of its contagion, and continually swell its number. The magnitude of the dangerous class in England

probably exceeds that of any European nation, and is largely increasing.

(Quoted in Philips, 2003)

CARDINAL BEATON'S HOUSE, COWGATE.

Figure 13.2 Unknown photographer, *Cardinal Beaton's House, Cowgate*, 1868, 10 x 8cm. © Edinburgh City Libraries. Licensor www.scran.ac.uk. This palatial sixteenth-century house had become part of a slum area in Edinburgh by the middle of the nineteenth century, with families or groups of people sleeping in each room. It was photographed in the 1860s as part of a project to record the city's picturesque ancient buildings before they were demolished in a slum-clearance initiative.

The middle and upper classes feared slum dwellers as criminals, and slums as a source of disease, as graphically described by Charles Dickens in *Bleak House* (1852–3):

> But [the fictional London slum called Tom-all-alone's] has his revenge. Even the winds are his messengers, and they serve him in these hours of darkness. There is not a drop of Tom's corrupted blood but propagates infection and contagion somewhere. It shall pollute, this very night, the choice stream (in which chemists on analysis would find the genuine nobility) of a Norman house, and his Grace shall not be able to say Nay to the infamous alliance. There is not an atom of Tom's slime, not a cubic inch of any pestilential gas in which he lives, not one obscenity or degradation about him, not an ignorance, not a wickedness, not a brutality of his committing, but shall work its retribution, through every order of society, up to the proudest of the proud, and to the highest of the high. Verily, what with tainting, plundering, and spoiling, Tom has his revenge.
>
> (Dickens, 1998 [1852–3], pp. 654, 657)

Although slums were associated with dirt, disease and disorder, these problems were not confined to those parts of the Victorian city. The sheer number of people living close together was believed to create an unnatural, unhealthy environment. The dense urban population generated filth: commentators complained of heaps of domestic refuse dumped in the streets or on vacant pieces of ground, of overflowing cesspools and privies, of the soot in the air and of the industrial effluent that polluted waterways and harbours. The streets were repositories for (literally) tons of manure, deposited by the hundreds of horses engaged in transporting people and goods. While slums were associated with old, dilapidated houses (see Figure 13.3), even new homes were overcrowded. The expanding populations were crammed into densely packed rows of back-to-back housing (which still characterise cities in northern England) or the tenements found in Scotland. Even urban graveyards overflowed, with bodies buried in shallow graves on top of older burials.

Victorian cities were often portrayed as sick bodies. A healthy body was one where the blood ran freely through the vessels that linked together the organs, ensuring that they functioned properly. Ill health was associated with stagnation. In the overcrowded dwellings of the

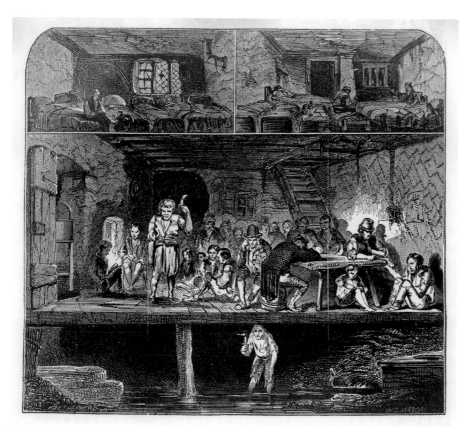

Figure 13.3 'Lodging houses in Field Lane', from Gavin, H. (1848) *Sanitary Ramblings: Being Sketches and Illustrations of Bethnal Green*, London, Churchill. Wellcome Library, London. Copyrighted work available under Creative Commons Attribution only licence CC BY 4.0 http://creativecommons.org/licenses/by/4.0/. This illustration – showing an imaginary cross-section of a lodging house – gives a good impression of the number of people who crammed into houses in slum areas. It also suggests that the natural water courses that served as sewers ran directly under the floorboards of houses.

city and in the cramped, narrow streets, the air became stagnant, full of the impurities thrown off by residents, by smoke and other pollutants. City rivers and streams became choked with filth. Even the traffic in the streets stagnated. *The Illustrated London News* of 1846 complained:

> the streets of London are choked by their ordinary traffic, and the life blood of the huge giant is compelled to run through veins and arteries that have never expanded since the days and dimensions of its infancy. What wonder is it that the circulation is an unhealthy one? That the quantity carried to each part of the frame is insufficient for the demands of its bulk and strength, that

there is dangerous pressure in the main channels and morbid disturbance of the current, in all causing daily stoppages of the vital functions …

(Quoted in Winter, 1993, p. 6)

While cities were metaphorically sick, urban residents were literally ill. From the 1820s, residents of cities regularly experienced **epidemics** of 'fever' (which would now be diagnosed as typhus or typhoid), smallpox, measles and other infectious diseases. In addition, there were high levels of **endemic** disease – illnesses present all the time within the population – such as tuberculosis and bronchitis. These diseases were familiar, but in 1831–32 the United Kingdom suffered its first visitation of Asiatic cholera. Cholera was endemic in India, but from the early nineteenth century the disease spread across Europe and America in a series of **pandemics**, reaching Britain in 1831, 1848, 1853 and 1866. Cholera was unfamiliar and terrifying: the onset was sudden – people could wake up well and be dead by nightfall – and it caused violent symptoms including acute vomiting, diarrhoea and muscle spasms. Doctors were helpless; none of their remedies alleviated or cured cholera.

Exercise 13.2

While all urban residents suffered from diseases, the poor suffered most. Turn to Reading 13.3, 'Henry Mayhew, "Description of Jacob's Island, London" (1849)' and Reading 13.4, 'A Medical Gentleman, "Low life in Victorian Edinburgh", Extract 2 (1850)', located at the end of the unit. These are extracts from the writings of a journalist and the anonymous medical practitioner whom you encountered in Exercise 13.1, respectively.

What do the authors suggest is the cause of illness in slums?

This should take around 15 minutes.

Specimen answer

Both authors link disease to filth, and especially to the air. In Reading 13.3 Mayhew graphically describes the filthy conditions and how these give off gases that poison the residents, producing a variety of symptoms as well as generally undermining their health. Reading 13.4

suggests that filth and lack of ventilation – so, a lack of fresh air –
produce fever.

The theory that dirt and disease were closely linked was widely held in
the first half of the nineteenth century. Most medical practitioners
believed that some diseases, including fever and cholera, were
generated or spread in filthy conditions. Rotting organic matter – such
as urban refuse – produced 'miasma' or bad air, which, in turn,
produced illnesses in those exposed to the air. However, other diseases,
such as smallpox, were thought to be contagious – they spread directly
from person to person through some unknown agent. There was
considerable debate about disease causation. A very few commentators
(most famously Florence Nightingale) were convinced that all disease
arose from filth, but most medical practitioners recognised a spectrum
of causation, with some diseases spread through infection and others
generated by the environment. There was also considerable debate
about what role was played by factors such as exposure to cold and
poor diet in making some people more susceptible to disease while
others remained healthy (Worboys, 2000).

13.2 Taking action against disease

Disease in cities was not a new phenomenon: in the seventeenth century, Londoners suffered from a severe outbreak of the plague or Black Death; in the eighteenth century, there were regular epidemics of smallpox. In the early nineteenth century, local government and charities began to take action to tackle outbreaks of fever. While charities organised temporary hospitals to care for the sick and distributed food and clothing, local government bodies cleaned up the urban environment, targeting the organic wastes that were believed to generate the miasma responsible for the disease. When Asiatic cholera threatened in 1831, the government set up a Board of Health to oversee local actions. It advised that local boards should be established in all towns and cities, which should organise efforts to remove accumulations of filth, record all cholera cases and provide free care to the poor in their own homes or in hospitals (Wohl, 1983). These efforts were temporary: when cholera disappeared, the local and central boards of health were disbanded and the facilities to deal with cholera were dismantled.

Medical care in Victorian Britain

In the mid-nineteenth century, medical care was provided by family members, general practitioners and physicians. Access to care depended on the ability to pay; the wealthy could afford to consult more than one practitioner and buy expensive medicines. The poor had to rely on self-prescribed over-the-counter remedies, although a fortunate few gained admission to charity hospitals and dispensaries. There, they received good-quality care from skilled practitioners but often had to serve as teaching material for medical students.

In the 1840s, concerns over high levels of disease and mortality in cities forced Parliament to consider the problem afresh. In the summer of 1848, Parliament passed the Public Health Act for England and Wales, creating the General Board of Health, the first government agency responsible for health issues, and giving local authorities a range of powers aimed at reducing levels of disease within their area. This was a major new initiative and raises the question of why the state agreed to take on this new responsibility, especially because, as you know from the unit 'The "age of equipoise" and the Great Exhibition of 1851' (Unit 8), the government was keen to promote a culture of self-help, voluntarism and minimal interference. In the past, historians pointed to the arrival of cholera as the trigger for action. Whereas outbreaks of fever affected communities on a regular basis, cholera was strange and frightening and it swept over large parts of the country causing many deaths – around 32,000 people died in the 1831–32 outbreak. (There was a second cholera outbreak in 1848–49 but it came after the Public Health Act – the bill was first presented to Parliament in February 1848 and the first death from cholera was recorded in September.) So cholera was a disease that demanded a greater response than other epidemics. A second theory is that the Public Health Act was a response to rising and increasingly intolerable levels of dirt in cities, which in turn caused disease.

Exercise 13.3

Which explanation for the inspiration behind the Public Health Act of 1848 do you find most convincing – cholera or 'intolerable dirt'? Jot down the reasons for your response.

This should take around 10 minutes.

Specimen answer

It is hard to see that a cholera outbreak in 1831–32 could have been a major driver for legislation passed in 1848 as there was such a long gap between the two events. The fear caused by cholera might have reinforced later demands for the government to act to control disease, but it is hard to believe that it was the main factor behind the legislation.

Concern about levels of dirt seems to be a more convincing argument, although it does prompt questions over when the levels of dirt became intolerable and who thought they were intolerable. The writings on slums that you read earlier show that at least some middle-class writers were shocked by filthy living conditions in towns – but how was this disgust translated into political action?

Discussion

We need to be cautious about making assumptions about levels of dirt in cities. We know that in the mid-nineteenth century middle-class people complained about dirt in cities. But we simply cannot tell to what extent cities were actually becoming dirtier, because there is no way of measuring this. We do know that, around this time, attitudes to dirt among the middle and upper classes were changing, and their concerns may therefore have reflected a new sensitivity to filth and bad smells.

In the mid-nineteenth century cleanliness was pursued much more vigorously than it had been previously. Middle-class householders waged an ever more intense battle to keep their homes clean. Elaborate carpets, furnishings and curtains had to be regularly swept, shaken, beaten, dusted or washed. Upper- and middle-class people washed their bodies more regularly than previous generations, in bathrooms kitted out with ever more elaborate baths and using greater quantities of soap. It is no coincidence that in 1830 the novelist Edwin Bulwer-Lytton (1803–1873) coined the phrase 'the great unwashed' to characterise the poor.

Sanitary Report on the Condition of the Labouring Population of Great Britain

It is now generally agreed that the catalyst for the Public Health Act of 1848 was the publication of the *Sanitary Report on the Condition of the Labouring Population of Great Britain* in 1842. The report was formally the work of the Poor Law Commissioners, though much of the work was done by their secretary, Edwin Chadwick. Chadwick, whom you encountered in the units 'Managing uncertainty: new forms of "knowledge"' (Unit 4 in Block 1) and 'Work, poverty and the new Poor Law' (Unit 10), was one of a number of Victorian reformers who have been described as 'moral entrepreneurs'. They sought to identify and analyse problems and thus created roles for themselves within government to mobilise reforms (Philips, 2003). As you will see, the way they defined problems helped to define their solutions. From 1839, Chadwick sent out queries about living and working conditions and levels of disease to Poor Law officials and medical practitioners across Britain. These reports were the basis for his analysis of conditions inside and outside the homes of working people and the attempts that had been made to improve sanitation by local authorities.

Exercise 13.4

Read the account below of the insanitary conditions found in public spaces and homes in Liverpool which was reproduced as part of the *Sanitary Report*. Then answer the following questions:

- What aspects of the urban environment does it identify as the source of disease?

- How does it compare to the accounts of slums you read earlier?

This should take around 10 minutes.

> [W]ith regard to the streets inhabited by the working classes, I believe that the great majority are without sewers, and that where they do exist they are of a very imperfect kind unless where the ground has a natural inclination, therefore the surface water and fluid refuse of every kind stagnate in the street, and add, especially in hot weather, their pestilential influence to that of the more solid filth … With regard to the courts, I doubt whether there is a single court in Liverpool which communicates with the street by an underground drain, the only means afforded for carrying off the fluid dirt being a narrow, open, shallow gutter, which sometimes exists, but even this is very generally choked up with stagnant filth.
>
> There can be no doubt that the emanations from this pestilential surface, in connexion with other causes, are a frequent source of fever among the inhabitants of these undrained localities. … In consequence of finding that not less than 63 cases of fever had occurred in one year in Union-court Banastre-street, (containing 12 houses,) I visited the court in order to ascertain, if possible, their origin, and I found the whole court inundated with fluid filth which had oozed through the walls from two adjoining ash-pits or cess-pools, and which had no means of escape in consequence of the court being below the level of the street, and having no drain. … I was informed by one of the inhabitants that the fever was constantly occurring there. The house nearest the ash-pit had been untenanted for nearly three years in consequence of the filthy matter oozing up through the floor, and the occupiers of the adjoining houses were unable to take their meals without previously closing the doors and windows.

(Flinn, 1965, p. 104)

Specimen answer

- The account focuses on the inadequate provision of drains and sewers in residential areas. As a result, filth and mud are present in and around homes, contaminated with material from the ash pits and cesspools where household waste and human excrement were stored. This makes the homes very unpleasant to live in and is the cause of fever.

- The account is similar in many ways to the accounts of slum dwelling written for a general audience. The language and descriptions are designed to shock – material is 'oozing' into homes; the stench is so great that people can't bear to eat. However, the account is very focused on the physical conditions and gives little sense of the people who lived there.

At the end of the *Sanitary Report*, Chadwick drew a simple conclusion:

> [t]he various forms of epidemic, endemic, and other disease caused, or aggravated, or propagated chiefly amongst the labouring classes by atmospheric impurities [are] produced by decomposing animal and vegetable substances, by damp and filth, and close and overcrowded dwellings prevail[ing] amongst the population in every part of the kingdom …

(Flinn, 1965, p. 422)

As such, he was able set out the actions need to solve the problem:

> The primary and most important measures, and at the same time the most practicable, and within the recognized province of public administration, are drainage, the removal of all refuse of habitations, streets, and roads, and the improvement of the supplies of water.

(Flinn, 1965, p. 423)

In the past, the *Sanitary Report* has been seen as a milestone in social reform, revealing to the middle classes the shocking living conditions suffered by the poor, presenting an objective analysis of the impact of these conditions on health, and proposing a rational and practical solution. According to the historian David Roberts, Chadwick's 'energy meant devastating and unanswerable reports upon which immediate action had to be taken' (quoted in Hamlin, 1998, p. 156).

Since the late 1990s, historians have taken a more critical view of Chadwick and his work. In 1998, Christopher Hamlin published a major study of the *Sanitary Report*, arguing that Chadwick's approach to the issue was informed by his role as secretary to the Poor Law Commissioners, who, as you know from Unit 10, were responsible for administering the new Poor Law. By the early 1840s, there was a good deal of concern about the costs of the Poor Law, including the amount spent on treating sick paupers. Poor Law medical officers often prescribed food and fuel, as well as medicines, for the sick poor. This ran directly counter to the fundamental principle of the Poor Law – that a bare minimum of relief should be offered in order to discourage applications for assistance.

In the *Sanitary Report*, Chadwick sought to prove that there was no point in giving food, fuel or clothing to the sick poor: that would not help them to recover from or avoid disease as this was the consequence of environmental conditions. As Chadwick declared in the report, 'high prosperity in respect to employment and wages, and various and abundant food, have afforded the labouring classes no exemptions from attacks of epidemic disease, which have been as frequent and as fatal in periods of commercial and manufacturing prosperity as in any others' (Flinn, 1965, p. 422). Preventing disease was therefore, in Chadwick's view, not the job of the Poor Law – it should be the responsibility of dedicated central and local government agencies (Hamlin, 1998).

The *Sanitary Report* was not intended to be an objective argument about how best to deal with insanitary conditions; rather, it was meant to prove the assumption that insanitary conditions were the primary cause of ill health among the general population. The evidence presented in the report was sent in response to requests for information on the diseases associated with defective living accommodation. Thus it was not surprising that the evidence collected confirmed a connection between dirt and disease. Chadwick made no effort to test his assumption by exploring the role of other factors –

contagion, poverty, inadequate diet, or exposure to cold – that might have made some groups more likely to become ill.

Activity 13.1

Now go to the module website and complete Activity 13.1 'Mortality from the filth diseases'. This should take around an hour.

13.3 Central government: public health policy

Accepting that there was a problem with high levels of disease and mortality within the population, especially those living in cities, was only the first step. The next issue was how to reduce levels of illness. This involved medical challenges – to devise strategies that were both effective and practical in reducing levels of disease – but also political challenges. At the start of the century, government was reluctant to take on responsibility for the health of the population in any permanent way. In the 1810s, bills to control smallpox had been thrown out, with MPs arguing that this was simply not a legitimate role for government (Brunton, 2008). By the second quarter of the nineteenth century, opinion had shifted sufficiently for Parliament to set up a temporary agency to oversee local responses to the first epidemic of cholera and, in 1840, to pass legislation offering free vaccination against smallpox to all children in England and Wales.

However, action to deal with health across the whole population was a more significant step. In the 1840s, a number of bills inspired by the *Sanitary Report* were rejected by Parliament and it was not until 1848 that a bill was finally passed. In the debates on the various bills in the 1840s, MPs generally accepted that the state should act as a guarantor of health, but there were fundamental divisions about the administration of public health reforms (see Figure 13.4). What role should existing local authorities take? Should they give up some of their existing powers to new local boards of health? What powers should be given to a new central government agency?

As a result, the Public Health Act of 1848 was a relatively limited piece of legislation. It broke new ground by creating the first permanent government agency dedicated to public health, the General Board of Health (GBH). But, like many government departments created at this time, it was very small: Chadwick was appointed as one of its three commissioners and the GBH also employed a few inspectors who reported on local sanitary conditions. The GBH also had limited powers. The 1848 Act was permissive, rather than mandatory, granting powers only to those local authorities who wanted to make sanitary improvements. Only in towns with unusually high mortality could the GBH force the authorities to undertake sanitary reform, and in practice these powers were rarely used.

SANATORY MEASURES.

Lord Morpeth Throwing Pearls before ———— Aldermen.

Figure 13.4 Unknown artist, 'Sanatory measures: Lord Morpeth throwing pearls before — Aldermen', 1848, cartoon from *Punch*. Photo: Chronicle / Alamy. This cartoon sums up the tensions between a wise central government, anxious to improve health, and local government members (with the arms of the city of London) presented as pigs, happy to continue wallowing in dirt.

The failure of sanitary reform

The work of the GBH was informed by Chadwick's interpretation of sanitary problems. In their reports, the agency's inspectors echoed his views on the dangers of filth and argued for the coordinated installation of improved water supplies and sewage systems. Old large brick sewers and open ditches, which had been constructed to carry off rainwater, should be replaced with high-pressure, small-diameter sewers that would carry away all filth, thus doing away with the need for cesspools to store wastes. As well as installing sewers, local authorities had to ensure that there was a plentiful water supply to shift refuse through the pipes. Building this infrastructure was a major undertaking, but tackling the problem in a piecemeal fashion, by attaching new sewers to existing drains, was strongly discouraged by the GBH inspectors for fear that it would create more problems. Only once the GBH had approved of plans to lay new sewers and bring in water supplies was the local authority allowed to raise a loan to pay for the works (Hamlin, 1998).

The General Board of Health may have been groundbreaking in political terms, but it failed to make much of an impact on insanitary conditions. The agency proved deeply unpopular with many of the groups who might have supported its work: with the medical profession (who had been excluded from its operations), with engineers (who disagreed with Chadwick's insistence on the use of particular types of sewers) and with many local government bodies. Between 1848 and 1853, only 103 local communities attempted to adopt Chadwick's water and drainage schemes. The GBH also ran into serious political problems. There was a perception that it was corrupt. According to an editorial in *The Times* newspaper:

> The inspectors, surveyors, and other officers of the General Board enjoy an obvious advantage in their communications with the Board itself. They are placed in judgment at the very outset upon the local authorities; they can report against all existing usages or original suggestions; they can frame their own proposals in accordance with opinions which they know to prevail at the Board; and if, therefore, they are permitted to compete … for the pending contracts, they clearly possess a superiority of position against which any independent rival might contend in vain.
>
> (*The Times*, 21 May 1853)

In addition, despite its very limited powers to enforce sanitary improvements, the agency was perceived to be despotic and overly powerful. As one newspaper put it: 'A little dirt and freedom may after all be more desirable than no dirt at all and slavery' (quoted in Porter, 1999, p. 120). This led to the end of the first General Board of Health: in 1854, in an effort to protect public health reforms and restore confidence, the original staff were dismissed and replaced. Nevertheless, the agency remained unpopular and in 1858 it was dissolved.

The GBH was both a product and a victim of contradictory views on the role of mid-nineteenth-century government. On the one hand, the mid-century was an age of laissez-faire government – there was a widespread desire to limit the role of central government, and especially to avoid any interference with market forces. Instead, successive governments sought to allow individuals maximum freedom to pursue their own interests. Yet at the same time, the governments of this period can be seen as radical and interventionist, pursuing a range of social reforms in response to specific problems, including Factory Acts to limit the working hours of women and children, Police Acts to deal with crime and disorder, and legislation on education. Victorian governments acknowledged that they had a responsibility to care for the weakest members of society – the poor – who were unable to help themselves, and needed to act in areas where the public good could not be guaranteed by private action, such as public health and the provision of policing. These conflicting pressures – to protect the weak but not to interfere with markets – meant that, in practice, social reforms were often very limited. In fact, public expenditure actually fell in the 1860s and 1870s before increasing again as governments launched a new wave of reforms.

The General Board of Health was reformed not because it had too much power but because the uncompromising attitudes of Edwin Chadwick, his dictatorial style of leadership and the manner in which the agency operated gave the impression that it was overly interventionist.

The success of public health

In many ways, the first General Board of Health represented a false start in public health policy. The departments that took over responsibility for health after 1854 – the GBH with a wholly new staff (1854–58), the Medical Office of the Privy Council, or MOPC (1859–71) and eventually the Local Government Board, or LGB (1871–1919) – were largely staffed by medical practitioners with an expert knowledge of public health matters. Until 1876, they were all led by Dr John Simon (1816–1904), who, like Chadwick, exerted strong leadership over the work of his departments. Simon's views on the causes of disease were much more in line with those of the majority of medical practitioners. Like Chadwick, he was concerned with the effects of poor sanitation. In his first annual report to the MOPC, he claimed that many deaths were the result of an 'absence of proper drainage and scavenging [street cleaning], impurity of water supply, over-crowded, ill-ventilated, uncleansed dwellings' (Simon, 1859, p. 27), but there were other causes of poor health:

unwholesome conditions, connected … with the pursuit of certain branches of industry; – neglect of children, incidentally (but not unavoidably) arising from the employment of mothers in factories; – omission or mal-performance of vaccination: – these few heads indicate our chief sanitary evils, and their average annual fatality may safely be reckoned at more than 100,000 deaths.

(Simon, 1859, p. 27)

Simon's views shifted over time in line with prevailing medical theory. By the 1860s and 1870s, the air was no longer seen as the main source of disease; instead, some sort of biological agent (often referred to as 'germs') or chemicals were believed to be the means of spreading infection, either through direct contact with an infected person or through contaminated food and water (Worboys, 2000). The bacteria and viruses now known to be responsible for disease were not identified until after 1880.

Simon oversaw the gradual expansion of public health policy. His staff of inspectors conducted research into a huge array of issues, including the causes of outbreaks of disease, the health problems associated with specific occupations, nutrition, diphtheria, the state of the River Thames and the quality of housing. This research, coupled with statistics on mortality provided through the Registrar-General's office (another product of the mid-century reforms, responsible for collecting and analysing data on births, marriages and deaths), was used to inform the drafting of new legislation. Under Simon, a succession of Acts gave local authorities powers to tackle disease through a range of strategies. Perhaps the most significant was the Sanitary Act of 1866, which allowed authorities to compel property owners to install drainage, to deal with overcrowded houses, to improve conditions in lodging houses and to act against smoke pollution. To help local authorities to control infectious disease, the Act included powers to disinfect homes and to remove patients to fever hospitals.

As well as expanding the scope of public health practice, legislation in the 1860s gradually changed the relationship between central and local government. Whereas early Public Health Acts were permissive – empowering local authorities to act if they so wished – later Acts compelled them to act. For example, local authorities were able to appoint a Medical Officer of Health (MOH) from the 1840s; under the Public Health Act of 1872 they were required to do so (Wohl, 1983).

The expansion of public health interventions was evident in Simon's summary of the work of government, written in 1868:

[p. 21]

> It would, I think, be difficult to over-estimate, ... the progress which during the last few years has been made in sanitary legislation. ... It is the almost completely expressed intention of our law that all such states of property and all such modes of personal action or inaction as may be of danger to the public health should be brought within scope [*sic*] of summary procedure and prevention. Large powers have been given to local authorities, and obligation expressly imposed on them ... to suppress all kinds of nuisance, and to provide all such works and establishments as the public health primarily requires; while auxiliary powers have been given ... in matters deemed of less than primary importance to health; as for baths and wash-houses, common lodging-houses, labourers' lodging-houses, recreation grounds, disinfection-places, hospitals, dead-houses, burial-grounds, &c. And in the interests of health the State has ... limited the freedom of persons and property in certain common respects.
>
> (Simon, 1868–9, pp. 20–1)

By seeking to win the support of local authorities, Simon succeeded where Chadwick had failed. His inspectors sought to educate and persuade rather than enforce the law in a heavy-handed manner. Such an approach was a feature of many Victorian inspectorates. In part, it was a necessity as they lacked the staff or the powers to mount large numbers of legal actions against local authorities who failed to live up to their responsibilities; in part, it was felt that education was a more effective way of obtaining compliance than coercion. Simon and his colleagues also benefited from changing attitudes: by the 1860s, there was far greater public support for government actions to protect the health of the people.

While the scope of public health reforms steadily expanded during the third quarter of the century, Simon and his colleagues were not exempt from the pressures for limited government. For many years, Simon had to fight against persistent efforts to limit the budget of his departments. He skilfully built up his staff of inspectors by employing them initially on short-term contracts and then persuading the Treasury to fund full-time posts. However, the expansion of public health reforms slowed significantly after 1871, when the Medical Office of the Privy Council was merged into the Local Government Board. This reflected a wider change in the mode of government, as influential individuals such as Simon were replaced by career civil servants. The LGB's leaders sought to limit the role of medical advisors and to end the research work. Frustrated by this new direction and by ever tighter financial control, Simon resigned in 1876. His successors were forced to focus on routine work, unable to pursue new initiatives (MacLeod, 1967).

Exercise 13.5

Look back over Section 13.3 and write a short paragraph summarising the main features of the early history of public health in central government.

This should take around 15 minutes.

Specimen answer

I hope that you noted that the early history of public health was not a story of smooth and inevitable progress. The growing acceptance that the state should act to protect the health of the population was countered by a desire to control the amount of government intervention and the amount of money spent on public health. The history is also one of shifting policy – from Chadwick's narrow schemes of sanitary reforms, through improved water and sewerage, to Simon's much broader programme of action to prevent disease.

13.4 Local government: public health in practice

Setting policy in central government was one thing, but its implementation rested with local government. The agencies responsible for actually carrying out public health reforms were a range of local bodies including parish authorities, boards of health and town councils. Until relatively recently, the work of local government received little attention from historians, who tended to accept Chadwick's critical narrative of a progressive central government frustrated by lazy and incompetent local authorities (see Figure 13.5). Simon also complained of the lack of action by local bodies:

> [When] we turn from contemplating the intentions of the Legislature to consider the degree in which they are realized, the contrast is curiously great. Not only have permissive enactments remained for the most part unapplied in places where their application has been desirable: not only have various optional constructions and organizations which would have conduced to physical well-being … remained in an immense majority of cases unbegun; but even nuisances which the law imperatively declares intolerable have, on an enormous scale, been suffered to continue …

> (Simon, 1868–9, p. 21)

We should treat such statements with some caution. A picture of local government incompetence was, perhaps unwittingly, promoted by government inspectors who were sent to report on towns with health problems, and not to those where sanitary matters were better administered. We also need to remember that it was in the interests of both Chadwick and Simon to portray local action as ineffective in order to justify giving greater powers to central government. Studies of public health reform at the local level that have been carried out from the late 1980s onwards have shown that, in towns and cities across Britain, local government agencies were active in improving many aspects of the urban environment well before the passing of the 1848 Act, and that these older forms of sanitary improvement continued for the rest of the century.

THE CITY NARCISSUS;
Or, The Alderman Enamoured of his Dirty Appearance.

Figure 13.5 Unknown artist, 'The city Narcissus; or, the alderman enamoured of his dirty appearance', 1849, cartoon from *Punch*. Photo: Chronicle / Alamy. This cartoon presents local government – in this case in London – as vain (the figure is admiring its reflection in the filthy water) and showing no concern for the lives of citizens. However, London faced particular problems in implementing public health reforms as a very complex, multi-layered administration had grown up in the huge city. London often had its own public health legislation to deal with this problem.

Sanitary reform

The importance of traditional sanitary measures is demonstrated by the work of inspectors of nuisances. These posts had a long history – they were originally created in medieval times – although far greater numbers of inspectors were appointed under the Nuisance Removal Acts from 1846 onwards. A 'nuisance' was anything that caused offence or discomfort; in the early nineteenth century, that could include disorderly behaviour or obstructing the pavement. As the century wore on, nuisances were increasingly associated with accumulations of dirt that offended the nose and eyes of townspeople and were believed to pose a threat to health. Inspectors of nuisances patrolled towns looking out for accumulated filth, inspected workplaces likely to create nuisances, such as slaughterhouses, and followed up complaints by the public (Hamlin, 2013).

Similarly, street cleaning was established well before the 1840s. In the eighteenth century, urban refuse was periodically gathered up from the streets and carted away, though sometimes only as far as the edge of cities. Over the nineteenth century, beginning in large cities and filtering down to villages, local authorities organised ever more regular and systematic street cleaning. Men with brooms, barrows and buckets swept up the filth from the streets. Domestic refuse was thrown into the dust carts as they passed on their regular rounds. In cities such as Edinburgh and Glasgow, the streets were cleaned every weekday and twice on Saturdays (the second refuse collection allowing workers to rest on the Sabbath); in small villages, streets were cleaned weekly. While very low-tech, this system removed huge amounts of rubbish. Around 40,000 tons of refuse were lifted every year from the streets of Edinburgh in the 1840s and 1850s. As well as making streets more pleasant and healthier, cleaning had an important economic benefit: the collected refuse was sold as agricultural fertiliser. Sales of 'town manures' brought in substantial sums until the late nineteenth century. Scottish towns could expect to earn between £1,000 and £2,000 each year, while large cities raised over £10,000 per annum, a level of income that offset a considerable part of the costs of street cleaning (Brunton, 2015).

These long-established sanitary practices – removing dirt from streets and dealing with particularly filthy spots – continued to form part of the backbone of disease control throughout the nineteenth century. In addition to the regular cleaning, extra efforts were made to clean up cities during epidemics. In the first half of the century, local authorities attempted to reduce mortality and bring to an end outbreaks of fever and cholera by intensifying existing sanitary measures. When threatened by an epidemic, street cleaners and nuisance inspectors made special efforts to remove accumulations of dirt, streets were washed down and drains were flushed and disinfected.

Historians of public health have focused much of their research on the creation of new sewers and water supplies, which were the most complex and expensive sanitary projects. However, local authorities carried out many small, cheaper and piecemeal improvements. For example, public lavatories and urinals were added to the urban environment a few at a time. They allowed pedestrians to relieve themselves in private rather than in quiet corners of the public streets. Bath and wash houses were built in poor neighbourhoods (where working-class housing had no bathrooms or even hot water) to give residents the opportunity to bathe and to launder clothes and bedding for a small fee.

From 1848, new public health legislation gave local authorities ever greater powers to take action against disease, funded through local rates or by borrowing from central government at low rates of interest. As you read in the quote from Simon at the start of this section, having legislation did not necessarily guarantee sanitary improvement. But why did the passage of new laws not result in sanitary improvements?

Activity 13.2

Now go to the module website and complete Activity 13.2 'Implementing sanitary improvements in British towns'. This should take around an hour.

At the local level, the spur to undertake action was always a specific problem – a serious outbreak of disease, or complaints from residents about insanitary areas or lack of water. Perhaps the most famous example of this is the 'Great Stink' of 1858 in London, when a combination of hot weather and the heavily polluted River Thames produced such bad smells that MPs were forced from the Houses of Parliament. Plans were promptly drawn up for the construction of a system of huge new sewers (Figures 13.6 and 13.7).

MAIN DRAINAGE OF THE METROPOLIS.—SECTIONAL VIEW OF THE TUNNELS FROM WICK LANE, NEAR OLD FORD, BOW, LOOKING WESTWARD.

Figure 13.6 Unknown artist, *Main Drainage of the Metropolis – Sectional View of the Tunnels from Wick Lane, near Old Ford, Bow, Looking Westward*, wood engraving, 18 x 24cm. Wellcome Library. Copyrighted work available under Creative Commons Attribution only licence CC BY 4.0 http:// creativecommons.org/licenses/by/4.0/. This engraving vividly conveys the scale and complexity of the task of building new sewer systems.

In practice, central government agencies did not drive public health reforms for much of the century. New legislation did not result in local authorities rushing to take on new projects. Even visits from government inspectors – usually in response to serious sanitary problems – did not guarantee results. Rather, legislation and advice from central government established a benchmark for good sanitary practice and set standards to which local authorities could aspire. Only in the last decades of the century, with the increasing passage of legislation compelling local authorities to adopt sanitary improvement, did central government begin to drive action on public health.

Figure 13.7 Crossness pumping station, Thamesmead, London. Photo: Eric Nathan / Alamy. The elaborately decorated pumping station at Crossness, opened in 1865 as part of London's sewer system, conveys the pride taken in sanitary engineering. Its infrastructure could be beautiful as well as functional.

Public health reform in Scotland also relied on initiatives from local, rather than central, government. Sanitary legislation passed for England and Wales did not apply in Scotland. Instead, reforms were carried out under Police Acts. ('Police' here referred to a wide range of civic improvements, not just law enforcement.) Under this legislation, Scottish towns and cities conducted an array of public health reforms very similar to those in English and Welsh communities. In a spirit of (literally) healthy competition, authorities in one city copied and improved on sanitary projects in another, in an effort to demonstrate that their community was more progressive and healthier than their neighbours'. A national Public Health Act was not passed in Scotland until 1867, when supervision of public health reform was added to the responsibilities of the central Poor Law agency – the Board of Supervision for the Relief of the Poor (Brunton, 2011).

From the public to the private

From the middle of the century, local public health practice was increasingly organised by Medical Officers of Health (MOsH). The first medical officer in England was appointed in Liverpool in 1847; the first Scottish MOsH were appointed in Edinburgh and Glasgow in 1862 and 1863. Early holders of these posts were medically qualified and usually had some interest in public health. From the 1870s, the post gradually became professionalised, with MOsH expected to hold a diploma in public health in addition to their medical qualification. Medical officers acted as local experts, overseeing public health initiatives and advising local authorities.

In cities, the local MOsH headed small departments that included sanitary inspectors and inspectors of nuisances. In their annual reports they analysed the diseases prevalent in their local communities and suggested actions to reduce mortality. Medical officers were responsible for sanitary matters – checking that streets were cleaned to an appropriate standard and ensuring that cowsheds and pigsties were kept reasonably clean (large numbers of animals were kept even in large cities). Although public health is usually associated with public facilities (such as water and sewerage) and public spaces (such as the streets), MOsH spent a good deal of their time monitoring the condition of private space inside houses. Their power to enter and examine homes is an indicator of the increasing acceptance of interventionist public health policies. They and their staff were responsible for enforcing regulations that specified that all houses were provided with water, drains, sinks and lavatories. MOsH and their staff not only inspected poor-quality housing but, by the 1870s, visited the homes of middle-class and respectable working-class residents to ensure that the new flushing lavatories had been correctly installed (Wohl, 1983).

Activity 13.3

Now go to the module website and complete Activity 13.3 'Medical Officer of Health reports'. This should take around an hour.

By the 1870s, medical officers were also intervening in private space in new ways – removing people suffering from infectious diseases to fever hospitals and disinfecting their furniture and belongings. This new strategy came out of a shift in medical theory. Instead of seeing disease as generated or transmitted through miasma, infections were now understood to be passed through specific agents – or 'germs' –

given off from the bodies of the sick. As a consequence, diseases could be contained not by a general clean-up of the environment (although such efforts did continue), but by ensuring infected people did not come into contact with others, and that all objects that had come into contact with patients were destroyed or disinfected. Middle- and upper-class families were expected to isolate patients in separate bedrooms in the home. Such care was impossible in the cramped houses of the poor, and from the 1870s local authorities set up fever hospitals, where patients suffering from smallpox, scarlet fever, diphtheria and other diseases were cared for in strict isolation (Mooney, 2015).

13.5 The public response to public health

It is hard to tell exactly what urban residents thought of public health reform: while individuals were happy to write to their local authority or a local newspaper and complain of specific problems, they rarely assessed the efforts made to improve public health. We can get some picture of the reaction to health reforms from the behaviour of urban residents, and this suggests a mixed reaction to sanitary reforms. New domestic refuse services provided by local authorities as part of more intensive street cleaning proved popular, with residents generally complying with the rules on where and when to deposit their rubbish. Similarly, when local authorities provided public lavatories and urinals, some proved so popular that long queues built up.

We might expect that sanitary reforms that required residents to make some special effort would have been met with greater resistance. However, local records suggest that urban dwellers generally seemed willing to cooperate, and not because they feared being brought before the courts and punished if they failed to act. Although local authorities had the power to prosecute offenders responsible for causing nuisances or ignoring sanitary regulations, they rarely took residents to court. Instead, inspectors took a pragmatic, even conciliatory, stance and sought to persuade offenders to comply (Crook, 2007). For example, when faced with complaints about pig keeping – a common urban activity, since pigs ate all sorts of scraps and refuse – owners were often asked to reduce the number of pigs, or move them further away from neighbouring houses, but not to get rid of them altogether.

Other sanitary reforms were something of a mixed blessing. Middle-class householders increasingly installed flushing lavatories in their homes from the middle of the century, embracing a technology that quickly and hygienically removed excrement from the home. But lavatories created a new domestic terror – sewer gas. It was widely believed that, in blocked drains, the rotting deposits generated gases and smells that seeped back into the home, causing disease. As homes were now connected to one another via drains, it was thought possible that blockages caused by filth originating from a neighbour's house, or even from poorer homes some streets away, might spread infections into respectable households (Figure 13.8). Householders were warned to be constantly vigilant, installing proper traps to ensure that gas could not enter homes and checking for possible leaks in their plumbing by dropping aromatic substances such as peppermint oil into their lavatories and checking where the smell could be detected (Allen, 2002).

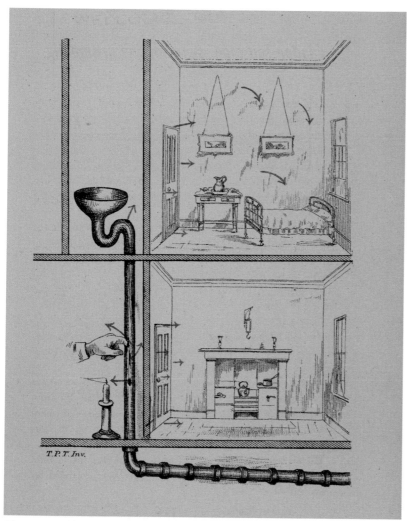

Figure 13.8 Illustration of the dangers of sewer gas in the home, from *Dangers to Health: A Pictorial Guide to Domestic Sanitary Defects,* 1878, London, J. & A. Churchill. Wellcome Library, London. Copyrighted work available under Creative Commons Attribution only licence CC BY 4.0 http:// creativecommons.org/licenses/by/4.0/. This diagram shows how gas, originating well outside the home, was believed to travel back to endanger sleeping residents.

But some public health reforms were deeply unpopular. When local authorities tried to establish temporary hospitals for fever or cholera patients, they ran into opposition from local residents, who feared that the hospital would concentrate the infection in one space, from where it would spread into surrounding homes. Similarly, a public lavatory might provide a welcome solution to the waste created by people defecating and urinating on the streets but, to any resident unfortunate enough to live close to the facility, it simply concentrated dirt and smells in one space. Such objections by residents often persuaded local authorities to rethink their plans and to find an alternative site for hospitals and public lavatories.

13.6. The impact of public health reform

How effective were these efforts to improve sanitary conditions and reduce mortality in cities? Records of deaths show that life expectancy declined sharply in cities in the 1820s and 1830s. From a figure of around 39 years in the 1800s, life expectancy fell to just 29 years in some rapidly growing cities in the 1830s and as low as 27 years in Glasgow, with the old centres of towns the most unhealthy areas. Rural areas and smaller towns with a slower rate of growth were generally healthier. Life expectancy rose very slowly or not at all through the 1840s and 1850s, then began to climb from the 1860s. By the 1870s, it had reached 38 years in provincial cities, but in Liverpool and Manchester average life expectancy was still around 34 years (Szreter and Mooney, 1998).

The deleterious impact of urban life on health can also be seen in the height of adults brought up in cities. The height of adults reflects their living conditions in childhood – if children receive a poor diet and suffer from repeated illnesses, then they grow less than their better-nourished and healthier contemporaries. Data from army and navy recruits suggests that average height increased in the late eighteenth century but then declined for those born between 1820 and 1840, especially among children born in large cities. The improvement in life expectancy is mirrored by data from the study of heights: on average, adults born after the 1850s were taller than the previous generation (Floud et al., 1990).

But were the taller, longer-lived urban residents a product of efforts to clean the streets, improve standards of housing and isolate fever patients? Or were other factors at play? Even with the comprehensive data collected by Victorian observers, these are difficult questions to answer. Until the 1970s, it was generally assumed by historians that the improved life expectancy and decline in mortality of the late nineteenth century was the product of sanitary reforms. Then this assumption was challenged by Thomas McKeown as part of a wider critique of modern medicine. In *The Modern Rise of Population*, McKeown identified the diseases that displayed significantly reduced mortality and categorised them according to their mode of transmission. He argued that the greatest decline in mortality was associated with respiratory disease, especially tuberculosis. Sanitary reforms could have had little effect on levels of this disease, so McKeown concluded that efforts to clean up

yyy

cities might have had a limited impact, but that the overall decline in mortality must have been the result of improved standards of living, which gave the population the ability to resist tuberculosis infection (McKeown, 1976).

McKeown's thesis was widely accepted until 1988, when it was severely criticised by Simon Szreter, who drew a different interpretation from the mortality data. Szreter challenged McKeown's focus on tuberculosis, pointing out that while there was a reduction in deaths from that disease, at the same time there was a significant increase in mortality from other respiratory diseases such as bronchitis and pneumonia. This undermined McKeown's argument about the impact of improved standards of living – if living standards were rising, there should have been a decline in deaths from all respiratory diseases, not just tuberculosis. Szreter pointed out that, in addition to a decline in deaths from tuberculosis, there was also reduced mortality from cholera, typhoid, smallpox and convulsions (which are associated with severe diarrhoea) in the late nineteenth century. These illnesses are transmitted through contaminated food and water, and their decline coincided with the widespread adoption of sanitary reforms. Szreter concluded that sanitary reforms had started to have some effect on levels of mortality as early as the 1860s, and had a greater impact as the century progressed (Szreter, 1988).

Exercise 13.6

Table 13.1 shows the number of deaths in England in 1880 from a selection of causes – it is the same selection that you analysed in Activity 13.1, although there was no data for 'old age' available in 1842.

Examine the table and pick out the five commonest causes of death. Then look back to your notes from Activity 13.1 and answer the following questions:

- How has this list changed since 1842?

- Does this support McKeown's or Szreter's argument?

This should take around 15 minutes.

Table 13.1 Causes of death in England, 1880

	Number of deaths in England	% of all deaths
All specified causes	525,916	100.0
Smallpox	648	0.1
Measles	12,328	2.3
Scarlatina	17,404	3.3
Whooping cough	13,662	2.6
Diarrhoea	29,519	5.6
Hydrocephalus	8,514	1.6
Convulsions	23,593	4.4
Typhus*	8,794	1.7
Apoplexy	14,287	2.7
Paralysis	11,904	2.3
Heart disease	33,218	6.3
Dropsy	3,192	0.6
Carcinoma	13,278	2.5
Pneumonia	25,166	4.8
Bronchitis	57,939	11.0
Phthisis	48,201	9.2
Childbirth	1,833	0.3
Old age	25,523	4.8

*In the original table, typhus is divided into typhus, typhoid and simple continued fever.

Source: Taken from the Forty-third Annual Report of the Registrar-General of births, deaths and marriages in England, *House of Commons Parliamentary Papers*, 1882, vol. XIX, pp. lxviii–lxxiii

Specimen answer

- The five main causes of death are: bronchitis, phthisis (tuberculosis), heart disease, diarrhoea and old age. Compared with 1842, phthisis remains an important cause of death but the other main killers – convulsions, pneumonia, typhus and scarlatina – are all less significant in 1880.

• The tables back up McKeown's argument about the importance of tuberculosis in changing mortality: the proportion of deaths from phthisis has dropped from over 17 per cent to over 9 per cent. However, the tables also confirm Szreter's point about the rising death toll from other respiratory diseases such as bronchitis, and show a significant decline in deaths from typhus and convulsions.

Discussion

The tables of mortality for 1842 and 1880 do not capture deaths from Asiatic cholera, which was absent from Britain in 1842 and had disappeared by 1880. They do reveal the continuing high mortality from diseases of infants; the death rate among infants remained high until the twentieth century.

Like many historical debates, the argument over whether declining mortality was due to public health measures or rising living standards has not been resolved. Data on wages and living standards suggests that the wages of men were rising from the 1800s, while those of women and children rose more slowly and their employment declined. However, it is not clear if additional household income was spent on more nourishing food. Research published since Szreter's article appeared in 1988 confirms that local authorities were putting considerable effort into controlling disease after 1850. Overall, it seems likely that both factors played some part in reducing mortality in the nineteenth century.

Recently, a number of historians have argued that public health reform was not just about cleaning up the urban environment but also about encouraging residents to change patterns of behaviour, turning them into responsible citizens who kept themselves and their homes clean and healthy. Providing wash houses meant that the poor had facilities to clean their bodies and clothing, and users were taught to behave in a decorous fashion. Male and female bathers were strictly segregated, cubicles enforced privacy, and attendants controlled the amount of water supplied and the time spent in the bath: bathing was about the serious business of getting clean, not about leisurely enjoyment (Crook, 2006). Similarly, public lavatories were partly a measure to stop residents leaving urine and facces in public spaces but they were also about teaching a new code of behaviours: that these activities should occur only in private spaces. Urinals were designed so that passers-by could not see inside and be shocked by the sight of exposed genitalia. This explains why the first conveniences were all for men – women were able to relieve themselves more discreetly thanks to their long skirts (Brunton, 2005). Even street cleaning was thought to educate the public: if residents lived on streets that were regularly cleaned, then they would be encouraged to follow this good example and make greater efforts to keep their homes clean. Ironically, the only residents thought to be immune to such influences were those living in the filthiest areas: slum dwellers, with their scnscs and moral sensibilities blunted by the conditions in which they lived, were beyond education and could not be expected to make appropriate use of public conveniences, sinks and other sanitary facilities.

Conclusion

The history of public health reform is not a straightforward story of progress. A programme of action to control and prevent disease in the urban environment was clearly desirable – but achieving that goal was fraught with tensions. By the 1840s, it was accepted by parliament that central government should set public health policy, but many questions remained. What level of intervention in the local implementation of that policy was appropriate and when did it become 'despotic' and high-handed? How much money should government invest in its new public health agencies, or would it be better to leave responsibility to local government?

The officials on local authorities also wrestled with difficult questions. Should they undertake major infrastructure projects to deal with insanitary conditions, or put up with old drainage systems? Should they build fever hospitals or public urinals to benefit the community, even if they upset particular groups of residents? While everyone (literally, everyone) had an interest in the progress of public health, many parties – MPs, civil servants, local administrators, some residents – also had good reasons for calling for caution, for progressing slowly. This tension shaped Victorian public health.

These types of issues were not confined to public health reforms. Similar tensions informed new legislation to reform education and Acts to improve conditions in factories – both were the subjects of very limited initial legislation, which gradually expanded over time. In welfare reform, the first central government agency, the Poor Law Commission, suffered a similar fate to the General Board of Health. As you know from Unit 10, it was disbanded in 1847 for being too interventionist (it was no coincidence that Chadwick was one of its secretaries) and replaced by the Poor Law Board. At the local level, at the same time that city authorities were taking on responsibility for health, they were also becoming responsible for the provision of policing and education, and would later take on responsibility for supplying gas, water and local transport. The growth of a specialist administration to organise public health practice was mirrored in the creation of posts for other experts such as borough surveyors, who oversaw the demolition of slums and the building of new streets.

In all these areas, the same questions arose again and again – how best to achieve the desired reforms; how much central government was too much; was it best to give local authorities more freedom to act? In many ways, these questions from the 'age of equipoise' are still at the heart of British political life.

Now turn to the module website to complete the independent study activities associated with this unit.

References

Allen, M. (2002) 'From cesspool to sewer: sanitary reform and the rhetoric of resistance, 1848–1880', *Victorian Literature and Culture*, vol. 30, no. 2, pp. 383–402.

Anon. (1980 [1850]) *Low Life in Victorian Edinburgh By a Medical Gentleman*, Edinburgh, Paul Harris Publishing, pp. 7–8, 35–6.

Bell, G. (1850) *Blackfriar's Wynd Analysed*, Edinburgh, Johnstone and Hunter.

Brunton, D. (2005) 'Evil necessaries and abominable erections: public conveniences and private interests in the Scottish city, 1830–1870', *Social History of Medicine*, vol. 18, no. 2, pp. 187–202.

Brunton, D. (2008) *The Politics of Vaccination: Practice and Policy in England, Wales, Ireland and Scotland, 1800–1874*, Rochester, NY, Rochester University Press.

Brunton, D. (2011) 'Health, comfort and convenience: the work of the Scottish Police Commissioners, 1800–1870', *Scottish Archives*, vol. 17, pp. 85–96.

Brunton, D. (2015) 'Regulating filth: cleansing in Scottish towns and cities, 1840–1880', *Urban History*, vol. 42, no. 3, pp. 424–39.

Crook, T. (2006) '"Schools for the moral training of the people": public baths, liberalism and the promotion of cleanliness in Victorian Britain', *European Review of History: Revue européenne d'histoire,* vol. 13, no. 1, pp. 21–47.

Crook, T. (2007) 'Sanitary inspection and the public sphere in late Victorian and Edwardian Britain: a case-study in liberal governance', *Social History*, vol. 32, no. 4, pp. 369–93.

Dickens, C. (1998 [1852–3]) *Bleak House*, Oxford, Oxford University Press.

Engels, F. (1968 [1844]) *The Condition of the Working Class in England in 1844*, Edinburgh, Neill & Co.

Flinn, M. W. (ed.) (1965) *Report on the Sanitary Condition of the Labouring Population of Great Britain,* Edinburgh, Edinburgh University Press.

Floud, R., Wachter, K. and Gregory, A. (1990) *Height, Health and History: Nutritional Status in the United Kingdom, 1750–1980*, Cambridge, Cambridge University Press.

Gunn, S. (2004) 'Urbanization', in Williams, C. (ed.) *A Companion to Nineteenth Century Britain, 1815–1900,* Maldon, MA and Oxford [Online]. Available at Blackwell Online Reference (Accessed 24 January 2017).

Hamlin, C. (1998) *Public Health and Social Justice in the Age of Chadwick: Britain 1800–1854*, Cambridge, Cambridge University Press.

Hamlin, C. (2013) 'Nuisances and community in mid-Victorian England: the attractions of inspection', *Social History*, vol. 38, no. 3, pp. 346–79.

McKeown, T. (1976) *The Modern Rise of Population*, London, Edward Arnold.

MacLeod, R. M. (1967) 'The frustration of state medicine 1880–1899', *Medical History*, vol. 11, no. 1, pp. 15–40.

Mayhew, H. (1849) 'A visit to the cholera districts of Bermondsey', *Morning Chronicle*, 24 September.

Mooney, G. (2015) *Intrusive Interventions: Public Health, Domestic Space, and Infectious Disease Surveillance in England, 1840–1914*, Rochester, NY, University of Rochester Press.

Philips, D. (2003) 'Three "moral entrepreneurs" and the creation of a "criminal class" in England, c. 1790s–1840s', *Crime, History and Societies*, vol. 7, no. 1, pp. 79–107 [Online]. Available at https://chs.revues.org/612 (Accessed 21 April 2017).

Porter, D. (1999) *Health, Civilization and the State: A History of Public Health from Ancient to Modern Times*, London, Routledge.

Simon, J. (1859) 'First Report of the Medical Officer of the Privy Council', *House of Commons Parliamentary Papers,* 1859 (I), no. 2512.

Simon, J. (1868–9) 'Eleventh Report of the Medical Officer of the Privy Council', *House of Commons Parliamentary Papers,* 1868–69, no. 4127.

Szreter, S. (1988) 'The importance of social intervention in Britain's mortality decline c.1850–1914: a re-interpretation of the role of public health', *Social History of Medicine*, vol. 1, no. 1, pp. 1–38.

Szreter, S. and Mooney, G. (1998) 'Urbanization, mortality, and the standard of living debate: new estimates of the expectation of life at birth in nineteenth-century British cities', *Economic History Review*, vol. 51, no. 1, pp. 84–112.

Wilson, J. M. (1870–2) *Imperial Gazetteer of England and Wales* [Online]. Available at http://www.visionofbritain.org.uk/descriptions/2121510 (Accessed 13 September 2016).

Winter, J. (1993) *London's Teeming Streets 1830–1914*, London, Routledge.

Wohl, A. (1983) *Endangered Lives: Public Health in Victorian Britain*, London, J. M. Dent & Sons.

Worboys, M. (2000) *Spreading Germs: Disease Theories and Medical Practice in Britain, 1865–1900*, Cambridge: Cambridge University Press.

Readings

Reading 13.1 A Medical Gentleman, 'Low life in Victorian Edinburgh', Extract 1 (1850)

Source: Anon. (1980 [1850]) *Low Life in Victorian Edinburgh By a Medical Gentleman*, **Edinburgh, Paul Harris Publishing, pp. 7–8, 35–6.**

[p. 8]

The wealthy see but little of these outcasts, who shun the light of the sun, burrowing themselves in their dark and noisome dens during the day, and emerging when night has spread around a gloom as dark as their own fate, and as black as their thoughts and deeds. Of their existence there can, however, be no doubt. At our very doors, crawling about our streets, lanes, and closes, to beg or steal, we have a population of thousands whose ignorance is only equalled by their utter destitution, – a population who know nothing of God or of religion, and who are not possessed of the commonest rudiments of education, to remove the gross darkness which envelops them like a cloud, which cuts them off from all association with their better-taught and better-fed fellowmen, and which almost necessitates that they should beg or steal, or else not live; which obscures their perceptions to a level with those of the beasts; till they sink from poverty and misery and crime into the grave ... And yet, from this scene of misery, cross but a single valley, pass along but one bridge, and enjoyment, recreation, and pleasure, refinement, pomp, and wealth everywhere surround you.

...

[p. 35]

In Toddrick's Wynd, and indeed in most of the wynds and closes of the High Street, great numbers of prostitutes are to be met with ...

[p. 36]

And in these very closes have robberies over and over again occurred by the girl leading her poor dupe into some dark corner, where her fancyman and his companions were lying in wait, who rushing out and seizing their victim by the throat, before he can raise any alarm, soon strip him of everything valuable, and then make hastily off before he can recover his senses. In this way, a few years ago, was an English traveller robbed of nearly £900, and, although a number of noted thieves were sent to prison, no clue sufficiently strong to convict was got against any of them.

Reading 13.2 George Bell, 'Blackfriar's Wynd analysed' (1850)

Source: Bell, G. (1850) *Blackfriar's Wynd Analysed*, **Edinburgh, Johnstone and Hunter.**

The next chamber is inhabited by a cinder-woman. She was a member of a respectable family; but she eloped with a sweetheart, who deserted her. She subsequently married a shopkeeper in Edinburgh. Her husband died, and she immediately took to drinking. As her business left her she drank the harder: her furniture was pawned, and then her clothes – her all was converted into whisky. She ... ultimately settled in the wretched abode which she at present inhabits. What an abode! it is hardly six feet square, has no fireplace, and is lighted by a small skylight. The floor is full of holes, and the walls are creviced; and altogether it is such a place as an owl might inhabit for the sake of the mice and other prey which have a domiciliary interest in the tenement. There is not a stick of furniture in this chamber ... we found [the cinder-woman] engaged in arranging a quantity of papers of all shapes, sizes, colours, &c. She had gathered them off the streets in the morning, and was preparing to sell them to the fish-venders.

Reading 13.3 Henry Mayhew, 'Description of Jacob's Island, London' (1849)

Source: Mayhew, H. (1849) 'A visit to the cholera districts of Bermondsey', *Morning Chronicle***, 24 September.**

On entering the precincts of the pest island, the air has literally the smell of a graveyard, and a feeling of nausea and heaviness comes over any one unaccustomed to imbibe the musty atmosphere. It is not only the nose, but the stomach, that tells how heavily the air is loaded with sulphuretted hydrogen [hydrogen sulphide – a poisonous gas smelling of rotten eggs]; and as soon as you cross one of the crazy and rotting bridges over the reeking ditch, you know ... that the air is thickly charged with this deadly gas. The heavy bubbles which now and then rise up in the water show you whence at least a portion of the mephitic [foul-smelling] compound comes, while the open doorless privies that hang over the water side on one of the banks, and the dark streaks of filth down the walls where the drains from each house discharge themselves into the ditch on the opposite side, tell you how the pollution of the ditch is supplied.

...

The inhabitants themselves show in their faces the poisonous influence of the mephitic air they breathe. Either their skins are white, like parchment, telling of the impaired digestion, the languid circulation, and the coldness of the skin peculiar to persons suffering from chronic poisoning, or else their cheeks are flushed hectically, and their eyes are glassy, showing the wasting fever and general decline of the bodily functions. The brown, earthlike complexion of some, and their sunk eyes, with the dark areolae round them, tell you that the sulphuretted hydrogen of the atmosphere in which they live has been absorbed into the blood; while others are remarkable for the watery eye exhibiting the increased secretion of tears so peculiar to those who are exposed to the exhalations of hydrosulphate of ammonia.

Reading 13.4 A Medical Gentleman, 'Low life in Victorian Edinburgh', Extract 2 (1850)

Source: Anon. (1980 [1850]) *Low Life in Victorian Edinburgh By a Medical Gentleman*, **Edinburgh, Paul Harris Publishing, p. 28.**

In the flat immediately above, the effects of filth and bad, or rather no ventilation, sufficiently appeared, for there fever revelled – there was its hot bed, from which it but bides its time to scatter its seed on all around, on old and young, and on the rich and fortunate in their turn, though preying first on the poor and wretched. Of a family of five, the father – it surely was God's providence – the breadwinner, was the only one who had escaped. The eldest girl had been first attacked; and then, in rapid succession, her brother and sister, and lastly the mother

...

Unit 14 Politics and the people

Stuart Mitchell

Contents

Aims

This unit will:

- introduce you to the history of politics at the uppermost political level and help you understand the ways in which parliamentary and **extra-parliamentary** political activities interacted

- describe the major electoral changes that occurred in the period between 1848 and the 1870s

- explain the different varieties of political history that historians have developed, and the types of concepts and perspectives that they have used in their work

- explore some of the historical debates about the extension of democracy and political participation, especially in relation to the Reform Act of 1867 (also known as the Second Reform Act).

Introduction

In 1867, Parliament took a remarkable step towards extending the adult male franchise through the passage of the Second Reform Act. The measure applied to England and Wales; Scotland and Ireland had separate Reform Acts the following year. Although the effect of the 1867 Act was slight in rural areas, it more than doubled the borough electorate in England and Wales, from 500,000 to almost 1.2 million, thereby bringing a substantial portion of the skilled urban working class into the constitutional democratic process (Lawrence, 2009). Piloted through Parliament by a minority Tory government led in the House of Commons by Benjamin Disraeli, the proposal – initially modest – was much altered and expanded in its parliamentary passage by Liberal amendments. These amendments, some of which caused considerable anxiety among Tory MPs, proved necessary to enact the bill, but in the process the legislation became more radical, to the extent that the prime minister, Lord Derby, dubbed it 'a leap in the dark' because no one at the time knew the impact it would have on Parliament and politics.

Such dramatic changes to the suffrage had numerous consequences for late nineteenth-century politics. In this unit, you will explore some of them. Section 14.1 examines the prelude to 1867 and historical explanations for the franchise reform. It begins by examining the precursors to reform in the aftermath of Chartism, before looking at the parliamentary manoeuvres (sometimes called **high politics**) that surrounded the Act's passage. Section 14.2 explores some of the ways in which the Second Reform Act altered the national political landscape, including how people participated in politics, and the extent to which it acted as a catalyst for further legislative moves, such as the introduction of the secret ballot in 1872.

This unit concentrates on national political history and, in consequence, most of it focuses on the central state and, more narrowly, Parliament. In so doing, it only fleetingly refers to working-class activities or the close detail of day-to-day local politics. Instead, it is designed to introduce you to some of the more notable and long-running debates between historians about national political change, one of which is whether or not the 1860s truly made the British Isles more democratic.

14.1 The advent of parliamentary reform

In the first 20 years after the passage of the Great Reform Act in 1832, the principal working-class movement agitating for extension of the franchise was, as you know from the unit 'The "age of equipoise" and the Great Exhibition of 1851' (Unit 8), Chartism. Regardless of how its achievements are assessed, it is clear that Chartism was an essentially *modern* movement born of a swelling population, industrialisation, swifter communication, rapidly increasing labour mobility, and a recognition by the labouring poor of shared political and economic interests that transcended locality. The historian James Vernon recites some striking figures to demonstrate its reach:

> [The] campaign against the slave trade provided the peak of eighteenth-century petitioning, with 500 petitions collecting more than 350,000 signatures in the single year of 1792. Compare this to the height of petitioning between 1838 and 1842, when there was an average of fourteen thousand petitions a year, with the Chartist petition of 1842 alone accounting for 3 million signatures … [Petitioning provided] a key mechanism for abstracting opinion from place and forging new affiliations between distant strangers …
>
> [Likewise,] incessant movement and tours around the country enabled these [radical] leaders to tie together divergent local struggles and organizations. In a single month during the Chartist agitation of 1839, [Feargus] O'Connor reportedly travelled fifteen hundred miles [2,400 km] and spoke at twenty-two public meetings – often for several hours. This type of charismatic organization was also enhanced by newspapers … The *Northern Star* [O'Connor's Chartist newspaper] sold forty thousand copies by 1839 and claimed a readership of three hundred thousand. Its format – which combined reporting on the local activities of Chartist groups, covering national politics, letters from its readers, and sensationalist crime stories – proved very effective at connecting the dots of the movement. …
>
> [Moreover,] the national reach and formal organizational structure of Chartism far outstripped its predecessors. By the late 1840s more than a thousand localities had had some form of Chartist organization, and between 1839 and 1858 these local branches

sent delegates to the annual convention of the National Charter Association.

(Vernon, 2014, pp. 81–3)

At the same time as highlighting its modern credentials, Vernon suggests that Chartism relied on the older political custom of petitioning to convey its demands. Petitions had a long heritage as a quasi-legal form of direct democracy, which allowed the public to approach the state irrespective of whether they were enfranchised. It was the coming together of this established communication technique with a rapidly evolving industrial economy that transformed what had previously been a ritual with comparatively limited reach into a tool of mass protest. Through its formidable organisation and its attempt to dissolve local boundaries (see Figure 14.1), Chartism served as an exemplar for future mass national movements. Furthermore, its modernity contrasted with a governmental system that, despite the central state's growing reach, was rooted in older, pre-modern arrangements – that is, in the centrality of parishes, dominated by local landowners, as the principal administrative units with which people had contact. Regardless of 1832's influx of middle-class voters, most members of the House of Commons (and all those in the House of Lords) continued to be drawn from the aristocracy and gentry. By the end of the 1840s, in the light of Chartism's organisational successes, that system looked increasingly anachronistic, even to some within it.

From Chartism to moral imperative

As you know from Unit 8, historians have argued about the development of radical politics after Chartism. If *Chartism* collapsed as a political force, it did not mean that individual *Chartists* retired from political campaigning after 1848's failures; many remained involved in radical causes such as secularism and republicanism. These causes did provide an organisational bridge, as Keith McClelland has argued, between the earlier campaigns for reform and those gathering momentum in the 1860s (McClelland, 2000).

Three developments were critical here. One was the emergence of so-called New Model Unions. These organisations, such as the Amalgamated Society of Engineers, created in 1851, were usually based in a single trade and they tended to attract the skilled working class. Increasingly, they functioned as a means to promote a political, as well

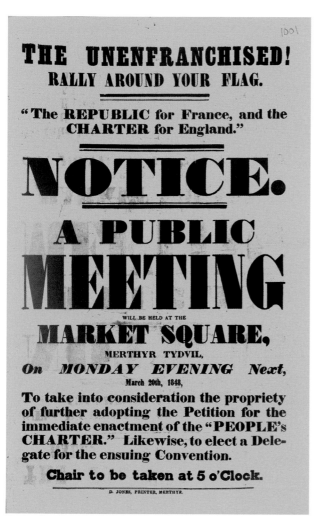

Figure 14.1 Chartist poster, March 1848. The National Archives, cat. HO 45/ 2410 (5) folio 1001. A typical example of the tangible links between Chartism as a local movement and a national one. Note the opportunity for attendees to elect Merthyr Tydfil's delegate to the National Convention.

as an economic, agenda by arguing that political rights were essential to ensuring the protection of workers' interests. Second, the Cooperative Movement, which flourished in England's north-west industrial heartlands in the 1850s and 1860s, benefited greatly from the patronage of ex-Chartists. It too was crucial in exemplifying working-class self-sufficiency and enterprise. The third change saw the repudiation of the mainstream Chartist notion that an alliance with middle-class reformers was undesirable (McClelland, 2000). Instead, there was an increased willingness on the part of both middle- and working-class reformers to work for a common goal: the extension of the franchise to all men, by stages if necessary. This understanding was assisted by the emergence of John Bright (whom you met in Unit 8) as the principal (middle-class) reform movement leader. Bright was already a political star; a passionate free trader, he had been the Anti-Corn Law League's most popular orator, able to attract large audiences throughout that campaign. Elected as Liberal MP for Birmingham in 1857, his decision to devote his talents to the electoral reform cause gave the movement both a figurehead and a singularly able spokesman in Parliament. Once again, Bright pulled in substantial crowds for his speeches, as we can see illustrated in Figure 14.2. It was not that Bright created the momentum for reform, but he played a highly significant role in shifting public, and elite, perceptions of it (McClelland, 2000).

SOIRÉE GIVEN TO MR. BRIGHT IN THE PHILHARMONIC HALL, LIVERPOOL, BY THE FINANCIAL REFORM ASSOCIATION—FROM A SKETCH BY G. HAYES.—SEE SUPPLEMENT, PAGE 584.

Figure 14.2 Unknown artist, 'Bright at Liverpool – Soirée Given to Mr Bright in the Philharmonic Hall, Liverpool, by the Financial Reform Association', engraving, from *The Illustrated London News*, 1859. Photo: © Illustrated London News Ltd / Mary Evans Picture Library

The events of 1848, as discussed in Unit 8, both in the UK and abroad, had drawbacks for advocates of broadening the franchise. Historians differ over whether Chartism was a genuine revolutionary threat – although its principal stated aim of universal manhood suffrage was decidedly constitutional in nature. Nevertheless, the authorities certainly *perceived* it as a menace to public order. Its open alignment with the revolutionaries who had overthrown the French **Orléanist** monarchy in 1848, as you can see in Figure 14.1 for instance, did nothing to dispel that anxiety. That the movement was suspected too of close links (some of which were more imagined than real) with Irish nationalism further blackened its reputation. Even as it declined as a national force, Chartism persisted as a byword among the political elites for political agitation designed to appeal to the mob and undisguised class aggression.

To make headway in parliamentary terms, the reform campaigners of the 1850s needed to distance themselves from the direct confrontation seen in 1848. This was where Bright's proselytising was crucial, because he promoted what Patrick Joyce has termed a moral narrative of constitutional renewal that emphasised notions of the nation or the people over the language of class (Joyce, 1996). He constructed a picture of Britain made economically great by the shared endeavour of its producers – an imagined nation that welded the middle and working classes together – but held back by a corrupt constitution sustained by an aristocratic caste, both Whig and Tory. As you know from Unit 8, this vision of the shared interests of capital and labour was a core part of the early Chartist movement, albeit one that coexisted with ideas of class differences. However, Bright's relentless focus on the shared interests of the nation of producers, and his sidelining of languages of class, was a clear shift in emphasis. By presenting capital and labour as the *productive* elements of society, those who ensured the progress of the nation, the political campaign for the working-class vote was given a strong moral imperative. In Bright's reasoning, it was a straightforward question of justice: workers, as an integral part of this rational, respectable, industrious nation, should be allowed full voting rights along with middle-class men; to fight reform was, by implication, to be against progress and enlightenment.

Bright's political narrative crystallised developments that were already in train. In the 1850s, reformers started to turn away from promoting the idea of universal manhood suffrage as an absolute right. Instead they tried to persuade the public to the cause by emphasising the individual character traits of working-class men, arguing that many had improved themselves and had acquired the right skills and qualities to use the vote fairly. Reformers built a moral, Christian case for change, emphasising the respectability and self-restraint of the labouring man in order to encourage legislators to extend the franchise to him. They claimed that working men would act independently and in the interests of their family in forming a political view, and that they would soberly and rationally enquire about politics through newspapers, libraries and voluntary associations. In so doing, the reformers helped to create an idealised model of *independent* citizenship, comprising virtues of 'dignified work, sole maintenance of the family, and free association on terms of equality with other men' that stressed the male roles of breadwinner and patriarchal head of the household (Tosh, 1994, p. 188). While this narrative may have persuaded some doubters that extending the franchise to more working men was morally appropriate, at the same time it marginalised women and made it harder for them to achieve similar voting rights.

In other words, reformers increasingly accepted, or feigned to accept, that the vote was a privilege to be earned by appropriately rational and respectable behaviours. This switch in tactics helped to ensure that the 1850s and 1860s were a period of relative calm, in extra-parliamentary terms. While outward tranquillity did not mean there was no underlying discontent, nonetheless the decline of Chartist activism contributed to a brief mid-century lull on the reform question. Although the reform campaign was becalmed as a serious national political force in the decade or so after 1848, this lull made its longer-term success more likely.

Exercise 14.1

Turn to Reading 14.1, 'Appeal to Non-Electors (1859)', located at the end of the unit. This is an extract from an article in the *Birmingham Daily Post* that quotes an address by the Manhood Suffrage Union. Despite the pause in full-scale agitation, there were several associations that existed to campaign for suffrage enlargement in this period – this was one of them. (In the mid-1860s, they tended to gravitate towards the umbrella organisation of the Reform League, of which more presently.) This article gives a snapshot of the arguments made for enfranchisement of the working class in the late 1850s.

As you read, consider the following questions:

- What were the demands of this group?

- What type of language did it employ?

- Would you view this as an attempt to construct a moral case for the enfranchisement of working men?

This should take around 15 minutes.

Specimen answer

- There were four demands: full manhood suffrage, repealing of the Septennial Act, equitable appointment of representatives, and elections by ballot.

- Avoiding confrontational language, the Manhood Suffrage Union's declaration was couched strongly in an idiom of respectability: references to sobriety, maturity, patriotism and earnestness are all prominent in the text.

- The vote was portrayed as a right that had already been earned, though not yet delivered, by possession of these virtues.

Discussion

The demand for full manhood suffrage was the principal demand, but the others are of interest, too. Repealing the Septennial Act (which allowed parliaments to sit for a maximum of seven years) would probably have made elections more frequent, while the demand for 'equitable appointment of representatives to population' was probably a demand for equally populated constituencies. You might have missed the call for elections by ballot: that was a request for secret voting.

The declaration fitted neatly with the prevailing moral orthodoxy and stressed that the enfranchisement of working men was no longer a threat to cool-headed governance (see, for instance, the Manhood Suffrage Union's attempt in lines 1–3 to divorce itself from inflammatory actions).

There were parliamentary attempts to extend the franchise in the years following Chartism's decline. In fact, there were Whig reform bills, introduced by John (later Lord) Russell, in 1852, 1854 and 1860, and a Tory one, promoted by Disraeli, in 1859. Although they were tepid in comparison with the measure eventually passed in 1867, none could muster enough support in the House of Commons to become law. One reason was that, after Chartism, there was insufficient extra-parliamentary pressure to suggest widespread insistence on changes to the suffrage. Another, though, was the dominance of the legislature by Lord Palmerston (1784–1865), who held office – variously as prime minister (1855–58 and 1859–65), foreign secretary and home secretary – almost continuously between 1846 and 1865. Palmerston was a doughty opponent of constitutional reform, who was backed by a solid cross-party bloc of landed opinion. As the reform campaign regained momentum in the 1860s, it increasingly held up Palmerston and his acolytes as the embodiment of a backward-looking landed oligarchy (government by a small group) that was hampering ordinary people's political rights.

By the early 1860s, however, more Liberal MPs, and a handful of Tories, began to accept the necessity, even desirability, of granting voting rights to at least part of the urban working classes. Both domestic and overseas events played a part in that shift. One was the Italian **Risorgimento**, or war of independence, of 1859–61. In the UK, this war acquired a romantic reputation as the Italian people's heroic struggle to remove their autocratic Habsburg and Bourbon rulers and establish a national, constitutional state. Further afield, but of greater significance because of its impact on the British textile industry, was the commitment of Abraham Lincoln (1809–1865, US president 1861–65) to slave emancipation in the American Civil War. These events gave credence to the type of liberalism that simultaneously was being promoted by Bright and his followers. The Lancashire cotton famine of 1861–65 (introduced in Unit 8 and also discussed in the unit 'Work, poverty and the new Poor Law': Unit 10), in which the supply of raw cotton to Britain was impeded by the northern states' blockade of the Confederacy's export trade, caused mass unemployment and eventually starvation among the north-west's cotton-workers, of whom there were over 350,000. With a few exceptions, the forbearance shown by Lancashire's unemployed hands in this lengthy period of inactivity, and their general abstention from protest riots, seemed an exemplar of reasoned moral restraint. In December 1862, following a mass meeting of cotton operatives at Manchester's Free Trade Hall, the 'Working People of Manchester' sent a public letter to Lincoln, which declared their support for, as they saw it, the latter's commitment to freedom and the end of slavery. Their example helped to convert several Liberal parliamentarians to ideas of franchise reform, not least the chancellor of the Exchequer, William Gladstone.

William Ewart Gladstone (1809–1898)

Gladstone (depicted in Figure 14.3) was one of the towering political figures of the nineteenth century and he appears in units across Blocks 2 and 3. Although he started political life as a Tory, he helped define nineteenth-century British Liberalism as a 'progressive', reforming movement. He was leader of the party for 30 years and prime minister for 13 of those.

Gladstone was born into a wealthy Liverpool trading family with Scottish origins, which had made its money in trade with the slave-owning colonies in the Americas. He was educated at Eton College and Oxford University, graduating from the latter in 1831 with a double first. Always committed to a political career, he first entered Parliament in 1833 as MP for Newark, a **pocket borough** controlled by the Tory Henry Pelham-Clinton, 4th Duke of Newcastle (1785–1851). Gladstone followed Prime Minister Sir Robert Peel in accepting the case for free trade and was president of the Board of Trade when the Corn Laws were repealed – a move that split the Tory Party. After a period in opposition, he returned to government under Lord Aberdeen as chancellor of the Exchequer. His reforming budgets were discussed in Unit 8.

Leader of the Liberals in the House of Commons during the debates on the Second Reform Act, Gladstone was prime minister in 1868–74, 1880–85, 1886 and 1892–94. As you will discover in Book 3, his later governments were dominated by the issue of Home Rule for Ireland. A profoundly religious man, his views were often expressed in strongly moral terms, and they polarised opinion.

Exercise 14.2

Turn to Reading 14.2, 'Speech of William Gladstone to the House of Commons (27 April 1866)', located at the end of the unit. In this speech, Gladstone outlined the reasons that caused him to reconsider the reform question.

How did he use the example of the cotton-workers to justify extending the franchise?

This should take around 15 minutes.

Specimen answer

There were clear echoes of the reform movement's argument in Gladstone's language. Lancashire's working people had shown themselves to be 'noble' and 'heroic' in their earnest resilience. They

Figure 14.3 Unknown artist, *Portrait of William Gladstone*, coloured engraving after a photograph by Mayall. Photo: © Mary Evans Picture Library / INTERFOTO / Sammlung Rauch

had thus proven themselves *morally* fit to exercise 'civil rights' (in other words, the vote).

Discussion

Historians need to be cautious about retrospective justifications, especially those made so publicly. Nevertheless, it appears that the cotton famine did help to convince Gladstone that respectable workers could be trusted with the vote, not just as individuals, but as a *class*. That they were able to exercise restraint as a 'mass' and a 'community' seems to have left a powerful impression on him. Moreover, it certainly fitted well with the version of political Liberalism that he was attempting to fashion in the late 1850s and early 1860s.

Gladstone grasped the difficulties of governing a modern industrial society better than Palmerston and older Whig landowners. In the 1850s, he became concerned that Britain's existing aristocratic system might easily become decadent, its economy stagnant, its labouring classes more mutinous, and the Liberals irreconcilably divided between the landed elite and those believing in the notion of progress. Though he was no enthusiast for franchise reform – indeed, he long actively opposed it – he was convinced that social stability and economic vitality depended on free trade and the reduction of financial burdens on the unenfranchised masses (Matthew, 1979). As you know from Unit 8, in his budgets in the 1850s and 1860s Gladstone shifted the burden of taxation from indirect taxes to income tax, which was paid only on incomes over £100. Gladstone's motives at that point were probably multiple. Although he believed government had the duty to represent all the people, the budgets were not a prelude to political reform; indeed, they might have been an attempt to delay it. In the popular acclaim for his budgets, however, he glimpsed the strategic possibility of a new Liberal Party constituency, which might include working-class men deemed independent and virtuous enough to participate in national politics. In that light, the cotton famine appears significant in providing the proof that Gladstone wanted: that enfranchising the respectable working man need not be a social catastrophe, and might be a political success, in party terms. Capitalising on his popularity, Gladstone announced his conversion to reform in May 1864 by declaring that 'every man who is not … incapacitated by some consideration of personal unfitness or of political danger, is morally entitled to come within the pale of the constitution'. Perhaps less noted, though, was his caveat warning against 'sudden, or violent, or excessive, or intoxicating change' (HC Deb 11 May 1864).

Dangers of democracy and the making of the Reform Act of 1867

Although, as you will see presently, historians disagree about the most important influences on the Reform Act of 1867, they generally agree that Palmerston's death in October 1865, and the appointment as prime minister of the reform-friendly Lord Russell, removed an impediment to reform. Simultaneously, the cluster of reform campaigns, of which the Manhood Suffrage Union you looked at in Exercise 14.1 was one, began coalescing into two nationwide pressure groups, the Reform League and the Reform Union. The former was established in early 1865 and was the more obviously working class of the two, counting among its leaders stalwarts of the New Model Unions. The latter was launched a year earlier, though its membership numbers were rapidly overtaken by those of the league; it was largely a middle-class group recruiting extensively from Liberal Party ranks. Although organisationally separate, these associations were prepared to work together (John Bright, for instance, addressed meetings of both league and union). They provided the spine of the first mass reform campaign since 1848. By 1866, then, an alignment of parliamentary and extra-parliamentary forces looked favourable for the extension of democracy.

Exercise 14.3

Reflect for a moment on what the phrase 'democratic rights' means to you. Note down anything that comes to mind.

Spend around 10 minutes on this.

Specimen answer

I imagine that you may have mentioned principles such as 'equal voting rights' or 'freedom of speech', or possibly you came up with more general terms such as 'fairness', 'transparency' or 'having a voice'.

Discussion

To understand the mid-nineteenth-century debates about democratic reform, however, historians need to be careful about imposing twenty-first-century assumptions onto the past. Instead, they must recognise the way in which people understood the term 'democracy' at the time. Nineteenth-century understandings of democracy – even among those arguing for franchise reform – were different from our ideas today.

Crucial to the nineteenth-century concept of democracy was the principle of citizenship: the right to vote conferred on someone membership of the political nation. Citizenship meant that an individual had rights and privileges that allowed them a voice, but also duties, including the duty to take an active interest in the well-being of the society of which they were a member. In formal terms, what was required of individuals in order that they might attain that citizenship was quite different from today. In order not to be a hostage to any one faction, class or economic imperative, individuals had to be able to think and act for themselves: they had to be independent.

In the nineteenth century being independent meant not being beholden to anyone else. This was demonstrated by the 'possession of independent means' or, to put it another way, owning property. In other words, the virtue of independence was habitually tied to property holding. In consequence, until the mid-century, most parliamentarians assumed that women and the property-less working classes should be excluded from full citizenship, and hence the franchise, because of their lack of independence. (You may remember from the unit 'The birth of the modern state' (Unit 5 in Block 1) that radical politicians argued that working men owned property in their labour – power that they sold in exchange for wages.) This did not mean that they were not represented in Parliament. Instead, different classes and local interests were balanced out by a concept known as *virtual representation*: the duty of MPs to look after the welfare of all their constituents, voters or not. Each voter, too, was supposed to act in the interests of others, so a male head of household was presumed to represent the interests of the female members of his family and younger men. There were ways in which those without a vote could participate in the political process – petitioning, for example, offered an opportunity for dialogue with political elites because Parliament felt that it had a duty to respond. It was this system that many tried to defend when the question of suffrage reform became more pressing in the 1860s.

Virtual representation made sense when politics was dominated by local landowners who had a duty to represent everyone in their locality. However, the pressures of industrialisation, population growth, urbanisation, quickening transport, improved literacy, and Liberal interventionism in policy areas from the Poor Law to policing had diminished local prerogatives and made principles such as virtual representation appear increasingly obsolete. In truth, Parliament was one of its last bastions, which perhaps explains some MPs' desperation to preserve the Commons in its unreformed state. For those determined to protect the old system, even limited democracy was a threat and something to defer as long as possible; the struggle between them and the reformers was to dominate parliamentary proceedings for most of 1866 and 1867.

Within five months of Palmerston's death, Gladstone – now Leader of the Commons – had introduced a Reform Bill, more modest in form than his 1864 declaration might have suggested, to enfranchise a greater proportion of the male artisan population in England and Wales. The core provisions of his bill, though bitterly contested at the time, were complicated (and mundane) so, for convenience's sake, Table 14.1 later in this unit lists them and compares them with the legislation eventually passed by his Commons' rival, Disraeli.

Exercise 14.4

Turn to Reading 14.3, 'The Reform Bill (1866)', located at the end of this unit. It is an extract from an article published in the *Quarterly Review*, which was a publication of some 60 years' standing and the foremost Tory-inclined intellectual journal of the nineteenth century.

The article gives a sense of the way in which the term 'democracy' was used by political elites. It was written by Robert Gascoyne-Cecil (1830–1903, prime minister 1885–86, 1886–92 and 1895–1902), the third Marquess of Salisbury (though in 1866 his proper title was Viscount Cranborne), who was probably traditionalist Toryism's weightiest intellectual. Here, Salisbury was reacting to Gladstone's Reform Bill.

As you read, consider the following questions:

- What were Salisbury's principal objections to the extension of democracy?

- In what terms did he conceptualise the matter of government?

This should take around 20 minutes.

Specimen answer

- Salisbury's major concerns about democracy lay in two areas: numbers and ignorance. The 1866 bill, had it become law, would have (on Salisbury's estimates) made the newly enfranchised portion of the working classes numerically superior to those with property, which posed significant dangers for that minority – those who had the biggest 'stake' in the country's success precisely because of that ownership. This was because workers would be tempted to vote en bloc in the interests of their class. Since the working classes consisted of 'men of less independence and lower culture', this could lead to the despotism of the working masses.

- In Salisbury's view, essentially the matter of government was one defined by class, and those class groups were, in turn, defined by the possession or otherwise of property.

Discussion

Salisbury's idea of government assumed that his readership would understand the idea of citizenship based on an individual's (or, rather, a man's) holdings of property. Only those who possessed it – in land especially – could be fully informed, independent citizens. Though not setting his face entirely against reform, in his view to give the vote to so many working people simultaneously could destroy the balance between different class interests in the constitution (Pinto-Duschinsky, 1967). Salisbury's views were based on ideas – which he assumed his audience understood and broadly agreed with – of virtual representation: the notion that property owners would make the best decisions not only for themselves, but for everyone. Although not mentioned in this passage, he also decried democracy for its encouragement of short-term populism and the tendency it provoked towards violence in times of want. Elsewhere in the article, Salisbury mentioned the aristocracy's fears of the working man 'put[ting] his heel upon their necks' – a vividly chilling image. It will not surprise you to learn that when, in 1867, his own party proposed an even more radical Reform Bill, Salisbury resigned from the Tory cabinet.

We should not assume that Salisbury's view was held solely by a backward-looking Tory minority; in fact, it was widely shared. Prominent among opponents of reform were a group on the Liberal benches who had been followers of the late prime minister, Lord Palmerston. The parliamentary speeches of their best orator, Robert Lowe (1811–1892, depicted in Figure 14.4), made similar arguments to Salisbury's. One of Lowe's more infamous interventions against the Reform Bill of 1866 recalled the mob-like fracas that regularly accompanied elections. Offering the vote to so many working men posed a moral threat to the conduct of national affairs because of the *type* of elector it would enfranchise: 'If you want venality, if you want ignorance, if you want drunkenness, and facility for being intimidated; or if, on the other hand, you want impulsive, unreflecting, and violent people, where do you look for them in the constituencies? Do you go to the top or to the bottom?' (HC Deb 13 March 1866).

You might be surprised that a government possessed of a fairly comfortable majority in the House of Commons, as the Liberals held in 1866, could be defeated on a major constitutional measure, but that is what happened. We should be careful, here, not to assume that the

Feb. 27, 1869.   VANITY FAIR.   208

No. 17.   STATESMEN, NO. 4.   Price 6d.

"An enemy to democracy, yet a professor of liberal principles, which tend to democracy ; the combination will one day make him Prime Minister of England."

Figure 14.4 Ape (pseudonym of Carlo Pellegrini), *Robert Lowe, Viscount Sherbrooke*, caricature in *Vanity Fair*, February 1869. Photo: © Mary Evans Picture Library

present-day nature of parliamentary parties was normal in the mid-nineteenth century. Victorian party allegiances were unreliable guides to voting behaviour. Instead, imagine the Liberal benches as a rather broad, and not altogether comfortable, coalition between traditional, landowning Whigs, reform-minded radicals, former **Peelites** (including Gladstone) and Irish MPs. Most of Lowe's allies came from the first of these groups. Parliamentary discipline – that is, following a stated party line – was very loose and, unlike today, MPs possessed considerable freedom to rebel. If, in 1864, Gladstone's conversion to reform was designed to please John Bright's radical faction of MPs, it came at the cost of alienating old Whig elements in the party. The Tory opposition was readily able to find allies on the Liberal benches. The government was narrowly defeated in June 1866. Without the confidence of the House, the Liberals shortly thereafter gave way to a minority Tory administration.

Benjamin Disraeli (1804–1881)

Disraeli was seen by many at the time as Gladstone's polar opposite. A wily political operator, he was known not for his principles or his moral sermons but for his wit. An outsider, who always seemed an oddity in a party still largely composed of country gentlemen, he helped to define a strand of Conservatism that still carries weight today.

Disraeli was born in London into a Jewish family that converted to Anglicanism when he was 12 years old. He trained as a solicitor but, like Gladstone, always aimed to be a writer and politician. He entered Parliament in 1837 and first made a name for himself by his eloquent arguments against the repeal of the Corn Laws. His views were best set out in a series of novels, of which the best-known are *Coningsby* (1844) and *Sybil* (1845), in which he pleaded for 'one nation' and an alliance between benevolent landowners and honest working men against the rapacious, rationalist middle class.

The departure of the Peelites after the repeal of the Corn Laws in 1846 left the Tory Party with few effective leaders, and Disraeli was able to make his mark, for instance with his tactics at the time of the Second Reform Act. He was briefly prime minister in 1868 following the retirement of Lord Derby, but the Conservatives lost the subsequent election. In 1874, however, they won convincingly and Disraeli was able to form a government that lasted until 1880. In office, most of his interest was taken up with foreign and imperial affairs. Long a favourite of Queen Victoria, he was made Earl of Beaconsfield in 1877.

The Conservative government, which was led by Lord Derby in the Lords and Disraeli in the Commons, came to power on the back of anti-reform sentiment, but it was clear that voting reform could not be postponed indefinitely. Agitation in the country, masterminded by the Reform League, became widespread after the failure of the Liberal bill. Whether these demonstrations frightened the new administration into reform has been a matter of historical debate, which I return to below. From a narrower parliamentary perspective, the Tories had been in power only sporadically over the previous 20 years, and their leaders, especially Disraeli, saw an opportunity to reverse their fortunes (see Figure 14.5 for one (satirical) take on this). By the end of 1866, the Conservatives were considering some version of reform, both as a way of placating the Reform League's protests and as a means to exploit Liberal divisions. In this, the personal animosity between Disraeli and Gladstone played no little part. Disraeli's unheralded movement towards reform, launched in February 1867, was primed to split the parliamentary Liberal Party: its radical wing, frustrated just eight months earlier, could hardly vote against its principles. Neither could Gladstone be seen to oppose actively a reform that he had strained to introduce in 1866.

From initially discreet beginnings, the legislation was subjected to several amendments from Liberal radicals, most of which the government accepted, which were designed to increase the electorate even further than the 1866 bill had envisaged – most notably, the abolition of **compounding** (see Table 14.1). In an attempt to weaken Gladstone's authority with his backbenchers, Disraeli conspicuously rejected only those suggestions that were proposed directly by his opposite number or his close allies. The result was reform of a considerably more drastic nature than the Tories had opposed in the previous year.

FUN.—December 1, 1866.

St. Stephe

REFORM

THE NEW "FRIEND OF THE WORKING-MAN;"

Or, the Party who may bring in a Reform Bill next Session after all.

Figure 14.5 Unknown artist, 'The new "friend of the working man;" or the party who may bring in a Reform Bill next session after all', from the satirical magazine *Fun*, 1 December 1866. Photo: © Mary Evans Picture Library. This cartoon is expressing surprise that Disraeli, having defeated Gladstone's 1866 bill, is now carrying the cause of working-class enfranchisement himself. Dressed in the clothes of a 'respectable' artisan, Disraeli is smuggling reform into St Stephen's Hall (in the Palace of Westminster).

Table 14.1 Main provisions of the Reform Bill 1866 and Reform Act 1867

	Boroughs	Counties	Redistribution
Reform Bill 1866 (Russell–Gladstone)	All men who met one of the following conditions: • £7 a year rental qualification • £10 a year lodger qualification • £50+ total savings qualification	All men who met one of the following conditions: • £14 a year rental qualification • £50+ total savings qualification	Disenfranchisement of 49 boroughs with populations of fewer than 8,000 people. All seats redistributed
Reform Act 1867 (Derby– Disraeli)	All men who met one of the following conditions: • any ratepaying adult occupiers • all lodgers in lodgings of 'annual value' of £10+ a year. The common practice of compounding (lodgers paying rates through their landlord) was abolished, thereby enfranchising more people (i.e. lodgers notionally became direct ratepayers)	All men who met one of the following conditions: • occupiers of land worth £5+ a year • ratepaying tenants occupying land to a rateable value of £12 a year	• 4 constituencies disenfranchised as corrupt • 42 small boroughs disenfranchised • 2 new double-member and 9 new single-member boroughs created • Birmingham, Leeds, Manchester, Liverpool, Salford and Merthyr Tydfil gained an additional MP • 10 counties (and Yorkshire's West Riding) gained 2 more members • Lancashire gained 3 new MPs

Source: Adapted from Hall et al., 2000, pp. 240–2

Table 14.1 lays out the major changes between the Liberal proposals of 1866 and the Act passed by the Conservatives the following year. It shows the terms on which people were given the vote and which areas gained greater representation – urban (boroughs) or rural (counties). The effects of the Tory measure were greatest in urban areas, especially industrial towns such as Manchester, Leeds and Merthyr Tydfil. In particular, the extension of the suffrage to all adult male ratepayers was a considerable concession. The changes to county franchises, though they went further than Gladstone's proposals, remained relatively modest, because the suffrage threshold of land/property value remained higher than that in the boroughs.

With the abolition of compounding, Disraeli's Act brought in many new voters: half a million more than originally forecast. It inducted far more of the working classes into political citizenship than Gladstone had envisaged and historians have attempted to divine the motives for its radicalism. Was this a far-sighted attempt to create a 'Tory democracy' in which the respectable working-class man would lend his vote to a more openly patriotic and social reform-minded Conservative Party in preference to the Liberals? Was it a bid to shore up Tory votes in the counties? Or was it perhaps merely a clever, if opportunistic, parliamentary ruse designed to offend Gladstone? It is likely that none of these reasons alone accounts for the Act's dramatic changes; I will return to some of these questions in the next section.

Why was the Reform Act passed?

Needless to say, the reasons for the Reform Act's passing have excited controversy among historians. To simplify, one interpretation, often associated with Asa Briggs' *Age of Improvement* (1959), depicted 1867 as a natural, progressive moment occurring within an environment of longer-term social and economic changes, such as increasing urbanisation and the emergence of New Model Unions. Thus legislators, animated by a principled concern for the national good, plus moral and political 'pressure from below', extended formal citizenship rights (symbolically represented by voting) to a working-class constituency that had, through its industry and moral continence, earned those privileges. For Briggs, it was primarily the spread of new liberal ideas, stimulated by new contexts, which underlay the reform measure. Opposing that view, historians of high party politics, notably Maurice Cowling (1967), presented the Act as resulting from an often cynical party political calculation that was broadly insulated from extra-parliamentary reform agitation. Disraeli and Derby, motivated largely by animosity towards Gladstone and a desire to shore up Tory votes nationally, while simultaneously embarrassing the Liberals, engaged in manoeuvres that ended with far more democratic legislation than they had initially intended.

These historiographical positions acquired labels of convenience that harked back to the period that they chose to investigate: Briggs' view was supposedly 'Whiggish'; Cowling's 'Tory'. Such black-and-white terms, though, served to distort the debate – turning what was essentially a difference of emphasis into a key disagreement. Briggs did not shrink from examining the parliamentary machinations that surrounded Gladstone's failure to secure reform and Disraeli's success; nor did Cowling maintain that Westminster was sealed off from public agitation and the climate of ideas (Craig, 2010). That said, both historians did concentrate principally on the motives and actions of a relatively small group of people. Subsequent scholars, sometimes called 'new political historians' – such as Robert Saunders (2011), Kristin Zimmerman (2003) and Keith McClelland (2000) – have sought to widen the compass of research to explore the politics, ideas and influence of the countrywide reform movement and its interaction with parliamentary elites. To assess the different factors that shaped the 1867 Act's passage, let's examine first the pressures on the legislature that emanated from the country, and then the high political causes.

In the first year and a half of its existence, from 1865, the Reform League's demonstrations and marches grew in size, echoing the organisational form of Chartism, though shorn of its more violent manifestations. Mindful of the way in which 1848 was still apprehended by the political class, the league was careful not to endorse, still less to encourage, anything other than orderly protest that posed no immediate hazard to public order. It was weight of numbers, twinned with the strength of their moral case, that reformers believed would deliver the vote. Beyond giving heart to radicals in the Liberal ranks, most historians have considered that the league's impact on parliamentary politics was small before the collapse of the Russell–Gladstone bill in mid-1866. That failure triggered an event known as the Hyde Park riot (Figure 14.6), where police denied a huge Reform League march entry to the park, in which a mass protest meeting had been planned. Undeterred, some of the marchers tore down sections of its railings and occupied the park regardless. Whether this event demonstrated genuine revolutionary potential on the part of the frustrated working classes is doubtful; nor, generally, did the parliamentary elite recognise it as a prelude to a national uprising. Nevertheless, it raised serious public order questions and, with mass protests continuing into the winter, probably contributed to an atmosphere in which formerly antagonistic parliamentarians began, from necessity, to seriously consider reform (Machin, 2001).

Figure 14.6 Rioting during the Reform League demonstration in Hyde Park, London, 4 August 1866. Engraving from *The Illustrated London News*. Photo: © Illustrated London News Ltd / Mary Evans Picture Library

Activity 14.1

Now go to the module website and complete Activity 14.1 'The Second Reform Act'. This should take about an hour and a half.

Following Saunders (2011), we should differentiate between the *likelihood* of reform in the mid-1860s and the measure eventually passed. It is difficult to see the Act itself as the product of politicians responding fearfully to extra-parliamentary action; Westminster's party choreography seems far more significant. However, that does not mean that popular agitation was unimportant. Here, it is important to distinguish between the burst of impatient protest in 1866–67 and the prolonged crusade to manufacture a moral case for the 'independent' working man's enfranchisement. If anything, the latter was more decisive, since it created both an environment in which some variety of reform became *steadily more likely*, regardless of which party held power, and a system of nationwide organisation to agitate for it. We should not forget either that ideas of national interest and social stability – not least, a desire to avoid yielding *full* manhood democracy – were important in politicians' calculations. Paradoxically, the countrywide campaign for limited enfranchisement on the basis of moral virtue was perhaps too successful. If its stated aim thereby became more likely, the old Chartist demand for universal manhood suffrage was as remote in 1867 as it was in 1848. Only a handful of MPs wanted every adult male to have the vote, and neither Gladstone nor Disraeli ever risked going that far.

It seems likely that the Conservatives hoped to gain certain party advantages from their reform package. I have already mentioned, for example, that the county franchise, where Tory support was strongest, was set at a much higher level than that for boroughs. Seat redistribution and expansion of borough boundaries seemingly created a buffer zone around the counties, which indicates that the government was thinking less about Disraeli's vision of 'Tory democracy' – at that point, anyhow, a vague notion – and more about shoring up Conservative votes in their heartlands (Jenkins, 1996). But if Disraeli hoped that public gratitude at his reform would deliver the 1868 general election to the Conservatives, he was to be disappointed, since the major issue in that contest was instead the disestablishment of the Church of Ireland and its result was a victory for Gladstone's Liberals.

Though franchise reform as a political issue waned rapidly in the aftermath of the 1867 Act, the consequences of the legislation and the debates that enveloped it were durable; they greatly conditioned public politics outside the narrow realm of Westminster. It is that phenomenon to which I will turn in Section 14.2.

Parliamentary reform in Scotland and Ireland

This unit has focused on the impact of the Reform Act of 1867 for England and Wales. As had been the case with the Reform Act of 1832 (as you may recall from the unit 'Imagined nations made real?': Unit 6 in Block 1), different laws were passed in 1868 to reform the representative systems of Scotland and Ireland.

Taking its population into account, Scotland had been significantly under-represented in Parliament, even after 1832. The Representation of the People (Scotland) Act of 1868 addressed this imbalance by creating seven additional seats for Scotland in the House of Commons, bringing the country's overall total to 60 seats. Seven small English constituencies were disenfranchised to facilitate this change, which meant that the overall number of seats in the House of Commons remained unchanged. Although the number of Scottish seats had increased, the country remained under-represented in Parliament after 1868 by approximately eight seats (McCord and Purdue, 2007). In terms of redefining voting qualifications, the Scottish Reform Act contained similar provisions to that of England and Wales, although the precise details differed somewhat. The Scottish Reform Act also had a significant impact on the size of the electorate, which more than doubled from approximately 105,000 to 240,000 (Mitchell, 2011).

The Representation of the People (Ireland) Act of 1868 did not alter the number of parliamentary seats returned for Ireland, so Ireland continued be under-represented in Westminster. More important reforms had taken place quite some time earlier. In response to population decline as a result of the Irish Famine of the 1840s, the Irish Franchise Act of 1850 had granted the right to vote to occupiers (rather than freeholders or leaseholders) of property valued at £12 in the county constituencies and £8 in borough constituencies. These changes had seen the Irish electorate triple in size. In contrast, the Reform Act of 1868 did not change the county franchise, although the rateable valuation in borough constituencies was reduced to £4. This measure saw the Irish electorate increase from approximately 197,000 to 225,000 (Mitchell, 2011), a very modest increase in comparison with the rest of the United Kingdom.

14.2 The impact of 1867

In Section 14.1, I examined the reform movement and the 1867 Act largely through the lens of democracy as manifested in a formal, national sense through voting rights. In that narrow sense, there is little doubt that the Reform Act of 1867 made England and Wales more democratic. However, historians such as Patrick Joyce and James Vernon have suggested that British politics may have become *less* democratic as it became more formal and organised. Think back to Exercise 14.3 and the discussion of Victorian ideas about democratic rights. Older forms of politics were generally public, whether hustings, petitioning or localised protests such as bread riots. Ostensibly, anyone – women and paupers included – could participate in them whether or not they had the vote. Over time, though, politics was taken off the streets. Partly that was a consequence of increasing literacy, which meant that some politics could be consumed through newspapers and pamphlets read in the home, in the library, or in clubs and meeting rooms. Partly it was about the organisation of political meetings in civic halls and meeting rooms, which had a limited capacity and often had to issue tickets for entry. Also, as you will see, it was brought about by state intervention (Vernon, 1993). I would like you to bear these arguments in mind as you go on to explore some of the consequences of the Reform Act.

Class, public order and the secret ballot

Admitting so many urban working-class men to political citizenship made politicians anxious about the administration of open elections and the public order threats that might result. You will recall from Unit 6 that both candidate nomination and voting were public spectacles, which attracted large crowds, usually consisting of a preponderance of *non*-electors (see Figure 14.7). These affairs were frequently rowdy and violent. That the 1868 general election produced a crop of stories about mob rule, intimidation, destruction of property and, in one case, murder, influenced the incoming Liberal administration to create a cross-party select committee to inquire into the running of elections. It was asked to offer suggestions to improve their moral conduct and render them less dangerous to public order (Lawrence, 2009).

Exercise 14.5

Turn to Reading 14.4, 'Extracts from the Select Committee Report on Parliamentary and Municipal Elections (1870)', located at the end of the unit, and consider these questions:

- What sort of practices did the committee find to be widespread at elections?

- What remedy did it suggest, and why?

This should take around 30 minutes.

Specimen answer

- The report's core findings were that corruption, intimidation, bribery, violence and drunkenness were present at many elections. Reminding MPs of the fears triggered by the extension of the franchise, the subtext may have been that the urban working classes were peculiarly susceptible to those tendencies. You might also have noticed the report's comments about Irish elections and the danger of 'spiritual intimidation' therein – insinuating the popular (English) phantom of Catholic influence over Irish politics.

- The committee's principal suggestion to combat malpractice and violence was the introduction of secret voting. The report's language is revealing, however, of the state's anxieties over public order in an age of greater democracy. Hence the ballot would promote the 'freedom', 'tranquillity' and 'purity' of the electoral process, so long as the secrecy of the vote was 'inviolable'.

Discussion

You might have picked up in this exercise some evidence to support the arguments made by Joyce and Vernon. The state was slowly moving towards intervention in the conduct of elections by making them private, rather than communal, matters. That required ending the public spectacle of open voting in order to make the process more bureaucratic and ordered. What the committee proposed was literally to take electoral politics off the streets.

The unruly election of 1868 might have persuaded Parliament that voting had become more corrupt and disorderly with the advent of an expanded franchise, but recent historical opinion has queried that notion. Jon Lawrence has argued that:

> What changed after 1867 was not so much the level of disorder, as the political and social context in which disorder was understood. In many boroughs non-voters were for the first time in a minority, at least among adult males, and traditional rituals that had symbolised their inclusion in the political system ... came to be seen as dangerous anachronisms which threatened to impede the smooth absorption of the new voters into orderly and rational electoral politics.
>
> (Lawrence, 2009, pp. 44–5)

More prosaically, 1868 saw the highest proportion of *contested* elections since the reform crisis of 1832, so the opportunities for disorder were greater (figures in Evans, 1983).

As you have seen, the 1867 reform heightened sensitivities among parliamentary elites about accommodating more working-class men into the system. In contrast to the beginning of the nineteenth century, when the central state's compass was restricted and public disorder was usually resolved locally, the mid-century state chose to intervene to correct alleged abuses.

The 1872 Act that introduced the secret ballot did not attract the mass agitation seen in 1866–67. Although the ballot had been an original Chartist demand, no significant external pressure was needed to drive the cause. Some middle-class radical opinion – led, once again, in Parliament by John Bright – had long been in favour of it (Machin, 2001). However, other Liberal parliamentarians, including Gladstone, believed that open voting was morally superior because they saw electors as trustees for their communities, each with an obligation to form a sound opinion before exercising their vote, and the system's public nature enabled non-electors to hold them accountable. Many MPs, still holding to the spirit of virtual representation, saw the reform as enabling people to vote on personal interest alone, an idea they thought selfish and repugnant. Some even saw the secret ballot as 'un-English' – because of its very secrecy – and, demonstrating the extent to which politics remained a male preserve, 'un-manly' – because it denied the virtue of sturdy and open independence that was deemed the mark of citizenship (Crook, 2011, p. 87). However, in the end, with little ideological pressure inside or outside of Parliament, the legislature's adoption of secret voting owed more to the changed circumstances after the 1867 Act. A suddenly larger electorate posed

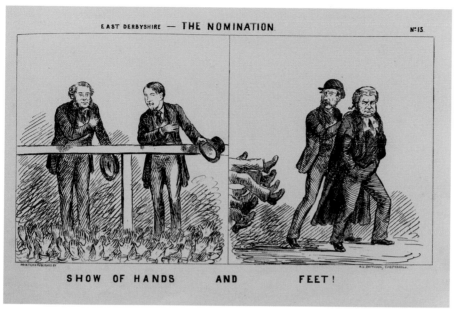

EAST DERBYSHIRE — THE NOMINATION.   N° 15.

SHOW OF HANDS   AND   FEET!

Figure 14.7 'East Derbyshire – the Nomination', a pro-Liberal cartoon by J. Priestman Atkinson (who worked for *Punch*), no. 15 from *East Derbyshire Election Cartoons, 1868*, Chesterfield, Richard John Smithson. University of Leicester Special Collections. The cartoons (20 in all) appeared week by week and were collected, after the election, into a bound volume. They are a rare form of local satirical output. The contest for East Derbyshire was a hard-fought affair, with the Liberal candidates victorious over their Conservative opponents by narrow margins. This image shows the essentially public nature of the nomination and, in the second half of the picture, as the candidates are pursued by the crowd, its associated risks.

considerable logistical difficulties, since open voting was a protracted process and most constituencies offered only one polling place. Furthermore, the notion of trusteeship as a rationale for public elections was difficult to maintain when, in many boroughs at least, electors began to outnumber male non-voters. Given the spectre of class violence and intimidation that haunted the 1868 poll, regardless of its extent, it was practical matters, not principles, which influenced Parliament most heavily.

Exercise 14.6

Study Figure 14.8. What impression does it give of voting using the secret ballot?

This should take around 10 minutes.

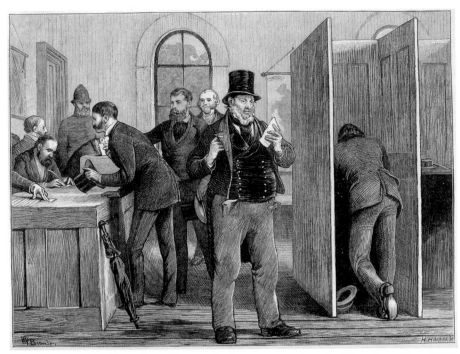

Figure 14.8 W. Bromley, 'Secret Ballot', engraving in *The Graphic*, 1873. Photo: © Illustrated London News Ltd / Mary Evans Picture Library

Specimen answer

The image is one of orderliness and respectability; the policeman in the corner seems entirely unnecessary. The voters are very far from the rough working men whose enfranchisement had so worried Lowe.

You might have noted the contrasts between this image and the picture of polling before the introduction of the secret ballot presented in Figure 14.7 – noting, of course, that 14.8 was an idealised image while 14.7 was satire.

Some historians have viewed the introduction of the secret ballot and what came with it – the suspension of public nomination at the hustings, the printing of standard ballot papers and formal regulation of the count – as a step in the development of the modern state. It fitted into a conception of modernity characterised by mass mobility, literacy, communications, innovation and economic growth. It is thus plausible to see the secret ballot's introduction as one of several Liberal devices to cope with the consequences of that modern condition –

although contemporary historical actors were unlikely to have seen their actions in such ambitious terms. The Act might be counted as an attempt to discipline the electoral process, thereby inducting the new mass electorate into political citizenship in a controlled fashion. Tom Crook, however, has noted that it rested on a paradox of sorts, whereby the idealised openness and transparency of liberal democracy required secrecy, promoted and enforced by the state, to sustain it (Crook, 2011). Whether this extension of state reach promoted or inhibited the exercise of democracy is a question I will return to later in the unit.

Gender and political participation

On 20 May 1867, in the commotion that accompanied the passage of Disraeli's Reform Bill, John Stuart Mill, political philosopher and Liberal MP, raised the prospect of female suffrage. He proposed an amendment that would have allowed women to vote on the same terms as men in county constituencies. Although it was defeated by 73 votes to 196, that the idea was treated (by most MPs) as a serious proposition represented the beginnings of a challenge to an exclusively masculine conceptualisation of political citizenship (see Figure 14.9 for *Punch*'s sardonic take). While the amendment was supported principally by Liberal radicals, Disraeli's (perhaps opportunistic) private support for the principle, though he did not vote in favour for fear of alienating the Tory cabinet, suggested that backing might in future be forthcoming from other parts of the party spectrum. Moreover, both local and national press gave the debate unusually thoughtful coverage and many in the social circles in which female suffrage was being advocated – such as readers of the *Englishwoman's Review* – were pleased with the level of support that Mill's efforts had garnered (Rendall, 2000).

Activity 14.2

Now go to the module website and complete Activity 14.2 'Gendered political language'. This should take around half an hour.

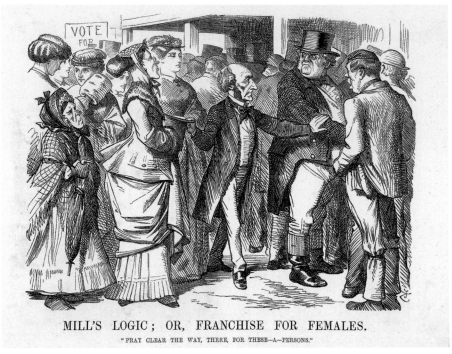

Figure 14.9 John Tenniel, 'Mill's logic; or, franchise for females – "Pray clear the way, there, for these-a-persons"', cartoon in *Punch*, March 1867. Photo: World History Archive / Alamy. Here, John Stuart Mill is asking an indignant John Bull to make way for women to cast their votes. The female figure second from left (foreground) is Lydia Ernestine Becker, an advocate of female suffrage.

With Liberal ranks increased at the 1868 general election, it was perhaps easier to squeeze onto the statute book legislation that favoured women's enfranchisement. In 1869, on the pretext of correcting anomalies in local election franchises, the Commons, with barely any tremor, agreed to extend the vote in municipal elections to single female householders. In that case, property ownership clearly trumped masculinity as a prerequisite for the franchise. Likewise, in 1870 Parliament passed two more pieces of legislation helpful to the cause of women's rights. The Education Act entitled them to vote for the new school boards, while the Married Women's Property Act enhanced their rights over property. Moreover, the coming of the secret ballot in 1872 emboldened female suffrage campaigners because it was no longer possible for their opponents to argue that unruly open elections, with their 'masculine' obligation for voters to pledge themselves publicly, would be unsuitable for women.

This is not to suggest that women had no agency or that they had to rely on the benevolent far-sightedness of a few individuals such as Mill. Prior to the 1867 Act, as Jane Rendall has noted, a pro-female suffrage movement – albeit a small one – had been developing. By 1866, it was large enough to sustain a journal in the form of the *Englishwoman's Review* (launched that year) and collect petition signatures; it was also crucial in driving Mill's attempt to amend the 1867 bill (Rendall, 2000). Furthermore, reform agitation in the mid-1860s was critical in drawing more women towards the campaign, so that by the late 1860s, with the creation of the National Society for Women's Suffrage, it was beginning to assume the dimensions of a popular movement.

If, however, the early 1870s appeared a propitious moment to push for greater concessions, it was to prove illusory. Splits in the National Society between its two largest chapters – Manchester and London – weakened the cause and, despite almost annual Commons debates on private members' bills from 1870 onwards (some of which progressed to second reading), there was no legislative movement towards women's enfranchisement for general elections. It was not until 1897, with the creation of the National Union of Women's Suffrage Societies under the leadership of Millicent Fawcett (1847–1929), that the campaign truly began to gather momentum.

Ordering democracy?

To focus exclusively on the vote and electoral mechanisms such as the ballot risks neglecting the other ways in which social and political developments in the 1860s led to changes in the practice of democracy. I have already observed that an emerging modern, democratic society posed problems for politicians keen to win over new voters. Here, I give two brief examples of their attempts to deal with those developments.

I have mentioned that the Liberal government's Education Act of 1870 provided an opportunity for women to participate in local politics by voting for school boards. However, the Act can also be viewed as an attempt by central government to promote the virtues of moral continence and respectability that Gladstonian Liberals in particular saw as critical for the functioning of the new democratic process. In short, voters needed to be educated. The Act did not, as sometimes assumed, establish a free and compulsory system of elementary education for all children in England and Wales. Rather, it used state and ratepayers' money to establish board schools wherever there was a gap in education provision left by the voluntary system of Anglican church schools. While no doubt inspired partly by Gladstone's conviction that education for all was one hallmark of a Christian society, it can also be seen as an effort to court a Nonconformist constituency that had grown in size in 1867, was inclined towards Liberalism, and had been sidelined by Anglicanism in the education field. Likewise, its effort to improve literacy rates and to inculcate independent virtues, and its introduction of a system of state inspection, are definite indications of the state's priorities in the changed circumstances of mass democracy. Educating the next generation of voters – and, incidentally, attempting to bring more people into the electorate by uplifting them morally – seems to demonstrate the close connection between electoral politics and the wider society envisaged by Liberal modernity.

After 1867, political parties too recognised the necessity to reach out to new electorates. Both the Liberals and the Conservatives started to develop national party organisations that sought to mobilise the voters by trying to impose a consistency of tactics and message on local branch organisations (usually through party agents). In 1874, the Liberal Central Association came into being, three years after the Conservative Central Office. What they had in common with central government's actions was that they too represented attempts to instruct and discipline modern democracy, albeit for the ends of political success. Hence, they contributed to an incremental shift away from locally focused, direct democracy, or the politics of the streets.

It would be wrong, I believe, to see these developments as part of a grand design by which the incorporation of more people into the formal political system required a comprehensive scheme to marshal and educate them in an orderly fashion. The state, political parties and other institutions (such as trade unions, trade associations, professional bodies and so on) responded to perceived problems of modern, industrial society in a frequently piecemeal and haphazard fashion. Indeed, sometimes, as you saw with the secret ballot, it required principles such as transparency to be discarded or applied in an inconsistent manner.

Nonetheless, the trend away from local, direct forms of democracy and towards central intervention and bureaucratisation is difficult to dispute. It is also hard to disagree with Vernon's argument that those trends took politics off the streets (though not entirely) and into a more private realm, symbolised by the decline of older, non-literate forms of political culture. However, whether that made Britain in consequence *less* democratic is more open to question. As you explored in Exercise 14.3, democracy is not a static concept. There is no doubt that the ways in which people *participated* in politics and exercised agency over political issues changed during the nineteenth century; to argue that those changes decreased their participation is far harder to prove. Philip Harling argues that, in fact, historians have perhaps been guilty of gazing for too long at the central state's actions, while overlooking the broadening of local electorates in the second half of the nineteenth century, which 'created new participatory opportunities for a good many women and working-class men on the local level' (Harling, 2004, p. 220). He reminds us that:

> All ratepayers who met a one-year residency qualification were given the local franchise in 1869, including thousands of rate-paying single women and widows, resulting in municipal electorates of some 18 to 20% of the *total* borough population. The 1870 Education Act entitled women ratepayers to vote for and serve on school boards, and from 1875 they were entitled to serve as Poor Law guardians, as well. The 1875 Public Health Act established district councils in many areas, to be elected on a ratepayer franchise. The 1888 Local Government Act dispersed many of the powers of justices of the peace to new ratepayer-elected county and county borough councils. ... By 1900 there were over a million women on the county and borough council and Poor Law electoral registers, ... and a growing number of women and working-class men stood for election, particularly for the school boards and boards of guardians.
>
> (Harling, 2004, p. 221)

Something similar may be said of political parties, labour organisations and pressure groups such as the National Society for Women's Suffrage. While it is true that they controlled and limited the ways in which people engaged with political issues, they still permitted more people, more regularly, and more deeply to participate through lecture classes, letter writing, canvassing, social events and the like.

Nor is it true that older forms of political participation disappeared entirely. Petitioning remained a viable form of protest. So did mass demonstrations, though they were far less inclined to rowdiness and occasional violence, and sometimes took new shapes such as the picket or the political rally. In fact, one could argue that, as popular demonstrations became more orderly, as in the Reform League's case, they were better attended to by political elites. Though we can readily see that the forms of political participation in the mid-nineteenth century altered, it would be a mistake to see that as necessarily betokening a less democratic, less participatory age.

Activity 14.3

Now go to the module website and complete Activity 14.3 'Visual satire'. This should take around an hour.

Conclusion

This unit has concentrated on the institutions and workings of central government, and has used the Reform Act of 1867 as a way of focusing on the conduct of politics at a national level, sometimes described as 'high politics'. That is, of course, not to claim that the reform crisis of the mid-1860s changed everything. Longer-term tendencies towards a more continent, ordered democratic era both existed before that point and persisted thereafter. If 1867 remains a peculiarly illuminating event, which in unleashing a new mass electorate was critical to subsequent developments, it can assume too great an importance if considered separately from these longer-term trends.

The unit has highlighted a number of historical debates, such as those about the changing nature of extra-parliamentary pressure for reform, the background to the 1867 Act, the role of gendered language in debates about democracy, and whether democracy became more limited as the century progressed. I have observed some of the ways in which politics at this time worked and tackled the question of differing historical interpretations of Victorian democracy. As with other topics that you have studied in this module, those interpretations will continue to develop as new historians add their perspectives.

> Now turn to the module website to complete the independent study activities associated with this unit.

References

Birmingham Daily Post (1859) 'Appeal to non-electors', 22 April.

Briggs, A. (1959) *The Age of Improvement, 1783–1867*, London, Longman.

Cecil, R. (1866) 'The Reform Bill', *Quarterly Review*, vol. 119, no. 23, April, pp. 552–3.

Cowling, M. (1967) *1867, Disraeli, Gladstone and Revolution: The Passing of the Second Reform Bill*, Cambridge, Cambridge University Press.

Craig, D. M. (2010) '"High politics" and the "new political history"', *The Historical Journal*, vol. 53, no. 2, pp. 453–75.

Crook, T. (2011) 'Secrecy and liberal modernity in Victorian and Edwardian England', in Gunn, S. and Vernon, J. (eds) *The Peculiarities of Liberal Modernity in Imperial Britain*, Berkeley, CA, University of California Press, pp. 72–90.

Evans, E. J. (1983) *The Forging of the Modern State: Early Industrial Britain, 1783–1870*, London, Longman.

Hall, C., McClelland, K. and Rendall, J. (2000) *Defining the Victorian Nation: Class, Race, Gender and the Reform Act of 1867*, Cambridge, Cambridge University Press.

HC Deb 11 May 1864, vol. 175, col. 324 [Online]. Available at http://hansard.millbanksystems.com/ (Accessed 12 May 2017).

HC Deb 13 March 1866, vol. 182, cols 147–8 [Online]. Available at http://hansard.millbanksystems.com/ (Accessed 12 May 2017).

HC Deb 27 April 1866, vol. 183, col. 147 [Online]. Available at http://hansard.millbanksystems.com/ (Accessed 12 May 2017).

Harling, P. (2004) 'The centrality of locality: the local state, local democracy, and local consciousness in late-Victorian and Edwardian Britain', *Journal of Victorian Culture*, vol. 9, no. 2, pp. 216–34.

Jenkins, T. (1996) *Disraeli and Victorian Conservatism*, Basingstoke, Macmillan.

Joyce, P. (1996) 'The constitution and the narrative structure of Victorian politics', in Vernon, J. (ed.) *Re-reading the Constitution: New Narratives in the Political History of England's Long Nineteenth Century*, Cambridge, Cambridge University Press, pp. 179–203.

Lawrence, J. (2009) *Electing Our Masters: The Hustings in British Politics from Hogarth to Blair*, Oxford, Oxford University Press.

McClelland, K (2000) 'England's greatness – the working man', in Hall, C., McClelland, K. and Rendall, J., *Defining the Victorian Nation: Class, Race, Gender and the Reform Act of 1867*, Cambridge, Cambridge University Press, pp. 71–118.

McCord, N. and Purdue, B. (eds) (2007) *British History 1815–1914*, Oxford, Oxford University Press.

Machin, I. (2001) *The Rise of Democracy in Britain, 1830–1918*, Basingstoke, Macmillan.

Matthew, H. C. G. (1979) 'Disraeli, Gladstone, and the politics of mid-Victorian budgets', *The Historical Journal*, vol. 22, no. 3, pp. 615–43.

Mitchell, S. (ed.) (2011) *Victorian Britain: An Encyclopedia*, Abingdon, Routledge.

Pinto-Duschinsky, M. (1967) *The Political Thought of Lord Salisbury*, London, Constable.

Rendall, J. (2000) 'The citizenship of women and the Reform Act of 1867', in Hall, C., McClelland, K. and Rendall, J., *Defining the Victorian Nation: Class, Race, Gender and the Reform Act of 1867*, Cambridge, Cambridge University Press, pp. 119–78.

Saunders, R. (2011) *Democracy and the Vote in British Politics, 1848–1867: The Making of the Second Reform Act*, Farnham, Ashgate.

Select Committee on Parliamentary and Municipal Election: Report, Proceedings, Appendices, Session 1870, Paper 115, pp. 4, 9.

Tosh, J. (1994) 'What should historians do with masculinity? Reflections on nineteenth-century Britain', *History Workshop Journal*, vol. 38, no. 1, pp. 179–202.

Vernon, J. (1993) *Politics and the People*, Cambridge, Cambridge University Press.

Vernon, J. (2014) *Distant Strangers: How Britain Became Modern*, Berkeley and Los Angeles, CA, University of California Press.

Zimmerman, K. (2003) 'Liberal speech, Palmerstonian delay, and the passage of the Second Reform Act', *English Historical Review*, vol. 118, no. 479, pp. 1176–1207.

Readings

Reading 14.1 Appeal to Non-Electors (1859)

Source: *Birmingham Daily Post* (1859) 'Appeal to non-electors', 22 April.

An address to the non-electors of the United Kingdom has been drawn up by the Executive Committee of the Manhood Suffrage Union. The address reads: –

…

'We trust that the advocates of manhood suffrage will specially avoid surrounding that topic with the needless and injurious asperities and antagonisms of bygone agitations. It is not a question of class, but of national interest, and it is of the highest importance that irritating topics, violent sentiments, and obstructive policy should be avoided. We think the question of Radical Reform may be argued upon the logical ground, that what is the real interest of the whole nation ought to involve the actual representation of every honest man in the nation. Put it therefore on this ground, and upon the patriotic ground that to advance the interests of the poor is to enhance the honour and dignity of the rich, and render stable the institutions of the country; and that in proportion as statesmen advance the political and material interests of the people they set free the people to advance their own moral and intellectual state, and thus ensure a condition of society which is the glory of States, and the bulwark of Governments.

'If we might venture to suggest to you subjects upon which to concentrate your thoughts and action at the present moment, we should point out: –

'The extension of the suffrage to every duly registered male adult, not undergoing punishment for crime, accompanied and rendered secure and effective by vote by ballot, the repeal of the Septennial Act, and an equitable appointment of representatives to population.

'We have, in conclusion, to express our hope and belief that electors and non-electors will alike join with us in a vigorous and patriotic effort to make the political institutions of our country subserve the social, intellectual, and moral advancement of the whole people.

…

'Be, therefore, non-electors, on your guard! Let every county, city, and borough in the kingdom have its compact and vigorous non-electors' committee, composed of earnest and practical men, and let every such committee make it its first and principal business to exact full and explicit declarations from every candidate on the subject of Parliamentary Reform. Do not be satisfied with vague and plausible, or conditional answers. Appoint men from each committee to put these questions, and, that nothing may be left to chance, have them previously prepared and written down. Where it is possible, appoint working men, but in all cases appoint men of mature age, and of discreet and sober character. Such men, however humble their speech or dress, will be listened to with respect, and do your cause honour. Above all, we think it exceedingly desirable that the non-electors should act for themselves in this matter – that they should have faith in their own leadership, and in their own power to carry out their own objects without the aid of professional agitation. This faith will enable them to hold their own against Whigs, Tories, and sham-Reformers. It will rid them of the charge of being the dupes and slaves of demagogues; and it is the only means whereby they can practically influence the coming elections. For when those who have votes see that they have only to deal with the sober and reasonable, but voteless artisans, mechanics, and labourers, with whom they come in daily contact; whose hopes are their hopes, and the common hopes of every true Englishman; whose interests are their interests; and whose prosperity is the foundation of their own prosperity, depend upon it their doubts as to the expediency of enfranchising the masses will vanish, and their very selfishness, if not higher motives, will assist to a speedy, practical, and satisfactory solution of the Reform question.

Reading 14.2 Speech of William Gladstone to the House of Commons (27 April 1866)

Source: HC Deb 27 April 1866, vol. 183, col. 147 [Online]. Available at http://hansard.millbanksystems.com/ (Accessed 12 May 2017).

My hon. Friend says we know nothing about the labouring classes. Is not one single word a sufficient reply? That word is Lancashire; Lancashire, associated with the sufferings of the last four years, so painful and bitter in themselves to contemplate, but so nobly and gloriously borne? The qualities then exhibited were the qualities not of select men here and there among a depraved multitude, but of the mass of a working community. The sufferings were sufferings of the mass. The heroism was heroism of the mass. For my own part, I cannot believe that the men who exhibited those qualities were only a sample of the people of England, and that the rest would have wholly failed in exhibiting the same great qualities had occasion arisen. I cannot see what argument could be found for some wise and temperate experiment of the extension of civil rights among such people, if the experience of the past few years does not sufficiently afford it.

Reading 14.3 The Reform Bill (1866)

Source: Cecil, R. (1866) 'The Reform Bill', *Quarterly Review,* **vol. 119, no. 23, April, pp. 552–3.**

It is a battle not of parties, but of classes. It is a struggle to decide whether the payers of direct taxation shall tax themselves, or shall be taxed at the will of those who do not pay it; whether the laws of property shall be made by the owners of property, or by those who have everything to gain and nothing to lose; whether the country shall be governed by those who have the most stake in it to stimulate them, and the most culture to guide them, or by those in whom both these qualifications are nearly or wholly absent. In short, it is a portion of the great political struggle of our century – the struggle between property, be its amount small or great, and mere numbers.

...

If those who dread the advance of democracy are right in their apprehensions, the success of the series of measures, of which the first is now before us, will imply results which every class, every industry, and every holder of property will feel; and those will feel them most whose stake in the welfare of their country is largest. It means Government by men of less independence and lower culture: it means laws which will fetter capital to favour labour, and will trammel the freedom of the owners of property to make it cheaper and more accessible to those who have it not: it means taxes levied and spent by the men that contribute to them least.

Reading 14.4 Extracts from the Select Committee Report on Parliamentary and Municipal Elections (1870)

Source: *Select Committee on Parliamentary and Municipal Election: Report, Proceedings, Appendices*, Session 1870, Paper 115, pp. 4, 9.

With regard to Parliamentary Elections in Boroughs your Committee have examined many witnesses, but the evidence does no more than confirm what has been frequently established before Committees of the House, Royal Commissions, and the Judges who have been engaged in the trial of Election Petitions. The returns in the Appendix to the Report of the Select Committee on Parliamentary and Municipal Elections in the last Session of Parliament show that both in former and in the last Elections various corrupt practices, of which bribery and treating were the chief, have prevailed, and to such an extent as to invalidate many Elections; and it cannot be supposed that either now or formerly have the whole of such practices been brought to light. It has been proved that in some instances rioting and violence to person and property have occurred on the nomination and polling days so as to interfere with the freedom of the Election, while in a much larger class of case Elections are accompanied by drunkenness and disorder.

It is difficult to arrive at the truth of the allegations of intimidation of workmen by masters, of tenants by landlords, of tradesmen by customers, and of working men by each other. This also applies to intimidation by ministers of religion. That intimidation in these forms is not extensively practised in a mode capable of legal proof, is evident from the rarity of cases in which a return has been set aside on this ground. But that it is practised, though in a manner difficult of proof before a legal tribunal, cannot be doubted. We have examined many witnesses who have alleged the existence of intimidation of each kind above described. As soon as this evidence has become known in the locality, applications have been received that witnesses on the other side should be examined, who have denied the charges brought against themselves, but have usually attributed similar practices to their opponents. It is certain, at least, that whether intimidation is extensively practised or not, the fear of it widely prevails among that class of voters who are liable to its influence. There exists during the canvass in most boroughs a system of working upon voters through private considerations, whether of interest, hope, or fear, for political purposes, and this system enables undue influence in a modified form to be constantly practised.

It remains to be considered, whether it is desirable that the ballot should be adopted in this country.

The principal objections which have been advanced against the ballot as applied to our own elections are: That the act of voting is a public duty, and should involve a public responsibility: That it would lead to hypocrisy and deception: That it would do little to restrain the practice of treating: That it would increase bribery, by making it more difficult to detect: That it would be wholly inoperative in the case of spiritual intimidation such as that which is alleged to exist so extensively in Ireland: That it would afford facilities for personation.

While we admit that there is force in many of these objections, we are, on the whole, of opinion that the ballot possesses many great advantages, and that the weight of evidence leads to the conclusion that this change in the mode of voting would not only promote the tranquillity both of Municipal and Parliamentary Elections, but will also protect voters from undue influence and intimidation, and introduce into elections a greater degree of freedom and purity than is secured under the present system. But in recommending the adoption of the ballot, we desire to express our opinion that, in order to secure the benefits we anticipate from its introduction into this country, it is necessary that the secrecy of the vote should be inviolable, except in the case of any voter who is found guilty of bribery, or whose vote, in due course of law, has been adjudged invalid.

Unit 15 Britain and empire, 1839–1886

Karl Hack

Contents

Aims

This unit will:

- explain Britain's interactions with vast swathes of the mid-nineteenth-century world

- help you to engage with some key terms and concepts in the history of British imperialism

- further develop your ability to recognise and analyse complex historical arguments

- use and analyse a range of secondary and primary sources, including visual sources.

Introduction

The unit 'The British Isles and the Atlantic World' (Unit 7 in Block 1) encouraged you to 'think Atlantically' as a way of understanding how slaves, people and trade criss-crossed an area that embraced Britain, West Africa, the Caribbean and North America. By 1839, however, slavery and the slave trade had been abolished, Britain's Caribbean territories were declining in importance, and its West African **enclaves** remained insignificant.

The Atlantic trade had been conducted under a mercantilist system: the process by which government tried to control trade in colonial produce so that it was carried only by British and colonial ships, and with high tariffs placed on foreign imports. By the 1840s this was being replaced by a move towards 'free trade': trade without tariffs and open to competition. In Britain, there was an increasing commitment to free trade between nations, and a greater confidence that this would lead to prosperity and peace in the future. As the Great Exhibition of 1851 demonstrated, there was also optimism that Britain, as the leading industrial nation and the 'workshop of the world', would lead the way in promoting the benefits of global free trade. Yet, instead, Britain's imperial reach increased vastly between 1839 and 1886, as new colonial territories were acquired, often through violent interventions. Why was this? How did it happen? Where did it happen?

This unit will help you to answer those questions. It covers the explosive expansion of British power and populations overseas between 1839 and 1886. There were, for instance, 22.6 million emigrants from the British Isles between 1815 and 1914 (Harper, 1999, p. 75). This period commenced with British territory much reduced after the loss of the 13 American colonies in 1783, and ended with Britain accounting for almost half the world's exports, almost half its merchant marine fleet and the majority of the world's settler colonies. You will learn how 'Britain' came to mean not simply a geographical location but a worldwide web of interconnections, people and interests, so much so that in 1883 John Seeley (1834–1895), Regius Professor of History at Cambridge University in 1869–95, could conjure up the image of a 'Greater Britain' (Seeley, 1909 [1883], p. 346): not just a ragbag of conquests but a society, state and economy that had spread to the far reaches of the globe.

You will focus in the unit on three types of overseas expansion, in three successive sections. Section 15.1 will cover economic aspects and the idea of 'the imperialism of free trade' – an example of how historians use specialist concepts and models to help them understand complex phenomena (in this case, imperialism). As you will see, such tools open up debate. Section 15.2 will examine British dominance in India. Section 15.3 will explore the emergence of what some historians have termed a 'British world' that bound together Britain and its settler colonies in Australia, Canada, South Africa and New Zealand.

By the end of the unit, you will have a firm outline grasp of Britain's changing place in the world. You will also be able to use this knowledge to consider how liberal ideas of global free trade coexisted with the expansion of empire.

15.1 The imperialism of free trade: an economic model of British imperialism

The theory of the imperialism of free trade was developed by historians who wanted to solve a paradox. From 1839 to 1886 Britain made numerous acquisitions of territory, from tiny ports that became coaling and trading posts such as Aden in modern-day Yemen (1839), to larger territories such as Upper Burma (1886). Indeed, between 1830 and 1880 Britain added 15.3 million square kilometres, 63 times the area of the 'mother country', to its possessions. Their combined population soared from 189 million to 271 million (Etemad, 2007, p. 155). The population of the United Kingdom (including all of Ireland) remained small by comparison, growing from 26.7 million to 37.7 million between 1841 and 1891 (Cook and Keith, 1984 [1975], pp. 232–3).

Yet this expansion happened despite increasing numbers of people in Britain opposing territorial acquisition, and despite suspicions about the very word 'empire'. In the mid-nineteenth century 'oriental' empires such as that of China were seen as corrupt and autocratic. Closer to home, the Ottoman Empire was seen as decaying. Rule over 'alien' races was seen as out of date and did not match Britain's sense of itself, after the abolition of Atlantic slavery, as a modern nation supporting ever-increasing freedom. In fact, a whole host of mid-nineteenth-century attitudes seemed to constitute an 'anti-imperial' mindset.

Empires also did not fit with new ideas in Britain about the efficient and minimal state. A number of colonial wars in the eighteenth century had left a fear among British politicians that colonies could be expensive to protect, while contributing little to their own defence. Adam Smith (whom you will recall from Block 1) had argued, in his 1776 book *An Inquiry into ... the Wealth of Nations*, that

> If any of these provinces of the British empire cannot be made to contribute towards the support of the whole empire ... Great Britain should free herself from the expense of ... supporting any part of their civil or military establishments [and] ... accommodate ... to the real mediocrity of her circumstances.
>
> (Smith, 1869 [1776], p. 550)

Smith's book formed part of a wider drive towards arguments that free trade would benefit a country more than mercantilism or monopolies of colonial trade, which he argued were expensive and difficult to maintain. His ideas became increasing popular in the mid-century as the nature of the global economy shifted. There were four main aspects behind this decisive shift from mercantilism to free trade. First, the loss of the American colonies, alongside the achievement of independence in the 1820s by most of Spain's South American colonies, made extra-imperial markets relatively more important than before. Second, liberal politicians and advocates of limited government became frustrated with the costs of defending colonies. For example, the expenses involved in crushing Maori resistance to settler expansion in the embryonic settler colony of New Zealand in the 1860s provoked debates about the value of empire. Third, as industrialisation took hold and British production rose sharply, it was in Britain's interests to encourage freer trade. Fourth, the new manufacturing interest and the growing middle classes wanted free trade. The free trade movement grew and, as you know from the unit 'The "age of equipoise" and the Great Exhibition of 1851' (Unit 8), interest groups from industrial cities and the Midlands petitioned Parliament in the hope of ending protectionist policies such as the Corn Laws. They also campaigned to end trading monopolies held by organisations such as the East India Company.

The confluence of these forces saw a dramatic acceleration in the British move towards free trade in the mid-nineteenth century. As you know, the Corn Laws were finally removed in 1846. Then in the 1850s William Gladstone as chancellor of the Exchequer slashed import duties on 400 items and concentrated revenue-raising tariffs on a few, such as tobacco, tea and spirits (Cain, 1999). Britain increasingly sought freer trade agreements with other countries. These included the 1860 Cobden–Chevalier Treaty, a trade agreement that saw British exports to France, and French exports of wine to Britain, double in the 1860s (Woodward, 1962, p. 179). On the back of this, British trade enjoyed fast growth. Champions of free trade such as Richard Cobden – the Manchester factory owner, Liberal MP and anti-Corn Law campaign organiser, whom you met in Unit 8 – argued that expanding free trade would also promote international peace.

Campaigners such as Cobden, and fellow Liberal John Bright, did not always have their way. Their kind of patriotism, which associated liberty with limited government, free trade and fair competition, was, at times, overridden by a popular desire to defend British interests. Bright lost his Manchester parliamentary seat in 1857 after opposing British involvement in the **Crimean War** (1853–56), though he was soon returned again, this time for Birmingham. But their free trade ideas were ascendant. The Navigation Acts, which since 1651 had sought to direct trade in key colonial produce to British and colonial-built ships, and to insist trade in listed goods went to Europe through Britain, were dismantled in 1849. This was the end of mercantilism: the centuries-long tradition of protecting colonial trade (see also Unit 7). British shipping, including, from the 1830s, larger sailing ships and increasing numbers of steamships, no longer needed such protection.

This movement towards freer trade also affected Britain's biggest imperial possession: India. After the loss of the American colonies, and decline in the importance of Caribbean sugar production following the abolition of the slave trade (1807) and slavery (1833), British imperialists began to look to the east, in particular to India. The East India Company (EIC) had secured the right to monopolise trade to the east, but the company had morphed into a territorial power during the eighteenth century. When its charter was renewed in the nineteenth century it lost monopoly rights, first to trade with India (1813) and then China (1833). By the 1840s the company was no longer a monopolist trading company. Instead, company ports such as Bombay (today known as Mumbai) and Singapore began acting as trading nodes for multiple traders and investors from London and the wider world.

Trade boomed as the cities in these networks increased in size and sophistication. Though textiles (mainly finished cotton goods) still accounted for half of Britain's exports in 1850, coal exports were surging, manufactures were strong, and expanding trade made sales of British services (shipping, insurance and banking, sometimes termed 'invisibles') ever more important (Cain and Hopkins, 1999).

We are left with a perplexing paradox. Political and economic thinking was moving towards freer trade and included a strong strand of scepticism about territorial empire. Yet, as noted at the beginning of this section, Britain kept adding new territory to its empire. How could that be?

In 1953, the historians John Gallagher and Ronald Robinson attempted to square this circle. They came up with the concept of the imperialism of free trade and their ideas are still highly influential. So, what is the imperialism of free trade?

Activity 15.1

Now go to the module website and complete Activity 15.1 'The imperialism of free trade'. This should take around an hour.

Gallagher and Robinson used the concept of the imperialism of free trade to argue that British attitudes to trade and empire remained constant through the nineteenth century and aimed at 'integrating new regions into the expanding economy' (Gallagher and Robinson, 1953, p. 5). They argued that Britain sought to expand and protect free trade and investment by whatever method was cheapest. The British preferred to do this using 'informal' methods of influence, but stood ready to use imperial methods to protect trade and investment when required. As Gallagher and Robinson said in their article, 'British policy followed the principle of extending control informally if possible and formally if necessary' (Gallagher and Robinson, 1953, p. 13).

In the mid-century, Britain was often able to get what it wanted without resorting to imperial control. This was in part because the Royal Navy ruled the waves virtually unchallenged after Napoleon Bonaparte (1769–1821, reigned as emperor 1804–14/15) had been finally defeated in 1815, and before a united Germany and Italy had been created (in 1871 and 1861, respectively). Hence free trade treaties, gentle pressure, threats, or short, sharp interventions – what became known as 'gunboat diplomacy' – could often ensure that a territory was integrated, or remained integrated, into a globalising world trade network without formal annexation. But as the century progressed this free rein came to an end, precipitating a scramble to convert informal influence into formal colonies. There were three factors that helped to drive this change across the mid-nineteenth century.

First, many western-dominated entrepôts (settlements offering major trade and service facilities) had developed in the mid-century. They acted as 'beachheads' or 'bridgeheads' (Darwin, 2009, pp. 3, 24) through which new capital and actors flowed into lightly developed areas. The sudden migration of money and people into these areas could have a destabilising effect, leading to social, economic or political breakdown. This breakdown then tempted Britain into more formal intervention to restore order. There was also a tendency for the 'man-on-the-spot' (an administrator, trader, missionary or settler) in these 'beachheads' to call on London to intervene in troubles, calls which became more frequent and harder to ignore as the 'beachhead' expanded. Hence the British government was drawn into interventions, especially after 1880, by events on the ground and the need to protect British investments.

Second, Britain's naval dominance went into *relative* decline after the mid-century, as France recovered from the Napoleonic Wars and as new nations such as Germany and Italy enlarged their navies. So informal dominance, screened by the Royal Navy and backed up through gunboat diplomacy, was at its peak only from 1815 to the 1860s.

Third, some powers, notably France and Germany, set about expanding their colonial territories, particularly in Africa and tropical areas from the 1880s, leading to a competitive scramble to stake out areas of informal dominance more formally. Therefore, while Britain's presence in Africa was mainly restricted to coastal enclaves and ports in the mid-century, by 1914, as you will see in 'Britain, empire and imperialism, 1880–1914' (Unit 20), almost all of Africa would be divided among European powers.

The Opium Wars

This leaves us with the question: how well does the imperialism of free trade work as an explanatory theory for the period covered here: 1839 to 1886? Let's test this by looking at one intervention – the First Opium War of 1839–42 – and the linked acquisition of Hong Kong. This and the Second Opium War of 1856–60 played a central part in the construction of a 'treaty port' system that would see western powers (and Japan) carve out niches or 'concession' areas within many Chinese ports. In some of these areas they also reserved the right to try their citizens under their own laws (known as 'extraterritorial' rights). How did Britain acquire rights to these areas?

From the seventeenth century the East India Company traded Chinese tea, porcelain and silk. Given low Chinese demand for British goods, the company paid mainly in silver, and was restricted to trading with select Chinese businesses ('the Hong') from factories (trading houses) at the Chinese port of Canton (Guangzhou). (Throughout the unit, where modern Chinese spelling differs from the historical spelling, the modern spelling is given in brackets after the first use.) From the 1780s, however, the EIC developed a monopoly of large-scale opium production in its Indian possessions. This illegal narcotic was shipped by independent traders who landed their illicit cargo at Lintin Island in the Pearl River Delta, not far from Canton.

From Lintin (see Figures 15.1 and 15.2), small Chinese-manned crafts – 'fast crabs' or 'scrambling dragons' – shuttled the opium ashore, bribing or skirting around Chinese authorities. Britain may have ended slavery in 1833, but its eastern and often Scottish traders had few qualms about smuggling this illegal narcotic. Boosted by the end of the EIC monopoly on trade with China in 1833, by 1838 British traders were shipping thousands of mango-wood chests of opium a year to China. Rather than British traders feeding silver into China's economy, they were now draining it out as payment for this opium (Perdue, 2010).

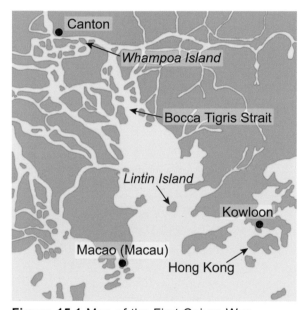

Figure 15.1 Map of the First Opium War

This silver drain might have continued, but revolutions in South America (1808–33) reduced the world supply of silver, which China needed to underpin its currency. Moves were made to keep silver from leaving the country by enforcing restrictions on the opium trade. Consequently, in March 1839 Special Commissioner Lin Zexu (1785–1850) arrived in Canton with instructions to enforce existing bans on opium. Lin locked up British and American merchants in the city. He made their food and water supplies, and their release, dependent on them handing over opium and signing a bond promising never to trade again in the drug. He then had the contents of 20,000 confiscated chests destroyed.

Figure 15.2 After William John Huggins, *The Opium Ships at Lintin*, nineteenth century. Photo: © De Agostini Picture Library / Bridgeman Images

The chief superintendent of British trade at Canton, Captain Charles Elliot (1801–1875), had promised opium traders that the British government would make good any losses that might result from the merchants handing their opium over to the Chinese. Elliot thought that the Chinese should pay for the destroyed stock. He blockaded Canton in pursuit of compensation, and a naval battle broke out in November 1839. At this point Lord Palmerston (whom you will recall from the unit 'Politics and the people': Unit 14) was foreign secretary. Never shy of protecting British interests, he dispatched a fleet and troops from India. Between then and August 1842 Royal Navy and EIC ships, including four steamships, won multiple engagements. The latter blew the vastly inferior Chinese war junks out of the water. The Chinese signed the Treaty of Nanking (Nanjing) in August 1842, agreeing to pay for British losses, to open five ports for the British to trade in and to acknowledge British sovereignty over Hong Kong island (see Figure 15.3), to which British merchant ships had withdrawn in 1839.

Figure 15.3 B. Clayton, after Piqua, *Victoria Town, Hong Kong Island*, 1847. Photo: © The Print Collector / Age Fotostock. This drawing shows Chinese junks and western ships, including a steamer. Hong Kong's population grew from less than 7,500 in 1842 to over 33,000 in 1850. It now formed part of the accelerating speed of flows of ships, people and information (especially as overseas telegraph lines expanded from the 1870s), through similar growing ports, and to and from British ports. Inland from the latter, the expanding railway system also accelerated the movement of people, goods and ideas (Osterhammel, 2014).

Judging British motives by the *results* of this conflict as evidenced by the Treaty of Nanking fits the imperialism of free trade theory: as you can see, gunboat diplomacy was used to secure the integration of China into world trade. But for historians, this raises further questions about methods. How far, for instance, are we entitled to deduce motives from a treaty (Nanking) signed after blood and treasure had been expended, and victory won? What do historical sources suggest about the original motivations for (and against) the actions Britain took?

Activity 15.2

Now go to the module website and complete Activity 15.2 'Understanding the causes of the First Opium War'. This should take around an hour.

Whatever the reasons that fuelled British intervention in China in 1839–42, it was controversial in Britain. When on 7–9 April 1840 the House of Commons debated censuring Palmerston's move to war, the final vote was close: 271 MPs favoured his actions, with 261 against.

Some free trade supporters actually opposed intervention, making their case in both Parliament and the newspapers. They variously argued that the government knew in advance of the change in Chinese policy, that the opium trade was evil (though, as laudanum, opium was used as a drug in Britain) and that war would damage the flow of trade.

Palmerston would later extend the idea of protecting British citizens abroad to a general principle, echoing the Roman idea of *civis Romanus sum* ('I am a Roman citizen'). That is, Roman citizens had been able to claim protection and Roman law wherever they might be in the empire by asserting their citizenship. This principle was asserted in the case of Don (David) Pacifico (1784?–1854), which mirrored the Opium War's muddying of economics, rights and prestige.

The case of Don Pacifico

In April 1847 the financier Mayer Amschel de Rothschild (1818–1874) visited Athens to discuss loans: the Greek government was not making payments due on its debt to European banks. Rothschild was Jewish and, to avoid causing him offence, the Greek government temporarily forbade the local practice of hanging an effigy of Judas Iscariot during the Orthodox Greek Easter celebrations. However, a mob (with the alleged encouragement of at least one Greek minister), annoyed about this interference, took revenge on a Gibraltar-born British subject, Don Pacifico, who was also Jewish. The mob looted Don Pacifico's house. He appealed to the Greek government for compensation, and then applied to the British government for support when the Greek government questioned this appeal. In response, Palmerston had the Royal Navy seize Greek naval vessels in Athens in June 1850. When challenged in the House of Commons on 25 June, Palmerston argued that 'a British subject, in whatever land he may be, shall feel confident that the watchful eye and the strong arm of England, will protect him against injustice', citing the Roman example (A Web of English History, n.d.).

Gladstone and Sir Robert Peel both spoke against the use of force against Greece. Gladstone worried about Britain setting itself up as a universal judge of others, and asked if Britain really wanted to be compared to a conquering empire such as Rome. Cobden feared the financial costs and moral hazards of a foreign policy inspired by an eagerness to fight. It was argued that Don Pacifico should have had recourse to Greek courts. But the House of Commons endorsed Palmerston's conduct and his argument found a high degree of press favour (Parry, 1989).

The Don Pacifico affair, as with the Opium Wars, demonstrates how difficult it can be to separate out motivations for intervention. These examples show how the imperialism of free trade (the Don Pacifico affair being linked to loans to Greece), British prestige, and rights to property and security of person had become intertwined. It was difficult to refuse to support intervention when significant British property was destroyed, loans were defaulted on, or British subjects harassed even when, as in this case, that subject was a Gibraltar-born man from Malta. Such mid-Victorian confidence in their ability to enforce their own standards on the world must be understood against the background of naval predominance, technological leadership and a sense of Britain being at the vanguard of modernisation.

Clearly, a desire to extend free trade and its infrastructure, and a desire to ensure new territories entered the world market, did contribute to the expansion of British imperial control and to its willingness to use gunboat diplomacy. It can also help to explain a preference by statesmen in London for informal influence, and for solutions short of territorial control. In many cases, the question is not whether the imperialism of free trade played a part, but what part that was in a wider cocktail of causes.

There is, however, an additional problem with the imperialism of free trade as an answer to our original paradox. Most of the peoples added to the empire in this period were not in areas easily explained by Gallagher and Robinson's theory. The main areas of demographic expansion were not 'informal' zones of economic influence, or areas that the British thought needed integrating into the world economy. The vast majority of the people in the empire were in India, which is the subject of the next section.

15.2 India

At its peak, Britain ruled over a fifth of the world's population. But in demographic terms India was more important than the rest of the empire combined. By 1880, 94 per cent of the empire's population (255 million out of 271 million) was in India. In 1872, just one Indian province, Bengal, contained more than 67 million people (Etemad, 2007, pp. 156, 166). Given these figures, it is not surprising that the majority of the British Empire's population increase in the preceding few decades was also in India.

But it is not obvious that British expansion in India was down to the imperialism of free trade. Yes, India was economically important. But imperialism in India had grown on the back of the East India Company's rights to a monopoly of trade between the east and Britain (see Figure 15.4 for the company's grandiose London building). So, if expansion here was not obviously about free trade, what might it have been about?

At one level, expansion was made possible by the EIC's tax-raising and military powers. The EIC had become a territorial power as it grabbed tax-gathering rights in Bengal (1756–64) and other areas. The secret to the company's power was its recruitment of large numbers of Indian 'sepoys' (infantry), trained by the British and paid well. With this army peaking at over 238,000 Indian and 45,000 British soldiers by 1857, the company squeezed out other European powers such as France, and established itself as the predominant power. It controlled vast swathes of territory directly, and entered alliances with Indian princely states, which together covered another third of the subcontinent. So in terms of soldiers and subjects and trade, the EIC was what made Britain the world's biggest overseas empire by far. It was also what made Victoria an empress, as she became empress of India (Kaiser-i-Hind) following Disraeli's Royal Titles Act of 1876.

Gallagher and Robinson cheekily inserted Indian acquisitions into the list of things that their theory of the imperialism of free trade could not explain. As such, they treated India as if it were marginal to the question of mid-century imperialism, when it was in fact one of the main areas of expansion. For example, their 1953 article noted that between 1840 to 1851 the large areas of Sind (annexed in 1842) and Punjab (annexed in 1849) were acquired. The latter alone had a population of 22.7 million by 1881.

Figure 15.4 Thomas Malton the Younger, *East India House*, c.1799, watercolour over etched outline, 22 x 31cm. Yale Center for British Art, Paul Mellon Collection, Acc. No. B2001.2.1001

So, if expansion in India was not obviously about 'free trade', what might it have been about? At one level, the answer is that India shows us how empire expanded due to threats and opportunities at imperial frontiers. Let's take the acquisition of Sind, in the north-west of the subcontinent, as an example. Sind's emirs (rulers) were viewed with suspicion after the British suffered setbacks in the nearby Anglo-Afghan War of 1839–42. As a result, an ambitious British general used the fact that the emirs had massed troops near the border with British India to justify annexing it. In this case and many more, annexation was motivated by the desire to fix perceived turbulence on India's frontiers, and by the ambitions of officers and administrators who exceeded their orders.

In addition to population increases, there was a second type of 'expansion' in India – an expansion of cultural and educational influence. From the 1830s to the 1850s debate raged between those of an 'Orientalist' turn – who favoured preserving princely states with minimum interference, and funding education in Indian languages – and the 'Anglicists'. The latter saw themselves as reformers and wanted to spread English-language education and replace 'backward' Indian customs. Thomas Macaulay's 'Minute on Education in India' of 1835 had referred to vernacular languages as 'fruitful of monstrous superstitions', that helped people to purify themselves 'after touching an ass'. He wanted 'to form a class who may be interpreters between us and the millions we govern; a class of persons, Indian in blood and colour, but English in taste, in opinions, in morals, and in intellect' (quoted in Burton, 2001, pp.18–21). The Anglicists and other reformers secured abolition (on paper at least) of suttee (*sati*), or the burning of a wife at her husband's funeral (1828), the ending of female infanticide (1870), and the production of a systematic Indian Penal Code (1860), thus reducing reliance on Indian *pandit*s (experts on custom and law, and the origin of the word 'pundit'). In some respects India was ahead of British reform efforts, with patronage replaced by open examinations for selection to the Indian Civil Service after 1853 (examinations in Britain followed in 1870).

In practice these reforms mainly affected the urbanised 9–10 per cent of Indians, rather than the overwhelming mass who were illiterate and rural (Brown, 1985, pp. 101–4). But in one respect these reforming, modernising and expansionary impulses would have a shattering impact.

Rebellion in India

Lord Dalhousie (1812–1860) was governor-general of India from 1849 until 1856. To press on with modernisation, he formed a Department of Public Works and accelerated the building of internal telegraphs, railways and irrigation. He departed in 1856 declaring India tranquil. It was anything but, due partly to his policy of 'lapse'. This involved taking over Indian-ruled states whenever he discerned poor government, or when a ruler died without natural heirs (even if that ruler had nominated a successor). In seven years, seven states were taken over, culminating in 1854 with Oudh (Awadh), from where much of the Bengal Army was recruited. To sepoys, often high-status Hindus seeking the standing as well as the pay that service brought, this policy of lapse was one of many slights. British officers increasingly seemed distant, and at worst disparaging, towards sepoys. Resentment also spread as new rifle cartridges that had to be bitten open were alleged to be greased with animal fat that was ritually polluting (beef fat in the case of Hindus; pork fat in the case of Muslims). A storm was brewing.

That storm broke in early 1857. Despite reassurances that cartridges would not be greased with polluting fat, there were recurrent mutinies until, at Meerut in May 1857, a group of sepoys killed their officers and took up arms. As the mutiny spread, people joined it for all sorts of reasons, so that it became part mutiny, part rebellion, part war of independence. European men, women and children in Delhi were slaughtered and a few towns were seized. At Lucknow and Cawnpore (Kanpur) handfuls of European soldiers and civilians held out. In the summer of 1857 things looked, and were, desperate for the British.

But with the mutineers divided in purpose and ill-coordinated, British troops slowly retook ground, until during 1858 the mutiny–rebellion petered out. What, then, were the British responses? How did these events change the value and perception of British India? Answering these questions requires us to understand how events were understood in Britain. In particular, what was the impact of the stories about the killings of Europeans, including women and children, which reached the British press over the summer of 1857?

The slaughter of women and children at Cawnpore in Oudh on 15 July 1857 was one of the most notorious atrocities. A few hundred Europeans had taken refuge in the barracks there, surrendering on 25 June in return for safe passage guaranteed by the local rebel leader, Nana Sahib (c.1820–c.1859). For reasons we are not sure about, their embarkation at the River Ganges degenerated into a firefight in which most of the men were killed and around 200 women and children taken prisoner. The latter were locked in the Bibighar ('House of Women') under Nana Sahib's orders. When a relief force led by General Henry Havelock (1795–1857) approached, Nana Sahib ordered the killing of the prisoners. The sepoys refused to fire more than the first volley, so Nana Sahib's bodyguard and local butchers finished the job and dropped the corpses into a well (Tickell, 2013). When Havelock's troops entered the city two days later, they discovered the house caked in blood.

Exercise 15.1

This exercise requires you to analyse two sources. The first (Figure 15.5) is *In Memoriam*, originally painted by Noël (Joseph) Paton (1821–1901) in 1858, as altered for exhibition in Scotland in 1859 and subsequently printed as an engraving by the Scottish publisher Alexander Hill in 1862. The second source is an *Illustrated London News* review (dated 15 May 1858) of the painting in its original form.

This should take about an hour.

Part 1

First, describe the image in Figure 15.5. In the light of what you have read above about the Indian mutiny and the slaughter at Cawnpore, what do you think the impact of this would have been on audiences in Britain?

Figure 15.5 William Henry Simmons, after Noël (Joseph) Paton, *In Memoriam*, 1862, engraving, 86 x 69cm. Victoria and Albert Museum, museum number: E.164-1970. © Victoria & Albert Museum, London

Specimen answer

Figure 15.5 combines two starkly contrasting foci, to give a sense of vulnerable European women and children rescued by valorous men: in this case Scottish Highlanders. The Highlanders, shown about to burst through the door, would have appealed to the patriotism of British audiences, particularly when exhibited in Scotland in 1859. Even with this sense of salvation and coming victory, the portrayal of the women and children invokes a sense of fear, vulnerability and danger. The central figure, ornately dressed in Indian patterns redolent of a privileged colonial life, is reading, while holding one younger girl whose garment appears to be slipping off her shoulder (perhaps hinting at the idea of violation to come), and another who is fearful.

Discussion

This image is a reworking of Paton's original painting. Paton had added the Highlanders to this painting for an exhibition in Scotland in 1859. No copies of the original exist. However, historians can find reviews of the first exhibition of Paton's work. These reviews can give us clues as to what the original painting looked like, its impact on audiences and why it was changed.

Part 2

Now read the following extract from a review of the original painting. What do you think the impact of the original image would have been? Note in particular who the review describes as poised at the doorway.

The Exhibition at the Royal Academy

More of the charnel-house! Ay, and in passages which curdle the blood with vain, indignant horror, and make one wish that the pen of history could for once be plunged in Lethe [forgetfulness]. Yet with such scenes Mr. Paton's brush patiently deals; and he describes his horrible picture as 'In Memoriam' (471), and inscribes beneath it, in quaint old letters, with illuminated initials, words of Divine consolation from Scripture: – 'Yea, though I walk through the Valley of the Shadow of Death, I will fear no evil; for Thou, Lord,' &c., which, in face of what is enacting above, read almost like mockery. There, in that miserable murder-hole, crouch the helpless English women and children of Cawnpore. Terror, anguish, despair are in every face; frantic, unavailing prayers, mingling with wild shrieks, seem to fill the very air; one little innocent alone sleeps, still unconscious of its impending doom. Above, in the background, brutal sepoys are glaring through the opened door and the little casement, in the very moment of rushing upon their victims. The subject is too revolting for further description. The picture is one which ought not to have been hung; and, in justice to the hanging committee, we believe that it was not without considerable compunction and hesitation that they consented to its being so.

(*The Illustrated London News*, 15 May 1858)

Specimen answer

The original painting was clearly shocking. It depicted sepoys at the doorway and window, with the intent of suggesting their imminent entry and killing, if not violation, of the women. This would have struck its audience as a representation of the historical events at the Bibighar, frozen in the seconds before the final massacre. Viewing this just months after the events of summer 1857 could have evoked immediate, if not visceral, sensations of shock, horror and anger. The reviewer might be accused of adding melodrama ('wild shrieks'), or might have been reflecting a real sense that the attempted effect is too soon and too raw.

Discussion

This exercise has encouraged you to think about the construction, use and role of images as historical sources, and to consider how the representation of events can be reframed for different audiences to convey different messages and invoke different emotions. Paintings, prints and illustrations are every bit as much constructed 'texts' as newspaper articles and books are. Decoding the 'text' becomes easier if we can discover more about the author, their intent and the context of creation.

The exercise has also invited you to consider the emotional impact of historical events such as the mutiny and the effect that images such as *In Memoriam* had on the British imagination at home. Emotion matters, and helped to shape public perceptions of India and demands for revenge (see Figure 15.6).

Both the original and revised versions of the painting were criticised, the former for being almost indecent in its horror, the latter for shrinking from the tragedy of the real event (Smith et al., 2016). It is difficult to fully comprehend the potentially distressing nature of viewing this painting at the time without standing in front of the canvas. I have stood in front of the later version (at Tate Britain's Empire and Art exhibition of 2016) and even this delivers an intense experience. The figures at the forefront are almost life-size, and their prominence draws the viewer to stand close, until you feel almost in the room with the women, the discarded clothing, the emotions on the children's faces, and the vulnerability. Yet when the more powerful original was shown, in the spring and summer of 1858, it was only months after the newspaper accounts of the rape, torture and murder of European women and children in the summer to autumn of 1857. This image hinted at these wider, in some respects exaggerated, press notions of widespread violation.

Figure 15.6 Sir John Tenniel, 'The British Lion's vengeance on the Bengal Tiger', cartoon from *Punch*, 1857. Photo: FALKENSTEINFOTO / Alamy

Some British newspapers, including *The Times*, called for vengeance as a step to justice and restoring order in India. And they got it. In the advance to relieve Europeans at Cawnpore and Lucknow, some officers hanged Indians, burned villages and killed with limited discrimination. At Cawnpore, Brigadier General James Neill (1810–1857) ordered that 'rebels' should lick a portion of the blood on the Bibighar floor before being hanged. Elsewhere, the Mughal practice of blowing rebels from the mouths of cannons was employed for demonstrative effect. William Howard Russell (1820–1907), in a diary entry of 25 September 1857, recalled the aftermath of retaking a town, with 'soldiers laden with loot or plunder: shawls, rich tapestry, gold and silver brocades, caskets of jewels, arms of splendid dresses. The men are wild with fury and lust of gold – literally drunk with plunder' (Russell, 2010 [1860], pp. 329–30).

But even as the mutiny drew thoughts in Britain of Old Testament-style retribution, and contrasts between virtuous Christian women and mutinous sepoys, the official line quickly moved from retribution to conciliation. Amnesty was offered for those who had not shed blood in rebelling. The Government of India Act, passed on 2 August 1858, swept away the old EIC, putting India under the control of the British crown. The cabinet-level position of secretary of state for India was created. Indeed, the viceroy and governor-general, Lord Charles Canning (1812–1862), was berated by *Punch* as 'Clemency Canning' for moving so quickly to stop the excesses of 1857.

Exercise 15.2

Turn to Reading 15.1, 'Extract from "Proclamation, by the Queen in Council, to the Princes, Chiefs, and People of India" (1 November 1858)', located at the end of the unit. Here, Queen Victoria sets out a new vision for India on 1 November 1858, by which point the revolt had been extinguished.

What do you notice about the tone of the declaration?

This should take around 30 minutes.

Specimen answer

The tone is conciliatory, promising clemency for all but the worst offenders. It is also respectful, committing to ensure a wide range of rights to religion and equal access to the law and official posts, and to respect existing treaties and the remaining princes.

Yet the proclamation also reeks of authority and control, starting as it does with a statement of who power is granted to (the viceroy and governor-general). Another way of describing this combination is that it is strongly paternalistic (showing the combined authority and yet care of a parent), as seen in the phrase 'to administer its Government for the benefit of all our subjects resident therein'. People will benefit, but by strong, just and concerned British rule.

The aftermath of the mutiny

So how did these ambitions for India turn out for the rest of the mid-century?

Gallagher and Robinson realised that, economically, India did not really fit their theory of the imperialism of free trade:

> Moreover, in this supposedly *laissez-faire* period India, far from being evacuated, was subjected to intensive development as an economic colony along the best mercantilist lines. In India it was possible ... to use the governing power to extort in the form of taxes and monopolies such valuable primary products as opium and salt. ... Direct governmental promotion of products required by British industry, government manipulation of tariffs to help British exports, railway construction at high and guaranteed rates of interest to open the continental interior ...
>
> (Gallagher and Robinson, 1953, p. 4)

The last point, the guarantee of interest to investors in railway bonds, was important. Indian investments were more likely to return a profit for British middle-class investors compared with investments in the USA, Latin America and the United Kingdom, where money could easily be lost. British investment fuelled 5,000 miles (8,000 km) of new railway in India in the 1860s, at a cost of around £100 million in bonds (Lloyd, 1984, p. 177). India was of growing value to Britain, with Britain increasingly earning a surplus in trade with India. Egyptian and American cotton were used to produce finished cloth and clothes in Britain to sell to India, which earned enough from tea, jute and other exports to fund these imports. India was also starting to assume a balancing position in Britain's external **balance of payments**, running a deficit with Britain and a surplus with the rest of the world. By the turn of the century some 60 per cent of India's imports were from Britain, and India and Ceylon (Sri Lanka) combined took about 10 per cent of Britain's overseas investment (Brown, 1985, pp. 95–6).

The British approach to ruling India nevertheless changed from the optimism of the Anglicists regarding their power to change Indian traditions to more gradual reform. The Indian princely states continued to constitute a third of India, operating with a degree of autonomy. David Cannadine has described the subsequent British respect of princely rank, and use of quasi-Indian forms of assemblies such as durbars (large gatherings presided over by the governor-general), as 'ornamentalism': rule by appearance and prestige as much as by force (Cannadine, 2001).

In military terms, although 1857 demonstrated the British ability to defeat opponents, it also precipitated military reorganisation. The Indian Army was recalibrated, from 238,000 Indians and 45,000 Europeans in 1857 to 130,000 Indians and 66,000 Europeans in 1880, with Europeans having control over the artillery (Brown, 1985, p. 95). The 2:1 Indian:British ratio gave British forces greater security, and those who had remained loyal in 1857–58 (such as Nepali Gurkhas) were dubbed **martial races** and made the new focus of recruitment. There was an explosion of classification, in censuses, in mapping and in pseudo-anthropology, as the British classified tribes with bizarrely precise delineation, attempting to dub peoples 'martial' or criminal tribes, and so on (Cohn, 1996). Thus reorganised, the Indian Army was deployed as an 'oriental' barrack in the eastern seas over the next decades, sending troops as far afield as China and East Africa.

Nevertheless, having gobbled up most of the subcontinent, the British Empire in India was coming to its territorial limits. Subsequent attempts to extend influence landward now had more to do with the desire to limit Russia's influence in India's neighbours (notably in Afghanistan and Persia [Iran]) than it did with any desire to expand.

On India's north-western frontiers Britain faced rulers whose power rested on influence over shifting tribal loyalties. Usually the British stuck to some mix of punitive raids and payments to encourage tribes to act in Britain's interests. When Britain did advance, it often ended badly. Afghanistan was invaded in 1839 to replace a leader thought too inclined towards the rulers of an expanding Russia. But as multiple tribes turned against them, British retreat from Kabul in 1841 turned into a rout. After a face-saving punitive mission, the British re-established peace with the original ruler. The Second Afghan War of 1878–80 also resulted in local defeats before Afghanistan promised to consult Britain over its foreign policy.

Yet securing India and its borders still kept huge numbers of Britons serving in the military in India. Hence, perhaps, the popularity of images of heroism, as in *Remnants of an Army* (Figure 15.7), painted by Lady Elizabeth Butler (1846–1933). The British Army had reorganised in the 1870s in three main areas. First, standard service terms were

Figure 15.7 Lady Elizabeth Butler, *Remnants of an Army*, 1879, oil on canvas, 132 x 234cm. Tate collection. Photo: © akg-images / Pictures From History. This painting portrays William Brydon arriving at the gates of Jalalabad in Afghanistan as apparently the sole survivor (in fact there were others) of a 16,500-strong evacuation from Kabul in January 1842.

reduced from 21 to 12 years (half of that in the reserves). Second, the buying of commissions ended. Third, British regiments were made 'territorial', corresponding with counties, usually with a pair of battalions, of which one might be overseas at any one time. In 1879 there were 59 infantry battalions at home and 82 overseas (Raugh, 2004, p. 176). In 1881 the UK had around 7.4 million families (Cook and Keith, 1984 [1975], p. 233) – if we divide this figure by the 66,000 British soldiers serving in the Indian Army, this represents up to one in 112 families with a member in the military in India. Given regular rotation, at least as many again would have had a family member who had served overseas within the recent past.

To this we can add up to a thousand or more British members of the higher Indian Civil Service, men who might oversee districts with tens of thousands of Indians, as well as the engineers, merchants, professionals and others who lived and worked in India. Nevertheless, the total British population in India was only 156,500 by 1921 (Brown, 1985, p. 65). But in terms of empire and overseas influence on Britain more generally, there were a myriad connections to empire through mariners, settlers, missionaries and export industries.

Given these connections, the impact of the mutiny and the Indian role in British trade and power, it is not surprising that India, and ex-India

Figure 15.8 Peter Archer, *Last Stand of the 66th (Berkshire) Regiment of Foot at the Battle of Maiwand, Second Afghan War*, 1986. Photo: The Wardrobe, Museum of the Infantry Regiments of Berkshire and Wiltshire. © Peter Archer. This painting echoes an 1884 print, which depicts the dog 'Bobbie' (now stuffed and in the Berkshire and Hampshire Regimental Museum in Salisbury), imaginatively placed at the episode during the Battle of Maiwand (June 1880) where the last 11 men from one group of the regiment died standing by their colours.

service soldiers, took a significant place in British culture. When Portsmouth doctor Arthur Conan Doyle (1859–1930) serialised his first Sherlock Holmes story, *A Study in Scarlet*, in 1888, India loomed large in the public imagination. Holmes' sidekick, Dr Watson, was a doctor invalided out of India after being wounded at Maiwand in the 1878–80 Second Afghan War (see Figure 15.8). The pair's second outing, in *The Sign of Four* (1890), relied on the idea of a pact – made by four soldiers during the chaos of the mutiny – to share stolen Indian treasure: echoing both memories of looting and a national obsession with the *Koh-i-noor* diamond. The *Koh-i-noor* had been given to Queen Victoria by Punjab's young ruler, Duleep Singh (1837–1893, maharaja 1843–49), after his kingdom's surrender in 1849; it was displayed at the Great Exhibition of 1851, and ultimately ended up in the crown jewels.

The Sign of Four also allowed Conan Doyle to display the Victorian tendency for racial stereotyping in a startling misrepresentation of the book's 'Andaman Islander', Tonga. In the story, Tonga is deployed in London as a blowpipe-armed assassin and thief by one of the original four villains. He becomes a 'type', an ugly criminal. Yet these Indian

Ocean islanders were the victims of the British establishment of a penal colony on their islands, through which they became associated with stories of violence and cannibalism that travelled to Britain and were picked up in popular culture. In practice, they knew neither the cannibalism attributed to them nor the blowpipe Conan Doyle imagines (Towheed, 2010).

As this demonstrates, an ambivalence about India persisted in mid-nineteenth century Britain. Queen Victoria employed Indian servants, and an Indian prince or graduate might be accepted in high society in Britain because of his class and educational status. But its peoples and customs more generally were classified and rigidified by martial race and **caste**, and were deployed in literature and documents as a source of the exotic or the threatening. In theory its peoples were granted equal access to the law and to government posts. In reality the slow expansion of higher education in India, and the need to come to England to sit Indian Civil Service examinations, limited their opportunities. Still, sufficient progress was made for the Indian National Congress to be formed, in December 1885, from civil servants and professionals seeking to represent Indian interests and to demand more access for Indians to further education and government posts: it was a call for more reform.

In short, India loomed even larger in the British Empire and British imaginations after the 'mutiny', offering emblems of trading prowess, of loyalty and treachery, of authoritarianism and progress, and of British heroism and horror.

15.3 The creation of a 'British world'

India would continue to be the most populous part of the empire, able to provide the largest number of troops. But there was no democracy in British India and, post-mutiny, the record of British rule did not fit the tendency to view British history as the progress of liberty. The development of the settler colonies was more easily fitted into a progressive Whig view of British history, which saw Britain as the 'mother of parliaments' and the expansion of British interests as a civilising process. At the same time, the settler colonies became increasingly important to the British economy and to the protection of Britain's strategic interests.

This increasing importance reflects the settler colonies' rapid expansion in this period. The most rapid demographic expansion of empire came, as you have seen, in India, home to 94 per cent of the empire's populace in 1880. But it was the settler colonies that contained most of the empire's territory, with nearly 80 per cent of its land mass (Etemad, 2007, p. 156). A significant amount of that area was relatively temperate and so amenable to replicating European crops, livestock and lifestyles. It also tended to have indigenous peoples whose population density was less than that of Asia. Yet little consideration was given to indigenous peoples. The governor of New South Wales in Australia went as far, in 1835, as to declare the continent's land *terra nullius*, 'empty land' in the sense that it was not improved or 'owned' and so it came under crown control. In these conditions, even small initial European settlements could grow exponentially and spawn new settlements modelled along similar lines. Hence the original penal colony of New South Wales (1788) was followed by successive new colonies in Tasmania (1825), Western Australia (1829), South Australia (1836), Victoria (1851) and Queensland (1859). Taken together, this meant that settlement colonies were transformed in this period.

In other ways, the significance of the settler colonies in the British Empire by the 1880s was more of a surprise. After the loss of the American colonies and their 3 million settlers in 1783, Britain's remaining settler areas had a European population of around 200,000 in total. These were tiny settlements, and it was generally assumed in Britain that they were likely to cause trouble with 'natives', with settlers not wanting to cough up taxes for their protection, and that there would be a tendency for them to follow the Americans in drifting away from their British 'mother' country.

Hence New South Wales was founded in 1788 as a dumping ground for prisoners who had piled up in naval 'hulks' (unseaworthy ships) in England, held there because prisons were full. New South Wales took these unwanted subjects, while also claiming lands of use for naval supplies. Initially, however, only tiny numbers of Europeans were involved, with even smaller numbers at the convict outpost established on the island of Van Diemen's Land (Tasmania) to the south. Meanwhile, New Zealand was in the 1830s still in the hands of Maoris and as yet the only Europeans there were no more than a smattering of whalers and settlers. Britain would only reluctantly extend sovereignty over the country in 1840, to secure this de facto colonisation in the context of tensions with Maoris and the threat of French intervention.

What would become Canada was the nearest to a settler jewel in the crown. French-speaking Lower Canada (conquered in 1756–63) was initially more populous than British Upper Canada and all the other British colonies in North America combined. But large-scale nineteenth-century emigration from Britain changed these small settlements into significant colonies. Upper and Lower Canada were combined in 1840, and in 1867 Britain's North American colonies combined to form one large federation, the Dominion of Canada, containing nearly 3.5 million people.

Cape Colony at the south-west tip of Africa, meanwhile, had been taken from the Dutch in 1806 and kept after the Napoleonic Wars as a strategic outpost on the route to India. But it and nearby Natal had very small British populations, which coexisted with a strong Dutch Boer settler presence and with far greater numbers of Africans living inland. The Boers even founded two states of their own in the interior of southern Africa, the Orange Free State and Transvaal.

Fifty years of emigration and population growth boosted this ragbag of settlements to a total population of around 1.25 million Europeans by 1830, just over a million of them living in the British North American provinces (Etemad, 2007, pp. 141, 155).

Exercise 15.3

This exercise is intended to help you visualise the areas Britain was expanding into in this period, especially settler areas.

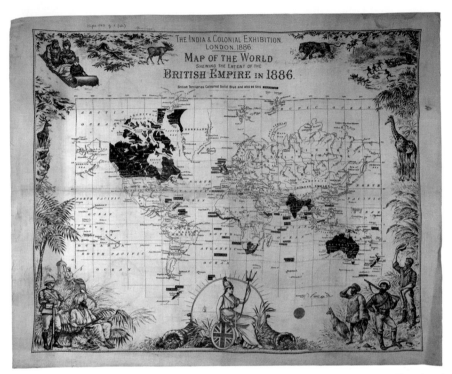

Figure 15.9 Map of the world showing the extent of the British Empire in 1886, linen, sold to accompany the India and Colonial Exhibition of 4 May–10 November 1886. British Library, London, Maps.183.q.1.(13). Photo: © The British Library Board

Study Figure 15.9. This map uses shading to illustrate the extent of the British Empire.

What impression does the use of shading give of the relative importance of different colonies? Are there any potential issues with the map's use of solid shading to highlight distinct areas of the British Empire?

This should take around 30 minutes.

Specimen answer

The shading makes it seem that Canada is by far the biggest, if not most important, territory, followed by Australia and then possibly India, with African and Caribbean territories marginal. It makes the settler empire seem vastly more significant. But there are no statistics here on trade or population, so there is a limit to how much we can tell from size of shading. In zooming in, you might also have wondered if the high number of the small port colonies (thinking back to Section 15.1 on the imperialism of free trade) made them important as a category despite their small size.

Discussion

Block shading of areas could be misleading in other ways. Might it, for instance, lead the unwary to wrongly assume that all the area within any one shaded zone was dominated in a similar way? In fact much of British North America was sparsely inhabited, and parts of some other shaded areas were only lightly administered, if at all.

There's much to be learned from the imagery on maps such as this. Here, exotic flora and fauna (such as palm trees, a giraffe for Africa and a kangaroo for Australia) are used to evoke the variety of Britain's empire. And note the expression of power in the way that the 'natives' are relegated to four Africans in front of a settler wagon, compared with the larger European settlers.

Causes of the growth of settler colonies

The tremendous growth in Britain's settler colonies was due in large part to accelerating population growth powered by increasing emigration. As you know from Unit 8 and from the unit 'Ireland and the Famine' (Unit 9), emigration was promoted as a solution to the famines in Scotland and Ireland in the 1840s. Some Scottish landlords subsidised the emigration of impoverished tenants and some local authorities did likewise for their poor. A British Government Colonial Land and Emigration Commission gave direct assistance to 340,000 emigrants between 1840 and 1869 (Magee and Thompson, 2010, p. 72), mainly aiding passage to Australia. An astonishing 6.5 million people emigrated from the British Isles between 1840 and 1873 (Lloyd, 1984, p. 145), with the greatest numbers going to the USA and about 30 per cent, or just under 2 million, going to empire territories.

Quicker journeys (by the 1840s voyages were increasingly undertaken in steamships and, from the 1860s, in purpose-built passenger steamships), the availability of land to be grabbed at the frontiers, and more regular mail services transformed both the image and the ease of settlement, increasing the flow of free settlers. Just how dramatic that transformation could be can be demonstrated by two examples concerning, first, Dorset labourers and, second, the explosive growth of Melbourne.

The first example is the emigrant cycle of the group known as the 'Tolpuddle Martyrs'. In 1834 labourer and Methodist preacher George Loveless (1797–1874) was transported to Tasmania for seven years and put to work on government farms. He was one of six men from the Dorset village of Tolpuddle convicted, against a backdrop of machine breaking and rick burning in other areas, of using secret oaths in their Friendly Society of Agricultural Labourers to agitate against local farmers who had cut labourers' wages to below 10 shillings a week.

But here is the twist in this story. Despite being pardoned and returned to England after a campaign by supporters, and given sufficient money by sympathisers to lease two Essex farms, in the 1840s Loveless and all but one of the others voluntarily emigrated to London, Ontario, in Upper Canada. There they kept quiet about their past and flourished, with all bar one obtaining land of their own (Marlow, 1974).

This personal transformation in the meaning of emigration, from punishment to aspiration, is also reflected in Charles Dickens' novel *Great Expectations* (first published in serialised form in 1860–61). At the start of the story Magwitch is a terrifying, shackled figure who is transported to Australia, but he makes his fortune in sheep farming (wool was New South Wales's main export by the 1820s), using it to act from afar as the benefactor of Pip, who had helped him when he was a prisoner.

'Booster' literature, quoting successful settlers, told people throughout the United Kingdom of the opportunities available in Australia and Canada. It was sometimes issued by companies that bought large tracts of land and provided some infrastructure or even transport on part of the route to encourage settlers, such as the Canada Company (formed 1826) and New Zealand Company (1838).

From the 1830s, a combination of opposition from local free settlers, prison reform at home and the declining value of transportation as a deterrent gradually undermined the transporting of convicts as a method of punishment. Transportation to New South Wales stopped in 1840 (by which time around 150,000 convicts had been processed). It lasted longer in some of the newer Australian colonies; the last to end it was sparsely populated Western Australia, in 1868.

By that date, 'responsible government' (exercised by ministers chosen from and 'responsible' to an elected assembly) was being extended to most settlement colonies. In the late 1840s governors in successive colonies, starting with Nova Scotia in North America, were told to act as little more than referees when it was not clear which group could control the assembly. The governors gradually restricted themselves to control over limited policy areas, notably foreign policy, and to powers to veto legislation or reserve it for consideration in London. In the Australian colonies, beginning with New South Wales in 1842, partly elected assemblies were set up; in 1856 fully elected lower houses of the assemblies, to whom ministers were responsible, were established in four of these colonies (Lloyd, 1984).

One final shift helped to change the nature of these colonies and their relationship with Britain, and can be illustrated by the transformation of Melbourne in southern Australia. Grazier John Batman (1801–1839) first signed treaties with Aboriginal groups there in 1835, when permanent settlement began. There were more than 10,000 settlers in Melbourne (still governed from New South Wales) in 1840, and 23,000 by 1851. Then, in 1851 – the year Melbourne became the capital of the new colony of Victoria – gold was discovered inland. A gold rush flooded Melbourne, whose population boomed to 126,000 by 1861 and 473,000 by 1891. Victoria provided 40 per cent of the world's gold at its peak, which, along with credit from London, financed Melbourne banks and public buildings to rival those of Birmingham and Manchester (Hunt, 2014, pp. 308–22). The gold rush period of 1853–1860 was one of the few times when Australasia as a whole took more British emigrants (over 273,000) than the USA (Magee and Thompson, 2010, p. 69). It also saw Victoria's wages outstrip those in Britain, manhood suffrage granted, and some trades secure an eight-hour workday. Melbourne continued to comprise around a third of Victoria's entire population. Along with other key littoral settlement cities, it both dominated the colony and linked it closely to Britain.

Britain's empire as a whole could be thought of as widely dispersed rural and industrial areas increasingly tightly bound together by such coastal cities, from Liverpool (Figure 15.10) and London through Cape Colony and Aden to Bombay, Trincomalee (in Ceylon), Singapore, Hong Kong and Melbourne. They had similar infrastructure, furnished with cricket and other sports clubs, Anglican churches, neoclassical law

Figure 15.10 Unknown artist, *Canning Dock, Liverpool*, 1841, engraving. Photo © The Print Collector / Alamy. Manchester is often thought of as the 'shock city' of industrialisation. But in this period Liverpool grew faster. Already a major eighteenth-century port for slaving and Atlantic trade, its role in emigration to North America and settler colonies, and in burgeoning world trade, saw its population grow from 77,000 (1801) to 376,000 (1851) and then 611,000 (1881). By mid-century Liverpool and the Mersey was second only to London for docks, second only to Glasgow and the Clyde for shipbuilding, and the premier European point for emigrating to North America. The *Liverpool Critic* announced in 1877 that its inhabitants were 'to a great extent, citizens of the world' (quoted in Hunt, 2014, p. 390).

courts, and banks. The settler ports among them, such as Melbourne, had the normal accoutrements of a British city plus milder climates and wider streets. They were also often fervently British. Melbourne, for instance, was enthusiastic in celebrating Queen Victoria's golden jubilee of 1887.

Far from assuming that the colonies and Britain would drift apart, as had seemed likely earlier, by the 1870s–80s imperial enthusiasts at home started casting about for ways to help keep Britain and the white settler colonies united so that, together, this 'Anglo-Saxon' federation could counterbalance the growing continental power of the USA, Russia and Germany. The idea of the settler colonies as part of a 'Greater Britain' had gradually grown in potency since the publication in 1868 of the book *Greater Britain* by Sir Charles Dilke (1843–1911). As Seeley put it in 1883, 'When we have accustomed ourselves to contemplate the whole empire together and call it England, we shall see that here too is a United States. Here too is a great homogenous people, one in blood, language, religion, and laws, but dispersed over a boundless space' (quoted in Hunt, 2014, p. 313).

Figure 15.11 The first white Australian Test cricket team to tour England, 1878. An Aboriginal team had toured in 1868. Photo: Pictorial Press Ltd / Alamy

The settler cities bound their hinterlands and Britain together, taking credit from London and emigrants from the four home nations, exporting commodities such as wool and importing British manufactures and tastes. Nothing better symbolises the growing sense of an interconnected 'British world' so well as sport (see Figure 15.11). An 'All England' cricket eleven played England's first international tour match at Melbourne in 1861. By 1873–74 England cricket legend W. G. Grace (1848–1915) was being paid a fortune to tour overseas, and in 1882 an Australian side returned home having beaten England at the Oval ground in south London on 29 August. This was the defeat that introduced the idea that winners of England–Australia Test matches possessed the 'Ashes', following the *Sporting Times* mock obituary for English cricket on 2 September:

In Affectionate Remembrance

OF
ENGLISH CRICKET,
WHICH DIED AT THE OVAL
ON
29th AUGUST, 1882,
Deeply lamented by a large circle of sorrowing
friends and acquaintances.
R. I. P.

*N.B. – The body will be cremated and the
ashes taken to Australia.*

This emerging sense of an interconnected 'British world' created 'cultural capital' through shared culture, laws and values (notwithstanding Irish and Scottish strands of difference), which in turn fostered trust that oiled emigration and investment. Settler colonies were able to raise debt from London more cheaply than foreign countries due to this cultural capital (Magee and Thompson, 2010; Belich, 2009). Churches, clubs, ethnic and religious societies (such as Caledonian societies), families and associates sustained networks with transnational reach and significance. The mid-century expansion of the telegraph, steamships, postal services and railways in Britain and the colonies further facilitated this. Meanwhile, proliferating news organisations shared information and increasingly employed the language of a common British, if not 'Anglo-Saxon' (tenuously including the USA) identity or 'race'. Also, as many as 40 per cent of emigrants returned home, making information sharing a two-way process. By the end of the period this was facilitating larger percentages of emigrants and of investment going to empire territories than ever before (Magee and Thompson, 2010, pp. viii–27, 64).

The increasing importance of this 'British world' can be seen in the 1886 Colonial and Indian Exhibition, for which the map depicted in Figure 15.12 was produced. The exhibition ran from May to November 1886 in South Kensington, attracting over 5.5 million visits. In contrast to the Great Exhibition of 1851, it was unashamedly an attempt to put empire – not trade and industry more generally – centre-stage. Against this background, at least three maps similar to Figure 15.12 were produced, all showing the British Empire in 1886. The one reproduced here was printed as a supplement to the weekly

Figure 15.12 'Imperial Federation – map of the world showing the extent of the British Empire in 1886.' Published as a supplement to the *Graphic* in July 1886. Map image courtesy of the Norman B. Leventhal Map Center at the Boston Public Library

illustrated newspaper, the *Graphic*, on 24 July 1886, and was probably intended to be used in schools and societies. The statistical boxes on the map were provided by Captain J. C. R. Colomb (1838–1909) – ex-Royal Marine officer, author of books on empire defence and member of the recently founded Imperial Federation League – who also wrote the article that accompanied it, extolling the need to give settler colonies more influence in London so that federalism would bind empire. So there are no bonus points for guessing the map was part of a wider propaganda effort intended to promote empire unity.

Activity 15.3

Now go to the module website and complete Activity 15.3 'Mapping the British Empire'. This should take around an hour.

In the summer of 1886 the Imperial Federation League held its first meeting, and Captain Colomb was also elected to Parliament. The following year Queen Victoria's golden jubilee saw celebrations in London, with the presence of premiers from settler colonies contributing to a first Colonial Conference at which the colonies discussed issues with British ministers. In short, this map fits a general context of rising pressure for Britain to coordinate with, and take seriously as partners, its settler colonies.

Conclusion

I have described three very different causes of imperial expansion, namely the imperialism of free trade, expansion at the frontier, and settler societies spreading and spawning new colonies. These manifested in three rather different types of empire: the empire of traders and influence, the empire of authoritarian rule in and around India, and the 'British world'.

Which of these three versions of Britain's empire were more important? Which had more impact on Britain and its culture in this period? Those are questions the sections above, and the associated visual and textual sources, equip you to probe. Indeed, academics have had heated debates about just how far Britons were empire-minded at this time. Bernard Porter has argued that many people scarcely noted empire, except as another set of foreign places. In contrast, John MacKenzie and others have argued that empire was intermeshed with British life and culture, and 'new imperial' historians have held that ideas flowed both ways, from empire to Britain as well as outwards (Porter, 2004; MacKenzie, 1984 and 2008; Howe, 2010).

What cannot be doubted is that the British Empire, and British commitment to the idea of free trade, both surged in this period, and that the voices calling for greater coordination among colonies increased strongly in the 1870s and 1880s. As you will see in Unit 20 of Block 3, this set the scene both for a more self-consciously 'jingoistic' attitude towards empire and power from the 1890s, and yet also for what we might now call 'humanitarian' voices against abuse and in favour of reform to continue growing.

Now turn to the module website to complete the independent study activities associated with this unit.

References

A Web of English History (n.d.) 'Palmerston's speech on affairs in Greece (25 June 1850)' [Online]. Available at http://www.historyhome.co.uk/polspeech/foreign.htm (Accessed 25 April 2017).

Belich, J. (2009) *Replenishing the Earth: The Settler Revolution and the Rise of the Anglo-World, 1783–1939*, Oxford, Oxford University Press.

Burton, A. (2001) *Politics and Empire in Victorian Britain: A Reader*, London, Palgrave.

Brown, J. (1985) *Modern India: The Origins of an Asian Democracy*, Oxford, Oxford University Press.

Cain, P. (1999) 'British free trade, 1850–1914: economics and policy', *Refresh*, no. 29 [Online]. Available at http://www.ehs.org.uk/dotAsset/11cabff5-3f6a-4d69-bba0-1086d69be6c7.pdf (Accessed 26 April 2017).

Cain, P. and Hopkins, A. (1999) *British Imperialism: Crisis and Deconstruction, 1914–1990*, vol. 2, London, Longman.

Cannadine, D. (2001) *Ornamentalism: How the British Saw Their Empire*, London, Allen Lane.

Cohn, B. (1996) *Colonialism and Its Forms of Knowledge: The British in India*, Princeton, NJ, Princeton University Press.

Cook, C. and Keith, B. (1984 [1975]) *British Historical Facts, 1830–1900*, London, Macmillan.

Darwin, J. (2009) *The Empire Project: The Rise and Fall of the British World-System, 1830–1970*, Cambridge, Cambridge University Press.

Etemad, B. (2007) *Possessing the World: Taking the Measurements of Colonisation*, London, Bergahn.

Gallagher, J. and Robinson, R. (1953) 'The imperialism of free trade', *Economic History Review*, vol. 6, no. 1, pp. 1–15.

Harper, M. (1999) 'British migration and the peopling of the British Empire', in Porter, A. (ed.) *The Oxford History of the British Empire*, vol. III: *The Nineteenth Century*, Oxford, Oxford University Press, pp. 75–86.

Howe, S. (ed.) (2010) *The New Imperial Histories Reader*, London, Routledge.

Hunt, T. (2014) *Ten Cities that Made an Empire*, London, Allen Lane.

Lloyd, T. O. (1984) *The British Empire, 1558–1983*, Oxford, Oxford University Press.

MacKenzie, J. M. (1984) *Propaganda and Empire: The Manipulation of British Public Opinion*, Manchester, Manchester University Press.

MacKenzie, J. M. (2008) '"Comfort" and "Conviction": a response to Bernard Porter', *Journal of Imperial and Commonwealth History*, vol. 36, no. 4, pp. 659–68.

Magee, G. B. and Thompson, A. S. (2010) *Empire and Globalisation: Networks of People, Goods and Capital in the British World, 1850–1914*, Cambridge, Cambridge University Press.

Marlow, J. (1974) *The Tolpuddle Martyrs*, St Albans, Panther Books.

Osterhammel, J. (2014) *The Transformation of the World: A Global History of the Nineteenth Century*, Princeton, NJ, Princeton University Press.

Parry, J. J. (1989) *Democracy and Religion: Gladstone and the Liberal Party, 1867–1875*, Cambridge, Cambridge University Press.

Perdue, P. (2010) 'The First Opium War: the Anglo-Chinese War of 1839–1842', MIT Visualizing Cultures, Massachusetts Institute of Technology [Online]. Available at http://ocw.mit.edu/ans7870/21f/21f.027/opium_wars_01/ow1_essay01.html (Accessed 26 April 2017).

Porter, B. (2004) *The Absent-minded Imperialists: Empire, Society and Culture in Britain*, Oxford, Oxford University Press.

Raugh, H. (2004) *The Victorians at War, 1815–1914*, Santa Barbara, CA, ABC-Clio.

Russell, W. H. (2010 [1860]) *My Diary in India, in the Year 1858–59*, Cambridge, Cambridge University Press.

Seeley, J. R. (1909 [1883]) *The Expansion of England: Two Courses of Lectures*, London, Macmillan.

Smith, A. (1869 [1776]) *An Inquiry into the Nature and Causes of the Wealth of Nations*, London, Macmillan.

Smith, A., Brown, D. B. and Jacobi, C. (eds) (2016) *Artist and Empire: Facing Britain's Imperial Past*, London, Tate Publishing.

Tickell, A. (2013) *Terrorism, Insurgency and Indian-English Literature, 1830–1947*, London, Routledge.

Towheed, S. (2010) 'Introduction' to Conan Doyle, A., *The Sign of Four*, Toronto, Broadview.

Victoria (1858) 'Proclamation, by the Queen in council to the princes, chiefs, and people of India (published by the governor-general at Allahabad, November 1st, 1858)' [Online]. Available at www.bl.uk/collection-items/proclamation-by-the-queen-in-council-to-the-princes-chiefs-and-people-of-india (Accessed 2 June 2017).

Woodward, L. (1962) *The Age of Reform, 1815–1870*, 2nd edn, Oxford, Oxford University Press.

Reading

Reading 15.1 Extract from 'Proclamation, by the Queen in Council, to the Princes, Chiefs, and People of India' (1 November 1858)

Source: Victoria (1858) 'Proclamation, by the Queen in council to the princes, chiefs, and people of India (published by the governor-general at Allahabad, November 1st, 1858)' [Online]. Available at www.bl.uk/collection-items/proclamation-by-the-queen-in-council-to-the-princes-chiefs-and-people-of-india (Accessed 2 June 2017).

And We, reposing especial trust and confidence in the loyalty, ability, and judgment of Our right trusty and well beloved Cousin and Councillor, Charles John Viscount Canning, do hereby constitute and appoint him… to be Our first Viceroy and Governor-General in and over Our said Territories… Our Principal Secretaries of State:

…

We desire no extension of Our present territorial Possessions; and while We will permit no aggression upon Our Dominions or Our Rights, to be attempted with impunity, We shall sanction no encroachment on those of others. We shall respect the Rights, Dignity, and Honour of Native Princes as Our own; and We desire that they, as well as Our own Subjects, should enjoy that Prosperity and that social Advancement which can only be secured by internal Peace and good Government.

We hold Ourselves bound to the Natives of Our Indian Territories by the same obligations of Duty which bind Us to all Our other Subjects; and those Obligations, by the Blessing of Almighty God, We shall faithfully and conscientiously fulfil.

Firmly relying Ourselves on the truth of Christianity, and acknowledging with gratitude the solace of Religion, We disclaim alike the Right and the Desire to impose our Convictions on any of Our Subjects. We declare it to be Our Royal Will and Pleasure that none be in any wise favored, none molested or disquieted by reason of their

Religious Faith or Observances; but that all shall alike enjoy the equal and impartial protection of the Law:

…

And it is Our further Will that, so far as may be, Our Subjects, of whatever Race or Creed, be freely and impartially admitted to Offices in Our Service, the Duties of which they may be qualified, by their education, ability, and integrity, duly to discharge. [p. 2]

We know, and respect, the feelings of attachment with which the Natives of India regard the Lands inherited by them from their Ancestors; and We desire to protect them in all Rights connected… We will that generally, in framing and administering the Law, due regard be paid to the ancient Rights, Usages, and Customs of India.

…

Our Clemency will be extended to all Offenders, save and except those who have been, or shall be, convicted of having directly taken part in the Murder of British Subjects. With regard to such, the Demands of Justice forbid the exercise of mercy.

To those who have willingly given asylum to Murderers… their lives alone can be guaranteed…

…

When, by the Blessing of Providence, internal Tranquillity shall be restored, it is Our earnest Desire to stimulate the peaceful Industry of India, to promote Works of Public Utility and Improvement, and to administer its Government for the benefit of all Our Subjects resident therein.

Glossary

A

absentee landlord

a landlord who does not live on their estate.

B

balance of payments

the difference in total value between payments into and out of a country over a period.

bourgeois hegemony

the leadership of the middle class through the exercise of cultural power, which is used to persuade others of the preeminence of 'middle-class' values of thrift and independence.

bourgeoisie

the middle class. Karl Marx used the term to refer to those who own the means of production, but it is often used to refer to the middle class more generally.

C

cash nexus

the reduction of all human relationships to monetary exchange. The term was used by critics of industrialisation in the nineteenth century to describe the ways that capitalism was perceived to be destroying social life.

caste

the hereditary classes of Hindu society, distinguished by degrees of ritual purity or pollution and of social status. The chief divisions are the high-caste Brahmins (originally associated with religious duties), Kshatriyas (associated with military and administrative duties), Vaishyas (merchants, tradesmen and farmers) and Shudras (labourers and service providers). Other subdivisions include the Dalits, ranked below the four main castes and often discriminated against.

chapel of ease

within episcopal churches (such as the Church of England and the Church of Ireland) this was a second, subsidiary church built in order to facilitate attendance, either because the main parish church was too small, due to population growth (as in growing urban parishes), or because it was too far away to be easily accessed.

Christian Socialism

a movement formed in 1848 by ex-Chartists and middle-class reformers, who argued that religion should inspire society and political reform. They blamed social problems on greed and acquisitiveness and promoted new forms of production in small cooperative workshops where profits were shared.

compounding

a system under which lodgers paid rates through their landlord and so, potentially, didn't qualify for the vote. It was abolished in 1867, meaning lodgers could vote if they paid enough in rates.

consecrated (ground)

property that has been set aside for a sacred purpose, for example burial according to the rites of the established churches in England and Ireland.

cotton famine

a depression in the cotton trade in Lancashire between 1861 and 1865. This was caused by over-production in the 1850s, which led to a mass of unsold cloth, and by an interruption to the flow of raw cotton to Lancashire as a result of the American Civil War.

Crimean War (1853–56)

a conflict in which Britain and France supported the Ottoman Empire against Russian pressure. It was so called because much of the fighting occurred around the Black Sea territory of Crimea, on Russia's southern flank.

D

diaspora

a large group of people living outside their original homeland.

domestic ideology

a set of ideas that associated men with public life and women with the home and domestic life. Domestic ideology considered women to be naturally suited to nurturing the family and taking care of its moral and physical well-being.

E

enclave

a territory that is surrounded by, or carved out of, another larger country or territory, and ruled separately.

endemic

a disease regularly found in a location.

epidemic

a disease that appears periodically and causes large numbers of cases of illness, but then disappears.

evangelise, evangelism

from the Greek word meaning 'bringing good news'; within Evangelicalism this was a process, often carried out by laypeople, of seeking the conversion of the unsaved through informal meetings in the open air and in unconsecrated buildings.

extra-parliamentary activity

political activity conducted, usually not by parliamentarians, outside of the legislature. Petitioning is one common example, as is the activities of pressure groups, mass campaigns such as Chartism, and local political parties.

F

Fabian socialists

members and supporters of the Fabian socialist movement, founded in the United Kingdom in 1884. Fabian socialists campaigned for a more equal and democratic society through reform rather than through revolution.

fair rent

the setting of rents according to land valuation, giving protection against arbitrary rent increases.

fixity of tenure

protection from eviction so long as rent is paid.

free sale

the right to the market value of a tenancy (that is, recompense for improvements made by the tenant).

H

high politics

a term used to describe the workings of national parliamentary politics. This used to be the main focus of political history, but is now balanced by a growing interest in local and popular politics.

I

income tax

a way for governments to generate income through the direct taxation of incomes. An income tax had been temporarily introduced in Britain in 1799 to pay for the wars with France but was suspended in 1816 after they ended. It was reintroduced by Sir Robert Peel in 1842.

J

joint stock company

an association of individuals who pool their capital in shares to set up in business. Limited companies became important as a way of funding businesses requiring large capital investment that was beyond the capacity of individuals and small partnerships – such as, for example, railways. Unlike in partnerships, where an individual's entire wealth was at risk, the liability of shareholders for any losses incurred by the business was limited to the capital they had put in. Later in the century they became a way for family firms to diversify ownership and encourage investment.

K

Kulturkampf

this literally translates from the German as 'culture struggle' and is often used to depict clashes in Europe in the nineteenth century between opposing ideological forces, such as Catholicism and modernity. In Unit 11 it has a more particular meaning, described by Colin Barr (2005, p. 473) as 'state action … that sought to regulate, control or suppress the activities of either the institutional Roman Catholic Church or individual Roman Catholics as Catholics'.

L

laissez-faire

this translates literally as 'let do'. A policy or attitude of leaving things to take their own course, without interference.

land agent

a person employed to manage an estate on behalf of a landlord.

liberal

being open to new ideas and able to debate them. In the nineteenth century liberal arguments were closely linked to the individual. Liberals thought that a progressive society depended on the education and self-improvement of individuals.

livestock

domesticated animals raised in an agricultural setting (for example cows).

lunatics

a term used in the nineteenth century to describe people suffering from mental illness and from congenital conditions affecting the brain. Other terms like 'idiot' and 'insane' were used alongside 'lunatic'.

M

Malthusian

of or pertaining to the ideas of the demographer Thomas Malthus.

Mansion House Fund

money raised from public donations to charitable campaigns organised by the Lord Mayor of London.

Married Women's Property Act 1870

an Act, applying to England and Wales, that no longer required women to relinquish control of their money and capital to their husband on marriage. The Act was extended in 1882 to allow women to keep control of all their property after marriage. An Act applying to Scotland was passed in 1880 and another in 1881.

martial race

a British term applied to ethnic or cultural groups they had found effective in battle, and usually also regarded as good and loyal recruits to British-led forces.

O

Orléanist

the 18-year rule of the House of Orléans in France. Its king, Louis-Philippe (1773–1850, reigned 1830–48), replaced the Bourbon monarch, Charles X (1757–1836, reigned 1824–30), in the French revolution of 1830. Despite attempting to rule as a more liberal, constitutional monarch than his predecessor, Louis-Philippe became increasingly unpopular as economic conditions worsened badly in the 1840s. He was forced to abdicate in the revolution of 1848.

outdoor relief

assistance for the poor in times of need, given in the form of money, clothes and food and delivered in their own homes.

P

pandemic

an outbreak of disease that spreads across many countries.

Papal rescript

an official statement of a process or procedure, issued by the pope in response to a request for change from individuals or groups within the Catholic Church.

parliamentary radicalism

the position adopted by a group of reformers elected as MPs after the widening of the franchise under the Reform Act of 1832. They used their position in Parliament to campaign for reform, particularly the repeal of the Corn Laws. Later, in the 1860s, parliamentary radicals such as John Bright campaigned for the extension of the franchise to working men.

Peelites

those who broke away from the Conservative Party in 1846 over the issue of the repeal of the Corn Laws and eventually joined the Liberal Party. They were named after Prime Minister Sir Robert Peel, who famously changed his mind over the Corn Laws and repealed them with Liberal support. After Peel, the most famous Peelite was William Gladstone.

Pentecost

a festival within the Jewish tradition commemorating Moses' presentation of the Ten Commandments. When taking part in this custom after Jesus' death, his disciples and other followers had a charismatic experience, attributed to the Holy Spirit, where flames of fire appeared above their heads and they were all enabled to speak and understand each other's languages. This event is seen as giving divine authority to the early Christian Church.

pocket borough

a parliamentary constituency prior to 1832 that was so under the influence of a powerful local landowner or businessman that the electoral vote was effectively a formality.

popular liberalism

a broad-based liberal movement organised on the idea that individual improvement leads to social progress.

proletariat

the working class. Karl Marx used the term to refer to those who do not own the means of production and have to sell their labour to earn a living.

R

rational recreation

spending one's free time in leisure pursuits which lead to self-improvement, such as reading, studying, and visiting museums and art galleries.

revival preaching

a style of preaching, popular within Evangelical Protestantism, that takes place in secular venues and the outdoors, and is aimed at promoting conversions among the unsaved, or a revival of religious commitment among existing church members. As such, it is often associated with emotional and ecstatic religious behaviour. It is a special preserve of laypeople because it does not involve the administration of the sacrament or the care of a congregation, two features of the ordained ministry.

Risorgimento

(Italian, literally 'resurgence'.) The term given to the series of events that led to the reunification of Italy in the nineteenth century. Historians often treat it as encompassing the period between the revolutions of 1848 and the occupation of Rome in 1870, of which the key stage was the so-called 'war of independence' of 1859–61.

S

slop shops

places to buy cheap, ready-made clothes.

sweated labour

working long hours for low pay in poor working conditions.

T

tillage

the preparation of agricultural land for growing crops.

W

'Whig' history

a term coined by the historian Herbert Butterfield in his work *The Whig Interpretation of History* (1931) to refer to a type of historical writing that describes the past in terms of an inevitable progression from a worse past to a better present. The term is often applied to works of history that lack critical awareness of the range of different developments possible at any given historical point.

Acknowledgements

Every effort has been made to contact copyright holders. If any have been inadvertently overlooked the publishers will be pleased to make the necessary arrangements at the first opportunity.

Grateful acknowledgements are made to the following sources:

Unit 10

Table 10.1: Taken from Hobsbawm, E. J. (1957) 'The British standard of living 1790–1850', *The Economic History Review*, New Series, vol. 10, no. 1.

Table 10.2: Adapted from Boyer, G. R. (1990) *An Economic History of the English Poor Law 1750–1850*, © Cambridge University Press 1990.

Table 10.4: Prom, C. J. (2010) 'Friendly Society discipline and charity in late-Victorian and Edwardian England', *The Historian*, © 2010 Phi Alpha Theta.

Figure 10.9: Adapted from Rowntree, B. S. (1908) *Poverty: A Study of Town Life*, Macmillan and Co.

Unit 12

Figure 12.2: Adapted from Morris, R. J. (1990) 'Occupational structure of five British towns, 1832–34, Occupational coding: principles and examples', *Historical Social Research / Historische Sozialforschung*, vol. 15, no. 1 (53), GESIS – Leibniz-Institute for the Social Sciences, Center for Historical Social Research.

Table 12.2: Taken from Morris, R. J. (2005) *Men, Women and Property in England, 1780–1870: A Social and Economic History of Family Strategies amongst the Leeds Middle Classes*, Cambridge University Press, Copyright © R. J. Morris 2005 adapted from Anderson, M. (1985), 'The emergence of the modern life cycle', *Social History* 10.

Unit 14

14.1 The advent of parliamentary reform: Vernon, J. (2014) *Distant Strangers: How Britain Became Modern*, University of California Press, Copyright © 2014 by the Regents of the University of California.

Table 14.1: Adapted from Hall, C., McClelland, K. and Rendall, J. (2000), *Defining the Victorian Nation: Class, Race, Gender and the British Reform Act of 1867*, Cambridge, Cambridge University Press.

Index

and Evangelicals 185
in Ireland 176, 178, 207
and Irish migrants 178, 186, 198
Papal Aggression (1850) 175, 196–200, 203, 206, 220–1
restored hierarchy 196–7, 198
Cawnpore, slaughter of women and children at 403–7
census (1851) 40–2
religious 178–80, 181, 190–1
central government
and public health reform 42, 44, 303–9, 314, 326–7
and social reform 42–3
Ceylon (Sri Lanka) 409
Chadwick, Edwin 132, 156, 306, 308, 310, 326
Sanitary Report 298–302, 303, 304, 305
Chambers, Thomas 147
charitable work 74, 194
charities 42–3, 44
and the cotton famine 144–5
and famine relief 74
and middle-class women 257
and the new Poor Law 145–7, 148
Charity Organisation Society (COS) 146–8, 157
Chartism 6, 7, 10–11, 24, 43, 92
and the Anti–Corn Law League 12–15
and equipoise 18–22
'First Chartist petition' 10–11, 17, 49–51
and franchise reform 342–3, 344, 345
and parliamentary reform 10, 17, 339–40, 341, 362
rally on Kennington Common 17, 18
and the Reform League 340
and the secret ballot 366
children
deaths from starvation 135, 137, 161–3
and education reforms 266
and the Factory Acts 8, 15, 142
infant death rate 324
Sunday schools for 184, 190
in workhouses 126, 132
China 390, 392, 410
Opium Wars 394–8
cholera 294, 295, 296, 297, 303
and mortality data 324
and sanitary reform 312, 319–20
Christian Socialists 26, 30, 33

church attendance
and the religious census (1851) 179–80, 181, 190–1
church and chapel culture 182–4
Church of England *see* Anglican Church (Church of England)
Church of Ireland 95, 176, 184, 187, 207, 212
Church of Scotland 176
church–state relationships 207–12
established churches 176–7, 207, 209
Nonconformists 207–12, 223–4
cities 8, 284–332
civic buildings 288–9
danger in 284, 289–95
Irish migrants in 86–9, 134, 178
Liberal governments and social reform 42–3
life expectancy in 284
middle–class civic spaces 262–6
population growth 286–7
positive attitudes to 284, 287–9
religion in 178, 180
slum dwellers 289–92, 325, 330–1
and disease 294–5, 331–2
street cleaning 312
street lighting 287–8
traffic in 293–4
urbanisation 286–7
Victorian cities as sick bodies 292–5
see also public health reform
citizenship
and democracy 350–3, 380
Roman citizenship and the imperialism of free trade 398–9
civic spaces
and the middle class 262–6, 267
civil registration
of births and marriages 210
civil service
Indian 402, 411, 413
reforms 44, 240, 267
Clarendon, George Villiers, Earl of 79
class
and the Anti–Corn Law League 11–12, 13–14, 15
and Chartism 11, 13, 15
and equipoise 18–20
and the Great Exhibition 27–8
historians writing about 233–5
and infectious diseases 317